10668340

HIMSS Dictionary of Health Information Technology Terms, Acronyms, and Organizations, Fourth Edition

HIMSS Dictionary of Health Information Technology Terms, Acronyms, and Organizations, Fourth Edition

CRC Press
Taylor & Francis Group
Boca Raton London New York

CRC Press is an imprint of the
Taylor & Francis Group, an **informa** business

CRC Press
Taylor & Francis Group
6000 Broken Sound Parkway NW, Suite 300
Boca Raton, FL 33487-2742

© 2017 by Taylor & Francis Group, LLC
CRC Press is an imprint of Taylor & Francis Group, an Informa business

No claim to original U.S. Government works

Printed on acid-free paper
Version Date: 20161029

International Standard Book Number-13: 978-1-4987-7241-9 (Paperback)

This book contains information obtained from authentic and highly regarded sources. Reasonable efforts have been made to publish reliable data and information, but the author and publisher cannot assume responsibility for the validity of all materials or the consequences of their use. The authors and publishers have attempted to trace the copyright holders of all material reproduced in this publication and apologize to copyright holders if permission to publish in this form has not been obtained. If any copyright material has not been acknowledged please write and let us know so we may rectify in any future reprint.

Except as permitted under U.S. Copyright Law, no part of this book may be reprinted, reproduced, transmitted, or utilized in any form by any electronic, mechanical, or other means, now known or hereafter invented, including photocopying, microfilming, and recording, or in any information storage or retrieval system, without written permission from the publishers.

For permission to photocopy or use material electronically from this work, please access www.copyright .com (http://www.copyright.com/) or contact the Copyright Clearance Center, Inc. (CCC), 222 Rosewood Drive, Danvers, MA 01923, 978-750-8400. CCC is a not-for-profit organization that provides licenses and registration for a variety of users. For organizations that have been granted a photocopy license by the CCC, a separate system of payment has been arranged.

Trademark Notice: Product or corporate names may be trademarks or registered trademarks, and are used only for identification and explanation without intent to infringe.

Library of Congress Cataloging-in-Publication Data

Names: Healthcare Information and Management Systems Society.
Title: HIMSS dictionary of healthcare information technology terms, acronyms, and organizations.
Other titles: Dictionary of healthcare information technology terms, acronyms and organizations | Healthcare Information and Management Systems Society dictionary of healthcare information technology terms, acronyms, and organizations
Description: Fourth edition. | Boca Raton : Taylor & Francis, 2017.
Identifiers: LCCN 2016041640 | ISBN 9781498772419 (pbk. : alk. paper)
ISBN 9781498709606 (ebook)
Subjects: LCSH: Medical informatics--Dictionaries. | Medical informatics--Terminology.
Classification: LCC R858 .H55 2017 | DDC 610.3--dc23
LC record available at https://lccn.loc.gov/2016041640

**Visit the Taylor & Francis Web site at
http://www.taylorandfrancis.com**

**and the CRC Press Web site at
http://www.crcpress.com**

Contents

About HIMSS

HIMSS is a global, cause-based, not-for-profit organization focused on better health through information technology (IT). HIMSS leads efforts to optimize health engagements and care outcomes using information technology. HIMSS produces health IT thought leadership, education, events, market research, and media services around the world. Founded 55 years ago, HIMSS and its related organizations are headquartered in Chicago with additional offices in the United States, Europe, and Asia. HIMSS represents over 64,000 individual members, 640 corporate members, and over 450 non-profit organizations that share our mission of transforming healthcare through the best use of information technology and management systems. To learn more about HIMSS and to find out how to join us and our members in advancing our cause, please visit our website at www.himss.org.

HIMSS Vision

Better health through information technology.

HIMSS Mission

Globally, lead endeavors optimizing health engagements and care outcomes through information technology.

Foreword

While the past three years seem to have flown by, it's still surprising to discover the influence of technology on terms in common use today. Ransomware, robotics, APIs, precision medicine, APMs, and IoT (Internet of Things) each describe emerging technologies that are impacting health and care. At the same time, the healthcare environment is rapidly shifting its focus from patients to consumers, EHRs to apps, data to analytics, and fee-for-service to value. Yet one thing remains constant—the use of acronyms is pervasive!

Publication of the fourth edition of the *HIMSS Dictionary of Health Information Technology Terms, Acronyms, and Organizations* is timely for helping us navigate this new and evolving space. And this updated publication also advances HIMSS's mission of leading healthcare transformation through the best use of health information technology.

Frequently, members tell us that the HIMSS HIT Dictionary is kept nearby on their desktop, becoming dog-eared with regular use. Whether it's a new organization, term, or acronym, this is THE reliable source. And for the first time, this fourth edition will include search word capability, providing additional value through ready-access from our virtual work space.

Whether you're a student learning about a new topic, a manager researching a proposal, or a health IT executive evaluating the best strategy, this is an essential resource to have at your fingertips. As innovation continues to influence healthcare, I invite you to join me in taking time to enhance our knowledge and start exploring this valuable tool.

Joyce Sensmeier, MS, RN-BC, CPHIMS, FHIMSS, FAAN

Joyce Sensmeier is vice president of Informatics at HIMSS where she is responsible for clinical informatics, standards, and interoperability programs and initiatives.

Introduction

Welcome to the fourth edition of the *HIMSS Dictionary of Health Information Technology Terms, Acronyms, and Organizations*, which follows the anniversary of the dictionary's first publication in June 2006, the second edition in 2009, and the third edition in 2013.

The fourth edition encompasses many terms found in the previous three editions. These have been updated to include new usage and new terms have been added that reflect the changes and evolution occurring within the health information technology industry. Some terms have been retired: obscure references, jargon, and definitions of ever-changing programming languages.

The changes made in this edition of the dictionary reflect a careful process of collection, review, refinement, and, finally, compilation of an editable document. The document was then revised and edited for the inclusion of an appropriate reference for each term. No one was permitted to define a term on his or her own—editors included. If an appropriate reference could not be found, the term was omitted.

This fourth edition contains 3200+ entries. Professional and organizational terms have been separated from the main terms of the dictionary into separate appendices. Acronyms have been incorporated into the alphabetical organization of the main terms to streamline the search for terms. An acronym reference list has been added for quick searches of the acronym's full name. In all, we hope our audience of HIT professionals, students, and others who come in contact with health information management and technology activities find this expanded and reorganized edition to be a useful tool in their everyday work.

We would like to thank HIMSS for undertaking the 2017 revision and publication of this valuable resource. Thanks also to people too numerous to mention for collaborating with us, giving us new ideas, suggesting changes in format, and helping us improve this dictionary. Thank you also to those who have purchased and used previous editions of the dictionary. Without your support of previous projects, this edition would not have happened.

Christine A. Hudak, PhD, CPHIMS, FHIMSS
Professor and Director, Health Informatics Program
Kent State University
Kent, Ohio

Acknowledgments

HIMSS sincerely thanks the Health IT Standards Dictionary Work Group, led by Dr. Christine A. Hudak, for the time and effort dedicated to the development of the fourth edition of this dictionary. Without their leadership, expertise, and consideration, this dictionary would not have become a reality. HIMSS would also like to thank all of the internal staff members who contributed their time and support throughout the review process, which greatly contributed to this dictionary's creation.

Chair, Health IT Standards Dictionary Work Group

Christine A. Hudak, PhD, CPHIMS, FHIMSS
Professor and Director, Health Informatics
Kent State University

Work Group Members

Deborah (Dee) Alexander
Senior Security and Clinical Applications Team Lead
AHS Information Services

Peggy Beaumont, MSN, BS, RN, CHTS-IM
Clinical Informatics Specialist
Beaumont Health System

Connie Berg, RN, BA, FHIMSS
Principal
CMB Consulting
Adjunct Instructor
Holy Names University

Darinda Blaskie, MSN, RN-BC
Manager, Nursing Quality and Informatics
Bronson Healthcare Group

Karen Boruff, PMP
Project Manager
California Association of HIEs

Juliana Brixey, PhD, MPH, MSN, RN
Associate Professor
UT Health SBMI/SON

Joseph Cawood, MSHI
Senior Clinical Information Support Specialist
Adventist Health

Jasvir (Jay) Dhamrhat
Desktop Support Specialist
Mount Sinai Hospital

Alison Greene, BA, MS, PhD
Managing Partner
Healthcare Interoperability Solutions LLC

Stacie Hengy, RN, BS
Quality Management Coordinator
Sky Ridge Medical Center

Thoma Hudson, MT (ASCP)
Clinical Regulatory Specialty
Parkview Health

Eunice Irvin
Student
College of St. Scholastica

Joanna Jung
Clinical Device Analyst
Partners Healthcare System, Inc.

Sindhu R. Kammath
Clinical Informaticist
UHS Inc.

Kelly Lester, MBA, RN
Senior Director, Meaningful Use
LifePoint Hospitals, Inc.

Harland Love, BSN, RN, PMP
Director, Clinical Applications
Texas Oncology

Clair Lunt, RN, MN, Med
Director, Healthcare Informatics
Mount Sinai Beth Israel

Christopher Morgan
Director, Dental Informatics
University of Louisville

Jonathan Ong, CHTS-IM/TR, PMP, CSM
Assistant Director, IT Analytics
SBH Health System

Brittany Partridge
Clinical Informatics Specialist
Seton Healthcare Family

Maryann Santitoro, CEHR
Senior Project Manager
University of Pennsylvania Health System

Joshua Tamayo-Sarver, MD, PhD, FACEP
CEP Director of Business Intelligence
CEP America

Steve Van Niman
Business Development
ARGO

Ronnie Wilkins
Graduate Student
Masters in Information Science
Health Informatics Concentration
North Carolina Central University

A

AA (Attribute authority): An entity, recognized by the Federal Public Key Infrastructure (PKI), Policy Authority, or comparable body as having the authority to verify the association of attributes to an identity.[1]

AAA (Authentication, authorization, and accounting): A term for a framework for intelligently controlling access to computer resources, enforcing policies, auditing usage, and providing the information necessary to bill for services. These combined processes are considered important for effective network management and security.[2] *See* **Authentication**, **Authorization**, and **Accounting**.

ABC (Activity-based costing): An accounting technique that allows an organization to determine the actual cost associated with each product and service produced by the organization, without regard to organizational structure.[3] Cost accounting approach concerned with matching costs with activities (called cost drivers) that cause those costs. It is a more sophisticated kind of absorption-costing and replaces labor-based costing systems. ABC states that (1) products consume activities, (2) it is the activities (and not the products) that consume resources, (3) activities are the cost drivers, and (4) activities are not necessarily based on the volume of production. Instead of allocating costs to cost centers (such as manufacturing, marketing, finance), ABC allocates direct and indirect costs to activities such as processing an order, attending to a customer complaint, or setting up a machine.[4]

ABC codes (Alternative billing codes): Terminology to describe alternative medicine, nursing, and other integrative healthcare interventions that include relative value units and legal scope of practice information.[5] ABC codes are five-digit Health Insurance Portability and Accountability Act (HIPAA) compliant alpha codes (e.g., AAAAA) used by licensed and non-licensed healthcare practitioners on standard healthcare claim forms (e.g., CMS 1500 Form) to describe services, remedies, and/or supply items provided and/or used during patient visits.[6]

Abend: Abnormal termination of software. **1.** A type of system error in which a task or program fails to execute properly (i.e., "ab-normally ends"). The term is also used as the name for a type of error message that indicates such a failure has occurred.[7] **2.** ABnormal END or ABortive END. System crash or other abnormal termination of a computer program caused by memory conflict or some other (usually unidentifiable) glitch.[4]

Abort: 1. Terminate. **2.** In data transmission, an *abort* is a function invoked by a sending station to cause the recipient to discard or ignore all bit sequences

A

transmitted by the sender since the preceding flag sequence.[8] To terminate a program or process abnormally and usually suddenly, with or without diagnostic information.[9]

Abstract message: Associated with a particular trigger event. Includes data fields that will be sent within a message, the valid response messages, and the treatment of application level errors or the failure of the underlying communications system.[10] The basic level of definition within HL7 is that of the abstract message associated with a particular trigger event. The abstract message definition includes the data fields that will be sent within a message, the valid response messages, and the treatment of application level errors or the failure of the underlying communications system. An HL7 abstract message is defined in terms of HL7 segments and fields.[10]

Abstract syntax: A form of representation of data that is independent of machine-oriented structures and encodings and also of the physical representation of the data. Abstract syntax is used to give a high-level description of programs being compiled or messages passing over a communications link.[9]

Abstract syntax notation: *See* **ASN.**

Abstracting: An application that facilitates the collection and maintenance of coded patient information with selected patient demographic, clinical, and admissions data from the medical record, usually post-discharge. This information can be used for internal control, analysis, regulatory reports, etc.[11]

Abstraction: 1. The process of extracting essential properties while omitting unessential details.[12] **2.** The process of taking away or removing characteristics from something in order to reduce it to a set of essential characteristics. In object-oriented programming, abstraction is one of three central principles (along with encapsulation and inheritance). Through the process of abstraction, a programmer hides all but the relevant data about an object in order to reduce complexity and increase efficiency.[2] *See* **Encapsulation** and **Inheritance.**

ACA (Affordable Care Act): On March 23, 2010, President Obama signed the Patient Protection and Affordable Care Act, which extends healthcare coverage to an estimated 32 million uninsured individuals and makes coverage more affordable for many others. Section 1561 requests the U.S. Department of Health & Human Services (HHS), in consultation with the Health Information Technology (HIT) Policy Committee, and the HIT Standards Committee (the Committees), to develop interoperable and secure standards and protocols that facilitate electronic enrollment of individuals in federal and state health and human services programs.[13]

Acceptable downtime: *See* **Maximum tolerable period of disruption** and **MAO.**

Acceptable risk: Level of risk at which, given costs and benefits associated with risk reduction measures, no action is deemed to be warranted at a given point in time.[14]

Acceptable use policy: *See* **AUP.**

Acceptance testing: A user-run testing event that demonstrates an application's ability to meet business objectives and system requirements. Also known as beta testing.[2]

Access: The ability and means to communicate with or otherwise interact with a system, to use system resources to handle information, to gain knowledge of the information the system contains, or to control system components and functions.[15]

Access control: The process of granting or denying specific requests for or attempts to: (1) obtain and use information and related information processing services; and (2) enter specific physical facilities.[16]

Access control decision function: *See* **ADF**.

Access control enforcement function: *See* **AEF**.

Access control information: *See* **ACI**.

Access control list: *See* **ACL**.

Access control policy: A way of limiting access to a system or to physical or virtual resources. In computing, access control is a process by which users are granted access and certain privileges to systems, resources, or information. In access control systems, users must present credentials before they can be granted access. In physical systems, these credentials may come in many forms, but credentials that cannot be transferred provide the most security.

Access control service: *See* **ACS**.

Access level: A category within a given security classification limiting entry or system connectivity to only authorized persons.[1]

Access mode: A distinct operation recognized by the protection mechanisms as a possible operation on an object. Read, write, and append are possible modes of access to a file, while execute is an additional mode of access to a program.[17]

Access point: The hub of a wireless network. Wireless clients connect to the access point, and traffic between two clients must travel through the access point.[18]

Access provider: *See* **ISP**.

Access to radiology information: *See* **ARI**.

Accountability: Refers to identifying the healthcare party (i.e., individuals, organizations, business units) or agent (e.g., software, device, instrument, monitor) that is responsible for data origination, amendment, verification, translation, stewardship, access and use, disclosure, and transmission and receipt.[19]

Accountable Care Organization: *See* **ACO**.

Accounting: Systematic and comprehensive recording of financial transactions pertaining to a business. Also refers to the process of summarizing, analyzing, and reporting these transactions to oversight agencies and tax collect entities.[20]

Accounting of disclosures: Refers to the right of individuals, with limitations, to a listing of the uses and disclosures of their identifiable health information for a period of time not to exceed six years prior to the date of the request.[21,22]

Accreditation: 1. Formal declaration by a designated approving authority that an information system is approved to operate in a particular security mode using a prescribed set of safeguards at an acceptable level of risk.[23] **2.** A process of review that healthcare organizations participate in to demonstrate the ability to meet predetermined criteria and standards of accreditation established by a professional accrediting agency. Accreditation represents agencies as credible and reputable organizations dedicated to ongoing and continuous compliance with the highest standard of quality.[24]

ACDF (Access control decision function) or ADF: A specialized function that makes access control decisions by applying access control policy rules to an access request, ADI (of initiators, targets, access requests, or that retained from prior decisions), and the context in which the access request is made.[17]

ACG (Ambulatory care group): Also known as an *adjusted clinical group*. A method of categorizing outpatient episodes: preventative, diagnostic, therapeutic, surgical, and/or rehabilitative that are based on resource use over time and are modified by principal diagnosis, age, and sex.[25] *See* **ADG** and **APG**.

ACI (Access control information): Information used for access control purposes, including contextual information.[26] An ACI controls user access by defining the access privileges of an ITIM group or ACI principal. Members of an ITIM group or an ACI principal can view and perform operations on attributes within a target class (context) as defined by the scope of the ACI.[27]

ACID (Atomicity, consistency, isolation, and durability): An acronym and mnemonic device for learning and remembering the four primary attributes ensured to any transaction by a transaction manager (which is also called a transaction monitor). The ACID concept is described in ISO/IEC 10026-1:1992 Section 4. Each of these attributes can be measured against a benchmark.[2] *See* **Atomicity**, **Consistency**, **Isolation**, and **Durability**.

ACK (General acknowledgment message): In data networking, an acknowledgment is a signal passed between communicating processes or computers to signify acknowledgment, or receipt, of response, as part of a communications protocol. The ACK message is used to respond to a message where there has been an error that precludes application processing or where the application does not define a special message type for the response.[10]

ACL (Access control list): A table that tells a computer operating system which access rights each user has to a particular system object, such as a file directory or individual file. Each object has a security attribute that identifies its access control list. The list has an entry for each system user with access privileges. The most common privileges include the ability to read a file (or all the files in a directory), to write to the file or files, and to execute the file (if it is an executable file, or program).[2]

ACO (Accountable Care Organization): Groups of doctors, hospitals, and other healthcare providers, who come together voluntarily to give coordinated high-quality care to the Medicare patients they serve. Coordinated care helps ensure that patients, especially the chronically ill, get the right care at the right time, with the goal of avoiding unnecessary duplication of services and preventing medical errors. When an ACO succeeds in both delivering high-quality care and spending healthcare dollars more wisely, it will share in the savings it achieves for the Medicare program.[28]

Acquisition modality: A system that acquires medical images, waveforms, or measurements while a patient or specimen is present (e.g., a computed tomography scanner, a specimen microscope, or a hemodynamic measurement system).[29]

Acquisition modality importer: A system that integrates a non-DICOM-ready modality into workflows.[29]

ACS (Access control service): 1. Includes embedded security management capabilities (provided as precursor information to this construct), and all other user-side access control and decision-making capabilities (policy enforcement point, policy decision point, obligation service, etc.) needed to enforce user-side system-object security and privacy policy. The ACS is responsible for creating trustworthy credentials forwarded in cross-domain assertions regarding security information and attributes. Access control services may be hierarchical and nested, distributed, or local.[22] **2.** A security service that provides protection of system resources against unauthorized access. The two basic mechanisms for implementing this service are ACLs and tickets.[18]

Active directory: *See* **AD.**

Active server pages: *See* **ASP.**

Activity-based costing: *See* **ABC.**

Activity tracker: A device or application for monitoring and tracking fitness-related metrics such as distance walked or run, calorie consumption, heartbeat, and quality of sleep. Most often refers to dedicated electronic monitoring devices that are synced to a computer or Smartphone for long-term data tracking.[8] *See* **Wearable technology.**

Actor: Information systems or components of information systems that produce, manage, or act on information associated with operational activities in the enterprise.[29]

Acute physiology and chronic health evaluation: *See* **APACHE.**

AD (Active directory): Microsoft's trademarked directory service, released as part of the Microsoft® Windows architecture. Like other directory services, such as Novell Directory Services (NDS), Active Directory is a centralized and standardized system that automates network management of user data, security, and distributed resources, and enables interoperation with other directories. Active Directory is designed especially for distributed networking environments.[2]

AD (Addendum): New documentation used to add information to an original entry. Addenda should be timely and bear the current date and reason for the additional information being added to the health record.[30]

Addendum: *See* **AD.**

A

Address: 1. The unique location of an Internet server. **2.** Identifies (as a computer peripheral or memory location) by an address or a name for information transfer.[31]

Address class: Five TCP/IP address classes (A, B, C, D, and E) were initially designed to accommodate networks of varying sizes. The class of address defines which bits are used for the network ID and which bits are used for the host ID. Also defines the possible number of networks and the number of hosts per network. Class A addresses are assigned to networks with a large number of hosts. The high-order bit in a class A address is always set to zero. The next seven bits (completing the first octet) complete the network ID. The remaining 24 bits (the last three octets) represent the host ID. This allows for 126 networks and 16,777, 214 hosts per network. (Class E is an experimental address that is reserved for future use. The high-order bits in a class E address are set to 1111.)[32]

Address resolution: The Address Resolution Protocol (ARP) feature performs a required function in IP routing. ARP finds the hardware address, also known as Media Access Control (MAC) address, of a host from its known IP address. ARP maintains a cache (table) in which MAC addresses are mapped to IP addresses.[18]

Address resolution protocol: *See* **ARP.**

ADE (Adverse drug event): An injury resulting from the use of a drug. Under this definition, the term ADE includes harm caused by the drug (adverse drug reactions and overdose) and harm from the use of the drug (including dose reductions and discontinuations of drug therapy). Adverse drug events may result from medication errors, but most do not.[33] ADEs are injuries resulting from drug-related medical interventions. ADEs can occur in any health care setting, including: inpatient, such as acute care hospitals, outpatient, and long-term care settings, such as nursing homes.[34]

ADG (Ambulatory diagnostic group): A method of categorizing outpatient episodes. *See* **ACG** and **APG.**[25]

Ad-hoc query: 1. A query that is not determined prior to the moment it is run against a data source. **2.** A non-standard inquiry created to obtain information as the need arises and contrasts with a query that is predefined and routinely processed.[35]

Administrative code sets: Code sets that characterize a general business situation, rather than a medical condition or service. Under HIPAA, these are sometimes referred to as non-clinical, or non-medical, code sets. Compare to code sets and medical code sets.[28]

Administrative record: A record concerned with administrative matters, such as length of stay, details of accommodation, and billing.[36]

Administrative safeguards: Administrative actions, policies and procedures to manage the selection, development, implementation, and maintenance of security measures to safeguard electronic protected health information;

and to manage the conduct of the covered entity's workforce in relation to the protection of that information.[14,37]

Administrative services only: *See* **ASO**.

Administrative simplification: Title II, Subtitle F, of HIPAA, which authorizes HHS to: 1. Adopt standards for transactions and code sets that are used to exchange health data; 2. Adopt standard identifiers for health plans, healthcare providers, employers, and individuals for use on standard transactions; and 3. Adopt standards to protect the security and privacy of personally identifiable health information. The Administrative Simplification Compliance Act (ASCA) prohibits payment of services or supplies that a provider did not bill to Medicare electronically. "Providers" is used in a generic sense here and refers equally to physicians, suppliers, and other healthcare providers. Providers are required to self-assess to determine whether they meet certain permitted exceptions to this electronic billing requirement.[28]

Administrative users access level: 1. The special rights given to the team of users who maintain and support a network. **2.** Level associated with an individual who may be accessing information (e.g., a clearance level) and information which may be accessed (e.g., a classification level).[38]

Admission date: The date the patient was admitted for inpatient care, outpatient service, or start of care.[28]

ADPAC (Automated data processing application coordinator): The person responsible for implementing a set of computer programs (application package) developed to support a specific functional area such as Immunology Case Registry, PIMS, etc.[39]

ADR (Adverse drug reaction): An unwanted response to a therapeutic drug. Health professionals must report all adverse events related to drugs or medical devices to the manufacturer and the FDA to aid in monitoring the safety of marketed medical products.[40]

ADR (ADT response message): Admission, discharge, and transfer response message.[10]

ADSL (Asymmetric digital subscriber line): A type of DSL broadband communications technology used for connecting to the Internet. ADSL allows more data to be sent over existing copper telephone lines (POTS), when compared to traditional modem lines. A special filter, called a *microfilter*, is installed on a subscriber's telephone line to allow both ADSL and regular voice (telephone) services to be used at the same time. ADSL requires a special ADSL modem and subscribers must be in close geographical locations to the provider's central office to receive ADSL service. Typically, this distance is within a radius of 2 to 2.5 miles.[41] ADSL supports data rates up to 20 Mbps when receiving data (known as the downstream rate) and 820 Kbps when sending data (known as the upstream rate).[42]

ADT (Admission, discharge, and transfer): Admission, discharge, and transfer message for patients in a healthcare facility.[28]

A

ADT response message: *See* **ADR.**

Advance directive: A document by which a person makes provision for healthcare decisions in the event that, in the future, he or she becomes unable to make those decisions. There are two main types of advance directive— the "Living Will" and the "Durable Power of Attorney for Health Care." There are also hybrid documents which combine elements of the Living Will with those of the Durable Power of Attorney.[28]

Advanced persistent threat: An attack that utilizes sophisticated resources to launch repeated assault against an organization's asset. Also an attack where an unauthorized person gains and retains access to computing resources for a long time undetected.[2]

Advanced technology attachment: *See* **ATA.**

Adverse drug event: *See* **ADE.**

Adverse drug reaction: *See* **ADR.**

Adverse event: *See* **AE.**

AE (Adverse event/adverse experience): Any untoward medical occurrence associated with the use of a drug or a medical product in humans, whether or not considered drug related.[43] Pre-marketing: Any untoward medical occurrence in a patient or clinical investigation subject administered a pharmaceutical product and which does not necessarily have a causal relationship with this treatment. Post-marketing/US: Any adverse event associated with the use of a drug in humans, whether or not considered drug related, including the following: An adverse event occurring in the course of the use of a drug product in professional practice; an adverse event occurring from drug overdose; an adverse event occurring from drug withdrawal; and any failure of expected pharmacologic action. Post-marketing/European Union: Any undesirable experience occurring to a patient treated with a pharmaceutical product whether or not considered related to the medicinal product.[10]

AE Title (Application Entity Title): An identifier utilized by picture archiving and communication systems (PACS) to uniquely name devices that can send and/or receive information to the imaging/PACS system.[44]

AEF (Access control enforcement function): A specialized function that is part of the access path between an initiator and a target on each access request and enforces the decision made by the access control decision function (ADF).[17]

Affinity domain policy: Clearly defines the appropriate uses of the Integrating the Healthcare Enterprise (IHE) Cross-Enterprise Document Sharing (XDS) affinity domain. Within this policy is a defined set of acceptable use privacy consent policies that are published and understood.[29]

Affordable Care Act: *See* **ACA.**

Agency specific data: All data pertinent to the agency where care is provided and which are used for patient care, such as procedures, hours of operations, visiting hours, standards of care, pharmacy formulary, etc.[3]

Aggregate: The collection or gathering of elements into a mass or whole.[3]

Aggregate data: 1. Data elements assembled into a logical format to facilitate comparisons or to elicit evidence of patterns.[45] **2.** A data type composed of multiple elements. An aggregate can be homogeneous (all elements have the same type), e.g., an array, a list in a functional language, a string of characters, a file; or it can be heterogeneous (elements can have different types), e.g., a structure. In most languages, aggregates can contain elements which are themselves aggregates, e.g., a list of lists.[46]

Aggregation logics: Logic for aggregating detailed data into categories.[47]

AHT (Average handling time/average handle time): The average duration of a call handled by a customer service associate.[48]

AIDC (Automatic identification and data capture): A broad category of technologies used to collect information from an individual, object, image, or sound without manual data entry. AIDC systems are used to manage inventory, delivery, assets, security, and documents. Sectors that use AIDC systems include distribution, manufacturing, transportation, medicine, government, and retail, among many others. AIDC applications typically fall into one of a few categories: identification and validation at the source, tracking, and interfaces to other systems. The actual technologies involved, the information obtained, and the purpose of collection vary widely. Current AIDC technologies include: barcodes, 2D barcodes, magnetic strips, smart cards, optical character recognition, radio frequency identification, biometrics applications including finger scanning, and voice recognition.[2]

AIMS (Anesthesia information management system): An information system that allows integrated communication with other hospital and provider systems throughout the perioperative period (such as clinical information systems used by nurses, clinical data repositories used by hospitals, and professional billing systems).[11] AIMS are a specialized form of electronic health record (EHR) systems that allow the automatic and reliable collection, storage, and presentation of patient data during the perioperative period. In addition to providing basic record-keeping functions, most AIMS also allow end users to access information for management, quality assurance, and research purposes. AIMS typically consist of a combination of hardware and software that interface with intraoperative monitors, and in many cases hospital clinical data repositories or EHRs. Although the primary role of an AIMS is to capture data during the intraoperative phase, most systems also can incorporate pre- and postoperative patient information.[49]

AIS (Automated information system): An assembly of computer hardware, software, firmware, or any combination of these, configured to automatically accomplish specific information-handling operations, such as communication, computation, dissemination, processing, and storage of information. Included are computers, word processing systems, networks, or other electronic information handling systems, and associated equipment.[2]

A

Alert: Written or acoustic signals to announce the arrival of messages and results and to avoid possible undesirable situations, such as contradictions, conflicts, erroneous entry, tasks that are not performed in time, or an exceptional result. A passive alert will appear on the screen in the form of a message. An active alert calls for immediate attention, and the appropriate person is immediately notified (e.g., by electronic pager).[36] *See* **Decision support system**.

Alert fatigue: Multiple false alarms by smart technology that cause workers to ignore or respond slowly to them.[50]

Alerting system: Computer-based system that automatically generates alerts and advice as a consequence of monitoring or other information-processing activities.[36]

Algorithm: Step-by-step procedure for problem-solving or calculating; a set of rules for problem solving. In data mining, it defines the parameters of the data mining model.[50]

Alias: In some computer operating systems and programming languages, an alias is an alternative and usually easier-to-understand or more significant name for a defined data object. The data object can be defined once and later a developer can define one or more equivalent aliases that will also refer to the data object. In some languages, this is known as an "equate" instruction.[2]

Alias domain name: The practice of establishing an e-mail protocol within another e-mail protocol, to allow for the local identification of users within a larger enterprise.[3]

ALOS (Average length of stay): Refers to the average number of days that patients spend in hospital. It is generally measured by dividing the total number of days stayed by all inpatients during a year by the number of admissions or discharges. Day cases are excluded.[51]

Alpha/beta testing: A pre-production development stage comprised of an initial trial (alpha test) by a select set of users. This initial test is to ensure that the system is stable enough for a rigorous trial (beta test) by additional users, or in a variety of settings.[52,53] *See* **Beta testing**.

Alternative payment models: *See* **APMs**.

ALU (Arithmetic logic unit): A major component of the central processing unit of a computer system. It does all processes related to arithmetic and logic operations that need to be done on instruction words. In some microprocessor architectures, the ALU is divided into the arithmetic unit (AU) and the logic unit (LU).[54]

Ambulatory care: Medical care, including diagnosis, observation, treatment, and rehabilitation that is provided on an outpatient basis. Ambulatory care is given to persons who are able to ambulate or walk about.[28]

Ambulatory care group: *See* **ACG**.

Ambulatory care information system: Information systems used to improve the quality of care and promote business systems integration in the ambulatory care setting.[55]

Ambulatory EMR: The EMR that supports the ambulatory/clinic/physician office environments. Provides all of the functions of an EMR: clinical documentation, order entry, clinical data repository, practitioner order entry, physician or nurse clinical documentation, etc.[11]

Ambulatory medical record: *See* **AMR.**

Amendments and corrections: Documentation meant to clarify health information within a health record. An amendment is made after the original documentation has been completed by the provider. All amendments should be timely and bear the current date of documentation. A correction is a change in the information meant to clarify inaccuracies after the original electronic document has been signed or rendered complete.[30]

American Recovery and Reinvestment Act of 2009: *See* **ARRA.**

American standard code for information interchange: *See* **ASCII.**

AMR (Ambulatory medical record): An electronic or paper-based medical record used in the outpatient or ambulatory care setting.[55]

Analog: Representing data by measurement of a continuous physical variable, as voltage or pressure, as opposed to digital, which represents data as discrete units.[8,41]

Analog signal: *See* **Digital signal.** In telecommunications, an analog signal is one in which a base carrier's alternating current frequency is modified in some way, such as by amplifying the strength of the signal or varying the frequency, in order to add information to the signal.[2]

Analog-to-digital conversion: An electronic process in which a continuously variable (analog) signal is changed, without altering its essential content, into a multi-level (digital) signal.[2]

Ancillary care: Refers to the wide range of healthcare services provided to support the work of a primary physician. These services can be classified into three categories: diagnostic, therapeutic, and custodial. Diagnostic services include laboratory tests, radiology, genetic testing, diagnostic imaging, and more. Therapeutic services range from rehabilitation to physical and occupational therapy, as well as massage, chiropractic services, and speech therapy. Custodial services include everything from hospice care and long-term post-acute care to nursing facilities and urgent care.[56]

Ancillary service information system: Information systems designed to store, manipulate, and retrieve information for planning, organizing, directing, and controlling administrative activities associated with the provision and utilization of radiology, laboratory, pharmacy, and other services.[57]

Anesthesia information management system: *See* **AIMS.**

Anonymization: A process that removes or replaces identity information from a communication or record. Communications and records may be made pseudonymous, in which case the same subject will always have the same replacement identity, but cannot be identified as an individual.[58]

A

Anonymized data: 1. Originally identifiable data which have been permanently stripped of identifiers. **2.** Data from which the patient cannot be identified by the recipient of the information.[38,59]

Anonymous FTP: Using the Internet's File Transfer Protocol (FTP), anonymous FTP is a method for giving users access to files so that they don't need to identify themselves to the server. Using an FTP program or the FTP command interface, the user enters "anonymous" as a user ID. Usually, the password is defaulted or furnished by the FTP server. Anonymous FTP is a common way to get access to a server in order to view or download files that are publicly available.[2]

Anti-tearing: The process or processes that prevent data loss when a smartcard is withdrawn during a data operation.[3]

Anti-virus software: *See* **Virus scanner**.

APACHE (Acute physiology and chronic health evaluation): 1. A severity-of-disease classification scoring system widely used in the United States. APACHE II is the most widely studied version of this instrument (a more recent version, APACHE IV, is proprietary, whereas APACHE II is publicly available); it derives a severity score from such factors as underlying disease and chronic health status.[3,11] Other points are added for 12 physiologic variables (e.g., hematocrit, creatinine, Glasgow Coma Score, mean arterial pressure) measured within 24 hours of admission to the ICU. The APACHE II score has been validated in several studies involving tens of thousands of ICU patients. **2.** A widely used web server platform written by the Apache Software Foundation (ASF). The Apache web server browser had a key role in the initial growth of the World Wide Web.[60]

APC (Ambulatory payment class): A payment type for outpatient prospective payment system (PPS) claims.[61]

APG (Ambulatory patient group): A reimbursement methodology developed by 3M Health Information Systems for the Health Care Financing Administration (HCFA); APGs are to outpatient procedures what DRGs are to inpatient days; APGs provide for a fixed reimbursement to an institution for outpatient procedures or visits and incorporate data regarding the reason for the visit and patient data; APGs prevent unbundling of ancillary services; *see also* **ACG** and **ADG**.[62]

API (Application program interface): 1. A set of standard software interrupts, calls, functions, and data formats that can be used by an application program to access network services, devices, applications, or operating systems. **2.** A set of pre-made functions used to build programs. APIs ask the operating system or another application to perform specific tasks. A variety of types of APIs exist, including messaging APIs for e-mail, telephony APIs for calling systems, Java APIs, and graphics APIs, such as DirectX.[3] *See* **Socket**, **SSL**.

APMs (Alternative payment models): Models that offer health care providers with different ways to deliver care to Medicare beneficiaries. APMs are outlined in MACRA as a path for participation in MACRA's Quality Payment Program (QPP). Accountable Care Organizations (ACOs), Patient Centered Medical Homes (PCMH), and bundled payment models are some examples of APMs.[28] *See* **MACRA, ACO.**

Application: A software program or set of related programs that provide some useful healthcare capability or functionality.[10]

Application architecture: Defines how applications are designed and how they cooperate; promotes common presentation standards to facilitate rapid training and implementation of new applications and functions. Good application architecture enables a high level of system integration, reuse of components, and rapid deployment of applications in response to changing business requirements.[59]

Application entity title: *See* **AE title**.

Application integration: Sometimes called *enterprise application integration* or EAI; the process of bringing data or a function from one application program together with that of another application program. Where these programs already exist, the process is sometimes realized by using middleware, either packaged by a vendor or written on a custom basis. A common challenge for an enterprise is to integrate an existing (or legacy) program with a new program or with a web service program of another company. In general, for new applications, the use of object-oriented programming and actual or de facto standard development tools and interfaces (such as Java or .NET) will help ensure that new application programs can be easily integrated with those that may be needed in the future. The Extensible Markup Language (XML) promises to serve as a tool for exchanging data among disparate programs in a standard way.[2]

Application layer: *See* **OSI**. Layer 7 of the OSI (open systems interconnection) model. Responsible for information transfer between two network applications. This involves such functions as security checks, identification of the two participants, availability checks, negotiating exchange mechanisms, and most importantly initiating the exchanges themselves.[10]

Application metadata: *See* **metadata**.

Application program interface: *See* **API**.

Application protocol services: These are services supporting application level protocols. Simple object access protocol (SOAP) will be supported. Other remoting protocols, such as remote method invocation, DICOM, etc., can be plugged into the application protocol service.[59]

Application role: A characteristic of an application that defines a portion of its interfaces. It is defined in terms of the interactions (messages) that the role sends or receives in response to trigger events. Thus, it is a role played by a healthcare information system component when sending or receiving health information technology messages; a set of responsibilities with respect to an interaction.[59]

Application server: 1. Program on a distributed network that provides business logic and server-side execution environment for application programs. **2.** A computer that handles all operations between a company's back-end applications or databases and the users' computers' graphical user interface or web browsers. **3.** The device that connects end users to software applications and databases that are managed by the server.[11,59]

Application service provider: *See* **ASP.**

Appointment: An appointment represents a booked slot or group of slots on a schedule, relating to one or more services or resources. Two examples might include a patient visit scheduled at a clinic, and a reservation for a piece of equipment.[10]

Archetype: 1. A named content type specification with attribute declarations. **2.** Model (or pattern) for the capture of clinical information—a machine readable specification of how to store patient data.[63,64]

Archetype instance: Metadata class instance of an archetype model, specifying the clinical concept and the value constraints that apply to one class of record component instances in an electronic health record extract.[65]

Archetype model: Information model of the metadata to represent the domain-specific characteristics of electronic health record entries, by specifying values or value constraints for classes and attributes in the electronic health record reference model.[65]

Archetype repository: Persistent repository of archetype definitions accessed by a client authoring tool, or by a run-time component within an electronic health record service.[65]

Architecture: 1. A term applied to both the process and the outcome of specifying the overall structure, logical components, and the logical interrelationships of a computer, its operating system, a network, or other conception. **2.** A framework from which applications, databases, and workstations can be developed in a coherent manner, and in which every part fits together without containing a mass of design details. Normally used to describe how a piece of hardware or software is constructed and which protocols and interfaces are required for communications. Network architecture specifies the function and data transmission needed to convey information across a network.[36,59]

Archive: Long-term, physically or digitally separate storage.[66]

Archiving: Data archiving is the process of moving data that is no longer actively used to a separate storage device for long-term retention. Archive data consists of older data that is still important to the organization and may be needed for future reference, as well as data that must be retained for regulatory compliance. Data archives are indexed and have search capabilities so files and parts of files can be easily located and retrieved.[2]

Arden syntax: A language created to encode actions within a clinical protocol into a set of situation-action rules for computer interpretation, and to facilitate exchange between different institutions.[67]

Argument: 1. The values that a formula uses; they may be entered by the user, or be functions provided by the software. **2.** The part of a command that specifies what the command is to do.[36,68]

ARI (Access to radiology information): Specifies a number of query transactions providing access to radiology information, including images and related reports, in a DICOM format, as they were acquired or created. Such access is useful, both to the radiology department and to other departments, such as pathology, surgery, and oncology.[29]

Arithmetic logic unit: *See* **ALU.**

ARP (Address resolution protocol): The term address resolution refers to the process of finding an address of a computer in a network. The address is "resolved" using a protocol in which a piece of information is sent by a client process executing on the local computer to a server process executing on a remote computer. The information received by the server allows the server to uniquely identify the network system for which the address was required and therefore to provide the required address. The address resolution procedure is completed when the client receives a response from the server containing the required address.[69]

ARPANET (Advanced research projects agency network): 1. Developed by the Defense Advanced Research Projects Agency (DARPA), this distributed network grew into the Internet. **2.** The first operational packet-switching network.[2]

ARRA (American Recovery and Reinvestment Act of 2009): An economic stimulus bill enacted by the 111th Congress that provides $30 billion for various health information technology investments. Some of this funding was allocated by CMS to encourage physicians and hospital providers to adopt certified EHRs.[11]

Array: A set of sequentially indexed elements having the same intrinsic data type. Each element of an array has a unique identifying index number.[70]

Artificial intelligence: A computer application that has been designed to mimic the actions of an intelligent human in a given situation, and to be capable of substituting for a human.[68]

ASA (Average speed of answer): The average amount of time (measured in seconds) from when a caller calls customer service (enters the customer service queue) to when the caller begins speaking to a customer service associate.[71]

ASCII (American standard code for information interchange): Extensively used bit standard information processing code that represents 128 possible standard characters used by PCs. In an ASCII file, each alphabetic, numeric, or special character is represented with a 7-bit number (a string of seven 0s or 1s), which yields the 128 possible characters.[3]

ASN (Abstract syntax notation): The International Organization of Standardization (ISO), the International Electrotechnical Commission (IEC), and the International Telecommunications Union-Telecommunications Sector (ITU-T) (formerly known as the International Telegraph and Telephone Consultative Committee [CCITT]) have established Abstract Syntax Notation One (ASN.1) and its encoding rules as a standard for describing and encoding messages. ASN.1 is a formal notation for abstractly describing data to be exchanged between distributed computer systems. Encoding rules are sets of rules used to transform data specified in the ASN.1 notation into a standard format that can be decoded by any system that has a decoder based on the same set of rules.[72]

ASO (Administrative services only): Sometimes referred to as an administrative services contract (ASC); a contract between an insurance company and a self-funded plan where the insurance company performs administrative services only and does not assume any risk; services usually include claims processing but may include other services such as actuarial analysis and utilization review.[25] An arrangement in which an organization funds its own employee benefit plan such as a pension plan or health insurance program but hires an outside firm to perform specific administrative services.[20]

ASP (Active server pages): A specification for a dynamically created web page with a *.ASP* extension that utilizes ActiveX scripting—usually VB Script or Jscript code. When a browser requests an ASP, the web server generates a page with HTML code and sends it back to the browser. So ASPs are similar to CGI scripts, but they enable Visual Basic programmers to work with familiar tools.[41]

ASP (Application service provider): 1. An entity that provides some type of specialty automation service or access, under a service agreement for a customer, with the business model of being able to provide expertise and reliability at a desired lower cost than the customer could provide for itself within a local data center. **2.** Network administration includes the deployment, maintenance, and monitoring of active network gear: switches, routers, firewalls, etc. Network administration commonly includes activities such as network address assignment, assignment of routing protocols, and routing table configuration, as well as configuration of authentication- and authorization-directory services. This function may be outsourced by the healthcare organization.[11]

Assembler: *See* **Compiler.** An assembler is a program that takes basic computer instructions and converts them into a pattern of bits that the computer's processor can use to perform its basic operations. Some people call these instructions assembler language and others use the term *assembly language.*[2]

Assembly services: A business request may include calls to various components providing multiple result sets. These result sets will be assembled together in the appropriate output format by the assembly service. This service will use assembly templates to carry out its function.[59]

Association: Linking a document with the program that created it so that both can be opened with a single command (e.g., double-clicking a '.doc' file opens Microsoft® Word and loads the selected document).[73]

Assurance: Measure of confidence that the security features, practices, procedures, and architecture of an IT system accurately mediate and enforce the security policy.[23]

Asymmetric cryptographic algorithm: Algorithm for performing encipherment or the corresponding decipherment, in which the keys used for encipherment and decipherment differ.[74]

Asymmetric digital subscriber line: *See* **ADSL**.

Asymmetric keys: A combination of public and private keys used to encrypt and decrypt data. The public key is shared with everyone and the private key is kept secret. One key is used to encrypt data, and the other key is used to decrypt it. Also known as public key cryptography.[2]

Asymmetric multiprocessing: Multiprocessing technique in which certain tasks are dedicated to specific processors. One processor executes the operating system, while another processor handles applications.[3]

Asynchronous communication: Communication in which the reply is not made immediately after the message is sent, but when the recipient is available. E-mail is an example of asynchronous communication.[68]

Asynchronous transfer mode: *See* **ATM**.

ATA (Advanced technology attachment): A type of disk drive that integrates the drive controller directly on the drive itself. Computers can use ATA hard drives without a specific controller to support the drive. The motherboard must still support an ATA connection, but a separate card (such as an SCSI card for an SCSI hard drive) is not needed. Some different types of ATA standards include ATA-1, ATA-2 (aka Fast ATA), ATA-3, Ultra ATA (33 MBps maximum transfer rate), ATA/66 (66 MBps), and ATA/100 (100 MBps). The term IDE, or "Integrated Drive Electronics," is also used to refer to ATA drives. Sometimes (to add extra confusion to people buying hard drives), ATA drives are labeled as "IDE/ATA." Technically, ATA uses IDE technology, but the important thing to know is that they refer to the same thing.[75]

ATCB (Authorized testing and certification body): An entity that tests and certifies that certain types of electronic health record (EHR) technology (base EHRs and EHR modules) are compliant with the standards, implementation specifications, and certification criteria adopted by the U.S. Department of Health & Human Services Secretary and meet the definition of certified EHR technology.[13]

ATM (Asynchronous transfer mode): A high-performance, cell-oriented, switching, and multiplexing technology that utilizes fixed-length packets to carry different types of traffic.[76] *See* **Frame relay**, **SONET**.

ATNA (Audit trail and node authentication): Establishes the characteristics of a Basic Secure Note: **1.** Describes the security environment (user

A

identification, authentication, authorization, access control, etc.). **2.** Defines basic security requirements for the communications of the node. **3.** Defines basic auditing requirements for the node. The profile also establishes the characteristics of the communication of audit messages between the Basic Secure Nodes and Audit Repository Nodes that collect audit information.[29] *See* **Profile. NOTE: ATNA is an Integrating the Healthcare Enterprise (IHE) Profile.**

Atomic concept: 1. Primitive concept. **2.** Concept in a formal system whose definition is not a compositional definition.[77,78]

Atomic data (atomic level data): Data elements that represent the lowest level of possible detail in a data warehouse. The elemental, precise data captured at the source in the course of clinical care, can be manipulated in a variety of ways. These data are collected once, but used many times.[2]

Atomicity: Atomicity is a feature of database systems dictating where a transaction must be all-or-nothing. That is, the transaction must either fully happen or not happen at all. It must not complete partially. Atomicity is part of the ACID model (Atomicity, Consistency, Isolation, Durability), which is a set of principles used to guarantee the reliability of database transactions. Atomicity is usually achieved by complex mechanisms such as journaling or logging, or via operating-system calls. The definition of what constitutes an atomic transaction is decided by its context or the environment in which it is being implemented.[54] *See* **ACID.**

Attachment unit interface: *See* **AUI.**

Attack (cyberattack): A cyberattack is deliberate exploitation of computer systems, technology-dependent enterprises, and networks. Cyberattacks use malicious code to alter computer code, logic, or data, resulting in disruptive consequences that can compromise data and lead to cybercrimes, such as information and identity theft. Cyberattack is also known as a computer network attack (CNA).[54]

Attack vectors: Means by which an unauthorized person gains access to a network to cause harm.[2]

Attempted security violation: An unsuccessful action to gain unauthorized access to computer resources.[3]

Attenuation: The measurement of how much a signal weakens over distance on a transmission medium. The longer the medium, the more attenuation becomes a problem without the regeneration of the signal. Signal regeneration is usually accomplished through the use of hubs (baseband) and amplifiers (broadband).[3]

Attester party: The person or entity that certifies and records legal responsibility for a particular unit of information.[65]

Attribute: 1. An attribute expresses characteristics of a basic elemental concept. Attributes are also known as *roles* or *relationship types*. Semantic concepts form relationships to each other through attributes.[10,79] Attributes are abstractions of the data captured about classes. Attributes capture separate aspects of the class and take their values independent of one another. Attributes assume data values that are passed in HL7 messages.[10]

Attribute authority: *See* **AA.**

Attribute certificate: 1. Data structure, digitally signed by an attribute authority, that binds some attribute values with identification about its holder. **2.** A digital document containing attributes associated to the holder by the issuer.[74]

Attribute relationship: Consists of two semantic concepts related to each other through an attribute. When an attribute-value pair has been assigned to a concept, that relationship becomes part of the concept's logical definition. For this reason, attribute relationships are called "defining characteristics" of semantic concepts.[79]

Attribute type: The last part of an attribute name (suffix). Attribute type suffixes are rough classifiers for the meaning of the attribute.[10] *See* **Data type** for contrast in definition.

Attribute-value pair: The combination of an attribute with a value that is appropriate for that attribute. Assigning attribute-value pairs to semantic concepts is known as "authoring" or "modeling" and is part of the process of semantic content development. Attributes and values are always used together as attribute-value pairs. Sometimes the entire relationship is referred to as an object-attribute-value triple, or "OAV" triple.[79]

Audit: Independent review and examination of records and activities to assess the adequacy of system controls; to ensure compliance with established policies and operational procedures; and to recommend necessary changes in controls, policies, or procedures.[66]

Audit data: Chronological record of system activities to enable the reconstruction and examination of the sequence of events and changes in an event.[114]

Audit repository: Stores audit events.[29]

Audit trail: 1. Chronological record of system activity which enables the reconstruction of information regarding the creation, distribution, modification, and deletion of data. **2.** Documentary evidence of monitoring each operation of individuals on health information. May be comprehensive or specific to the individual and information. Audit trails are commonly used to search for unauthorized access by authorized users.[59]

Audit trail and node authentication: *See* **ATNA.**

Auditing: Specific activities that make up an audit. This can be manual, automated, or a combination.[22]

AUI (Attachment unit interface): The AUI (attachment unit interface) is the 15-pin physical connector interface between a computer's network interface card (NIC) and an Ethernet cable.[2]

AUP (Acceptable use policy): A document stipulating constraints and practices that a user must agree to for access to a corporate network or the Internet.

A

Many businesses and educational facilities require that employees or students sign an acceptable use policy before being granted a network ID.[2]

Authenticated document: A status in which a document or entry has been signed manually or electronically by one or more individuals who attest to its accuracy. No explicit determination is made that the assigned individual has performed the authentication. While the standard allows multiple instances of authentication, it would be typical to have a single instance of authentication, usually by the assigned individual.[10]

Authentication: Security measure, such as the use of digital signatures, to establish the validity of a transmission, message, or originator, or a means of verifying an individual's authorization to receive specific categories of information. The process of proving that a user or system is really who or what it claims to be. It protects against the fraudulent use of a system, or the fraudulent transmission of information.[3]

Authenticity: Assurance that a message, transaction, or other exchange of information is from the source it claims to be from. Authenticity involves proof of identity.[80]

Authority certificate: Certificate issued to a certification authority or to an attribute authority.[74] A certificate authority (CA) is a trusted entity that issues electronic documents that verify a digital entity's identity on the Internet. The electronic documents, which are called digital certificates, are an essential part of secure communication and play an important part in the public key infrastructure (PKI).[2]

Authorization: A security mechanism used to determine user/client privileges or access levels related to system resources, including computer programs, files, services, data, and application features. Authorization is normally preceded by authentication for user identity verification.[54]

Authorization decision: 1. Evaluating applicable policy, returned by the Policy Decision Point (PDP) to the Policy Enforcement Point (PEP). **2.** A function that evaluates to "Permit," "Deny," "Indeterminate," or "Not Applicable." **3.** A set of obligations by Organization for the Advancement of Structured Information Standards (OASIS).[22]

Authorized access: Mechanisms by which access to data is granted by challenges to the requesting entity, to assure proper authority based on the identity of the individual, level of access to the data, and rights to manipulate that data.[22] Process of granting or denying a user the access to a secure system. Most computer security systems are based on a two-step process: (1) Authentication to ensure that the entity requesting access to the system is what or who it claims to be, and (2) authorization to allow access only to those resources which are appropriate to that entity's identity.[4]

Authorized testing and certification body: *See* **ATCB**.

Automated data processing application coordinator: *See* **ADPAC**.

Availability: Assurance that the systems responsible for delivering, storing, and processing information are accessible when needed, by those who need them, and that the information it provides will be of acceptable integrity.[118] The property that data or information is accessible and useable upon demand by an authorized person.[81]

Average handling time: *See* **AHT**.

Average length of stay: *See* **ALOS**.

Average speed of answer: *See* **ASA**.

AVR (Analysis, visualization, and reporting): Ability to analyze, display, report, and map accumulated data, and share data and technologies for analysis and visualization with other public health partners.[82]

B

B2B (Business-to-business): On the Internet, B2B (business-to-business), also known as e-biz, is the exchange of products, services, or information (aka e-commerce) between businesses, rather than between businesses and consumers.[2]

B2B2C (Business-to-business-to-consumer): An emerging e-commerce model that combines business-to-business (B2B) and business-to-consumer (B2C) for a complete product or service transaction. B2B2C is a collaboration process that, in theory, creates mutually beneficial service and product delivery channels.[2]

B2C (Business-to-consumer): An Internet and electronic commerce (e-commerce) model that denotes a financial transaction or online sale between a business and consumer. B2C involves a service or product exchange from a business to a consumer, whereby merchants sell products to consumers.[2]

BAA (Business associate agreement): Also known as HIPAA business associate agreement (BAA). Under the U.S. Health Insurance Portability and Accountability Act of 1996, a HIPAA business associate agreement (BAA) is a contract between a HIPAA covered entity and a HIPAA business associate (BA). The contract safeguards protected health information (PHI) in accordance with HIPAA guidelines.[2]

Back door: Typically, unauthorized hidden software or hardware mechanism used to circumvent security controls. Also, alternate spelling, backdoor; an undocumented way of gaining access to a computer system. A backdoor refers to a potential security risk.[1]

Backbone: The high-speed, high-performance main transmission path in a network; a set of paths that local or regional networks connect to as a node for interconnection. The top level in a hierarchical network. Stub networks and transit networks which connect to the same backbone are guaranteed to be interconnected.[9]

Background: A task running in the background (a background task) is detached from the terminal where it was started (and often running at a lower priority); opposite of foreground. This means that the task's input and output must be from/to files (or other processes).[9]

Background process: A program that is running without user input. A number of background processes can be running on a multitasking operating system, such as Linux, while the user is interacting with the foreground process. Some background processes, such as daemons, for example, never require user input. Others are merely in the background temporarily while the user is busy with the program presently running in the foreground so that other processes can be sleeping and taking up swap space, until activated, which thus makes it currently a background process.[35]

Backup: A copy of files and programs made to facilitate recovery, if necessary.[1]

Backup domain controller: *See* **BDC**.

BAN (Body area network): A communication standard optimized for low-power devices and operation on, in, or around the human body (but not limited to humans) to serve a variety of applications, including medical, consumer electronics/personal entertainment, and others.[83]

Bandwidth: The difference between the highest and lowest frequencies of a transmission channel (the width of its allocated band of frequencies). The term can also mean data rate or capacity—the amount of data that is, or can be, sent through a given communications circuit per second.[9]

Bar code: A printed horizontal strip of vertical bars of varying widths, groups of which represent decimal digits and are used for identifying commercial products or parts. Bar codes are read by a bar code reader and the code interpreted either through software or a hardware decoder.[9]

Bar code medication administration: *See* **BCMA**.

Bar coding: A code consisting of a group of printed and variously patterned bars and spaces, and sometimes numerals, which are designed to be scanned and read into computer memory as identification for the object it labels. Bar coding is used by materials management, nursing, and pharmacy in inpatient and outpatient settings.[11]

Baseband: A transmission medium through which digital signals are sent without frequency shifting. In general, only one communication channel is available at any given time.[9]

Baseline: Compiled performance statistics for use in the planning and analysis of systems and networks.[3]

Baseline configuration: A set of specifications for a system, or Configuration Item (CI) within a system, that has been formally reviewed and agreed on at a given point in time, and which can be changed only through change control procedures. The baseline configuration is used as a basis for future builds, releases, and/or changes.[1]

BASIC (Beginner's all-purpose symbolic instruction code): Programming language. Originally devised as an easy-to-use programming language, it became widespread on home microcomputers in the 1980s, and remains popular to this day in a handful of heavily evolved dialects.[9]

Basic input output system: *See* **BIOS**.

BAT: A text file containing operating system commands which are executed automatically by the command-line interpreter. In UNIX, this is called a "shell script" since it is the UNIX shell which includes the command-line interpreter. Batch files can be used as a simple way to combine existing commands into new commands. In Microsoft® Windows, batch files have a filename extension, ".bat" or ".cmd." A special example is autoexec.bat, which MS-DOS runs when Windows starts.[9]

Batch: Since the advent of the personal computer, the term "batch" has come to mean automating frequently performed tasks that would otherwise be done interactively by storing those commands in a "batch file" or "script."[9]

Batch job: A batch job in SAP (Systems, Applications, and Products) is a scheduled background program that usually runs on a regular basis without any user intervention. Batch jobs are provided with more allocated memory than the ones that are done in the foreground. They are used to process high volumes of data that would normally consume long-term memory if run in the foreground, as well as for running programs that require less user interaction.[54]

Batch mode: A non-interactive mode of using a computer, in which customers submit jobs for processing and receive results on completion.[36]

Batch processing: A system that takes a sequence (a "batch") of commands or jobs, executes them, and returns the results, all without human intervention. This contrasts with an interactive system where the user's commands and the computer's responses are interleaved during a single run.[9]

Baud: The unit in which the information carrying capacity or "signaling rate" of a communication channel is measured. One baud is one symbol (state-transition or level-transition) per second. This coincides with bits per second only for two-level modulation with no framing or stop bits.[9]

BCMA (Bar code medication administration): An inventory control system that uses barcodes to prevent human errors in the distribution of prescription medications. The goal of BCMA is to make sure that patients are receiving the correct medications at the correct time by electronically validating and documenting medication administration. The information encoded in barcodes allows for the comparison of the medication being administered with what was ordered for the patient.[2]

BCP (Business continuity plan): The documentation of a predetermined set of instructions or procedures that describe how an organization's mission/business functions will be sustained during and after a significant disruption.[1]

BDC (Backup domain controller): A server in a network of Microsoft® Windows® computers that maintains a copy of the Security Account Manager (SAM) database and handles access requests that the Primary Domain Controller (PDC) doesn't respond to. There may be zeros or more BDCs in a network. They increase reliability and reduce load on the PDC.[9]

Beaconing: Token ring network signaling process that informs computers on the network that a serious error has occurred. A problem area ablation process.[3]

Beaming: Transfer of data or software programs between devices, such as cell phones, personal computers, and printers, using either infrared or radio-wave transmission.[84]

BEC (Business email compromise): A sophisticated email scam targeting businesses engaged in foreign transaction or wire transfer.[85]

Bedside workstation: Workstation in a patient room or examination room.[36]

Beginner's all-purpose symbolic instruction code: *See* **BASIC.**

Behavioral health: *See* **BH.**

Behavioral Risk Factor Surveillance System: *See* **BRFSS.**

Benchmarking: Refers to testing a product or service against a reference point to quantify how much better or worse it is compared to other products. Benchmarking is the standard way of comparing one product to another. With technology in particular, benchmarking against competing products is often the only way to get an objective measure of quality. This is because many technology products increase rapidly in measures such as speed and storage size when compared to the previous version from the same company, making comparisons between the versions virtually useless.[54]

Best of breed system: The best system in its referenced niche or category. Although it performs specialized functions better than an integrated system, this type of system is limited by its specialty area. To fulfill varying requirements, organizations often use best of breed systems from separate vendors. However, maintaining multiple systems provides little cross connectivity, which creates maintenance and integration challenges.[54]

Best of suite: An application buying philosophy between "best of breed" and "single vendor" that emphasizes integration of segments, or suites, of applications, each segment normally purchased from a different vendor. Each suite is then interfaced. Examples of suites include financial applications, clinical applications, and revenue cycle applications.[11]

Best practice: An industry-wide agreement that standardizes the most efficient and effective way to accomplish a desired outcome. A best practice generally consists of a technique, method, or process. The concept implies that if an organization follows best practices, a delivered outcome with minimal problems or complications will be ensured. Best practices are often used for benchmarking and represent an outcome of repeated and contextual user actions.[54]

Beta testing: The final stage in the testing of new software before its commercial release, conducted by testers other than its developers.[86] Evaluation of a prerelease (potentially unreliable) version of a piece of software (or possibly hardware) by making it available to selected users ("beta testers") before it goes on general distribution.[9]

BH (Behavioral health): A branch of interdisciplinary health which focuses on the reciprocal relationship between the holistic view of human behavior and the well-being of the body as a whole entity.[87]

Big data: Any voluminous amount of structured, semi-structured, and unstructured data that can be mined for information. Big data can be characterized by the volume of data, the variety of types of data, and the velocity at which the data must be processed.[2]

Big data storage: A storage infrastructure that is designed specifically to store, manage, and retrieve massive amounts of data, or big data. Big data storage enables the storage and sorting of big data in such a way that it can easily be accessed, used, and processed by applications and services working on big data. Big data storage is also able to flexibly scale as required.[54]

BGI (Binary gateway interface): Provides a method of running a program from a web server. Uses a binary Dynamic Link Library (DLL), which is loaded into memory when the server starts.[3]

BGP (Border gateway protocol): A protocol for exchanging routing information between gateway hosts in a network of autonomous systems. BGP is often the protocol used between gateways hosts on the Internet. The routing table contains a list of known routers, the addresses they can reach, and a cost metric associated with the path to each router so that the best available route is chosen.[2]

BIA (Business impact analysis): An analysis of an information system's requirements, functions, and interdependencies used to characterize system contingency requirements and priorities in the event of a significant disruption.[1]

Binary base two: A number representation consisting of zeros and ones used by practically all computers because of its ease of implementation using digital electronics and Boolean algebra.[9]

Binary gateway interface: *See* **BGI**.

Binding: 1. The linking of a protocol driver to a network adapter. **2.** An affirmation by a certificate authority/attribute authority (or its acting registration authority) of the relationship between a named identity and its public key or biometric template.[66]

BinHex: A Macintosh format for representing a binary file using only printable characters. The file is converted to lines of letters, numbers, and punctuation. Because BinHex files are simply text, they can be sent through most electronic mail systems and stored on most computers. However, the conversion to text makes the file larger, so it takes longer to transmit a file in BinHex format than if the file was represented some other way.[9]

Bioinformatics: The use of computer science, statistical modeling, and algorithmic processing to understand biological data. Bioinformatics is an example of how computer science has revolutionized other fields.[54]

Biomedical informatics: The interdisciplinary field that studies and pursues the effective uses of biomedical data, information, and knowledge for scientific inquiry, problem solving, and decision making, motivated by efforts to improve human health.[88]

Biometric authentication: A user identity verification process that involves biological input, or the scanning or analysis of some part of the body. Biometric authentication methods are used to protect many different kinds of systems—from logical systems facilitated through hardware access points to physical systems protected by physical barriers, such as secure facilities and protected research sites.[54]

Biometric identifier: An identifier based on some physical characteristic, such as a fingerprint.[61]

Biometric information: The stored electronic information pertaining to a biometric. This information can be in terms of raw or compressed pixels, or in terms of some characteristic.[66,89]

Biometric system: A technological system that uses information about a person (or other biological organism) to identify that person. Biometric systems rely on specific data about unique biological traits in order to work effectively. A biometric system will involve running data through algorithms for a particular result, usually related to a positive identification of a user or other individual.[54]

Biometric verification: An identity authentication process used to confirm a claimed identity through uniquely identifiable biological traits, such as fingerprints and hand geometry. It is designed to allow a user to prove his or her identity by supplying a biometric sample and associated unique identification code in order to gain access to a secure environment.[54]

Biometrics: Pertaining to the use of specific attributes that reflect unique personal characteristics, such as a fingerprint, an eye blood-vessel print, or a voice print, to validate the identity of a person.[38] A physical or behavioral characteristic of a human being.[1] Biometrics is a technological and scientific authentication method based on biology and used in information assurance (IA). Biometric identification authenticates secure entry, data, or access via human biological information such as DNA or fingerprints. Biometric systems include several linked components for effective functionality. The biometric system connects an event to a single person, whereas other ID forms, such as a personal identification number (PIN), may be used by anyone.[54]

BIOS (Basic input output system): The part of the system software of the IBM PC and compatibles that provides the lowest level interface to peripheral devices and controls the first stage of the bootstrap process, including installing the operating system. The BIOS is stored in ROM, or equivalent, in every PC. Its main task is to load and execute the operating system which is usually stored on the computer's hard disk.[9]

BioSense Platform: At the core of CDC's National Syndromic Surveillance Program (NSSP) is its BioSense Platform. It provides public health officials a common cloud-based health information system with standardized tools and procedures to rapidly collect, evaluate, share, and store information. Health officials can use the BioSense Platform to analyze and exchange syndromic data—improving their common awareness of health threats over time and across regional boundaries. They can exchange information faster and better coordinate community actions to protect the public's health. The BioSense Platform was developed through an active collaboration of CDC and other federal agencies, state and local health departments, and public health partners. The platform hosts an array of user-selected tools and has features that are continually being enhanced to reflect their needs.[82]

Biosurveillance: Surveillance programs in areas such as human health, hospital preparedness, state and local preparedness, vaccine research and procurement, animal health, food and agriculture safety, and environmental monitoring, that integrate those efforts into one comprehensive system.[22] *See* **Surveillance**.

Bit: A contraction of the term Binary Digit. The smallest unit of information in a binary system of notation.[1]

Bitcoin: A form of digital currency that requires encryption to regulate funds generation and transfer without any oversight from a central bank.[90]

Bit depth: The number of bits used to represent each pixel in an image, determining its color or tonal range.[3]

Bitmap: A data file or structure which corresponds bit for bit with an image displayed on a screen, probably in the same format as it would be stored in the display's video memory or maybe as a device independent bitmap. A bitmap is characterized by the width and height of the image in pixels and the number of bits per pixel which determines the number of shades of gray or colors it can represent. A bitmap representing a colored image (a "pixmap") will usually have pixels with between one and eight bits for each of the red, green, and blue components, though other color encodings are also used. The green component sometimes has more bits than the other two to cater to the human eye's greater discrimination in this component.[9]

Bits per second: *See* **BPS**.

Blacklisting: The process of the system invalidating a user ID based on the user's inappropriate actions. A blacklisted user ID cannot be used to log on to the system, even with the correct authenticator. Blacklisting and lifting of a blacklisting are both security-relevant events.[1] A control to prevent unwanted applications and programs from gaining access to an organization's computing resources.[2]

Block algorithms: Formulas that encrypt data one block at a time.[3]

Blockchain: A technology for transactional applications that can be used to share a ledger across a business network. This ledger is the source of all transactions across the business network and is shared among all participants in a secure, encrypted environment.[91] This technology grew out of the Bitcoin technological innovation. Blocks, or transaction records, are added to the chain in a linear, chronological order. Each node (or participant connected to the network) gets a copy of the blockchain, which gets downloaded automatically upon joining.[20] Though mostly used in banking and finance, there are potential applications for this technology in reimbursements and other healthcare activities.

Blog: Any kind of diary published on the web, usually written by an individual (a "blogger") but also by corporate bodies.[9]

Bluetooth: A specification for short-range radio links between mobile devices, mobile phones, digital cameras, and other portable devices.[9]

Body area network: *See* **BAN**.

Boolean logic/Boolean algebra: Form of logic seen in computer applications in which all values are expressed either as true or false. Symbols used to designate this are often called Boolean operators. They consist of equal to (=), more than (>), less than (<), and any combination of these, plus the use of "AND," "OR," and "NOT."[9]

Boot partition: Partition that contains the operating system files.[3]

Border gateway protocol: *See* **BGP**.

Born in the cloud: Refers to a specific type of cloud service that does not involve legacy systems, but was designed only for cloud delivery. This category of cloud services is instructive in changing how companies view reliance on cloud vendors.[54]

Bounce: An electronic mail message that is undeliverable and returns an error notification (a "bounce message") to the sender is said to "bounce."[9]

Bourne shell: The original command-line interpreter shell and script language for UNIX written by S.R. Bourne of Bell Laboratories in 1978. This term has been superseded for interactive use by the Berkeley C shell, *csh*, but still widely used for writing shell scripts.[9]

BPS (Bits per second): The basic unit of speed associated with data transmission.[3]

Breach of security: Any action by an authorized or unauthorized user that violates access rules and regulations, and results in a negative impact upon the data in the system or the system itself; or that causes data or services within a system to suffer unauthorized disclosure, modification, destruction, or denial of service.[3]

Breakthrough use case: A use case selected for implementation which crosses boundaries and levels, intended to stimulate investment, and delivers both immediate and long-term benefits.[22]

BRFSS (Behavioral Risk Factor Surveillance System): The nation's premier system of health-related telephone surveys that collect state data about U.S. residents regarding their health-related risk behaviors, chronic health conditions, and use of preventive services. Established in 1984 with 15 states, BRFSS now collects data in all 50 states as well as the District of Columbia and three U.S. territories. BRFSS completes more than 400,000 adult interviews each year, making it the largest continuously conducted health survey system in the world.[82]

Bridge: A device which forwards traffic between network segments based on data link layer information. These segments would have a common network layer address. Every network should only have one root bridge.[9] Bridging router, *See* **Brouter.**

Bring your own cloud: *See* **BYOC.**

Bring your own device: *See* **BYOD.**

Broadband: A class of communication channels capable of supporting a wide range of frequencies, typically from audio up to video frequencies. A broadband channel can carry multiple signals by dividing the total capacity into multiple, independent bandwidth channels, where each channel operates only on a specific range of frequencies.[9]

Broadcast: A transmission to multiple, unspecified recipients. On Ethernet, a broadcast packet is a special type of multicast packet which all nodes on the network are always willing to receive.[9]

Broadcast storm: Result of the number of broadcast messages on the network reaching or surpassing the bandwidth capability of the network.[3] A broadcast on a network that causes multiple hosts to respond by broadcasting themselves, causing the storm to grow exponentially in severity.[9]

Brouter (Bridging router): A device that bridges some packets (i.e., forwards based on data link layer information) and routes other packets (i.e., forwards based on network layer information). The bridge/route decision is based on configuration information.[9]

Browser: A program that allows a person to read hypertext. The browser gives some means of viewing the contents of nodes (or "pages") and of navigating from one node to another.[9]

Browsing: Act of searching through information system storage or active content to locate or acquire information without necessarily knowing the existence or format of information being sought.[1]

Brute force attack: A technique where software creates many possible combinations of characters in an attempt to guess passwords to gain access to a network or a computer.[50]

Buffer: An area of memory used for storing messages. Typically, a buffer will have other attributes such as an input pointer (where new data will be written into the buffer), and output pointer (where the next item will be read from) and/or a count of the space used or free. Buffers are used to decouple processes so that the reader and writer may operate at different speeds or on different sized blocks of data.[9]

Bug: An unwanted and unintended property of a program or piece of hardware, especially one that causes it to malfunction. Antonym of feature. The identification and removal of bugs in a program is called "debugging."[9]

Bus: 1. A structure that is used for connecting processors and peripherals, either within a system or in a local area network (LAN). **2.** The internal wiring between and within the central processing unit (CPU) and other motherboard subsystems.[3,36] A set of electrical conductors (wires, PCB tracks, or connections in an integrated circuit) connecting various "stations," which can be functional units in a computer or nodes in a network. A bus is a broadcast channel, meaning that each station receives every other station's transmissions and all stations have equal access to the bus.[9]

Business associates: Persons or business that provides services to assist covered entities with healthcare activities and function. Protected by HIPAA Privacy Rules and Business Associate Agreements (BAAs) that outlines assurances for the use of the information, covered providers and health plans are able to disclose protected health information to these "business associates." Covered entities may disclose protected health information (PHI) to an entity in its role as a business associate only to help the covered entity carry out its healthcare functions. PHI cannot be used for the business associate's independent use or purposes, except as needed for the proper management and administration of the business associate. *See* **Covered Entity, BAA.**

Business continuity plan: *See* **BCP.**

Business impact analysis: *See* **BIA.**

Business intelligence system: Represents the tools and systems that play a key role in the strategic planning process of the corporation. These systems allow a company to gather, store, access, and analyze corporate data to aid in decision-making.[41] *See* **Decision support system.**

Business interruption: Anticipated interruption to normal business, functions, operations, or processes such as due to a strike or unanticipated such as due to a power failure.[4]

Business-to-business: *See* **B2B.**

Business-to-business-to-consumer: *See* **B2B2C.**

Business-to-consumer: *See* **B2C.**

BYOC (Bring your own cloud): A concept/trend in which employees are allowed to use public or private third-party cloud services to perform certain job roles. BYOC often involves the piecing together of enterprise and consumer software—both in the cloud and on the premises—to get the job done.[54]

BYOD (Bring your own device): An enterprise policy used to permit partial or full integration of user-owned mobile devices for business purposes.[92]

Byte: A component in the machine data hierarchy larger than a bit and usually smaller than a word; now nearly always eight bits and the smallest addressable unit of storage. A byte typically holds one character.[9]

C

CA (Certification authority): The official responsible for performing the comprehensive evaluation of the technical and nontechnical security features of an IT system and other safeguards, made in support of the accreditation process, to establish the extent that a particular design and implementation meet a set of specified security requirements.[23]

Cache: 1. An area of temporary computer memory storage space that is reserved for data recently read from a disk, which allows the processor to quickly retrieve it, if it is needed again. A part of random access memory (RAM). **2.** A small, fast memory holding recently accessed data, designed to speed up access.[59]

Caching services: Service used to manage the cache and provide functions related to cache responses based on configured settings. The settings may include time to live, persistence, cache cycling, parameter/role/facility-based caching, etc.[59]

CAD (Computer-aided detection): Combining elements of artificial intelligence and digital image processing with radiological image processing to assist in the interpretation of medical images. Designed to decrease observational oversights, thus reducing false negative rates.[93] Also known as *computer-aided diagnosis (CADx)*.

CAH (Critical-access hospital): Rural community hospitals that receive cost-based reimbursement. To be designated a CAH, a rural hospital must meet defined criteria that were outlined in the Conditions of Participation 42 CFR 485 and subsequent legislative refinements to the program through the Balanced Budget Refinement Act of 1999 (BBRA), Benefits Improvement and Protection Act (BIPA, 2000), the Medicare Modernization Act, the Medicare Improvements for Patients and Providers Act (MIPPA, 2008), and the Patient Protection and Affordable Care Act (ACA, 2010).[94]

CAL (Computer-assisted learning): Any use of computers to aid or support the education or training of people. CAL can test attainment at any point, can provide faster or slower routes through the material for people of different aptitudes, and can maintain a progress record for the instructor.[58] *See* **CBL**.

Canadian Health Outcomes for Better Information and Care: *See* **C-HOBIC**.

Canonical: Of, or relating to, a set of core, standard, irreducible, or foundational concepts, works, or documents.[95]

CAP (Common alerting protocol): A digital format for exchanging emergency alerts with a single, consistent message that are simultaneously delivered over many different communications systems.[96]

Capability: Nonfunctional, observable system qualities that do not represent specific functions, and cannot be satisfied by any one component. These are emerging properties that are observed in a collection of components working together.[59]

Capacity: 1. The ability to run a number of jobs per unit of time.[59] **2.** The maximum amount or number that can be received or contained.[46]

Capitation: Pre-established payment of a set dollar amount to a provider on a per member basis for certain contracted services, for a given period of time. Amount of money paid to provider depends on number of individuals registered to their patient list, not on volume or type of service provided.[48]

Capture: 1. The method of taking a biometric sample from an end user. **2.** Process or means of obtaining and storing external data for use at a later time, such as a digital x-ray of a patient.[2,66]

Card reader: The generic term for an input device that reads flash memory cards. It can be a standalone device that connects to a computer via USB or it may be integrated into a computer, printer, or multifunction device. In fact, most multifunction printer/scanner/copiers now have built-in card readers.[75]

Cardiac catheterization workflow: *See* **CATH**.

Cardinality: 1. The number of rows in a table, or the number of indexed entries in a defined index. **2.** The number of elements in a set.[10] *See* **Multiplicity**.

Care coordination: The deliberate organization of patient care activities between two or more participants (including the patient) involved in a patient's care to facilitate the appropriate delivery of healthcare services. Organizing care involves the marshaling of personnel and other resources needed to carry out all required patient care activities, and is often managed by the exchange of information among participants responsible for different aspects of care.[97]

Care management: A set of activities that assures that every person served by the treatment system has a single approved care (service) plan that is coordinated, not duplicative, and designed to assure cost-effective and good outcomes. Care managers will oversee a patient's journey through treatment.[98]

Care plan: *See* **Plan of care**.

Care transitions: Movement of patients between different formal or informal healthcare providers over the course of an illness, encompassing the set of actions or processes designed to ensure the patient has continuity of care. Every change from provider or setting is another care transition.[3]

Carrier sense multiple access with collision detection: *See* **CSMA/CD**.

CASE (Computer-assisted software engineering): A computer-assisted method to organize and control the development of software. CASE allows developers to share a common view, allow checkpoint process, and serves as a repository.[2]

Case mix management: An application that provides integrated information from admission, discharge, transfer, utilization review, patient billing, and abstracting to monitor and understand the mix of types of patient services delivered.[11]

Casemix systems: An early form of analytic decision support system, which, for the first time, combined clinical and financial data for analysis. Sparked by the introduction of prospective payment (DRGs), the first system was developed at Rush-Presbyterian-St. Luke's, and was popularized by a system developed by New England Medical Center.[3]

Case-sensitive, Case sensitivity: Computer command which specifies that each letter of a word or term must be typed exactly as required or shown as a capital (uppercase) letter or a common (lowercase) letter. Usually, passwords are case-sensitive for better security. Also, a database search can be made case-sensitive for greater accuracy.[4]

CAT (Computerized axial tomography): An x-ray procedure that combines many x-ray images with the aid of a computer to generate cross-sectional views and, if needed, three-dimensional images of the internal organs and structures of the body.[99] Also known as *CT*.

CAT-1-7 (Categories 1-7): Categories of unshielded twisted pair cable (UTP). Allows voice grade only transmission rates below 100 Mbps up to 100 meters, or 328 feet, in length per segment. Higher categories support 10 Gigabit Ethernet, full-motion video, and teleradiology.[2]

Categories 1-7: *See* **CAT-1-7.**

Categorization: Process by which an individual information product can be associated with other products, using vocabularies designed to help citizens locate and access information. There can be multiple attributes assigned to a product (e.g., multiple categorizations). Categorization is used to provide context to a specific product, and to define relationships across a group of information products.[100] *See* **Classification.**

CATH (Cardiac catheterization workflow): Establishes the continuity and integrity of basic patient data in the context of the cardiac catheterization procedure. This profile deals specifically with consistent handling of patient identifiers and demographic data, including that of emergency patient presentation where the actual patient identity may not be established until after the beginning of the procedure, or even a significant time after the completion of the procedure. It also specifies the scheduling and coordination of procedure data across a variety of imaging, measurement, and analysis systems, and its reliable storage in an archive form where it is available to support subsequent workflow steps, such as reporting. It also provides central coordination of the completion status of steps of a potentially multi-phase (diagnostic and interventional) procedure.[29] *See* **Profile.** **NOTE: CATH is an Integrating the Healthcare Enterprise (IHE) Profile.**

Cause and effect diagram: A display of the factors that are thought to affect a particular problem or system outcome. The tool is often used in a quality improvement program or in brainstorming to group people's ideas about the causes of a particular problem in an orderly way. Also known as the *fishbone diagram* because of the shape that it takes when illustrating the primary and secondary causes.[101,102]

CBL (Computer-based learning): Any kind of learning with the help of computers. Computer-based learning makes use of the interactive elements of the computer applications and software and the ability to present any type of media to the users. Computer-based learning has many benefits, including the advantage of users learning at their own pace and also learning without the need for an instructor to be physically present.[103] *See* CAL.

CCC (Clinical care classification): Standardized, coded nursing terminology system that identifies the discrete elements of nursing practice. CCC provides a unique framework and coding structure for capturing the essence of patient care in all healthcare settings.[104]

CCD (Continuity of care document): A specification that is an XML-based markup standard (developed between HL7 and ASTM) intended to specify the encoding, structure, and semantics of a patient summary clinical document for exchange, used for sharing patient summary data.[10]

C-CDA (Consolidated clinical document architecture): Standard developed through joint efforts of Health Level Seven (HL7), Integrating the Healthcare Environment (IHE), the Health Story Project, and the Office of the National Coordinator (ONC) in order to consolidate CDA implementation guides from various Standards Development Organizations (SDOs) conflicting information.[13] *See* **CDA.**

CCO (Chief compliance officer): Responsible for legal processes and procedures, maintaining industry standards, and ensuring compliance with healthcare regulations.[11]

CCoM (Clinical context management): A standard for single sign-on designed to reduce administrative overload and improve interoperability and workflow.[56] Single sign-on allows a clinical user to access multiple applications on his or her computer via a single username and password, permitting browsing/search of a single patient's details across these applications. Context management allows a user to gain a unified view of a specific focus, a patient or patient encounter, for example, across multiple clinical applications at a single point of use.

CCOW (Clinical context object workgroup): Using a technique called context management, CCOW provides the clinician with a unified view on the information held in separate and disparate healthcare applications referring to the same patient, encounter, or user. This means that when a clinician signs onto one application within the group of disparate applications tied together by the CCOW environment, that same sign-on is simultaneously executed on all other applications within the group. Similarly, when the clinician selects a patient, the same patient is selected in all the applications. CCOW then builds a combined view of the patient on one screen. CCOW works for both client-server and web-based applications.[10,105]

CCR (Continuity of care record): 1. A standard specification developed jointly by ASTM International, the Massachusetts Medical Society (MMS), the Healthcare Information and Management Systems Society (HIMSS), the American Academy of Family Physicians (AAFP), and the American Academy of Pediatrics (AAP). It is intended to foster and improve continuity of patient care, reduce medical errors, and assure at least a minimum standard of health information transportability when a patient is referred or transferred to, or is otherwise seen by another provider. **2.** An XML document standard for a summary of personal health information that clinicians can send when a patient is referred, and that patients can carry with them to promote continuity, quality, and safety of care.[106]

CD (Committee draft): The second internal technical committee balloting stage for international standards from ISO.[38]

CD (Compact disc): Optical disk used to store digital data, originally developed for storing digital audio files.[8]

CDA (Clinical document architecture): 1. An XML-based document markup standard that specifies the structure and semantics of clinical documents for the purpose of exchange. **2.** Known previously as the patient record architecture, CDA provides an exchange model for clinical documents, such as discharge summaries and progress notes, and brings the healthcare industry closer to the realization of an electronic medical record. By leveraging the use of XML, the HL7 Reference Information Model (RIM), and coded vocabularies, the CDA makes documents both machine-readable (so documents are easily parsed and processed electronically) and human-readable so documents can be easily retrieved and used by the people who need them.[10,11]

CDMA (Code division multiple access): A wireless technology that includes digital voice service with 9.6 Kpbs to 14.4 Kpbs data services, and includes enhanced calling features, such as caller ID, but lacks an "always-on" data connection feature. CDMA is used as the access method in many mobile phone standards, similar to GSM.[3]

CDPD (Cellular digital packet data): A specification for supporting wireless access to the Internet and other public packet-switched networks. Cellular telephone and modem providers that offer CDPD support make it possible for mobile users to get access to the Internet at up to 19.2 kbps. Because CDPD is an open specification that adheres to the layered structure of the Open Systems Interconnection (OSI) model, it has the ability to be extended in the future. CDPD supports both the Internet Protocol and the ISO Connectionless Network Protocol (CLNP).[2]

CDR (Clinical data repository): **1.** A structured, systematically collected storehouse of patient-specific clinical data. **2.** A centralized database that allows organizations to collect, store, access, and report on clinical, administrative, and financial information, collected from various applications within or across the healthcare organization that provides an open environment for accessing/viewing, managing, and reporting enterprise information.[70]

CD-ROM (Compact Disc, read-only-memory): An adaptation of the Compact Disc (CD) that is designed to store computer data in the form of text and graphics, as well as hi-fi stereo sound. The original data format standard was defined by Philips and Sony in the 1983 Yellow Book. Other standards are used in conjunction with it to define directory and file structures, including ISO 9660, HFS (Hierarchal File System, for Macintosh computers), and Hybrid HFS-ISO. The format of the CD-ROM is the same as for audio CDs: a standard CD is 120 mm (4.75 inches) in diameter and 1.2 mm (0.05 inches) thick and is composed of a polycarbonate plastic substrate (underlayer—this is the main body of the disc), one or more thin reflective metal (usually aluminum) layers, and a lacquer coating.[2]

CDS (Clinical decision support): The use of automated rules based on clinical evidence to provide alerts, reminders, clinical guidelines, and other knowledge to assist in healthcare delivery.[45]

CDSS (Clinical decision support system): An application that uses pre-established rules and guidelines that can be created and edited by the healthcare organization, and integrates clinical data from several sources to generate alerts and treatment suggestions.[3] Also known as CDSS.

CDT (Current dental terminology): Official coding system for dentists to report professional services and procedures to third parties for payment. CDT is produced by the American Dental Association (ADA).[45]

CDW (Clinical data warehouse): Grouping of data accessible by a single data management system, possibly of diverse sources, pertaining to a health system or sub-system; and enabling secondary data analysis for questions relevant to understanding the functioning of that health system, and hence can support proper maintenance and improvement of that health system.[107]

CE (Coded element): A data type that transmits codes and the text associated with the code.[10]

Cellular digital packet data: *See* **CDPD**.

CEN (European Committee for Standardization): Major provider of European standards and technical specifications. CEN is the only recognized European organization for the planning, drafting, and adoption of European standards in all areas of economic activity with the exception of electrotechnology (CENELEC) and telecommunication (ETSI).[108]

Centers for Medicare & Medicaid Services (CMS) Electronic Health Record Incentive Program: Program that provides incentive payments to eligible professionals, eligible hospitals, and critical-access hospitals (CAHs) as they adopt, implement, upgrade, or demonstrate meaningful use of certified EHR technology.[28] *See* **Meaningful use.**

Central processing unit: *See* **CPU** and **Microprocessor.**

CERT (Computer emergency response team): A trusted authority and team of system specialists and other professionals, who are dedicated to improving the security and resilience of computer systems and networks, and are a national asset in the field of cybersecurity.[109]

Certificate: In cryptography, a **public key certificate** (also known as a **digital certificate** or **identity certificate**) is an electronic document used to prove ownership of a **public key.**[8,74] *See* **Public key certificate.**

Certificate authority: An independent licensing agency that vouches for a patient/person's identity in encrypted electronic communication. Acting as a type of electronic notary public, a certified authority verifies and stores a sender's public and private encryption keys and issues a digital certificate, or seal of authenticity, to the recipient.[59]

Certificate distribution: Act of publishing certificates and transferring certificates to security subjects.[74]

Certificate extension: Extension fields (known as extensions) in X.509 certificates that provide methods for associating additional attributes with users or public keys, and for managing the certification hierarchy. **Note:** Certificate extensions may be either critical (i.e., a certificate-using system has to reject the certificate if it encounters a critical extension it does not recognize) or noncritical (i.e., it may be ignored if the extension is not recognized).[74]

Certificate generation: Act of creating certificates.[74]

Certificate issuer: Authority trusted by one or more relying parties to create and assign certificates and which may, optionally, create the relying parties' keys.[74] **Note 1:** Adapted from ISO 9594-8:2001. **Note 2:** "Authority" in the Certificate Authority (CA) term does not imply any government authorization; it only denotes that the certificate authority is trusted. **Note 3:** *Certificate issuer* may be a better term, although *CA* is very widely used.

Certificate management: Procedures relating to certificates (i.e., certificate generation, certificate distribution, certificate archiving, and revocation).[74]

Certificate policy: *See* **CP.**

Certification: 1. Comprehensive evaluation of the technical and nontechnical security features of an IT system and other safeguards, made in support of the accreditation process, to establish the extent that a particular design and implementation meets a set of specified requirements. **2.** Procedure by which a third party gives assurance that all, or part of, a data processing system conforms to specified requirements. **3.** A defined process to ensure that EHR technologies meet the adopted standards, certification criteria, and other technical requirements to achieve meaningful use of those records in systems.[13,23,74]

Certification authority: *See* **CA.**

Certification practices statement: *See* **CPS.**

Certification profile: Specification of the structure and permissible content of a certificate type.[74]

Certification revocation: Act of removing any unreliable link between a certificate and its related owner (or security subject owner) because the certificate is not trusted any more, even though it is unexpired.[74]

Certified EHR technology: A qualified electronic health record that is certified pursuant to Section 3001(c) (5) of the Public Health Service Act (PHSA) as meeting standards adopted under Section 3004 that are applicable to the type of record involved (as determined by the Secretary of HHS, such as an ambulatory electronic health record for office-based physicians or an inpatient hospital electronic health record for hospitals).[37,110]

CF (Conditional formatting/coded formatted element): 1. A tool that allows a user to apply formats to a cell or range of cells and have that formatting change, depending on the value of the cell or the value of a formula.[111] **2.** Coded element with formatted values data type. This data type transmits codes and the formatted text associated with the code.[10,111]

CGI (Common gateway interface): 1. A standard or protocol for external gateway programs to interface with information servers, such as HTTP servers. Part of the overall HTTP protocol.[3,75] **2.** In the computer graphics world, CGI typically refers to Computer Generated Imagery. This type of CGI refers to 3D graphics used in film, TV, and other types of visual media. Most modern action films include at least some CGI for special effects, while other movies, such as Pixar animated films, are built completely from computer generated graphics.[75]

Channel: A path for the transmission of signals between a transmitting and receiving device.[3]

Channel sharing unit/data service unit: *See* **CSU/DSU.**

CHAP (Challenge handshake authentication protocol): An authentication protocol used to log in a user to an Internet access provider.[3]

Character: A member of a set of elements that is used for representation. Organization or control of data.[38]

Character-based terminal: A type of computer terminal and system that supports only alphabetical or numeric characters, with the visual displays and "mouse"-driven, bitmap software that most systems now utilize; the opposite of graphical user interface (GUI).[3]

Characteristic: Abstraction of a property of an object or a set of objects.[77]

Check digit: Number added to a code (such as a bar code or account number) to derive a further number as a means of verifying the accuracy or validity of the code as it is printed or transmitted. A code consisting of three digits, for example, such as 135 may include 9 (sum of 1, 3, and 5) as the last digit and be communicated as 1359.[4]

CHG (Charge posting): Specifies the exchange of information from the department system scheduler/order filler actor to the charge processor actor regarding charges associated with particular procedures, as well as communication between the ADT/patient registration and charge processor actors about patient demographics, accounts, insurance, and guarantors. The charge posted transaction contains all of the required procedure data to generate a claim. Currently, these interfaces contain fixed field formatted, or HL7-style, data. The goal of including this transaction in the IHE Technical Framework is to standardize the charge posted transaction to a charge processor, thus reducing system interface installation time between clinical systems and charge processors. Additionally, the charge posted transaction reduces the need of the billing system to have knowledge of the radiology internals. The result is that the charge processor will receive more complete, timely, and accurate data.[29] *See* **Profile. NOTE: CHG is an Integrating the Healthcare Enterprise (IHE) Profile.**

Chief compliance officer: *See* **CCO.**

Chief information/informatics officer: *See* **CIO.**

Chief medical information/informatics officer: *See* **CMIO.**

Chief nursing informatics/information officer: *See* **CNIO.**

Chief security officer: *See* **CSO.**

Chief technology officer: *See* **CTO.**

Child document: Subordinate to another, such as a parent document.[10]

CHIN (Community health information network): The service model for delivery of medical information across a local community, shared between providers, which was promulgated in the early 1990s. The movement failed to take hold due to concerns about aligning costs with benefits, with confidentiality of patient and propriety information, and other factors.[112] *See* **RHIO.**

C-HOBIC (Canadian Health Outcomes for Better Information and Care): Joint project between the Canadian Nurses Association (CNA) and Canada Health Infoway to begin the process of collecting standardized clinical outcomes that are reflective of nursing practice for inclusion in electronic health records.[113]

Chronic care model: Model developed by Edward Wagner and colleagues that provides a solid foundation from which healthcare teams can operate. The model has six dimensions: community resources and policies; health system organization of healthcare; patient self-management supports; delivery system redesign; decision support; and clinical information system. The ultimate goal is to have activated patients interact in a productive way with well-prepared healthcare teams. Three components that are particularly critical to this goal are adequate decision support, which includes systems that encourage providers to use evidence-based proto-cols; delivery system redesign, such as using group visits and same-day appointments; and use of clinical information systems, such as disease registries, which allow providers to exchange information and follow patients over time.[114]

Chronic disease: A sickness that is long-lasting or recurrent. Examples include diabetes, asthma, heart disease, kidney disease, and chronic lung disease.[114]

CHV (Consumer health vocabulary initiative): Open-access, collaborative initiative that links everyday words and phrases about health to technical terms or jargon used by healthcare professionals.[115]

CIA (Confidentiality/integrity/availability): The *CIA triad* is one of the core principles of information security.[8]

CIO (Chief information officer/chief informatics officer): Person responsible for the overall planning and management of the information technology department, including establishing strategic long-term goals and determining long-term systems needs and hardware acquisitions to accomplish business objectives.[11] Healthcare executive generally responsible for the health informatics platform to support the efficient design, implementation, and use of health information technology within a healthcare organization.[8]

Cipher text: Data produced through the use of encipherment, the semantic content of which is not available.[74]

Circuit switched: A type of network connection that establishes a continuous electrical connection between calling and called users for their exclusive use until the connection is released (e.g., telephone system); ideal for communications that require data to be transmitted in real-time.[3] *See* **Packet switching**.

CIS (Clinical information system): A system dedicated to collecting, storing, manipulating, and making available clinical information important to the delivery of healthcare. Clinical information systems may be limited in scope to a single area (e.g., lab system, ECG management system) or they may be comprehensive and cover virtually all facets of clinical information (e.g., electronic patient; the original discharge summary residing in the chart, with a copy of the report sent to the admitting physician, another copy existing on the transcriptionist's machine).[59]

CISC (Complex instruction set computer or computing): Computers designed with a full set of computer instructions that were intended to provide needed capabilities in the most efficient way. Later, it was discovered that, by reducing the full set to only the most frequently used instructions, the computer would get more work done in a shorter amount of time for most applications. Since this was called Reduced Instruction Set Computing (RISC), there was a need to have something to call full-set instruction computers, which resulted in the term CISC.[2]

Claim attachment: Any variety of hardcopy forms or electronic records needed to process a claim, in addition to the claim itself.[116]

Claim status category codes: A national administrative code set that indicates the general category of the status of healthcare claims. This code set is used in the Accredited Standards Committee (ASC) X12 248 claim status notification transaction, and is maintained by the healthcare code maintenance committee.[116]

Claim status codes: A national administrative code set that identifies the status of healthcare claims. This code set is used in the Accredited Standards Committee (ASC) X12 277 claim status notification transaction, and is maintained by the healthcare code maintenance committee.[116]

Class: A term used in programs written in the object-oriented paradigm. A class description will contain the code which describes the features (i.e., the data [properties] and behaviors [methods] of an object).[36]

Classification: The systematic placement of things or concepts into categories that share some common attribute, quality, or property. A classification structure is a listing of terms that depicts hierarchical structures.[36]

Clear text: *See* **Plain text**.

Clearance level: The security level of an individual who may access information.[3]

Client: A single term used interchangeably to refer to the user, the workstations, and the portion of the program that runs on the workstation. If the client is on a local area network (LAN), the client can share resources with another computer (server).[59]

Client application: A system entity, usually a computer process acting on behalf of a human user, which makes use of a service provided by a server.[66]

Client information: Personal information relating to healthcare.[14]

Client records: All personal information that has been collected, compiled, or created about clients, which may be maintained in one or more locations and in various forms, reports, or documents; including information that is stored or transmitted by electronic media.[14]

Client registry: The area where a patient/person's information (i.e., name, date of birth, Social Security number, health access number) is securely stored and maintained.[59]

Client/server model: 1. A client application is one that resides on a user's computer, but sends requests to a remote system to execute a designated procedure using arguments supplied by the user. The computer that initiates the request is the client, and the computer responding to the request is the server. **2.** A model for computing that splits the processing between clients and servers on a network, assigning functions to the machine most able to perform the function.[3]

Clinical algorithm: Flow charts to which a diagnostician or therapist can refer for a decision on how to manage a patient with a specific clinical program.[97]

Clinical care classification: *See* **CCC**.

Clinical context management: *See* **CCoM.**

Clinical context object workgroup: *See* **CCOW.**

Clinical data: All relevant clinical and socioeconomic data disclosed by the patient and others, as well as observations, findings, therapeutic interventions, and prognostic statements, generated by the members of the healthcare team.[3]

Clinical data information systems: Automated systems that serve as tools to inform clinicians about tests, procedures, and treatment in an effort to improve quality of care through real-time assistance in decision making, and to increase efficiency and decrease unnecessary utilization.[3]

Clinical data repository: *See* **CDR.**

Clinical data warehouse: *See* **CDW.**

Clinical decision support: *See* **CDS.**

Clinical decision support system: See **CDSS.**

Clinical document architecture: *See* **CDA.**

Clinical documentation system: An application that allows clinicians to chart treatment/therapy/health assessment results for a patient. This application provides the flow sheets and care plan documentation for a patient's course of therapy.[11]

Clinical informaticist: A person who evaluates clinical data relative to improving patient safety, clinical outcomes, and protocols and guidelines for clinical services. The functions are usually performed by people with clinical degrees.[11] Also known as Clinical Informatician.

Clinical informatics: 1. Promotes the understanding, integration, and application of information technology in healthcare settings. **2.** The application of informatics and information technology to deliver healthcare services.[55,88]

Clinical laboratory information system: Information system that manages clinical laboratory data to support laboratory management, laboratory data collection and processing, patient care, and medical decision making. **Note:** May be part of a hospital information system, or may be independent.[36] Also known as **LIS.**

Clinical observation: Clinical information, excluding information about treatment and intervention.[36] **Note:** Clinical information that does not record an intervention is, by nature, a clinical observation.

Clinical observation access service: *See* **COAS.**

Clinical pathway: A patient care management tool that organizes, sequences, and times the major interventions of nursing staff, physicians, and other departments for a particular case type, subset, or condition.[102]

Clinical performance measure: A method or instrument to estimate or monitor the extent to which the actions of a healthcare practitioner or provider conform to practice guidelines, medical review criteria, or standards of quality.[28]

Clinical practice guidelines: A set of systematically developed statements, usually based on scientific evidence, to assist practitioners and patient decision making about appropriate healthcare for specific clinical circumstances.[101]

Clinical protocol: A set of rules defining a standardized treatment program or behavior in certain circumstances.[36]

Clinical quality measures: *See* **CQM.**

Clinical record: *See* **EHR.**

Clinical status: Description of the individual by means of results for a specified set of measurable quantities.[36]

Clinical terminology: Terminology required directly or indirectly to describe health conditions and healthcare activities.[117]

Clinical terminology system: Consists of a collection of words or phrases organized together to represent the entities and relationships that characterize the knowledge within a given biomedical domain.[118]

Clinical/medical code sets: Code sets used to identify medical conditions and the procedures, services, equipment, and supplies used to deal with them. Nonclinical or nonmedical or administrative code sets to identify, or characterize, entities and events in a manner that facilitates an administrative process.[117]

Clock speed: Measure of how quickly a computer completes basic computations and operations. This is measured as a frequency in hertz (Hz) and most commonly refers to the speed of the computer's central processing unit.[119]

Closed card system: A smartcard system in which the cards can only be used in a specified environment, such as a college campus.[3]

Closed loop medication administration: An environment in which the medication process is electronic from initial entry by physicians using CPOE, to pharmacies for order validation and bar coding the medications, to the automatic dispensing machines, to the actual administration of the medication at the point of care by the nurse, the point at which the nurse scans the patient bar code and the medication bar code. This initiates clinical decision support for the five rights of medication administration: right patient, right time, right drug, right dose, and right route.[11]

Cloud (Cloud computing): A model for enabling ubiquitous, convenient, on-demand network access to a shared pool of configurable computing resources (e.g., networks, servers, storage, applications, and services) that can be rapidly provisioned and released with minimal management effort or service provider interaction.[120]

CM (Composite message/composite data type): A field that is a combination of other meaningful data fields. Each portion is called a component.[10]

CMD (Command): File type: External Command Menu. Dot (.) CMD is similar to a DOS.bat (batch file) or an .exe (executable file). A way of giving command line (like DOS) prompts to the computer (e.g., to map the drive).[8]

CMET (Common message element type): Reusable data types, which can be included in any number of messages without repeating the common internal structure.[10]

CMIO (Chief medical information officer/chief medical informatics officer): A person that provides overall leadership in the ongoing development, implementation, advancement, and optimization of electronic information systems that impact patient care. Works in partnership with the organization's IT leadership to translate clinician requirements into specifications for clinical and research systems.[11] Healthcare executive generally responsible for the health informatics platform required to work with clinical information technology staff to support the efficient design, implementation, and use of health technology within a healthcare organization.[8]

CMYK (Cyan, magenta, yellow, and black): 1. Printing processes, such as offset lithography, use CMYK inks; digital art must be converted to CMYK color for print. **2.** The 'K' in CMYK stands for Key, since in four-color printing cyan, magenta, and yellow printing plates are carefully keyed or aligned with the key of the black key plate.[8,120]

CNCL: Cancelled.

CNIO (Chief nursing information officer/chief nursing informatics officer): Leads the strategy, development, and implementation of information technology to support nursing, nursing practice, and clinical applications, collaborating with the chief nursing officer on the clinical and administration decision-making process.[11]

COA (Compliance-oriented architecture): The virtues of service-oriented architectures (SOAs) as applied to the specific business challenge of compliance. The result is a flexible architecture that can meet compliance challenges now and in the future. Compliance requirements can be expressed as a set of core services.[121]

COAS (Clinical observations access service): Standardizes access to clinical observations in multiple formats, including numerical data stored by instruments, or entered from observations.[121]

COB: Close of business.[3]

COB (Coordination of benefits): 1. The process by which a payer handles claims that may involve other insurance companies (i.e., situations in which an insured individual is covered by more than one insurance plan). **2.** Process of determining which health plan or insurance policy will pay first and/or determining the payment obligations of each health plan, medical insurance policy, or third-party resource when two or more health plans, insurance policies, or third-party resources cover the same benefits.[122]

Code: 1. Concept identifier that is unique within a coding system. **2.** A representation assigned to a term so that the term may more readily be electronically processed.[45,78]

Code 128: A one-dimensional bar code symbology, using four different bar widths, used in blood banking and other healthcare and nonhealthcare applications.[112] *See* **ISBT 128.**

Code division multiple access: *See* **CDMA.**

Code meaning: Element within a coded set.[123]

Code set: 1. A set of elements which is mapped onto another set according to a coding scheme. **2.** Clinical or medical code sets identify medical conditions, and the procedures, services, equipment, and supplies used to deal with them. Nonclinical or nonmedical or administrative code sets identify, or characterize, entities and events in a manner that facilitates an administrative process.[38,124]

Code set maintaining organization: Under the Health Insurance Portability and Accountability Act (HIPAA), this is an organization that creates and maintains the code sets adopted by the HHS Secretary for use in the transactions for which standards are adopted.[116]

Code value: Result of applying a coding scheme to a code meaning.[123]

Codec (Compression/decompression): An algorithm, or specialized computer program, that reduces the number of bytes consumed by large files and programs.[120]

Coded element: *See* **CE.**

Coded formatted elements: *See* **CF.**

Coded with exceptions: *See* **CWE.**

Coding: The activity of using a coding scheme to map from one set of elements to another set of elements. The products of classification and coding are often used for similar purposes and sometimes considered the same; however, coding and classification are distinct concepts.[36]

Coding scheme: The collection of rules that maps the elements of one set onto the elements of a second set.[38]

Coding system: Combination of a set of concepts (coded concepts), a set of code values, and at least one coding scheme mapping code values to coded concepts.[78]

Cognitive computing: The simulation of human thought processes in a computerized model. Cognitive computing involves self-learning systems that use data mining, pattern recognition, and natural language processing to mimic the way the human brain works. The goal is to create automated IT systems that are capable of solving problems without human assistance. This is used in numerous artificial intelligence (AI) applications.[2] An example of this technology occurring in healthcare is with IBM's Watson Health, a cognitive computing system that mines big data to identify trends and assist in clinical decisions.[91] *See* **Artificial intelligence.**

Collect and communicate audit trails: Means to define and identify security relevant events and the data to be collected and communicated, as determined by policy, regulation, or risk analysis.[22]

Collect/collection: The assembling of personal information through interviews, forms, reports, or other information sources.[22]

Collision detection: *See* **CSMA/CD.**

Command: A sequence of words and/or symbols that instructs the computer to perform a specific task.[36]

Committee draft: *See* **CD.**

Common alerting protocol: *See* **CAP.**

Common gateway interface: *See* **CGI.**

Common message element type: *See* **CMET.**

Common object request broker architecture: *See* **CORBA.**

Common services: A type of software service that can be shared across multiple applications. These include services such as messaging, security, logging, auditing, mapping, etc. Common services are part of the health information access layer.[59]

Common vulnerabilities and exposures: *See* **CVE.**

Common weakness enumeration: *See* **CWE.**

Communication bus: Part of the health information access layer that allows applications to communicate according to standard messages and protocols.[59]

Communication network: Configuration of hardware, software, and transmission facilities for transmission and routing of data carrying signals between electronic devices.[36]

Communications security: *See* **COMSEC.**

Communities of interest: Inclusive term to describe collaborative groups of users who must exchange information in pursuit of shared goals, interests, missions, or business process; and must have a shared vocabulary for the information exchanged. Communities provide an organization and maintenance construct for data.[125]

Community health information network: *See* **CHIN.**

Compact disc: *See* **CD.**

Compact disk read only memory: *See* **CD-ROM.**

Comparability: The ability of different parties to share precisely the same meaning for data.[45]

Comparison: The process of comparing a biometric with a previously stored reference.[66]

Compatibility: Suitability of products, processes, or services for use together under specific conditions to fulfill relevant requirements without causing unacceptable interactions.[36]

Competence: Demonstrated performance and application of knowledge to perform a required skill or activity to a specific, predetermined standard.[101]

Compiler: 1. Programs written in high-level languages are translated into assembly language or machine language by a compiler. Assembly language programs are translated into machine language by a program called an assembler. Every CPU has its own unique machine language. Programs must be rewritten or recompiled, therefore, to run on different types of computers. **2.** A program that translates a program written in a high-level programming language to a machine-language program, which can then be executed.[8,36] *See* **Assembler.**

Complex instruction set computer processor: *See* **CISC.**

Compliance: Adherence to those policies, procedures, guidelines, laws, regulations, and contractual arrangements to which the business process is subject.[14]

Compliance date: Under the Health Insurance Portability and Accountability Act (HIPAA), this is the date by which a covered entity must comply with a standard, an implementation specification, or a modification. This is usually 24 months after the effective date of the associated final rule for most entities; 36 months for small health plans. For future changes in the standards, the compliance date would be at least 180 days after the effective date, but can be longer for small health plans or for complex changes.[116]

Component: An object-oriented term used to describe the building block of GUI applications. A software object that contains data and code. A component may or may not be visible.[36]

Component object model: Used by developers to create reusable software components, link components together to build applications, and take advantage of Windows services.[70]

Composite message: *See* **CM.**

Compression/decompression: *See* **Codec.**

Compromise: Disclosure of information to unauthorized persons, or a violation of the security policy of a system in which unauthorized intentional or unintentional disclosure, modification, destruction, or loss of an object may have occurred.[66]

Computer-aided detection: *See* **CAD.**

Computer-assisted coding: Software solutions using natural language processing (NLP), which is an exclusive patented algorithmic software to electronically analyze entire medical charts to precode with both CPT procedure and ICD diagnostic nomenclatures.[11]

Computer-assisted learning: *See* **CAL** and **CBL.**

Computer-assisted medicine: Use of computers directly in diagnostic or therapeutic interventions (e.g., computer-assisted surgery).[126]

Computer-assisted software engineering: *See* **CASE.**

Computer-based patient record: Term coined by the Institute of Medicine in its publication *The Computer-based Patient Record: An Essential Technology for Health Care* (Washington, DC: National Academy Press, 1991, p. 11, rev. 1997). It may be used synonymously with *electronic medical record* or *electronic health record.* It is electronic patient medical record information that resides in a system specifically designed to support users by providing accessibility to complete and accurate data, alerts, reminders, clinical decision support systems, links to medical knowledge, and other aids.[45] *See* **EHR**.

Computer emergency response team: *See* **CERT**.

Computer-on-wheels: *See* **COW**.

Computer readable card: A card capable of storing information in a form that can be read by a computer. Information may be written to the card on manufacture, or may be added during the use of the card. If the card contains a processor, the card is known as a *smartcard*.[36]

Computer security: The protection of data and resources from accidental or malicious acts, usually by taking appropriate actions.[38]

Computer system: An integrated arrangement of computer hardware and software operated by customers to perform prescribed tasks.[36]

Computer telephony integration: *See* **CTI**.

Computerized axial tomography: *See* **CAT**.

Computerized practitioner order entry: *See* **CPOE**.

Computing environment: The total environment in which an automated information system, network, or a component operates. The environment includes physical, administrative, and personnel procedures, as well as communication and networking relationships, with other information systems.[23]

COMSEC (Communications security): Measures and controls taken to deny unauthorized persons information derived from telecommunications and ensure the authenticity of such telecommunications. Communications security includes cryptosecurity, transmission security, emission security, and physical security of COMSEC material.[23]

Concentrator: Network device where networked nodes are connected. Used to divide a data channel into two or more channels of lower bandwidth.[3] *See* **Hub**.

Concept: 1. An abstraction or a general notation that may serve as a unit of thought or a theory. In terminology work, the distinction is made between a concept and the terms that reference the concept. Where the concept is identified as abstract from the language and the term is a symbol that is part of the language. **2.** A clinical idea to which a unique concept has been assigned. Each concept is represented by a row in the concepts table. Concept equivalence occurs when a postcoordinated expression has the same meaning as a precoordinated concept or another postcoordinated expression.[36,79] **Note 1:** Informally, the term "concept" is often used when what is meant is "concept representation." However, this leads to confusion when precise meanings are required. Concepts arise out of human individual and social conceptualizations of the world around them. Concept representations are artifacts constructed of symbols.[33] **Note 2:** Concept representations are not necessarily bound to particular languages. However, they are influenced by the social or cultural context of use often leading to different categorizations.[33]

Concept harmonization: Activity for reducing or eliminating minor differences between two or more concepts that are closely related to each other.[36] **Note:** Concept harmonization is an integral part of standardization.

Concept identifier: Concept name, code, or symbol, which uniquely identifies a concept.[33]

Concept status: A field in the concepts table that specifies whether a concept is in current use. Values include "current," "duplicate," "erroneous," "ambiguous," and "limited."[79]

Concept unique identifier: *See* **CUI**.

Concepts table: A data table consisting of rows, each of which represents a concept.[79]

Concurrent versioning system: *See* **CVS**.

Conditional formatting: *See* **CF**.

Confidentiality: 1. Obligation of an entity that receives identifiable information about an individual as part of providing a service to that individual to protect that data or information; including not disclosing the identifiable information to unauthorized persons, or through unauthorized processes. **2.** A property by which information relating to an entity or party is not made available or disclosed to unauthorized individuals, entities, or processes.[22,38]

Confidentiality/integrity/availability: *See* **CIA**.

Configuration: The components that make up a computer system, including the identity of the manufacturer, model, and various peripherals; the physical arrangement of those components (what is placed and where). The software settings that enable two computer components to communicate with each other.[3]

Configuration control: Process of controlling modifications to an IT system's hardware, firmware, software, and documentation to ensure the system is protected against improper modifications prior to, during, and after system implementation.[23]

Configuration management: Management of security features and assurances through control of changes made to hardware, software, firmware, documentation, test, test fixtures, and test documentation, throughout the lifecycle of the IT.[23]

Configuration manager: The individual or organization responsible for configuration control or configuration management.[23]

Configuration services: This service is used to configure an electronic health record (EHR). This includes configuration of the EHR data repository, the system, the metadata, the service components, EHR indexes, schema support, security, session, caching mechanism, etc.[59]

Conformance: The precise set of conditions for the use of options which must be implemented in a standard. There are two types of conformance: dynamic and static. Dynamic conformance requirements of a standard are all those requirements (including options) which determine the possible behavior permitted by the standard. Static conformance is a statement of what conforming implementation should be capable of doing (i.e., what is implemented).[38]

Conformance assessment process: The complete process of accomplishing all conformance testing activities necessary to enable the conformance of an implementation or system to one or more standards to be assessed.[36]

Conformance testing: Testing to determine whether a system meets some specified standard. To aid in this, many test procedures and test setups have been developed, either by the standard's maintainers or external organizations, specifically for testing conformance to standards. Conformance testing is often performed by external organizations, sometimes the standards body itself, to give greater guarantees of compliance. Products tested in such a manner are then advertised as being certified by that external organization as complying with the standard.[8]

Connected health: Model of healthcare delivery using technology to provide services including information and education.[50]

Connectivity: The potential to establish links to, or interact with, another computer system or database.[3]

Consensus: General agreement, characterized by the absence of sustained opposition to substantial issues by any important part of the concerned interests, and by a process that involves seeking to take into account the views of all parties concerned, and to reconcile any conflicting arguments.[36]

Consensus standards: These are standards developed or adopted by consensus standards bodies, both domestic and international. Such work and the resultant standards are usually voluntary.[38]

Consent: Under the Privacy Rule, consent is made by an individual for the covered entity to use or disclose identifiable health information for treatment, payment, and healthcare operations purposes only. This is different from consent for treatment, which many providers use and which should not be confused with the consent for use or disclosure of identifiable health information. Consent for use and/or disclosure of identifiable health information is optional under the Privacy Rule, although it may be required by state law, and may be combined with consent for treatment unless prohibited by other law.[22]

Consent directive: The record of a healthcare consumer's privacy policy that grants or withholds consent for: one or more principals (identified entity or role); performing one or more operations (e.g., collect, access, use, disclose, amend, or delete); purposes, such as treatment, payment, operations, research, public health, quality measures, health status evaluation by third parties, or marketing; certain conditions (e.g., when unconscious); specified time period (e.g., effective and expiry dates); and certain context (e.g., in an emergency).[22]

Consenter: An author of a consent directive; and may be the healthcare consumer or patient, a delegate of the healthcare consumer (e.g., a representative with healthcare power of attorney), or a provider with legal authority to either override a healthcare consumer's consent directive, or create a directive that prevents a patient's access to protected health information (PHI) until the provider has had an opportunity to review the PHI with the patient.[22]

Consistency: The transaction takes the resources from one consistent state to another.[8] *See* **ACID**.

Consistent presentation of images: *See* **CPI**.

Consistent time: *See* **CT**.

Consumer health vocabulary initiative: *See* **CHV**.

Content coverage: The ability of a coding system to capture the meaning of a document.[3]

Content profile: An Integrating the Healthcare Enterprise (IHE) content profile specifies a coordinated set of standards-based information content, exchanged between the functional components of communicating healthcare IT systems and devices. An IHE content profile specifies a specific element of content (e.g., a document) that may be conveyed through the transactions of one or more associated integration profiles.[127]

Continuity: Strategic and tactical capability, preapproved by management, of an organization to plan for and respond to conditions, situations, and events in order to continue operations at an acceptable predefined level.[89]

Continuity of care document: *See* **CCD**.

Continuity of care record: *See* **CCR**.

Continuity strategy: Approach by an organization intended to ensure continuity and ability to recover in the face of a disruptive event, emergency, crisis, or other major outage.[89]

Control: Means of managing risk, including policies, procedures, guidelines, practices, or organizational structures, which can be of an administrative, technical, management, or legal nature.[128]

Control chart: A graphic display of the results of a process over time and against established control limits. The dispersion of data points on the chart is used to determine whether the process is performing within prescribed limits, and whether variations taking place are random or systematic.[101]

Control rights: The right of an individual to know where his or her data are stored, to authorize who can access his or her own data, to correct his or her own record, to make certain segments inaccessible via standard processes, and to know that the data keeper observes the laws and professional ethical tenets.[3]

Control unit: *See* **CU.**

Controlled access: Authorized user access limited to specific data and resources, according to that user's authorization.[3]

Controlled resource: A resource to which an access control mechanism has been specifically applied.[3]

Controlled vocabulary: An established list of standardized terminology for use in indexing and retrieval of information.[129]

Conventional memory: On DOS systems, the portion of memory that is available to standard DOS programs to run.[41]

Convergence: The end point of any algorithm that uses iteration or recursion to guide a series of data processing steps. An algorithm is usually said to have reached convergence when the difference between the computed and observed steps falls below a predefined threshold.[130]

Cookies: A small amount of data generated by a web site and saved to the web browser. The purpose is to remember information about the web session, similar to a preference file created by a software application.[75]

Coordination of benefits: *See* **COB.**

Coprocessor: A chip designed specifically to handle a particular task, such as math calculations or displaying graphics on-screen; faster at its specialized function than the main processor; relieves the processor of some work.[3]

CORBA (Common object request broker architecture): A language-independent object model and specification for a distributed applications development environment.[3]

Core-based statistical area: *See* **CBSA.**

Core values: An organization's essential and enduring tenets—a small set of general guiding principles.[131]

Corporate executives or C-level: *See* **CxO.**

Cost-benefit analysis: A comparison of the costs of a proposed course of action with its benefits, considering tangible and intangible economic impacts, and the time value of money.[52]

Cost containment: The process of planning in order to keep costs within certain constraints.[36]

Cost effectiveness: A system contributing to cost savings in healthcare by efficiently collecting, storing, and aggregating data; and by providing decision support and augmented practices with appropriate and timely information.[52]

Countermeasure response administration: *See* **CRA.**

Covered entity: Health plans, healthcare clearinghouses, and healthcare providers who transmit any health information in electronic form, in connection with a transaction that is subject to Health Insurance Portability and Accountability Act (HIPAA) requirements, as those terms are defined and used in the HIPAA regulations, 45 CFR Parts 160 and 164.[14]

Covered function: Functions that make an entity a health plan, a healthcare provider, or a healthcare clearing house.[116]

COW (Computer-on-wheels): Allows a single computer to operate in **multiple places** around the hospital or other healthcare setting. This method is used to save space as there is minimal space to accommodate a computer in every patient room.[132]

CP (Certificate policy): Named set of rules that indicates the applicability of a certificate to a particular community and/or class of application with common security requirements.[74]

CPI (Consistent presentation of images): Specifies a number of transactions that maintain the consistency of presentation for grayscale images and their presentation state information (including user annotations, shutters, flip/rotate, display area, and zoom). It also defines a standard contrast curve, the Grayscale Standard Display function, against which different types of display and hardcopy output devices can be calibrated. It thus supports hardcopy, softcopy, and mixed environments.[3] *See* **Profile. NOTE: CPI is an Integrating the Healthcare Enterprise (IHE) Profile.**

CPOE (Computerized practitioner order entry): 1. An order entry application specifically designed to assist practitioners in creating and managing medical orders for patient services and medications. This application has special electronic signature, workflow, and rules engine functions that reduce or eliminate medical errors associated with practitioner ordering processes. **2.** A computer application that accepts the provider's orders for diagnostic and treatment services electronically, instead of the clinician recording them on an order sheet or prescription pad.[11] Also known as *computerized physician order entry, computerized patient order entry,* and *computerized provider order entry.*

CPR (Computer-based patient record): *See* **EHR.**

CPRS (Computer-based patient record system): *See* **EHR.**[3]

CPS (Certification practices statement): Statement of the practices that a certification authority employs in issuing certificates.[74]

CPT (Current procedural terminology): 1. The official coding system for physicians to report professional services and procedures to third parties for payment. It is published by the American Medical Association.[48] **2.** A medical code set, maintained and copyrighted by the AMA, that has been selected for use under HIPAA for non-institutional and non-dental professional transactions.[45,124]

CPU (Central processing unit): 1. The component in a digital computer that interprets and executes the instructions and data contained in software. Microprocessors are CPUs that are manufactured on integrated circuits, often as a single-chip package. **2.** Brain of the computer. Main system board (motherboard) integrated chip that directs computer operations. Performs the arithmetic, logic, and controls operations in the computer.[3]

CQM (Clinical quality measures): Tools that measure and track the quality of healthcare services provided by eligible professionals (EPs), eligible hospitals, and critical access hospitals (CAHs) within the U.S. healthcare system.[28]

CRA (Countermeasure response administration): Systems that manage and track measures taken to contain an outbreak or event, and to provide protection against a possible outbreak or event. This public health information network (PHIN) functional area also includes multiple dose delivery of countermeasures: anthrax vaccine and antibiotics; adverse events monitoring; follow-up of patients; isolation and quarantine; and links to distribution vehicles (such as the Strategic National Stockpile).[82]

Crash: A data system error condition leading to a total termination of all computing activities, and requiring a restart procedure for recovering normal operational status.[3]

Crawler: A program that automatically fetches web pages. Crawlers are used to feed pages to search engines.[3] *See* **Web crawler.**

Credential: Evidence attesting to one's right to credit or authority; in this standard, the data elements associated with an individual that authoritatively binds an identity (and, optionally, additional attributes) to that individual.[66]

Crisis management team: Group of individuals functionally responsible for directing the development and execution of the response and operational continuity plan, declaring an operational disruption or emergency/crisis situation, and providing direction during the recovery process, both pre- and postdisruptive incident. The crisis management team may include individuals from the organization, as well as immediate and first responders, stakeholders, and other interested parties.[89]

Critical-access hospital; *See* **CAH.**

Critical path: A tool that supports collaborative, coordinated practices. It provides for multidisciplinary communication, treatment and care planning, and documentation of caregiver's evaluations and assessments.[52]

Criticality assessment: A process designed to systematically identify and evaluate an organization's assets based on the importance of its mission or function, the group of people at risk, or the significance of a disruption on the continuity of the organization.[89] *See* **Risk assessment.**

CRM (Customer relationship management): The approach of establishing relationships with customers on an individual basis, then using collected information about customers and their buying habits to treat different customers differently.[3]

Cross-enterprise document sharing: *See* **XDS.**

Cross map: A reference from one concept in one terminology to another in a different terminology. A concept may have a single cross map or a set of alternative cross maps.[79]

Cross-platform: Refers to software or network functionality that will work on more than one platform or type of computer.[3]

Crosstalk: Signal overflow from one wire to an adjacent wire, with the possibility of causing information distortion.

Crosswalk: *See* **Data mapping.**

CRUD (Create, read, update, and delete): The basic processes that are applied to data.[2,62]

Cryptographic algorithm cipher: Method for the transformation of data in order to hide its information content, prevent its undetected modification, and/ or prevent its unauthorized use.[74]

Cryptography: The art of keeping data secret, primarily through the use of mathematical or logical functions that transform intelligible data into seemingly unintelligible data and back again.[3]

CSMA/CD (Carrier sense multiple access with collision detection): 1. A network control protocol in which a carrier-sensing scheme is used; and a transmitting data station that detects another signal while transmitting a frame stops transmitting that frame, transmits a jam signal, and then waits for a random time interval (known as "backoff delay" and determined using the truncated binary exponential backoff algorithm) before trying to send that frame again. Ethernet is the classic CSMA/CD protocol.[8] **2.** A protocol for carrier transmission access in Ethernet networks. On Ethernet, any device can try to send a frame at any time. Each device senses whether the line is idle and therefore available to be used. If it is, the device begins to transmit its first frame. If another device has tried to send at the same time, a collision is said to occur and the frames are discarded. Each device then waits a random amount of time and retries until successful in getting its transmission sent.[2]

CSO (Chief security officer): The person with the responsibility for the security of the paper-based and electronic health information, as well as the physical and electronic means of managing and storing that information.[133]

CSU/DSU (Channel sharing unit/data service unit): A unit that shapes digital signals for transmission. The CSU is a device that performs protective and diagnostic functions for a telecommunications line.[3]

CT (Consistent time): Mechanisms to synchronize the time base between multiple actors and computers. Various infrastructure, security, and acquisition profiles require use of a consistent time base on multiple computers. The consistent time profile provides a median synchronization error of less than one second.[29] *See* **Profile. NOTE: CT is an Integrating the Healthcare Enterprise (IHE) Profile.**

CTI (Computer telephony integration): Systems that enable a computer to act as a call center, accepting incoming calls and routing them to the appropriate device or person.[3]

CTO (Chief technology officer): 1. Has overall responsibility for managing technical vendor relationships and performance, as well as the physical and personnel technology infrastructure, including technology deployment, network and systems management, integration testing, and developing technical operations personnel. **2.** Develops technical standards and ensures compatibility for the enterprise-wide computer environment.[11]

CTS (Common terminology services): Specification developed as an alternative to a common data structure.[10]

CU (Control unit): Portion of the CPU that coordinates all computer operations through the machine cycle: fetch, decode, execute, and store.[3]

CUI (Concept unique identifier): The class of names that uniquely identifies an instance of entity. Some examples of unique identifiers are the keys of tables in database applications and the International Standard Book Number (ISBN).[3]

Cure letter: A letter sent by one party to another, proposing or agreeing to actions that a party will take to correct legal errors or defects that have occurred under a contract between the parties or other legal requirement.[14]

Current procedural terminology: *See* **CPT.**

Custom, customized: Software that is designed or modified for a specific user or organization; may refer to all or part of a system. *See* **Vanilla.**[3]

Customer-centric: Placing the customer at the center or focus of design or service.[8]

Customer-driven: Systems design focused on user acceptance; focused on customer requirements.[8]

Customer relationship management: *See* **CRM.**

CVE (Common vulnerabilities and exposures): A list of standardized names for vulnerabilities and other information security exposures. CVE aims to standardize the names for all publicly known vulnerabilities and security exposures.[26]

CVS (Concurrent versioning system): Keeps track of all work and changes in a set of files.[8]

CWE (Coded with exceptions): Specifies a coded element and its associated detail. The CWE data type is used (1) when more than one table may be applicable or (2) when the specified HL7 or externally defined table may be extended with local values or (3) when the text is in place, the code may be omitted.[134]

CWE (Common weakness enumeration): A community-developed formal list of software weaknesses, idiosyncrasies, faults, and flaws.[26]

CxO (Corporate executives or C-level): A short way to refer, collectively, to corporate executives at what is sometimes called the C-level, whose job titles typically start with "Chief" and end with "Officer."[2]

Cybersecurity: The practice of keeping computers and electronic information safe and secure by preventing, detecting, and responding to attacks or unauthorized access against a computer system and its information.[13]

Cyberspace: The realm of communications and computation. A term used to refer to the electronic universe of information available through the Internet.[3]

Cyberspace shadow: The model in cyberspace of a person or of an organization (e.g., a person's medical files).[3]

D

DaaS (Data as a service): A cloud strategy used to facilitate the accessibility of business-critical data in a well-timed, protected, and affordable manner. DaaS depends on the principle that specified, useful data can be supplied to users on demand, irrespective of any organizational or geographical separation between consumers and providers.[54]

Dashboard: A user interface or web page that gives a current summary, usually in graphic, easy-to-read form, of key information relating to progress and performance, especially of a business or website.[46]

Data: 1. Items representing facts, text, numbers, graphics, images, sound, or video. Data are the raw material used to create information. **2.** Discrete entities that are described objectively without interpretation. **3.** Data are information that has been translated into a form that is more convenient to move or process.[2]

Data access: Refers to a user's ability to access or retrieve data stored within a database or other repository. Users who have data access can store, retrieve, move, or manipulate stored data, which can be stored on a wide range of hard drives and external devices.[2]

Data aggregation: 1. A process by which information is collected, manipulated, and expressed in summary form. **2.** Combining protected health information by a business associate, on behalf of more covered entities than one, to permit data analysis related to the healthcare operations of the participating covered entities.[22,135]

Data analytics: The systematic use of data to drive fact-based decision making for planning, management, measurement, and learning. Analytics may be descriptive, predictive, or prescriptive. In healthcare, data analytics is being used to drive clinical and operational improvements to meet business challenges.[136] Data analytics focuses on inference, the process of deriving a conclusion based solely on what is already known by the researcher.[2]

Data architecture: A set of rules, policies, standards, and models that govern and define the type of data collected and how it is used, stored, managed, and integrated within an organization and its database systems. It provides a formal approach to creating and managing the flow of data and how it is processed across an organization's IT systems and applications.[2]

Data as a service: *See* **DaaS**.

Data capture: The retrieval of information from a document using methods other than data entry. The utility of data capture is the ability to automate this information retrieval where data entry would be inefficient, costly, or inapplicable.[137]

Data center: 1. A centralized repository, either physical or virtual, for the storage, management, and dissemination of data and information organized around a particular body of knowledge or pertaining to a particular business. **2.** Computer facility designed for continuous use by several users, and well-equipped with hardware, software, peripherals, power conditioning, backup, communication equipment, security systems, etc.[2,4]

D

Data circuit-terminating equipment: *See* **DCE**.

Data classification: Conscious decision to assign a level of sensitivity to data as they are being created, amended, enhanced, stored, or transmitted. The classification of the data, whether established by federal or state law or by the entity holding the data, will determine the extent the data needs to be protected, controlled, and/or secured, and is indicative of its value in terms of information assets.[22]

Data cleaning/cleansing: Manipulating data extracted from operational systems to make data usable by the data warehouse.[138]

Data collection: A systematic approach to gathering information from a variety of sources to get a complete and accurate picture of an area of interest.[2]

Data compression: A reduction in the number of bits needed to represent data. Compressing data can save storage capacity, speed file transfer, and decrease costs for storage hardware and network bandwidth.[2]

Data condition: A description of the circumstances in which certain data are required.[28]

Data content: All the data elements and code sets inherent to a transaction, and not related to the format of the transaction.[116]

Data corruption: A deliberate or accidental violation of data integrity.[3]

Data definition language: *See* **DDL**.

Data dictionary: A document or system that characterizes the data content of a system.[28]

Data diddling: Unauthorized data alteration; a common form of computer crime.[3]

Data element: 1. The smallest named unit of information in a transaction or database. **2.** A unit of data for which the definition, identification, representation, and permissible values are specified by means of a set of attributes.[38,116]

Data elements for emergency department systems: *See* **DEEDS**.

Data encryption standard: *See* **DES** and **DEA**.

Data entry: Direct input of data in the appropriate data fields of a database, through the use of a human data-input device such as a keyboard, mouse, stylus, or touch screen, or through speech recognition software. *See also* **Data capture** and **Data logging**.[4]

Data exchange: Securing transmissions over communication channels.[3]

Data field: In the structure of a database, the smallest component under which data is entered through data capture or data entry. All data fields in the same database have unique names, several data fields make up a data record, several data records make up a data file, and several data files make up a database.[4]

Data flow diagram: A two-dimensional diagram that explains how data is processed and transferred in a system. The graphical depiction identifies each source of data and how it interacts with other data sources to reach a common output. This type of diagram helps business development and design teams visualize how data is processed and identify or improve certain aspects.[4]

Data governance: The overall management of the availability, usability, integrity, and security of the data employed in an enterprise. A sound data governance program includes a governing body or council, a defined set of procedures, and a plan to execute those procedures.[2]

Data granularity: *See* **Granularity**.

Data integration: A process in which heterogeneous data is retrieved and combined as an incorporated form and structure. Data integration allows different data types (such as data sets, documents, and tables) to be merged by users, organizations, and applications, for use as personal or business processes and/or functions.[54]

Data integrity: 1. Assurance of the accuracy, correctness, or validity of data, using a set of validation criteria against which data are compared or screened. **2.** The property that data have not been altered or destroyed in an unauthorized manner or by authorized users; it is a security principle that protects information from being modified or otherwise corrupted, either maliciously or accidentally.[45,52]

Data interchange: The process of transferring data from an originating system to a receiving system.[36]

Data Interchange Standards Association: A body that provides administrative services to ASC X12 and several other standards-related groups.[28]

Data leakage: The practically undetectable loss of control over, or possession of, information.[3]

Data link layer: Second layer in the OSI model. Consists of upper logical link control (LLC) and lower media access control (MAC) portions. Handles data flow control, the packaging of raw data in its frames, or frames into raw data bits, and retransmits frames as needed.[3]

Data logging: The process of using a computer to collect data through sensors, analyze the data and save and output the results of the collection and analysis. Data logging also implies the control of how the computer collects and analyzes the data.[139]

Data manipulation language: *See* **DML**.

Data mapping: A process used in data warehousing by which different data models are linked to each other using a defined set of methods to characterize the data in a specific definition. This data linking follows a set of standards, which depends on the domain value of the data model used.[54]

Data mart: 1. A well-organized, user-centered, searchable database system. A data mart picks up where a data warehouse stops, by organizing the information according to the user's needs (usually by specific subjects), with ease of use in mind. **2.** A repository of data that serves a particular community of knowledge workers. The data may come from an enterprise-wide database or a data warehouse. **3.** Collection of data focusing on a specific topic or organization unit or department created to facilitate strategic business decisions.[59,140]

Data messaging: *See* **Messaging**.

Data migration: The process of transferring data between data storage systems, data formats, or computer systems.[2]

Data mining: A decision support approach of analyzing data, and then extracting actionable information in the form of new relationships, patterns, clusters, predictive models, and trends.[3]

Data model: 1. A conceptual model of the information needed to support a business function or process. **2.** Describes the organization of data in an automated system. The data model includes the subjects of interest in the system (or entities) and the attributes (data elements) of those entities. It defines how the entities are related to each other (cardinality) and establishes the identifiers needed to relate entities to each other. A data model can be expressed as a conceptual, logical, or physical model.[59,116]

Data modelling: A method used to define and analyze data requirements needed to support the business functions of an enterprise. Data modeling defines the data elements, their relationships, and their physical structure in preparation for creating a database.[3]

Data object: A collection of data that has a natural grouping and may be identified as a complete entity.[123]

Data origin authentication: Corroboration that the source of data is received as is claimed.[3]

Data originator: The person who generates data, such as the patient for symptoms, the physician for examination and decisions, the nurse for patient care, etc.[3]

Data processing: The converting of raw data to machine-readable form and its subsequent processing (as storing, updating, rearranging, or printing out) by a computer.[31]

Data provenance: 1. The ability to trace and verify the creation of data, how it has been used or moved among different databases, as well as altered throughout its lifecycle.[141] **2.** Evidence and attributes that describe the origin of health information as it is captured in a health system.[142]

Data quality: 1. A comprehensive view of the usefulness of data to support decision making. The measurements of data quality include completeness, correctness, comprehensibility, and consistency in support of intended use. **2.** The features and characteristics that ensure data are accurate, complete, and convey the intended meaning.[3,45]

Data registry: An information resource by a registration authority that describes the meaning and representational form (metadata) of data units, including data element identifiers, definitions, units, allowed value domains, etc. HIPAA's standards for electronic transactions call for a master data dictionary to be developed and maintained to ensure common data definitions across standards selected for implementation.[45]

Data repository: *See* **Repository** and **Data warehouse**.

Data service unit: *See* **DSU**.

Data set: A collection of discrete items of related data that may be accessed individually or in combination or managed as a whole entity such as Uniform Hospital Discharge Data Set (UHDDS). Analyzing data sets during data mining can discover patterns and use those patterns to forecast or predict the likelihood of future events.[2,143] *See* **PNDS, NMDS,** and **NMMDS**.

Data standards: Consensual specifications for the representation of data from different sources and settings; necessary for the sharing, portability, and reusability of data.[144]

Data structure: Interrelationships among data elements that determine how data are recorded, manipulated, stored, and presented by a database.[4]

Data subject: The person whose information is stored in a computer system.[3]

Data synchronization: The process of maintaining the consistency and uniformity of data instances across all consuming applications and storing devices. It ensures that the same copy or version of data is used in all devices—from source to destination.[54]

Data tagging: A formatted word that represents a wrapper for a stored value. The data tag is a small piece of scripting code, typically JavaScript, which transmits page-specific information via query string parameters. The process begins when a page containing a data tag is requested from the server. The tag is a piece of scripting code executed when the page is loaded into the browser. The data tag constructs the query string by scanning the document source for HTML, beginning with a specific identifier.[145]

Data terminal ready: *See* **DTR**.

Data transformation: The process of converting data or information from one format to another, usually from the format of a source system into the required format of a new destination system. The usual process involves converting documents, but data conversions sometimes involve the conversion of a program from one computer language to another to enable the program to run on a different platform. The usual reason for this data migration is the adoption of a new system that is totally different from the previous one.[54]

Data type: 1. A category of data. The broadest data types are alphanumeric and numeric. Programming languages allow for the creation of several data types, such as integer (whole numbers), floating point, date, string (text), logical (true/false), and binary. Data type usually specifies the range of values, how the values are processed by the computer, and how the data type is stored. **2.** The categories of data that will be persisted in the EHR. They include voice, waveforms, clinical notes, and summaries, diagnostic imaging, lab, and pharmacy information.[35,59]

Data use agreement: Confidentiality agreement between a covered entity and the recipient of health information in a limited data set.[22]

Data user: The person or organization that has justified need for certain data to perform his or her legitimate tasks.[3]

Data validation: A process used to determine if data are accurate, complete, or meet specified criteria. Data validation may include format checks, check key tests, reasonableness checks, and limit checks.[38]

Data visualization: A decision support methodology for turning data into information by using the high capacity of the human brain to visually recognize patterns and trends using a wide variety of data plotting, graphing, and exploration techniques.[3]

Data warehouse: 1. A repository where all types of data (clinical, administrative, and financial) are stored together for later retrieval. Data mining and decision support systems are uses of a data warehouse. When the perspective of the strategy or user shifts from the enterprise view of aggregate data to the individual user or knowledge worker (who may need access to a specialized or local database), then the system is referred to, instead, as a data mart. **2.** A collection of clinical and/or financial data in a database designed to support management decision making.[59]

Database: 1. A file created by a database manager that contains a collection of information. The basic database contains fields, records, and files; a field is a single piece of information, a record is one complete set of fields, and a file is a collection of records. **2.** A collection of stored data, typically organized into fields, records, files, and associated descriptions (schema).[36]

Database administrator: The person responsible for a database system, particularly for defining the rules by which data are accessed, modified, and stored.[3]

Database design: This includes logical (entity relationship) and physical (table, column, and key) design tools for data. Physical data modeling is becoming almost mandatory for applications using relational database management systems (RDBMSs).[146]

Database management system: *See* **DBMS.**

Datum: Any single observation or fact. A medical datum generally can be regarded as the value of a specific parameter (e.g., a patient, at a specific time).[36]

Daughterboard: A board that attaches to another board, such as the motherboard or an expansion card. A daughter card may contain additional memory to an accelerator card.[3]

DBMS (Database management system): 1. A program that lets one or more computer users create and access data in a database. On personal computers, Microsoft® Access® is a popular example of a single or small group user

DBMS. Microsoft's SQL server is an example of a DBMS that serves database requests from a larger number of users. **2.** A set of programs used to define, administer, store, modify, process, and extract information from a database.[11]

DDL (Data definition language): A language used to define data structures and modify data. For example, DDL commands can be used to add, remove, or modify tables within a database. DDLs used in database applications are considered a subset of SQL, the Structured Query Language. However, a DDL may also define other types of data, such as XML.[75] Also known as *data description language.*

DEA (Data encryption algorithm): A method for encrypting information.[46] *See* **DES.**

Debugging: The process of discovering and eliminating errors and defects, or bugs, in program code.[3]

Decipherment decryption: Process of obtaining, from a cipher text, the original corresponding data.[74]

Decision support (analytic): Recommendations for intervention based on computerized care protocols.[50]

Decision support system: *See* **DSS.**

Decision tree: A data mining predictive model-building algorithm that segregates data into factors with high association to the predicted variable. The resulting set of decision rules branch off each other and resemble a tree.[3]

Decompression: The expansion of compressed image files.[3] *See* **Lossless compression** and **Lossy.**

Decryption: The process of decoding a message so that its meaning becomes obvious. The reverse process of encryption in which cipher text is transformed back into the original plain text using a second complex function and a decryption key.[3]

Dedicated line: A telephone or data line that is always available. This line is not used by other computers or individuals, is available 24 hours a day, and is never disconnected.[3]

DEEDS (Data elements for emergency department systems): The recommended data set for use in emergency departments; it is published by the Centers for Disease Control and Prevention (CDC).[82] Subsequently Health Level Seven (HL7) Data Elements for Emergency Department Systems (DEEDS) was created to improve interoperability of emergency care data.[10]

Default gateway: TCP/IP configuration option that specifies a device or computer to send packets out of a local subnet.[3] *See* **Gateway.**

Default route: A routing table entry used to direct packets addressed to networks not explicitly listed in the routing table.[3]

Definition: Statement that describes a concept and permits differentiation from other concepts within a system.[38]

Degaussing: Exposure to high magnetic fields. One method of destroying data on a hard drive, USB thumb drive, smart phone, or floppy disk. Also commonly used to improve the picture resolution on electronic displays. Many display manufacturers include an internal coil that will degauss the display when it is turned on. Display monitors and televisions with cathode ray tube (CRT) technology are particularly subject to the buildup of magnetic fields.[2]

De-identified health information: Removal of individual identifiers so that they cannot be used to identify an individual. De-identified health information is not protected by HIPAA.[22]

Deliberate threat: Threat of a person or persons to damage a computer system consciously and willingly.[3]

Deliverable: Any tangible outcome that is produced by the project. These can be documents, plans, computer systems, buildings, aircraft, etc. Internal deliverables are produced as a consequence of executing the project, and are usually only needed by the project team. External deliverables are those that are created for clients and stakeholders.[70]

Demodulation: Reverse of modulation. The analog-to-digital signal conversion process occurring in a modem at a receiving site. Analog signals are used to transfer data over phone lines. Digital signals are in a format that can be used by a computer.[3]

Demographic data: Data that describe the characteristics of enrollee populations such as within a managed care entity. Demographic data include but are not limited to age, sex, race/ethnicity, and primary language.[28]

Denial-of-service attack: An attack in which a user (or a program) takes up so much of a shared resource that none of the resource is left for other users or uses.[3]

Derivative: Any re-use of information at the application level. Captures the notion of "collect once, use many times." For example, detailed data information from an accounting system can be used for financial planning. Loosely adapted from mathematics, investing.[4]

Derivative file: A subset from an original identifiable file.[28]

DES (Data encryption standard): A common standard for data encryption and a form of secret key cryptography (SKC), which uses only one key for encryption and decryption versus public key cryptography (PKC) that uses two keys, i.e., one for encryption and one for decryption.[54]

Description logics: A family of knowledge representation languages that can be used to represent the terminological knowledge of an application domain in a structured and formally well-understood way. The name *description logic* refers, on the one hand, to concept descriptions used to describe a domain; and, on the other hand, to the logic-based semantics which can be given by a translation into first-order predicate logic.[147]

Descriptor: The text defining a code in a code set.[117]

Design: 1. Phase of software development following analysis and concerned with how the problem is to be solved. **2.** The process and result of describing how a system or process is to be automated. Design must thoroughly describe the function of a component and its interaction with other components. Design usually also identifies areas of commonality in systems and optimizes reusability.[59]

Designated approving authority: Official with the authority to formally assume the responsibility for operating a system or network at an acceptable level of risk.[23]

Designated code set: A medical code set or an administrative code set that is required to be used by the adopted implementation specification for a standard transaction.[28]

Designated record set: A group of records maintained by or for a covered entity that comprises the medical records and billing records about individuals maintained by or for a covered health care provider; enrollment, payment, claims adjudication, and case or medical management record systems maintained by or for a health plan; or other records that are used, in whole or in part, by or for the covered entity to make decisions about individuals.[37]

DHCP (Dynamic host configuration protocol): Standard protocol that allows a network device to obtain all network IP configuration information automatically from host-based, pooled IP addresses. Alleviates manual static IP address assignment.[3]

DI (Diagnostic imaging): Also called *medical imaging.* The use of digital images and textual reports prepared as a result of performing diagnostic studies, such as x-rays, CT scans, MRIs, etc.[148]

Diagnostic and Statistical Manual: *See* **DSM.**

DICOM (Digital imaging and communications in medicine): 1. A standard for the electronic communication of medical images and associated information. DICOM relies on explicit and detailed models of how patients, images, and reports involved in radiology operations are described and how the above are related. The DICOM standards contain information object definitions, data structure, data dictionary, media storage, file format, communications formats, and print formats. **2.** An ANSI-accredited standards development organization that has created a standard protocol for exchanging medical images among computer systems.[45]

Dictionary: In computer science programming languages, a dictionary is an abstract data type storing items or values. A value is accessed by an associated key. Basic operations are new, insert, find, and delete.[149]

Digital: Data is in terms of two states: positive and nonpositive. Positive is expressed or represented by the number 1 and nonpositive by the number 0. Thus, data transmitted or stored with digital technology is expressed as a string of 0's and 1's. Each of these state digits is referred to as a bit and a string of bits that a computer can address individually as a group is a byte.[2]

Digital certificate: An electronic "passport" that allows a person, computer, or organization to exchange information securely over the Internet using the public key infrastructure (PKI). A digital certificate may also be referred to as a public key certificate. Just like a passport, a digital certificate provides identifying information, is forgery resistant, and can be verified because it was issued by an official, trusted agency. The certificate contains the name of the certificate holder, a serial number, expiration dates, a copy of the certificate holder's public key (used for encrypting messages and digital signatures), and the digital signature of the certificate-issuing authority (CA) so that a recipient can verify that the certificate is real.[2]

Digital envelope: Data appended to a message that allow the intended recipient to verify the integrity of the content of the message.[38]

Digital imaging and communications in medicine: *See* **DICOM**.

Digital radiography: A form of x-ray imaging in which digital x-ray sensors are used instead of traditional photographic film. Advantages include time efficiency through bypassing chemical processing and the ability to digitally transfer and enhance images. Also less radiation can be used to produce an image of similar contrast to conventional radiography.[8]

Digital signal: Transmission signal that carries information in the discrete value form of 0 and 1.[3] *See* **DS-2-3**.

Digital signature: A mathematical technique used to validate the authenticity and integrity of a message, software, or digital document. In many countries, including the United States, digital signatures have the same legal significance as the more traditional forms of signed documents.[2] *See* **Private key** and **Public key**.

Digital signature standard: Specifies algorithms for applications requiring a digital signature, rather than a written signature. A digital signature is represented in a computer as a string of bits. A digital signature is computed using a set of rules and a set of parameters that allow the identity of the signatory and the integrity of the data to be verified. Digital signatures may be generated on both stored and transmitted data. Signature generation uses a private key to generate a digital signature; signature verification uses a public key that corresponds to, but is not the same as, the private key. Each signatory possesses a private and public key pair. Public keys may be known by the public; private keys are kept secret. Anyone can verify the signature by employing the signatory's public key. Only the user that possesses the private key can perform signature generation.[150]

Digital subscriber line: *See* **DSL**.

Digital subscriber line access multiplexer: *See* **DSLAM**.

Digitize: To convert an analog signal to a digital signal.[3]

Digitized signature: An electronic image of an actual written signature. A digitized signature looks much the same as the original, but it does not provide the same protection as a digital signature, as it can be forged and copied.[3]

Dimension table: A building block of a star schema data model; it contains the descriptive data regarding the data in a fact table that are used for column headings, query constraints, and OLAP dimensions.[3]

Direct address: A direct address is similar to a typical email address which can be issued to an individual, organization, or machine but is different because a direct address serves as a secure messaging system that provides for identity management and message encryption to enable the secure sending and receiving of personal health information and other sensitive communication exchange.[151] The DIRECT Project standard requires the use of a direct address.

Direct connection: A permanent communication connection between a computer system (either a single CPU or a LAN) and the Internet. This is also called a leased-line connection because the telephone connection is leased from the phone company. A direct connection is in contrast to a dial-up connection.[3]

Direct exchange: Describes the push of health information from a sender to a known receiver, similar to a how an email or fax is pushed from one endpoint to another.[151]

Direct memory access: *See* **DMA**.

Direct messaging: One type of secure messaging that is generally recognized as an effective, secure, encrypted communication mechanism for use in the point-to-point exchange of sensitive clinical and administrative data.[151]

DIRECT Project: Launched in March 2010 as a part of the Nationwide Health Information Network, the DIRECT Project was created to specify a simple, secure, scalable, standards-based way for participants to send authenticated, encrypted health information directly to known, trusted recipients over the Internet. Participants include EHR and PHR vendors, medical organizations, systems integrators, integrated delivery networks, federal organizations, state and regional health information organizations, organizations that provide health information exchange capabilities, and health information technology consultants. Two primary DIRECT Project specifications are the Applicability Statement for Secure Health Transport and the XDR and XDM for Direct Messaging.[13]

Direct sequence spread spectrum: *See* **DSSS**.

Directory: A system that the computer uses to organize files on the basis of specific information.[3]

Directory services markup language: *See* **DSML**.

Disaster recovery system: The processes, policies, and procedures related to preparing for recovery or continuation of technical infrastructure critical to an organization after a natural or human-induced disaster.[11]

Disclosure history: Under the Health Insurance Portability and Accountability Act (HIPAA), this is a list of any entity that has received personally identifiable healthcare information for uses unrelated to treatment and payment.[37]

Disclosure/disclose: The release, transfer, provision of, access to, or divulging in any other manner of information outside the entity holding the information.[22]

D

Discovery/e-discovery: Electronic discovery, or e-discovery, is a type of cyber forensics (also referred to as computer or digital forensics) and describes the process by where law enforcement can obtain, secure, search, and process any electronic data for use as evidence in a legal proceeding or investigation. Electronic discovery may be limited to a single computer or a network-wide search.[41]

Discrete data: Information that can be categorized into a classification. Discrete data is based on counts. Only a finite number of values is possible, and the values cannot be subdivided meaningfully. For example, the number of parts damaged in shipment.[152]

Disease registry: A large collection or registry that contains information on different chronic health problems affecting patients within the system. A disease registry helps to manage and log data on chronic illnesses and diseases. All data contained within the disease registry are logged by healthcare providers and are available to providers to perform benchmarking measures on healthcare systems.[13]

Disease staging: A classification system that uses diagnostic findings to produce clusters of patients based on etiology, pathophysiology, and severity. It can serve as the basis for clustering clinically homogeneous patients to assess quality of care, analysis of clinical outcomes, utilization of resources, efficacy of alternative treatments, and assignment of credentials for hospital privileges. Staging was also designed as a quality assurance tool for evaluating ambulatory care by comparing levels of severity at the time of hospitalization for patients receiving their health benefits from government and private insurers.[153] *See* **Severity system.**

Disk operating system: *See* **DOS.**

Disk striping with parity: Fault-tolerant storage technique that distributes data and parity across three or more physical disks. Storage technique that stripes data and parity in 64K blocks across all disks in the array. Striping provides fast data transfer and protection from a single disk failure by regenerating data for a failed disk through the stored parity. Minimum of three physical disks are required for disk striping with parity.[1] Also known as *RAID 5*.

Disk striping without parity: Storage technique that distributes data across two or more physical disks in 64K blocks across all disks in the array. Striping provides fast data transfer. Minimum of two physical disks are required for disk striping without parity.[3] Also known as *RAID 0.*

Distinguished name: A name given to a person, company, or element within a computer system or network that uniquely identifies it from everything else.[154]

Distributed computing environment: A client-server environment in which data are located in many servers that might be geographically dispersed but connected by a wide area network (WAN).[3]

Distributed database: A database that is stored in more than one physical location. Parts or copies of the database are physically stored in one location, and other parts are stored and maintained in other locations.[3]

Distributed processing: The distribution of computer processing work among multiple computers, linked by a communications network.[3]

Dithering: The attempt by a computer program to approximate a color from a mixture of other colors when the required color is not available. For example, dithering occurs when a color is specified for a web page that a browser on a particular operating system cannot support. The browser will then attempt to replace the requested color with an approximation composed of two or more other colors it can produce. It may appear somewhat grainy.[2]

DLC (Data link control): A data link control is a service that ensures reliable network data communication by managing frame error detection and flow control. DLC is based on the Data Link layer of the Open Systems Interconnection (OSI) model.[54]

DLL (Dynamic link library): A file of code containing functions that can be called from other executable code (either an application or another DLL). Programmers use DLLs to provide code that they can reuse and to parcel out distinct jobs. Unlike an executable file, a DLL cannot be directly run. DLLs must be called from other code that is already executing.[3]

DMA (Direct memory access): Rapid data movement between computer subsystems. Accomplished through the use of the DMA controller without the use of the CPU.[3]

DMA controller (Direct memory access controller): Integrated computer chip that handles direct memory operations without CPU intervention. Allows the CPU to concentrate on other computer operations.[3]

DML (Data manipulation language): A family of computer languages, including commands permitting users to manipulate data in a database. This manipulation involves inserting data into database tables, retrieving existing data, deleting data from existing tables, and modifying existing data. DML is most often incorporated into structured query language (SQL) databases.[54]

DNS (Domain name server): An online database that resolves human readable names to IP addresses. The DNS is a distributed database used by TCP/IP applications to map between host names and IP addresses, and to provide electronic mail routing information. The DNS provides the protocol to allow clients and servers to communicate with each other.[3]

DNSSEC (Domain name system security extension): A set of Internet Engineering Task Force (IETF) standards created to address vulnerabilities in the Domain Name System (DNS) and protect it from online threats. The purpose of DNSSEC is to increase the security of the Internet as a whole by addressing DNS security weaknesses. Essentially, DNSSEC adds authentication to DNS to make the system more secure.[2]

Document management: Software systems allowing organizations to control the production, storage, management, and distribution of electronic documents, yielding greater efficiencies in the ability to reuse information and to control the flow of the documents, from creation to archiving.[11]

Document type definition: *See* **DTD**.

Documentation and procedures test: A testing event that evaluates the accuracy of user and operations documentation and determines whether the manual procedure will work correctly as an integral part of the system.[52]

Documentation integrity: The accuracy of the complete health record. It encompasses information governance, patient identification, authorship validation, amendments, and record corrections. It also includes auditing the record for documentation validity when submitting reimbursement claims.[28]

Domain: Used synonymously with "domain name," it also has a definition specific to local networks. A domain contains a group of computers that can be accessed and administered with a common set of rules. For example, a company may require all local computers to be networked within the same domain so that each computer can be seen from other computers within the domain or located from a central server. Setting up a domain may also block outside traffic from accessing computers within the network, which adds an extra level of security.[75]

Domain information model: The model describing common concepts and relationships for a problem domain.[36]

Domain name server: *See* **DNS**.

DOS (Disk operating system): The first widely installed operating system for personal computers.[2]

Dot pitch: A measurement (in millimeters) of the distance between dots on a monitor. The lower the number, the higher the clarity of the display.[2]

Dots per square inch: *See* **DPI**.

Download: To retrieve a file from another computer.[3]

DPI (Dots per square inch): A measure of the resolution of a printer, scanner, or monitor. It refers to the number of dots per inch. The more dots per inch, the higher the resolution.[3]

Draft international standard: *See* **DIS**.

Draft standard for trial use: *See* **DSTU**.

Draft supplement for public comment: A specification candidate for addition to an IHE Domain Technical Framework (e.g., a new profile) that is issued for comment by an interested party.[127]

Draft technical report: *See* **DTR.**

DRAM (Dynamic random access memory): RAM that must be continuously refreshed to maintain the current RAM value. Most RAM in microcomputers is dynamic RAM, although there is a trend toward synchronous dynamic random access memory (SDRAM).[3]

DRG (Diagnosis related group): A classification system that groups patients according to diagnosis, type of treatment, age, and other relevant criteria. Under the prospective payment system, hospitals are paid a set fee for treating patients in a single DRG category, regardless of the actual cost of care for the individual.[28]

Drilldown: Exploration of multidimensional data allows moving down from one level of detail to the next, depending on the granularity of data in the level.[107]

Driver: A piece of software that tells the computer how to operate an external device, such as a printer, hard disk, CD-ROM drive, or scanner.[3]

Drop: Wiring run made from a modular wall plate to a communications wiring closet. Unshielded twisted pair (UTP) is the most common medium used in drops. Also identified as the connection between a computer and thick-net cabling.[3]

Drop-down list (or menu): A menu of commands or options that appears when you select an item with a mouse. The item you select is generally at the top of the display screen, and the menu appears just below it, as if you had it dropped down or you had pulled it down.[31]

Drug information system: A computer-based system that maintains drug-related information, such as information concerning appropriate dosages and side effects, and may access a drug interaction database. A drug information system may provide, by way of a directed consultation, specific advice on the usage of various drugs.[36]

Drug interaction database: Database containing information on drug interactions.[36]

Drug reference terminology: A collection of drug concepts and information such as definitions, hierarchies, and other kinds of knowledge and relationships related to the drug concepts.[45]

Drug therapy: The use of drugs to cure a medical problem, to improve a patient's condition, or to otherwise produce a therapeutic effect.[36]

DS-2-3: A type of digital signal that represents a sequence of values. A logic signal is a digital signal with only two possible values that describes an arbitrary. A digital signal is a physical quantity that alternates between a discrete set of waveforms. Alternatively, a digital signal may be considered to be the sequence of codes represented by such a physical quantity. The physical quantity may be a variable electric current or voltage, the intensity, phase or polarization of an optical or other electromagnetic field, acoustic pressure, the magnetization of a magnetic storage media, etc. Digital signals are present in all digital electronics, notably computing equipment and data transmission.[8]

DSA (Digital signature algorithm): *See* **Digital signature.**

DSG (Document digital signature): *See* **Digital signature.**

DSL (Digital subscriber line): A communications medium used to transfer digital signals over standard telephone lines. Along with cable Internet, DSL is one of the most popular ways ISPs provide broadband Internet access.[75]

DSLAM (Digital subscriber line access multiplexer): A device used by Internet Service Providers (ISPs) to route incoming DSL connections to the Internet. Since a "multiplexer" combines multiple signals into one, a DSLAM combines a group of subscribers' connections into one aggregate Internet connection.[75]

DSM (Diagnostic and Statistical Manual of Mental Disorders): Manual produced by the American Psychiatric Association. Used by clinicians and researchers to diagnose and classify mental disorders. The criteria are concise and explicit, intended to facilitate an objective assessment of symptom presentations in a variety of clinical settings—inpatient, outpatient, partial hospital, consultation-liaison, clinical, private practice, and primary care.[155]

DSML (Directory services markup language): A proposed set of rules for using extensible markup language (XML) to define the data content and structure of a directory and maintain it on distributed directories. It permits XML and directories to work together, enabling applications to use directories efficiently.[54]

DSMO (Designated Standard Maintenance Organization): An organization, designated by the Secretary of the U.S. Department of Health & Human Services, to maintain standards adopted under Subpart I of 45 CFR Part 162. A DSMO may receive and process requests for adopting a new standard or modifying an adopted standard.[28]

DSSS (Direct sequence spread spectrum): Also known as direct sequence code division multiple access (DS-CDMA), one of two approaches to spread spectrum modulation for digital signal transmission over the airwaves. In direct sequence spread spectrum, the stream of information to be transmitted is divided into small pieces, each of which is allocated to a frequency channel across the spectrum. A data signal at the point of transmission is combined with a higher data-rate bit sequence (also known as a chipping code) that divides the data according to a spreading ratio. The redundant chipping code helps the signal resist interference and also enables the original data to be recovered if data bits are damaged during transmission.[2]

DSTU (Draft standard for trial use): A standard or implementation specification released to allow implementers to test the standard.[2] At the end of the trial period, the standard may be balloted, revised, or withdrawn.[156]

DSU (Data service unit): A device used for interfacing data terminal equipment (DTE) to the public telephone network.[157]

DSU/CSU (Data service unit/channel service unit): A hardware device about the size of an external modem that converts a digital data frame from the communications technology used on a local area network (LAN) into a frame appropriate to a wide-area network (WAN) and vice versa. For example, if you have a web business from your own home and have leased a digital line (perhaps a T-1 or fractional T-1 line) to a phone company or a gateway at an Internet service provider, you have a CSU/DSU at your end and the phone company or gateway host has a CSU/DSU at its end.[2]

DT (Date data type) (YYYYMMDD): 1. International method of writing the date. **2.** International format defined by ISO (ISO 8601) to define a numerical date system as follows: YYYY-MM-DD where YYYY is the year (all the digits, i.e., 2012), MM is the month (01 [January] to 12 [December]), DD is the day (01 to 31).[63]

DTD (Document type definition): A specific document defining and constraining definition or set of statements that follow the rules of the Standard Generalized Markup Language (SGML) or of the Extensible Markup Language (XML), a subset of SGML. A DTD is a specification that accompanies a document and identifies what the markup codes are that, in the case of a text document, separate paragraphs, identify topic headings, and so forth and how each is to be processed. By mailing a DTD with a document, any location that has a DTD "reader" (or "SGML compiler") will be able to process the document and display or print it as intended. This means that a single standard SGML compiler can serve many different kinds of documents that use a range of different markup codes and related meanings. The compiler looks at the DTD and then prints or displays the document accordingly.[2]

DTE (Data terminal equipment): An end instrument that converts user information into signals for transmission or reconverts the received signals into user information.[157]

DTR (Draft technical report): Standards that are in the process of review but are implementable in their current form.[158]

Dual-use technology: Technology that has both civilian and military applications (e.g., cryptography).[3]

Dumb terminal: Device that consists of a keyboard and a monitor, and a connection to a server PC, minicomputer, or a mainframe computer. Dumb terminals have no "intelligence" (data processing or number crunching power) and depend entirely on the computer to which they are connected for computations, data storage, and retrieval. Dumb terminals are used by airlines, banks, and other such firms for inputting data to, and recalling it from, the connected computer.[4]

Durability: A database property that ensures transactions are saved permanently and do not accidentally disappear or get erased, even during a database crash. This is usually achieved by saving all transactions to a nonvolatile storage medium. Durability is part of the ACID acronym, which stands for atomicity, consistency, isolation, and durability. ACID is a set of properties guaranteeing the reliability of all database transactions.[54] *See* **ACID**.

DVD (Digital video disk or digital versatile disk): A type of optical media used for storing digital data. It is the same physical size as a CD, but has a larger storage capacity. Some DVDs are formatted specifically for video playback, while others may contain different types of data, such as software programs and computer files.[75]

Dynamic host configuration protocol: *See* **DHCP**.

Dynamic link control: *See* **DLC**.

Dynamic link library: *See* **DLL**.

Dynamic RAM: *See* **DRAM**.

D

E

e-[text] or e-text: Short for "electronic," "e" or "e" is used as a prefix to indicate that something is Internet-based, not just electronic. The trend began with e-mail in the 1990s, and now includes eCommerce, eHealth, e-GOV, etc.[31]

E-1-3 European digital signal: 2.048-3.139.254 Mbps digital transmission that is similar to Integrated Service Digital Network (ISDN).[3]

EAI (Enterprise application integration): 1. The use of software and architectural principles to bring together (integrate) a set of enterprise computer applications. It is an area of computer systems architecture that gained wide recognition from about 2004 onward. EAI is related to middleware technologies, such as message-oriented middleware (MOM), and data representation technologies, such as eXtensible markup language (HTML, XML). Newer EAI technologies involve using web services as part of service-oriented architecture as a means of integration. **2.** A presentation-level integration technology that provides a single point of access to conduct business transactions that utilize data from multiple disparate applications.[8] *See* **System integration**.

EAP (Extensible authentication protocol): A general protocol for authentication that also supports multiple authentication methods, such as token cards, one-time passwords, certificate, public key authentication, and smartcards.[11]

Early event detection: *See* **EED**.

EBB (Eligibility-based billing): Process in which a payer bills a customer based on his or her eligibility. Clients are responsible for their own eligibility and data accuracy.[3]

EBCDIC (Extended binary coded decimal interchange code): A character set coding scheme that represents 256 standard characters. IBM mainframes use EBCDIC coding, while personal computers use American Standard Coding for Information Interchange (ASCII) coding. Networks that link personal computers to IBM mainframes must include a translating device to mediate between the two systems.[159]

EC (Electronic commerce): Consists of the buying and selling of products or services over electronic systems such as the Internet and other computer networks.[160] Also known as *eCommerce*.

ECG (electrocardiogram): Specifies a mechanism for broad access throughout the enterprise to electrocardiogram (ECG) documents for review purposes. The ECG documents may include "diagnostic quality" waveforms, measurements, and interpretations. This integration profile allows the display of this information without requiring specialized cardiology software or workstations, but with general purpose computer applications, such as a web browser. This integration profile is intended primarily for retrieving resting 12-lead ECGs, but may also retrieve ECG waveforms gathered during stress, Holter, and other diagnostic tests. This integration profile only addresses ECGs that are already stored in an information system. It does not address the process of ordering, acquiring, storing, or interpreting the ECGs.[29] *See* **Profile. NOTE: ECG is an Integrating the Healthcare Enterprise (IHE) Profile.**

ECHO: Describes the workflow associated with digital echocardiography (diagnostic test that uses ultrasound waves to create an image), specifically transthoracic echo, transesophageal echo, and stress echo. As with the Cath Workflow integration profile, this profile deals with patient identifiers, orders, scheduling, status reporting, multi-stage exams (especially stress echo), and data storage. It also specifically addresses the issues of acquisition modality devices that are only intermittently connected to the network, such as portable echo machines, and addresses echo-specific data requirements.[29] *See* **Profile. NOTE: ECHO is an Integrating the Healthcare Enterprise (IHE) Profile.**

ECN (Explicit congestion notifier): A 2-bit IP packet header field that allows reduction of the number of Transmission Control Protocol (TCP) retransmissions in the Internet.[3]

e-Consent: Explicit agreement from a patient to allow another party to view his or her data captured in an electronic health record.[67]

ED (Encapsulated data): The coupling or encapsulation of the data with a select group of functions that defines everything that can be done with the data.[8]

ED (Evidence documents): Defines interoperable ways for observations, measurements, results, and other procedure details recorded in the course of carrying out a procedure step to be output by devices, such as acquisition systems and other workstations; to be stored and managed by archival systems; and to be retrieved and presented by display and reporting systems. This allows detailed nonimage information, such as measurements, computer-aided detection (CAD) results, procedure logs, etc., to be made available as input to the process of generating a diagnostic report. The evidence documents may be used either as additional evidence for the reporting physician, or in some cases, for selected items in the evidence document to be included in the diagnostic report.[29] *See* **Profile. NOTE: ED is an Integrating the Healthcare Enterprise (IHE) Profile.**

EDC (Electronic data capture system): A computerized system designed for the collection of clinical data in electronic format for use mainly in human clinical trials.[8]

EDDS (Electronic document digital storage): Document management systems available online.[31] *See* **Decision support, clinical and analytic** and **Decision support system**.

EDI (Electronic data interchange): 1. Even before HIPAA, the American National Standards Institute (ANSI) approved the process for developing a set of EDI standards known as the X12. EDI is a collection of standard message formats that allows businesses to exchange data via any electronic messaging service. **2.** The electronic transfer of data between companies using networks to include the Internet. Secure communications are needed in healthcare to exchange eligibility information, referrals, authorization, claims, encounter, and other payment data needed to manage contracts and remittance.[21]

EDI Gateway (Electronic data interchange gateway): An electronic process to send data (claims, membership, and benefits) back and forth between providers and insurance companies.[48]

EDIT: In the Centers for Medicare & Medicaid Services, the logic within the Standard Claims Processing System (or PSC Supplemental Edit Software) that selects certain claims, evaluates or compares information on the selected claims or other accessible source, and, depending on the evaluation, takes action on the claims, such as pay in full, pay in part, or suspend for manual review.[14]

EED (Early event detection): This component of the Public Health Information Network (PHIN) preparedness uses case and suspect case reporting, along with statistical surveillance of health-related data, to support the earliest possible detection of events that may signal a public health emergency.[82]

EDXL (Emergency data exchange language): A standard message distribution framework for data sharing among emergency information systems.[161]

EDXL–HAVE (Emergency data exchange language–hospital availability exchange): Describes a standard message for data sharing among emergency information systems using the XML-based Emergency Data Exchange Language (EDXL).[161]

EEPROM (Electronically erasable programmable read only memory): A reprogrammable memory chip that can be electronically erased and reprogrammed via a reader/writer device.[3]

Effective date: This is the date that a federal agency final rule is effective, which is usually 60 days after it is published in the *Federal Register*.[116]

EGA (Enhanced graphics adapter): Color display system providing 16 to 64 colors at a resolution of 640×480.[3]

E-GOV: The E-Government Act of 2002 was signed into law by President George W. Bush in July 2002: "This legislation builds upon the Administration's expanding E-Government initiative by ensuring strong leadership of the information technology activities of Federal agencies, a comprehensive framework for information security standards and programs, and uniform safeguards to protect the confidentiality of information provided by the public for statistical purposes. The Act also assists in expanding the use of the Internet and computer resources in order to deliver Government services, consistent with the reform principles I outlined on July 10, 2002, for a citizen-centered, results-oriented, and market-based Government."[162]

eHealth (also written e-health): A term for healthcare practice which is supported by electronic processes and communication; the term eHealth encompasses a whole range of services that is at the edge of medicine/healthcare and information technology, including electronic medical records, telemedicine, and evidence-based medicine.[3]

EHR (Electronic health record): 1. A longitudinal electronic record of patient health information generated by one or more encounters in any care delivery setting. Included in this information are patient demographics, progress notes, problems, medications, vital signs, past medical history, immunizations, laboratory data, and radiology reports and images. The EHR automates and streamlines the clinician's workflow. The EHR has the ability to generate a complete record of a clinical patient encounter, as well as supporting other care-related activities directly or indirectly via interface; including evidence-based decision support, quality management, and outcomes reporting. **2.** Health-related information on an individual that conforms to nationally recognized interoperability standards and that can be created, managed, and consulted by authorized clinicians and staff across more than one healthcare organization. *See also* **CPR** and **EMR**.[13,55]

EIDE (Enhanced or extended integrated drive electronics): A standard interface for high-speed disk drives that operates at speeds faster than the standard Integrated Drive Electronics (IDE) interface. It allows the connection of four IDE devices.[3]

EIN (Employer identification number): 1. Employers, as sponsors of health insurance for their employees, often need to be identified in healthcare transactions, and a standard identifier for employers would be beneficial for electronically exchanged transactions. Healthcare providers may need to identify the employer of the participant on claims submitted electronically to health plans. **2.** The HIPAA standard is the EIN, the taxpayer-identifying number for employers that is assigned by the Internal Revenue Service. This identifier has nine digits with the first two digits separated by a hyphen, as follows: 00-000000.[116]

EIP (Enterprise information portal): 1. A framework for integrating information, people, and processes across organization boundaries. Provides a secure unified access point. **2.** An Internet-based approach to consolidate and present an organization's business intelligence and information resources through a single access point via an intranet.[8] Also known as an *Internet portal enterprise portal.*

EIS (Enterprise information system): A class of decision-support systems that provide predefined and easy-to-use data presentation and exploration functionality to top-level executives.[3]

EIS (Executive information system): A class of decision-support systems that provide predefined data presentation and exploration functionality to top-level executives. The system is intended to facilitate and support the information and decision-making needs of senior executives by providing ready access to both internal and external information relevant to meeting the strategic goals of the organization. Commonly considered a specialized form of decision-support systems (DSS). The emphasis of EIS is on graphical displays with reporting and drill-down capabilities. In general, an EIS is an enterprise-wide DSS that allows executives to analyze, compare, and highlight trends and important variables, as well as monitor performance and identify opportunities and problems.[11]

Electromagnetic interference: *See* **EMI**.

Electronic attestation: Verifies the identity of an individual by linking signature verification data to that person. The purpose of attestation is to show authorship and assign responsibility for an act, event, condition, opinion, or diagnosis. Every entry in the health record must be identified with the author and should not be made or signed by someone other than the author. Attestation functionality must meet applicable legal, regulatory, and other applicable standards or requirements.[11]

Electronic certificate: *See* **Digital certificate**.

Electronic claim: 1. Electronic transactions sent to payers to receive payments for healthcare services covered by the payers. These are the HIPAA 837 transactions, responsible for remittance advice for claims payment made by payers. **2.** Any claim submitted for payment to the health plan by a central processing unit, tape diskette, direct data entry, direct wire, dial-in telephone, digital fax, or personal computer download or upload.[3,11] *See* **EDI Gateway**.

Electronic commerce: *See* **EC** and **eCommerce**.

Electronic data: Recorded or transmitted electronically, while nonelectronic data would be everything else. Special cases would be data transmitted by fax and audio systems, which is, in principle, transmitted electronically, but which lacks the underlying structure usually needed to support automated interpretation of its contents.[116]

Electronic data capture system: *See* **EDC**.

Electronic data interchange: *See* **EDI**.

Electronic data interchange gateway: *See* **EDI Gateway**.

Electronic forms management: A software system that automatically generates forms and can be populated by importing data from another system and/or can export data that has been entered into another system.[11]

Electronic health record: *See* **EHR**.

Electronic health record provider: Entity in legitimate possession of electronic health record data, and in a position to communicate it to another appropriate entity.[65]

Electronic media: 1. Electronic storage media, including memory devices in computers (hard drives) and any removable/transportable digital memory media, such as magnetic tapes or disks, optical disks, or digital memory cards. **2.** Transmission media used to exchange information already in electronic storage media; including, for example, the Internet (wide open), extranet (using Internet technology to link a business with information accessible only to collaborating parties), leased lines, dial-up lines, private networks, and the physical movement of removable/transportable electronic storage media. Certain transmissions, including paper via facsimile and voice via telephone, are not considered to be transmissions via electronic media because the information being exchanged did not exist in electronic form before the transmission.[14]

Electronic media claims: *See* **EMC**.

Electronic medical record: *See* **EMR**.

Electronic medical record adoption model: *See* **EMRAM**.

Electronic medication administration record: *See* **eMAR**.

Electronic patient record: *See* **EHR**.

Electronic personal health record: *See* **ePHR** and **PHR**.

Electronic prescribing: *See* **E-prescribing**.

Electronic protected health information: *See* **ePHI**.

Electronic remittance advice: *See* **ERA**.

Electronic signature: 1. Creates the logical manifestation of a signature, including the possibility for multiple parties to sign a document and have the order of application recognized and proven and supply additional information, such as time stamp and signature purpose, specific to that user. **2.** Verifying a signature on a document verifies the integrity of the document and associated attributes and verifies the identity of the signer. Several technologies are available for user authentication, including passwords, cryptography, and biometrics.[3]

Electronic text: *See* **e-[text]** or **e-text**.

Electronically erasable programmable read-only memory: *See* **EEPROM**.

Eligible professional: *See* **EP**.

Eligibility-based billing: *See* **EBB**.

E-mail (Electronic mail): Electronic messages sent via networks between users on other computer systems. A service that permits a message or response to be created on one computer and sent over a network to another machine, another person, a group, or a computer program.[3]

eMAR (Electronic medication administration record): An electronic record keeping system that documents when medications are given to a patient during a hospital stay. This application supports the five rights of medication administration (right patient, right medication, right dose, right time, and right route of administration) and can be used with bar coding functionality, although bar coding is not required. eMAR functionality is normally found within a nursing documentation application.[11]

EMC (Electronic media claims): This term usually refers to a flat file format used to transmit or transport claims.[116]

Emergency: Sudden demand for action; a condition that poses an immediate threat to the health of the patient. This definition is further clarified to mean "any potential denial of critical health services, or information, that could reasonably result in personal injury or death to an individual or the public."[22,68,106]

Emergency access: Granting of user rights and authorizations to permit access to protected health information and applications in emergency conditions outside of normal workflows. (Emergency room access is considered to be a normal workflow.)[22]

Emergency care system: An application that assists emergency department clinicians and staff in the critical task of managing patients quickly and efficiently; directs each step of the patient management/patient flow and patient documentation process, including triage, tracking, nursing and physician charting, disposition, charge capture, and management reporting.[11]

Emergency data exchange language: *See* **EDXL.**

Emergency permission: Permission granted to certain caregivers in advance that allows self-declaration of an emergency and assumption of an emergency role. Emergency permissions defined in standard ways, compliant with appropriate ANSI standards and Health Level Seven (HL7) healthcare permission definitions, are suitable for federated circumstances, where the person declaring the emergency is not a member of the organization possessing the requested information.[22]

Emergency repair disk: *See* **ERD.**

Emergency respond data architecture: *See* **ERDA.**

EMI (Electromagnetic interference): Any disruption caused by electromagnetic waves.[3]

Emissions security: *See* **EMSEC.**

Emoticons: A combination word for "emotional icon," it is a small picture created with the normal keys on a keyboard meant to denote the writer's mood in an e-mail message.[68]

EMPI (Enterprise master patient index): A system that maintains online listings of patients and medical records across multiple facilities and/or hospitals. It includes admission, registration, and discharge dates, as well as all data pertinent for re-registration. It provides for quick access to previous records and the ability to send new patient information to them.[11]

Employee Retirement Income and Security Act: *See* **ERISA.**

Employee welfare benefit plan: A plan, fund, or a program maintained by an employer, or an employee organization, that provides medical, surgical, or hospital care.[22]

Employer identification number: *See* **EIN.**

EMR (Electronic medical record): 1. An application environment that is composed of the clinical data repository, clinical decision support, controlled medical vocabulary, order entry, computerized practitioner order entry, and clinical documentation applications. This environment supports the patient's electronic medical record across inpatient and outpatient environments, and is used by healthcare practitioners to document, monitor, and manage healthcare delivery. **2.** Health-related information on an individual that can be created, gathered, managed, and consulted by authorized clinicians and staff within one healthcare organization.[11,13] *See* **EHR.**

EMRAMSM (Electronic medical record adoption model): A tool developed by HIMSS Analytics guiding hospitals to improved clinical outcomes.[11]

EMSEC (Emanations security): Measures taken to deny unauthorized persons information derived from intercept and analysis of compromising emanations from crypto-equipment of an IT system.[23]

Emulation: A software program that allows a computer to imitate another computer with a differing operating system.[3]

EN (European standard): Developed by the European Committee for Standardization (CEN). CEN is a major provider of European standards and technical specifications.[8]

EN 46000 Medical device quality management systems standard: Technically equivalent to ISO 13485:1996, an international medical device standard. The two are similar enough that if an organization is prepared to comply with one, it could easily comply with the other.[163]

Encapsulated data type: *See* **ED.**

Encapsulation: In object-oriented programming, the inclusion within a program object of all the resources needed for the object to function—basically, the methods and the data. The object is said to "publish its interfaces." Other objects adhere to these interfaces to use the object without having to be concerned with how the object accomplishes it. An object can be thought of as a self-contained atom. The object interface consists of public methods and instantiated data.[2]

Encipherment encryption: Cryptographic transformation of data to produce ciphertext.[74]

Encoded data: Data represented by some identification of classification scheme, such as a provider identifier or a procedure code.[61]

Encoder: This application enables health information management personnel to find and use complete and accurate codes and code modifiers for procedures and diagnosis to optimize billing and reimbursement. For example, 1234 is bronchitis, whereas 1235 is bronchitis with asthma, and 1236 is bronchitis with stomach flu.[11]

Encoding-decoding services: This service will encode and/or decode messages from and to different coding formats, such as Unicode, UTF-8, Base64, etc.[59]

Encounter: 1. An instance of direct provider/practitioner to patient interaction, regardless of the setting, between a patient and practitioner vested with primary responsibility for diagnosing, evaluating, or treating the patient's condition, or both, or providing social worker services. **2.** A contact between a patient and practitioner who has primary responsibility for assessing and treating the patient at a given contact, exercising independent judgment. Encounter serves as a focal point linking clinical, administrative, and financial information. Encounters occur in many different settings—ambulatory care, inpatient care, emergency care, home healthcare, field, and virtual (telemedicine).[106]

Encounter data: Detailed data about individual services provided by a capitated managed care entity. The level of detail about each service reported is similar to that of a standard claim form. Encounter data are also sometimes referred to as "shadow claims."[28]

Encryption: 1. An application/technology that provides the translation of data into a secret code. Encryption is the most effective way to achieve data security. To read an encrypted file, you must have access to a secret key or password that enables you to decrypt it. Unencrypted data is called plain text; encrypted data is referred to as cipher text. **2.** Means of securing data by transforming/generating them into apparently meaningless random characters between source and destination. A process by which a message is encoded so that its meaning is not obvious. It is transformed into a second message using a complex function and a special encryption key.[11]

Encryption-decryption services: This encrypts and decrypts messages. It could use X.509 certificates and other cryptography mechanisms.[59]

End user: In information technology, the term end user is used to distinguish the person for whom a hardware or software product is designed by the developers, installers, and servicers of the product.[2]

End user license agreement: *See* **EULA.**

Enhanced or extended integrated drive electronics: *See* **EIDE.**

Enhanced small device interface: *See* **ESDI.**

ENP® (European nursing care pathways): Provides nursing knowledge for nursing professionals in terms of a nursing language implemented in a classification system for the illustration of the nursing process. The nursing classification ENP® consists of the vertical level of the classes nursing diagnoses, characteristics, resources, nursing objectives and nursing interventions, and intervention guiding specifications. Within the individual classes, the organizing principle is either hierarchical or coordinate. In the ENP® system, every single ENP® nursing diagnosis, supported by nursing literature, relates horizontally and class-spanning to other objects (characteristics, etiologies, resources, nursing objectives, and nursing interventions). According to the ENP® developers, these nursing diagnosis-related pathways represent up-to-date nursing knowledge and can be understood as a knowledge management system for nursing due to semantic networks. ENP® is among the precombined nursing classifications and is conceived for front-end use.[164]

Enterprise: A business organization.[31]

Enterprise application integration: *See* **EAI**.

Enterprise architecture: 1. A strategic resource that aligns business and technology, leverages shared assets, builds internal and external partnerships, and optimizes the value of information technology services. **2.** A business-focused framework developed in accordance with the Clinger-Cohen Act of 1996 that identifies the business processes, systems that support processes, and guidelines and standards by which systems must operate.[13,165]

Enterprise architecture integration: Tools and techniques that promote, enable, and manage the exchange of information and distribution of business processes across multiple application systems, typically within a sizeable electronic landscape, such as large corporations, collaborating companies, and administrative regions.[59]

Enterprise information portal: *See* **EIP**.

Enterprise information system: *See* **EIS**.

Enterprise master patient index: *See* **EMPI**.

Enterprise master person index: A system that coordinates client identification across multiple systems, namely, by collecting and storing IDs and person-identifying demographic information from source system (track new persons, track changes to existing persons). These systems also take on several other tasks and responsibilities associated with client ID management.[59]

Enterprise network: A network consisting of multiple servers and domains over a small or large geographical area.[3]

Enterprise network services: Examples are security, messaging, administration, host connectivity, and wide area network communication.[3]

Enterprise resource planning: *See* **ERP**.

Enterprise scheduling: Ability to schedule procedures, exams, and appointments across multiple systems and/or locations spanning an entire jurisdiction.[59]

Enterprise user authentication: *See* **EUA**.

Entity: Something that has a distinct, separate existence, though an entity needs not be a material existence.[8]

Entity identity assertion: Ensures that an entity is the person or application that claims the identity provided.[22]

Entity-relationship diagram: *See* **ERD**.

Entries: Health record data in general (clinical observations, statements, reasoning, intentions, plans, or actions) without particular specification of their formal representation, hierarchical organization, or of the particular record component class(es) that might be used to represent them.[65]

EOB (Explanation of benefits): A document detailing how a claim was processed according to the insured's benefits.[48]

EOP (Explanation of payment): Generated to the provider in reply to a claim submission.[48]

EP (Eligible professional): According to the Centers for Medicare & Medicaid Services (CMS), eligible professionals may receive incentive payment under either the Medicare or Medicaid Incentive Programs. Eligible professionals (EPs) under the Medicare EHR Incentive Program include doctors of medicine or osteopathy, doctors of dental surgery or dental medicine, doctors of podiatry, doctors of optometry, and chiropractors. Medicaid eligible professionals include physicians (primarily doctors of medicine and doctors of osteopathy), nurse practitioners, certified nurse-midwives, dentists, and physician assistants who furnish services in a Federally Qualified Health Center or Rural Health Clinic that is led by a physician assistant.[37]

ePHI (Electronic protected health information): Any protected health information (PHI) that is created, stored, transmitted, or received electronically.[22]

ePHR (Electronic personal health record): A universally accessible, layperson comprehensible, lifelong tool for managing relevant health information, promoting health maintenance, and assisting with chronic disease management via an interactive, common data set of electronic health information and eHealth tools. The ePHR is owned, managed, and shared by the individual or his or her legal proxy(s) and must be secure to protect the privacy and confidentiality of the health information it contains. It is not a legal record unless so defined, and is subject to various legal limitations.[55] *See* **PHR**.

Episode of care: Services provided by a healthcare facility or provider for a specific medical problem or condition or specific illness during a set time period. Episode of care can be given either for a short period or on a continuous basis or it may consist of a series of intervals marked by one or more brief separations from care.[166]

E-prescribing (Electronic prescribing): The use of computing devices to enter, modify, review, and output or communicate drug prescriptions.[3]

EPROM (Erasable programmable memory): Reusable firmware that can be programmed. Previous contents are erased by applying ultraviolet light through the window in the chip.[3]

ERA (Electronic remittance advice): Any of several electronic formats for explaining the payments of healthcare claims.[116]

Erasable programmable memory: *See* **EPROM.**

ERD (Emergency repair disk): Disk that contains machine-specific repair process information on registry (system, software, security, security accounts manager) and system files for use when failures occur.[3]

ERD (Entity relationship diagram): 1. A diagram showing entities and their relationships. Relates to business data analysis and database design. **2.** An entity relationship (ER) model shows how the sets of information contained in architectures are related to each other.[3,8]

ERDA (Emergency respond data architecture): A data architecture developed to support real-time information sharing and interoperability during emergency situations of all types.[167]

ERISA (Employee Retirement Income and Security Act of 1975): Most group health plans covered by ERISA are also health plans under the Health Insurance Portability and Accountability Act.[22]

ERP (Enterprise resource planning): Management information systems that integrate and automate many of the business functions associated with the operations or production aspects of an enterprise, such as general ledger, budgeting, materials management, purchasing, payroll, and human resources.[8]

Error chain: Generally, refers to the series of events that led to a disastrous outcome, typically uncovered by a root cause analysis. A more specific meaning of error chain, especially when used in the phrase "break the error chain," relates to the common themes or categories of causes that emerge from root cause analyses. These categories go by different names in different settings, but they generally include (1) failure to follow standard operating procedures; (2) poor leadership; (3) breakdowns in communication or teamwork; (4) overlooking or ignoring individual fallibility; and (5) losing track of objectives. Used in this way, "break the error chain" is shorthand for an approach in which team members continually address these links as a crisis or routine situation unfolds; the checklists that are included in teamwork training programs have categories corresponding to these common links in the error chain (e.g., establish team leader, assign roles and responsibility, monitor your teammates).[97]

Error proofing: Used to ensure products and processes are completed correctly the first time. Often relies on mechanisms built into tools or systems that automatically signal when problems occur or prevent the process from continuing until the proper conditions are met.[163] Also known as *mistake proofing.*[94]

E

Ethernet: 1. The most common type of connection computers use within a local area network (LAN). An Ethernet port looks much like a regular phone jack, but it is slightly wider. This port can be used to connect the computer to another computer, a local network, or an external DSL or cable modem. **2.** A family of computer networking technologies and protocols for local area networks (LANs) commercially introduced in 1980. **3.** A frame-based computer networking technology for LANs. The name comes from the physical concept of ether. It defines wiring and signaling for the physical layer and frame formats and protocols for the media access control (MAC)/data link layer of the Open Systems Interconnection (OSI) model. Ethernet is mostly standardized as IEEEs 802.3. It has become the most widespread LAN technology in use during the 1990s to the present.[8,11]

ETL (extraction, transformation, loading): Short for *extract, transform, load,* three database functions that are combined into one tool to pull data out of one database and place it into another database. **Extract** is the process of *reading data* from a database. **Transform** is the process of *converting the extracted data* from its previous form into the form it needs to be in so that it can be placed into another database. Transformation occurs by using rules or lookup tables or by combining the data with other data. **Load** is the process of *writing the data* into the target database. ETL is used to migrate data from one database to another, to form data marts and data warehouses, and also to convert databases from one format or type to another.[41]

EUA (Enterprise user authentication): A means to establish one name per user that can then be used on all of the devices and software that participate in this integration profile, greatly facilitating centralized user authentication management and providing users with the convenience and speed of a single sign-on. This profile leverages Kerberos (RFC 1510) and the HL7 clinical context object work group (CCOW) standard (user subject).[29] *See* **Profile. NOTE: EUA is an Integrating the Healthcare Enterprise (IHE) Profile.**

EULA (End user license agreement): A legal contract between a software application publisher and the user of that application. Often referred to as the software license, EULA is similar to a rental agreement in which the user agrees to pay for the use of the software and promises the publisher to comply with all restrictions stated in the EULA. Users are prompted to "accept" the terms of the EULA during the installation process.[2]

European committee for standardization: *See* **CEN.**

European digital signal: *See* **E-1-3.**

European nursing care pathways®: *See* **ENP®.**

European standard: *See* **EN.**

Event: Action or activity that occurs within a system and/or network scope, inclusive of its boundaries.[22]

Event aggregation: Consolidation of similar log entries into a single entry, containing a count of the number of occurrences of the event.[22]

Event correlation: Relationships between two or more log entries.[22]

Event filtering: Suppression of log entries from analysis, reporting, or long-term storage because their characteristics indicate that they are unlikely to contain information of interest.[22]

Event reduction: Removal of unneeded data fields from all log entries to create a new log that is smaller.[22]

Evidence documents: *See* **ED**.

Evidence-based medicine: 1. The conscientious, explicit, judicious and reasonable use of modern, best evidence in making decisions about the care of an individual. It integrates clinical experience and patient values with best available research information.[168] **2.** Evidence-based medicine asks questions, finds and appraises the relevant data, and harnesses that information for everyday clinical practice. Evidence-based medicine follows four steps: formulate a clear clinical question from a patient's problem; search the literature for relevant clinical articles; evaluate (critically appraise) the evidence for its validity and usefulness; and implement useful findings in clinical practice.[3]

Evidence-based practice: *See* **Evidence-based medicine**.

Exceeds authorized access: To access a computer with authorization and to use such access to obtain or alter information in the computer that the accessor is not entitled to obtain or alter.[17]

Exception: A transaction that does not receive authorization by the accepted rules and procedures.[3]

Exchange format: The representation of the data elements and the structure of a message, while in transfer between systems.[36]

Exclusive branching: Splits a process in several branches, only one of which can be selected, based on the fulfillment of a condition associated with a given branch.[169]

Exclusive choice: The divergence of a branch into two or more branches, such that when the incoming branch is enabled, the thread of control is immediately passed to precisely one of the outgoing branches, based on a mechanism that can select one of the outgoing branches.[170] *See* **Simple merge**.

Executive information system: *See* **EIS**.

Expert system: Artificial intelligence based system that converts the knowledge of an expert in a specific subject into a software code. This code can be merged with other such codes (based on the knowledge of other experts) and used for answering questions (queries) submitted through a computer. Expert systems typically consist of three parts: (1) a knowledge base which contains the information acquired by interviewing experts, and logic rules that govern how that information is applied; (2) an inference engine that interprets the submitted problem against the rules and logic of information stored in the knowledge base; and an (3) interface that allows the user to express the problem in a human language such as English.[4]

Explanation of benefits: *See* **EOB.**

Explanation of payment: *See* **EOP.**

Explicit congestion notification: *See* **ECN.**

Expression: The textual means to convey a concept to the user. It can be a major concept, a synonym, or a lexical variant.[31]

Extended ASCII (Extended American standard code for information interchange): Extensively used 8-bit standard information processing code with 256 characters.[3]

Extended binary coded decimal interchange code: *See* **EBCDIC.**

Extended industry standard architecture: *See* **EISA.**

Extensibility: 1. System design feature that allows for future expansion without the need for changes to the basic infrastructure. **2.** The ability to economically modify or add functionality.[59,140]

Extensible authentication protocol: *See* **EAP.**

Extensible markup language: *See* **XML.**

Extensible stylesheet language: *See* **XSL.**

External customer: A person or organization that receives a product, service, or information; not part of the organization supplying the product, service, or information.[62]

Extraction, transformation, loading: *See* **ETL.**

Extranet: Restricted network of computers that allows controlled access to a firm's internal information to authorized outsiders (customers, suppliers, joint venture partners, etc.) by connecting them (usually via Internet) to the firm's intranet.[4]

F

Fact table: In data warehousing, a fact table consists of the measurements, metrics, or facts of a business process. It is often located at the center of a star schema or a snowflake schema, surrounded by dimension tables.[8] In a dimensional database, a fact table is used to store measures of business activity, which are quantitative or factual data about the entity represented by the fact table.[171]

Failback: The process of restoring operations to a primary machine or facility after they have been shifted to a secondary machine or facility during failover.[2]

Failover: A backup operational mode in which the functions of a system component (such as a processor, server, network, or database, for example) are assumed by secondary system components when the primary component becomes unavailable through either failure or scheduled downtime. Used to make systems more fault-tolerant, failover is typically an integral part of mission-critical systems that must be constantly available.[2]

Failsafe: Pertaining to avoidance of compromise in the event of a failure.[38]

Family set: Group of backup tapes consisting of a single run of backup information.[38]

FAQ (Frequently asked questions): A collection of information on any subject for which questions are typically asked. FAQ postings provide quick answers without the need or expense of a staff person answering the question on the phone or in writing and are viewed as a time-saving feature of web sites, which provides a return on investment.[3]

FAR (False acceptance rate): A statistic used to measure biometric performance when operating in the verification task. The percentage of times a system produces a false accept, which occurs when an individual is incorrectly matched to another individual's existing biometric.[15]

Fast healthcare interoperability resources: *See* **FHIR**.

Fast SCSI (Fast small computer system interface): Ten Mbps high-speed 8-bit bus interface for connecting devices to the computer bus.[3]

Fast small computer system interface: *See* **Fast SCSI**.

FAT Client: In a client/server system, a client that performs most of the necessary data processing itself, rather than relying on the server. Also called *thick, heavy,* or *rich client.*[84]

FCOE (Fiber channel over Ethernet): An encapsulation of fiber channel frames over Ethernet networks. This allows a fiber channel to use 10 gigabit Ethernet networks (or higher speeds) while preserving the fiber channel protocol.[11]

FDDI (Fiber distributed data interface): A set of ANSI and ISO standards for data transmission on fiber optic lines in a local area network (LAN) that can extend in range up to 200 km (124 miles). The FDDI protocol is based on the token ring protocol. In addition to being large geographically, an FDDI local area network can support thousands of users. FDDI is frequently used on the backbone for a wide area network (WAN). FDDI is a type of physical network based on fiber optics. It is supported by Digital Imaging and Communications in Medicine (DICOM) standard.[2]

Federal Health Architecture: *See* **FHA.**

Federal Privacy Act of 1974 HIPAA: U.S.C. Section 552a. The Federal Privacy Act established a framework within which the government collects and uses information about individuals. Medicare recipients are protected because Medicare contractors are prohibited from releasing personal information, such as a person's health insurance claim number, claim data, diagnoses, etc., without written or verbal permission from the beneficiary or their official representative. Privacy rights of individuals were further strengthened in various revisions and through the Health Insurance Portability and Accountability Act (HIPAA).[3]

Fee for service: *See* **FFS.**

Feeder systems: Operational systems that will feed patient/person data to the EHR in the form of real-time single messages, multiple messages, or batch file uploads.[59] *See* **Source systems**. These systems may also be known as legacy systems and are often involved in extract-transform-load processes.[52] *See* **ETL.**

FFS (Fee for service): Contract method to pay a contracted fee for services performed by providers.[31] FFS is a reimbursement model which has begun to wane. It is being replaced by newer models for health care delivery such as Accountable Care Organizations.[28] *See* **ACO.**

FHA (Federal Health Architecture): The Federal Health Architecture (FHA) is an E-Government Line of Business (LoB) initiative designed to bring together the decision makers in federal health IT for inter-agency collaboration—resulting in effective health information exchange (HIE), enhanced interoperability among federal health IT systems, and efficient coordination of shared services. FHA also supports federal agency adoption of nationally recognized standards and policies for efficient, secure HIE. Established as an Office of Management and Budget E-Government LoB in 2004, FHA reaches out to more than 20 federal agencies to advance the national agenda for health IT.[13]

FHIR (Fast healthcare interoperability resources): A next generation standards framework created by HL7®, FHIR combines the best features of HL7's V2, HL7 V3, and CDA product lines that leverage emerging web standards which apply a tight focus on ease of implementation. Furthermore, it defines a set of resources for health. These resources represent granular clinical concepts that can be exchanged to quickly and effectively solve problems in healthcare and related process. The resources cover the basic elements of healthcare—patients, admissions, diagnostic reports, medications, and problem lists, with their typical participants—and also support a range of richer and more complex clinical models. The simple direct definitions of the resources are based on thorough requirements gathering, formal analysis, and extensive cross-mapping to other relevant standards.[10]

Fiber channel: A gigabit-speed network technology primarily used for storage networking.[11]

Fiber channel over Ethernet: *See* **FCOE**.

Fiber distributed data interface: *See* **FDDI**.

Fiber optic cable: A pure glass cable used for the transmission of digital signals. It generates no radiation of its own and is resistant to electromagnetic interference. It is used in areas where security is of prime importance because tapping into the cable is detectable. Can be used over longer distances than copper cable.[3]

Fiber optics: Extremely fast communications technology that uses glass or plastic medium to transmit light pulses produced by LEDs or ILDs to represent data. Fiber optics are immune to electronic magnetic interference, but susceptible to chromatic dispersion. Information is transmitted through the fiber as pulsating light. The light pulses represent bits of information. Fiber optics give users of telecommunications added capacity, better transmission quality, and increased clarity.[3]

Fiber transceiver: Device that converts fiber optic signals to digital signals and vice versa. Usually used to make a connection from a fiber run to an Ethernet segment.[3]

Field: When a unit of data can be subdivided, the individual subdivisions are known as fields, or data elements.[3]

Field components: A field entry may also have discernible parts or components. For example, the patient's name is recorded as last name, first name, and middle initial, each of which is a distinct entity separated by a component delimiter.[10]

Field level security: Data protection and/or authorization of specified fields or data elements within files, rather than of entire files.[3]

FIFO (First in, first out): An abstraction related to ways of organizing and manipulating data relative to time and prioritization.[8]

File: Electronic data collected in related records. Files have unique names and entities that allow for them to be stored, moved, and edited. Often, a file's suffix describes its type, such as a Microsoft document file (.doc) or an executable file (.exe).[3]

File extension: A group of characters appended to the end of a disk file name. File extensions usually consist of a full stop (dot) and one to three characters. Examples: .doc, .docx, or .pdf format.[36]

File server: A networked computer that provides file handling and storage for users with network access. A computer that each computer on a network can use to access and retrieve files that can be shared among the attached computers. Access to a file is usually controlled by the file server software, rather than by the operating system of the computer that accesses the file.[3]

File transfer protocol: *See* **FTP.**

Filmless radiology: Use of devices that replace film by acquiring digital images and related patient information, and transmit, store, retrieve, and display them electronically.[172]

Filter: A program that accepts a certain type of data as input, transforms the data in some manner, and then outputs the transformed data. Also defined as a pattern through which data passed. Only data that matches the pattern is allowed to pass through the filter.[41]

FIPS (Federal information processing standard): Under the Information Technology Management Reform Act (Public Law 104-106), the Secretary of Commerce approves standards and guidelines that are developed by the National Institute of Standards and Technology (NIST) for federal computer systems. These standards and guidelines are issued by NIST as Federal Information Processing Standards (FIPS) for use government-wide. NIST develops FIPS when there are compelling federal government requirements such as for security and interoperability and there are no acceptable industry standards or solutions.[173]

Firewall: 1. Used to prevent unauthorized access by blocking and checking all incoming network traffic. A firewall permits only authorized users to access and transmit privileged information and denies access to unauthorized users. **2.** Objective is to control the incoming and outgoing network traffic by analyzing the data packets and determining whether the packets should be allowed through based on a predetermined rule set.[3]

Firmware: Computer instructions written to a read-only memory (ROM), programmable memory (PROM), or erasable programmable memory (EPROM) chip.[3]

First in, first out: *See* **FIFO.**

Fitbit: A physical activity tracker designed to help you become more active and live a healthier lifestyle. It is a 21st-century pedometer.[171]

Fixed wireless: Refers to wireless devices or systems that are situated in fixed locations, such as an office or home, as opposed to devices that are mobile, such as cell phones. The point-to-point signal transmissions occur through the air over a terrestrial microwave platform rather than through copper or fiber cables; therefore, fixed wireless does not require satellite feeds or local phone service. The advantages of fixed wireless over traditional cabling infrastructure include the ability to connect with users in remote areas without the need for laying new cables and the capacity for broad bandwidth that is not impeded by fiber or cable capacities.[3]

Flash drive: Portable memory in a space the size of a key. Also called memory key, jump drive, thumb drive, stick, removable drive, and other names.[8]

Flash memory: Nonvolatile memory that provides read-only operations for computer boot-up. Contents can be updated. Smartcard memory technology that emulates a hard disk, except that the data are stored electronically, and there are no moving parts.[3]

Flat files: 1. Files in which each record has the same length, whether or not all the space is used. Empty parts of the record are padded with a blank, or zero, depending on the data type of each field. **2.** Refers to a file that consists of a series of fixed-length records that include some sort of record type code.[116]

Flat table: One data element per field, tables are in the simplest form.[52]

Flexibility: The ability to support architectural and hardware configuration changes.[59]

Flexible spending account: *See* **FSA**.

Flip-flop: Digital signal circuit that can store one bit of information or be in a cleared state. One-bit memory.[3]

Flow chart: A diagram that combines symbols and abbreviated narratives to describe a sequence of operations and/or a process. The flow chart is a tool typically associated with the waterfall methodology of software development.[2]

Flow sheet: A tabular summary of information that is arranged to display the values of variables as changed over time.[36]

Foreground: Application or task that is executing and accepting user input and subsequent output on a multitasking machine.[3] *See also* **Background**.

Foreign key: A primary key of one data table that is placed into another data table to represent a relationship between those tables. Foreign keys resolve relationships and support navigation among data structures.[3] *See* **Primary key**.

Formal system: In a concept representation, a set of machine processable definitions in a subject field.[174]

Format: Specifications of how data or files are to be characterized.[61]

Fortezza card: A credit card-sized electronic module that stores digital information that can be recognized by a network or system. It is used to provide data encryption and authentication services.[3]

FQDN: *See* **Fully specified name**.

Frame: A packet that can be 64- to 1518-bytes long and contain header/data/trailer information, in addition to a preamble to mark the start of a frame.[3] Frame is a term used to refer to the existence of data at the Data Link Layer of the OSI Model.[41] *See* **OSI**.

Frame relay: A packet-oriented communication switching method used for local area network (LAN) interconnections and wide area network (WAN) connections. Used in both private and public networks. Frame relay networks in the United States support data transfer rates at T-1 (1.544 Mbps) and T-3 (45 Mbps) speeds.[3] *See* **ATM** and **SONET**.

Framework: 1. A structured description of a topic of interest, including a detailed statement of the problem(s) to be solved and the goals to be achieved. An annotated outline of all the issues that must be addressed while developing acceptable solutions to the problem(s). A description and analysis of the constraints that must be satisfied by an acceptable solution, and detailed specifications of acceptable approaches to solving the problem(s). **2.** Provides a unified view of the needs and functionality of a particular service or application, thus allowing a coherent approach to the specification of protocols and protocol elements, as needed to realize the implementation of the service or application.[36,66]

Free text: Unstructured, uncoded representations of information in text format (e.g., sentences describing the results of a patient's physical condition). The term implies that the user is free to enter text that is not filtered.[36] *See* **Filter.**

Frequently asked questions: *See* **FAQ.**

FTP (File transfer protocol): 1. A standard high-level protocol for transferring files of different types between computers over a TCP/IP network. FTP can be used with a command line interface or graphical user interface. **2.** The name of a utility program available on several operating systems, which makes use of this protocol to access and transfer files on remote computers.[3]

Full duplex: Communication channel/circuit that allows simultaneous two-way data transmission.[3]

Fully specified name: A phrase that describes a concept uniquely and in a manner that is intended to be unambiguous. In the context of networking, the term fully qualified domain name may be used similarly. A fully qualified domain name (FQDN) is the complete domain name for a specific computer, or host, on the Internet.[15,79]

Functional requirements: A statement of the system behavior needed to enforce a given policy. Requirements are used to derive the technical specifications of a system. Describes the performance expectations for a system. This term is often used synonymously with the term functional specifications.[3] Role an individual is acting under when executing a function.[175] A precise description of a computer system's functional requirements containing an overall picture of the proposed system's conditions, prerequisites, and restraints.[52]

G

Gantt chart: A type of bar chart used in process or project planning, and control to display planned work targets for completion of work in relation to time. Typically, a Gantt chart shows the week, month, or quarter in which each activity will be completed, and the person or persons responsible for carrying out each activity.[101]

Gap analysis: The comparison of a current condition to the desired state. Gap analysis is a term also used within process analysis to describe the variance between current and future state processes.[163]

Garbage in, garbage out: *See* **GIGO**.

Gateway: 1. A computer or a network that allows access to another computer or network. **2.** A phrase used by web masters and search engine optimizers to describe a web page designed to attract visitors and search engines to a particular web site. A typical gateway page is small, simple, and highly optimized. **3.** A technical term for the software interface between a web-based shopping cart (or order form) and a merchant account.[8] *See* **Electronic commerce**.

GB (Gigabyte): Approximately one billion (1024 megabytes) bytes. Unit of computer storage capacity.[3]

GBps (Gigabytes per second): Transmission of a billion bits per second.[3]

GELLO (Guideline Expression Language, Object Oriented): An object-oriented query and expression language for clinical decision support.[105] **Note: GELLO is an HL7 standard**.[176]

General order message: The function of this message is to initiate the transmission of information about an order. This includes placing new orders, cancellation of existing orders, discontinuation, holding, etc. Messages can originate with a placer, filler, or interested third party.[16] Also known as *ORM messages*.

Genomics: The study of all of a person's genes (the genome), including interactions of those genes with each other and with the person's environment. Genomics includes the scientific study of complex diseases that are typically caused more by a combination of genetic and environmental factors than by individual genes.[177] *See* **Precision medicine**.

GIF (Graphics interchange format): Standard for encoding, transmitting, decoding, and providing photo quality images. Introduced by CompuServe in 1987 to allow network transmission of photo-quality graphics images.[3]

GIFanim: An animated picture created by including two or more .gif images in one file.[3]

GIG (Global information grid): A globally interconnected, end-to-end set of information capabilities, associated processes, and personnel for collecting, processing, storing, disseminating, and managing information on demand.[165]

Gigabit: 1. A measure of computer storage that is approximately equal to one billion bits, most commonly used to describe telecommunications transfer speeds. For example, gigabit Ethernet allows LAN transfer of about one billion bits, or discrete signal pulses, per second. **2.** A gigabit Ethernet is a term describing various technologies for transmitting Ethernet frames at a rate of gigabit per second (1,000,000,000 bits per second), as defined by IEEE 802.3-2008 standard.[3,11]

Gigabyte: *See* **GB.**

Gigahertz: One billion cycles per second.[3]

GIGO (Garbage in, garbage out): Synonymous with the entry of inaccurate or useless data and processed output of worthless/useless information. A concept common to computer science and mathematics: the quality of output is determined by the quality of the input.[2]

Global information grid: *See* **GIG.**

Global system for mobile communications: *See* **GSM.**

Global unique device identification database: *See* **GUDID.**

Global unique identifier: *See* **GUID.**

Gnutella: A file-sharing network.[2] *See* **P2P.**

Graduated security: A security system that provides several levels of protection based on threats, risks, available technology, support services, time, human concerns, and economics.[66]

Granular: 1. An expression of the relative size of a unit. The smallest discrete information that can be directly retrieved. In security, it is the degree of protection. Protection at the file level is considered coarse granularity, whereas protection at the field level is finer granularity. **2.** Refers to a high degree of detail. In particular, a vocabulary that is highly granular provides names and definitions for the individual data elements within the context of a broader concept.[45]

Granularity: The level of depth represented by the data in a fact or dimension table in a data warehouse. High granularity means a minute, sometimes atomic grade of detail, often at the level of the transaction. Low granularity zooms out into a summary view of data and transactions.[178]

Graphical user interface: *See* **GUI.**

Grid computing: Uses the resources of many separate computers connected by a network (usually the Internet) to solve large-scale computation problems.[8] Also known as Beowulf computing.

GroupWare: Network software that defines applications used by a group of people. Allows users on different systems to collaborate and interact. Electronic mail is an example.[3]

GSM (Global system for mobile communications): 1. A worldwide digital standard used in nearly all countries in the world except Japan and the United States. GSM is a pure digital service that can transmit IP packets to the Internet and uses an array of fixed antennas in geographical cells that connect various mobile devices to the network. **2.** GSM uses 1900 MHz in the United States, and 800 to 900 MHz in Europe and Asia. GSM providers also offer wireless application protocol (WAP) services, such as connection of a GSM phone to a laptop with a PC card or cable at a data rate of 9.6 Kbps.[3]

GUDID (Global unique device identification database): A Food and Drug Administration (FDA) publicly accessible database that would hold information about each medical device marketed in the United States.[43]

GUI (Graphical user interface): 1. User interface that employs graphical images for the execution of resources as opposed to command line entry. Employs windows, icons, and menus in lieu of text to run programs and give commands to the computer. It is usually a window system accessed through a pointing device, such as a mouse. **2.** Options on how the mouse interacts with the objects on the screen allow a point-and-click interface to identify or activate an icon, or a drag-and-drop interface to move an item to another location. **3.** A type of display format that enables users to choose commands, initiate programs, and other options by selecting pictorial representation (icons) via a mouse or a keyboard.[3]

GUID (Global unique identifier): A Microsoft® term for a number that its programming generates to create a unique identity for each entity. GUIDs are widely used in Microsoft products to identify interfaces, replica sets, records, and other objects.[2]

G

H

Hacker: Computer-savvy individual most commonly thought of as a malicious person who hacks or breaks through security to steal or alter data and information (Black hat hacker). Can also be any of a group of computer aficionados who band together in clubs or organizations or who use their skills as a hobby or for good (White hat hacker).[50]

Hacktivist/hacktivism: The act of hacking a website or computer network in an effort to convey a social or political message. The person who carries out the act of hacktivism is known as a hacktivist.[54] In contrast to a malicious hacker who hacks a computer with the intent to steal private information or cause other harm, hacktivists engage in similar forms of disruptive activities to highlight political or social causes. For the hacktivist, hacktivism is an Internet-enabled strategy to exercise civil disobedience. Acts of hacktivism may include website defacement, denial-of-service attacks (DoS), redirects, website parodies, information theft, virtual sabotage, and virtual sit-ins.

Half duplex: Communication channel/circuit that allows data transmission in one direction at a time, but not in both directions simultaneously.[3]

HAN (Health alert network): To ensure that each community has rapid and timely access to emergent health information; a cadre of highly trained professional personnel; and evidence-based practices and procedures for effective public health preparedness, response, and service on a 24/7 basis.[82]

Hand-held: A portable computer that is small enough to hold in one's hand. Used to refer to a variety of devices ranging from personal data assistance, such as Smart phones, to more powerful devices that offer many of the capabilities of desktop or laptop computers. Hand-helds are used in clinical practice for such tasks as ordering prescriptions, accessing patients' medical records, and documenting patient encounters.[84]

Hard copy: File printed to a paper document.[3]

Hard disk: Part of a unit, often called a "disk drive" or "hard disk drive," that stores and provides relatively quick access to large amounts of data on an electromagnetically charged surface or set of surfaces.[3]

Hardware: The physical equipment of a computer system, including the central processing unit, data-storage devices, terminals, and printers.[36]

Hardware address: Unique low-level address burned into each piece of network hardware.[3]

Harmonization: 1. Harmonization of national standards is the prevention or elimination of differences in the technical content of standards having the same scope, particularly differences that may cause hindrances to trade. Processes to achieve harmonization include convergence, modeling, mapping, translation, and other technical specifications. **2.** The coordination processes by standard development organizations to make standards work together. Processes to achieve harmonization include convergence, modeling, mapping, translation, and other techniques.[36,45]

Hashing: Iterative process that computes a value (referred to as a hashword) from a particular data unit in such a manner that, when the hashword is protected, manipulation of the data is detectable.[3]

Hashtag: A type of label or metadata tag used on social network and blogging services to make it easier for users to find messages with a specific theme or content or community.[7] Users create and use hashtags by placing the hash character "#" in front of a word or unspaced phrase. Hashtags tie public conversation from different users into a single stream that can be found by searching for a hashtag, clicking on one, or using a third-party monitoring tool.[179]

HCPCS (Healthcare Common Procedure Coding System): For Medicare and other health insurance programs to ensure that healthcare claims are processed in an orderly and consistent manner, standardized coding systems are essential. The HCPCS Level II Code Set is one of the standard code sets used for this purpose. The HCPCS is divided into two principal subsystems, referred to as level I and level II of the HCPCS.[28]

hData: A specification for lightweight, scalable information exchange. hData creates network-facing interfaces based on REST and Atom that can enable interactions with existing health data systems.[10]

Heads-up display: *See* **HUD.**

Health alert network: *See* **HAN.**

Health informatics: The intersection of clinical informatics and public health informatics. It is one of several fields which compose the interdisciplinary field known as biomedical informatics. Health informatics is "the interdisciplinary study of the design, development, adoption and application of IT-based innovations in healthcare services delivery, management and planning."[180]

Health information: Information, whether oral or recorded in any form or medium, that **(1)** is created or received by a healthcare provider, health plan, public health authority, employer, life insurer, school or university, or healthcare clearinghouse; and **(2)** relates to the past, present, or future physical or mental health or condition of an individual; the provision of healthcare to an individual; or the past, present, or future payment for the provision of healthcare to an individual.[22]

Health information confidentiality: The obligation to protect the confidentiality of patient health information is imposed by a myriad of state laws and the federal Health Insurance Portability and Accountability Act of 1996 (HIPAA) as amended under the Health Information Technology for Economic and Clinical Health Act (the "HITECH Act"). Protected health information (PHI) can only be used or disclosed by covered entities and their business associates for purposes of treatment, payment, or healthcare operations without the patient's consent.[181]

Health information exchange: *See* **HIE.**

Health information organization: *See* **HIO.**

Health information privacy: An individual's right to control the acquisition, uses, or disclosures of his or her identifiable health data.[22] *See* **HIPAA.**

Health information security: Refers to physical, technological, or administrative safeguards or tools used to protect identifiable health data from unwarranted access or disclosure.[22]

Health information service provider: *See* **HISP.**

Health information system: Computer systems that capture, store, process, communicate, and present any healthcare information, including patient medical record information (PMRI).[45]

Health information technology: *See* **HIT.**

Health Information Technology Expert Panel: *See* **HITEP.**

Health Information Technology for Economic and Clinical Health Act: *See* **HITECH Act.**

Health Information Technology Policy Committee: *See* **HITPC.**

Health Information Technology Standards Committee: *See* **HITSC.**

Health insurance exchange: *See* **HIEx.**

Health Insurance Portability and Accountability Act of 1996: *See* **HIPAA.**

Health IT: *See* **HIT.**

Health outcome: *See* **Outcome.**

Health plan identifier: *See* **HPID.**

Healthcare Clearing House: Organization that processes health information received from another entity in a nonstandard format or containing nonstandard data content, into standard data elements or a standard transaction, or vice versa.[22]

Healthcare Common Procedure Coding System: *See* **HCPCS.**

Healthcare data card: A machine readable card conformant to ISO 7810, intended for use within the healthcare domain.[123]

Healthcare effectiveness data and information set: *See* **HEDIS.**

Healthcare evaluation: Methods for determining the success of healthcare delivery.[36]

Healthcare information framework: High-level logical model of healthcare system.[36]

Healthcare Information Technology Standards Committee: *See* **HITSC.**

Healthcare terminology: A collective term used to describe the continuum of code set, classification, and nomenclature (or vocabulary). A code is a representation assigned to a term so that it may more readily be processed. A classification arranges or organizes like or related terms for easy retrieval. A nomenclature, or vocabulary, is a set of specialized terms that facilitates precise communication by eliminating ambiguity. The term *controlled* *vocabulary* suggests only the set of individual terms in the vocabulary. A *structured vocabulary*, or *reference terminology*, relates terms to one another (with a set of relationships) that qualifies them (with a set of attributes) to promote precise and accurate interpretation.[45]

HealthKit: Apple's software platform for collecting data from various health and fitness apps, and then making that data easily available to Apple users through the company's new Health app.[182] HealthKit is being built to send data directly into hospital and doctor charts.[183]

HEDIS (Healthcare effectiveness data and information set): A tool used by health plans to measure performance on important dimensions of care and service. Altogether, HEDIS consists of 81 measures across 5 domains of care.[184]

Hexadecimal: Base 16 numbering system where 4 bits are used to represent each digit. Uses the 0–9 digits and A–F letters for the representations of the 10–15 digits.[3]

HIE (Health information exchange): 1. The sharing action between any two or more organizations with an executed business/legal arrangement that have deployed commonly agreed-upon technology with applied standards for the purpose of electronically exchanging health-related data between the organizations. **2.** A catch-all phrase for all health information exchanges, including RHIOs, QIOs, AHRQ-funded communities, and private exchanges. **3.** A concept evolved from the community health information exchanges of the mid-1990s. HIE provides the capability to electronically move clinical information among disparate healthcare information systems, and maintain the meaning of the information being exchanged. The goal of HIE is to facilitate access to and retrieval of clinical data to provide safer, more timely, efficient, effective, equitable, patient-centered care. HIE is also used by public health authorities to assist in the analysis of the health of populations.[13,48,55]

HIEx (Health insurance exchange): A set of state-regulated and standardized healthcare plans in the United States from which individuals may purchase health insurance eligible for federal subsidies. All exchanges must be fully certified and operational by January 1, 2014, under federal law.[8]

Hijacking: The ability of a hacker to misuse a system by gaining entry through the computer of a user who failed to logoff from a previous use. A user failing to log off is not the only way hijacking can take place. A hijacker does not need physical access to perform an attack.[2,3]

HIO (Health information organization): An organization that oversees and governs the exchange of health-related information among organizations according to nationally recognized standards. The purpose of an HIO is to perform oversight and governance functions for health information exchanges (HIEs).[13]

HIPAA (Health Insurance Portability and Accountability Act of 1996): According to the Centers for Medicare & Medicaid Services (CMS) web site, Title I of HIPAA protects health insurance coverage for workers and their families when they change or lose their jobs. Title II of HIPAA, the Administrative Simplification (AS) provisions, requires the establishment of national standards for electronic healthcare transactions and national identifiers for providers, health insurance plans, and employers. The AS provisions also address the security and privacy of health data. The standards are meant to improve the efficiency and effectiveness of the nation's healthcare system by encouraging the widespread use of electronic data interchange in healthcare. Also known as the *Kennedy-Kassebaum Bill, K2, Public Law 104-91.*[8]

HIPAA administrative code sets: Code sets that characterize a general business situation, rather than a medical condition or service.[3] Also called *nonmedical code sets.*

HIPAA administrative simplification: HIPAA, Title II, Subtitle F, gives the U.S. Department of Health & Human Services the authority to mandate the use of standards for the electronic exchange of healthcare data; specify what medical and administrative code sets should be used within those standards; require the use of national identification systems for healthcare patients, providers, payers (or plans), and employers (or sponsors); and specify the types of measures required to protect the security and privacy of personally identifiable healthcare information.[3]

HIPAA chain of trust: A term used in the HIPAA Security Notice of Proposed Rulemaking (NPRM) for a pattern of agreements that extend protection of healthcare data by requiring that each covered entity sharing healthcare data provide comparable protections offered by the original covered entity.[3]

HIPAA clearinghouse (or healthcare clearinghouse): Under HIPAA, this is a public or private entity that reformats health information, especially billing transactions, from a nonstandard format into a standard and approved format.[3]

HIPAA data dictionary: A data dictionary that defines and cross-references the contents of all X12 transactions included in the HIPAA mandate. The dictionary is maintained by the X12N/TG3.[3]

HIPAA standard: Any data element or transaction that meets each of the standards and implementation specifications adopted or established by the Secretary of the U.S. Department of Health & Human Services.[3]

HIPAA standard setting organization: An organization accredited by the American National Standards Institute (ANSI) to develop information transactions or data elements for health plans, clearinghouses, and/or providers.[3]

HIPAA unique identifier: A standard unique health identifier for each individual, employer, health plan, and healthcare provider, for use in the healthcare system.[3]

HIS (Health information system): A comprehensive, knowledge-based system, capable of providing information to all who need it to make sound decisions about health.[19]

HISP (Health information service provider): Term used by the DIRECT project to describe both a function (the management of security and transport for directed exchange) and an organizational model (an organization that performs HISP functions on behalf of the sending or receiving organization or individual).[185]

HIT (Health information technology): An area of information technology (IT) that involves the design, development, creation, use, and maintenance of information systems for the health and healthcare markets.[2] It involves the application of information processing with both computer hardware and software that deals with the storage, retrieval, sharing, and use of health and healthcare data, information, and knowledge for communication and decision making. As an industry, it has gained prominence in the last several years as healthcare has modernized to adopt IT. Enterprise resource planning, revenue cycle management, and other business applications have been joined by electronic health records (EHRs), population health platforms, personal health devices, and other health-oriented applications to represent health IT.[186]

Hit analysis: An analysis that uses the collected detail transactions of an organization's web site to determine how, when, why, and what visitors did during their web site visits. Within the analysis, the number of clicks, or hits, is shown from various perspectives; includes which search engine may have referred them to the site, how long they stayed, and how many different pages were viewed.[3]

HITECH Act (Health Information Technology for Economic and Clinical Health Act): Part of the American Recovery and Reinvestment Act of 2009 (ARRA) that addresses privacy and security concerns related to the transmission of electronic health information. The HITECH Act broadened the scope of privacy and security measures for personal health records (PHRs) under Health Insurance Portability and Accountability Act (HIPAA), and also increased certain legal liabilities for noncompliance.[37]

HITEP (Health Information Technology Expert Panel): Expert panel charged with recommending a standardized Quality Data Model for data representation to enable quality measurement through improved data flows within and across care settings.[187]

HITPC (Health Information Technology Policy Committee): A federal advisory committee charged with making recommendations to the National Coordinator for Health IT for the development and adoption of a nationwide health information infrastructure, including standards for the exchange of patient medical information.[37]

HITSC (Health Information Technology Standards Committee): A federal advisory committee charged with making recommendations to the National Coordinator for Health Information Technology on standards, implementation specifications, and certification criteria for the electronic exchange and use of health information.[37]

Hospital Availability Exchange: *See* **EDXL-HAVE**.

Host: For companies or individuals with a web site, a host is a computer with a web server that serves the pages for one or more web sites. A host can also be the company that provides that service, which is known as hosting.[2,3]

Host file: Text file that maps remote host names to IP addresses. Acts as a local DNS equivalent to provide a static type of DNS service.[3]

HPID ([Unique] health plan identifier): The U.S. Department of Health & Human Services (HHS) proposed a 2012 rule to establish a unique health plan identifier under the HIPAA standards for electronic healthcare transactions. The adoption of HPID and other entity identifier (OEID) would increase standardization within HIPAA standard transactions and would eliminate problems that several hospitals and healthcare providers experience frequently, such as improper routing of transactions, rejected transactions due to insurance identification errors, difficulty in determining patient eligibility and other claims processing challenges.[188]

HTML (Hypertext markup language): 1. American Standard Code for Information Exchange (ASCII)-based language used for creating files to display documents or web pages to web browsers. **2.** Hypertext markup language is the standard provided by World Wide Web Consortium (W3G) used for web pages on the Internet.[36]

HTTP (Hypertext transfer protocol): 1. Communication link protocol used by web servers and browsers to transfer/exchange HTML documents or files (text, graphic images, sound, video, and other multimedia files) over the Internet. **2.** Protocol with lightness and speed necessary for a distributed collaborative hypermedia information system. It is a generic, stateless, object-oriented protocol, which may be used for many similar tasks, such as name servers and distributed object-oriented systems, by extending the commands or "methods" used.[3,10] *See* **S-HTTP**.

HTTP over SSL/HTTPS: A secure way of using HTTP. It supplements HTTP's transport layer, the insecure transmission control protocol (TCP), with Secure Socket Layer (SSL), a secure transport layer. HTTPS is a web protocol developed by Netscape and built into its and other browsers, which encrypts and decrypts user page requests, as well as the pages that are returned by the web server.[59]

Hub: Electronic network device to which multiple networked computers are attached. Divides a data channel into two or more channels of lower bandwidth. Hubs function at the physical layer (first layer) of the open systems interconnection (OSI) model. These devices have long since been replaced by switches, but it is possible to see variants (e.g., switching hubs/intelligent hubs).[41] *See* **Concentrator**.

HUD (Heads-up display): Any transparent display that presents data without requiring users to look away from their usual viewpoints. A form of wearable technology, HUD is most commonly used in commercial aircraft, automobiles, and other professional applications.[8]

Hybrid network: Type of LAN topology in which networked nodes are connected to a hub, where star and ring topologies are combined into one overall topology.[3]

Hybrid smartcard: A card that combines both optical and smartcard technologies.[3]

Hype cycle: Hype Cycle of Emerging Technology (Gartner Group), a five-stage progression concerning "the visibility" of an emerging technology (e.g., in the popular press): 1. Technology trigger; 2. peak of inflated expectations; 3. trough of disillusionment; 4. slope of enlightenment; and 5. plateau of productivity. Relative values on a 0–10 scale: 0, 9, 2, 3, 4. Used to convey the sense that new technologies are always oversold at first. Though they eventually are useful, they seldom live up to initial expectations.[146]

Hypertext markup language: *See* **HTML**.

Hypertext transfer protocol: *See* **HTTP**.

Hz (Hertz): One cycle per second. Processing speeds for CPUs are measured in MHz.[3]

I

I/O (Input/output device): Allows computer to communicate with external devices, such as printers.[36]

I/O bus: A signal route to which a number of input and output devices can be connected in parallel.[58]

IAM (Identity access management): Set of services to include authentication, user provisioning (UP), password management, role matrix management, enterprise single sign-on, enterprise access management, federation, virtual and meta-directory services, and auditing.[22]

IAP (Internet access provider): Company that provides basic Internet connection access. No additional services are provided, such as e-mail hosting.[3]

ICC (Integrated circuit chip): Another name for a chip, an integrated circuit is a small electronic device made from semiconductor material. Integrated circuits are used for a variety of devices, including microprocessors, audio and video equipment, and automobiles. Integrated circuits are often classified by the number of transistors and other electronic components they contain.[3]

ICD (International Classification of Diseases): ICD is the standard diagnostic tool for epidemiology, health management, and clinical purposes, including the analysis of the general health situation of population groups. Also used to monitor the incidence and prevalence of diseases and other health programs and to classify diseases and other health problem records on the many types of health and vital records include death certificates and health records. And, used for reimbursement and resource allocation decision-making by countries. It is published by the World Health Organization. The latest edition currently in practice in the United States is ICD-10, endorsed in 1990 by the World Health Assembly but not implemented within the US healthcare system until 2015.[189]

ICIDH (International Classification of Improvements, Disability, and Health): Classification system issued by the World Health Organization, for common language for clinical use, data collection, and research.[45]

ICMP (Internet control message protocol): An extension to the Internet protocol, or IP, that supports packets containing error, control, and information messages. The PING command uses ICMP to test an Internet connection.[3]

Icon: A picture or symbol that graphically represents an object or a concept.[31]

ICON: An informational tool to describe nursing practice and provides data representing nursing practice in comprehensive health information systems. A combinatorial terminology for nursing practice that includes nursing phenomena, nursing actions, and nursing outcomes, and facilitates cross-mapping of local terms and existing vocabularies and classifications.[190]

ICR (Intelligent call routing): Capability that automatically routes each call, based on caller profile, to the best available agent to handle the need, anywhere in the network.[3] *See* **PING.**

ICR (Intelligent character recognition): The computer translation of manually entered text characters into machine-readable characters.[3]

IDE (Integrated drive electronics): A standard electronic interface used between a computer motherboard's data paths or bus and the computer's disk storage devices. The IDE interface is based on the IBM PC Industry Standard Architecture (ISA) 16-bit bus standard, but it is also used in computers that use other bus standards.[2]

Identification: The process of discovering the true identity of a person or item from the entire collection of similar persons or items.[66]

Identification authentication: 1. The process of determining the identity of a user who is attempting to access a physical location or computer resource. Authentication can occur through a variety of mechanisms, including challenge/response, time-based code sequences, biometric comparison, or other techniques. **2.** Use of a password, or some other form of identification, to screen users and to check their authorization.[66]

Identifier: Unique data used to represent a person's identity and associated attributes. A name or a card number are examples of identifiers.[66]

Identity: The set of physical and behavioral characteristics by which an individual is uniquely recognizable.[66]

Identity access management: *See* **IAM.**

Identity digital management: *See* **IDM.**

Identity management system: *See* **IDMS.**

Identity proofing: The process of providing sufficient information (e.g., identity history, credentials, documents) to a personal identity verification (PIV) registrar when attempting to establish an identity.[66]

Identity verification: The process of confirming or denying that a claimed identity is correct by comparing the credentials of a person requesting access with those previously proven and stored in the personal identity verification (PIV) card/system, and associated with the identity being claimed.[66]

IDM (Identity digital management): Composed of the set of business processes, and a supporting infrastructure, for the creation, maintenance, and use of digital identities within a legal and policy context.[22]

IDMS (Identity management system): 1. Composed of one or more systems or applications that manage identity verification, validation, and issuance process. **2.** Software that is used to automate administrative tasks such as resetting user passwords. It enables users to reset their own passwords. There is also identity management "password synchronization" software that enables users to access resources across the system with a single password, or single sign-on. In an enterprise setting, identity management is used to increase security and productivity, while decreasing cost and redundant effort.[11,66]

IDN (Integrated delivery network): A formal system of providers and sites of care that provides both health care services and a health insurance plan to patients in a particular geographic area. The functionalities included in an IDN vary but can include acute care, long-term health, specialty clinics, primary care, and home care services—all supporting an owned health plan.[191]

IDR (Intelligent document recognition): 1. Based on intelligent character recognition, the IT system automatically identifies structural features of a document to allow for a more rapid creation of the document text. **2.** Provides the ability to make sense of and help manage the unstructured, untagged information that is coming into the corporation or organization. It can provide the front-end understanding needed to feed business process management (BPM) and business intelligence (BI) applications, as well as traditional accounting and document or records management systems.[192,193]

IDS (Integrated delivery system): *See* **IDN.**

IGP (Interior gateway protocol): Used to advertise routing information within an autonomous system.[3]

IHE (Integrating the Healthcare Enterprise): An initiative by healthcare professionals and industry to improve the way computer systems in healthcare share information. IHE promotes the coordinated use of established standards such as DICOM and HL7 to address specific clinical need in support of optimal patient care. Systems developed in accordance with IHE communicate with one another better, are easier to implement, and enable care providers to use information more effectively.[29] *See* **Appendix B.**

IHE profile: Provides a common language for purchasers and vendors to discuss the integration needs of healthcare sites and the integration capabilities of healthcare IT products. IHE profiles offer developers a clear implementation path for communication standards supported by industry partners and are carefully documented, reviewed, and tested. They give purchasers a tool that reduces the complexity, cost, and anxiety of implementing operating systems.[29]

IIF (Information in identifiable form): Any representation of information that permits the identity of an individual to whom the information applies to be reasonably inferred by either direct or indirect means.[66]

IIS (Immunization information systems): Confidential, population-based, computerized databases that record all immunization doses administered by participating providers to persons residing within a given geopolitical area.[82]

IIS (Internet information server): Server that provides HTTP and FTP services to web browsers.[3]

IKE (Internet key exchange): A key management protocol standard that is used in conjunction with the IPSec standard. IPSec is an IP security feature that provides robust authentication and encryption of IP packets.[3]

ILD (Injection laser diode): Also known as an injection laser or diode laser, it is a semiconductor device that produces coherent radiation (in which the waves are all at the same frequency and phase) in the visible or infrared (IR) spectrum when current passes through it. Laser diodes are used in optical fiber systems, compact disc (CD) players, laser printers, remote-control devices, and intrusion detection systems.[2]

Image compression: Used to reduce the amount of memory required to store an image (e.g., an image that has a resolution of 640×480 and is in the RGB color space at 8 bits per color requires 900 Kbytes of storage). If this image can be compressed at a compression ratio of 20:1, the amount of storage required is only 45 Kbytes. There are several methods of image compression, including iVEX, JPEG, MPEG, H.261, H.263, and Wavelet.[3]

Imaging: The process of capturing, storing, displaying, and printing graphical information, such as the capturing of paper documents for archival purposes. Can be used to store and call up documents from centralized image storage systems.[3]

Immunization information systems: *See* **IIS**.

Impact analysis: Process of analyzing all operational functions and the effect that an operational interruption might have upon them.[89]

Implementation: The carrying out, execution, or practice of a plan, a method, or any design for doing something. Implementation is the action that must follow any preliminary thinking in order for something to actually happen.[59]

Implementation guide: 1. A document explaining the proper use of a standard for a specific purpose. **2.** Method for standardized installation and maintenance of computer software and hardware. The implementation guidelines include recommended administrative processes and span the devices' lifecycle.[8,116]

Implementation specification: Specific instructions for implementing a standard.[116]

In-band: Communications that occur together in a common communications method or channel. For example, a privacy label that applies to a clinical document will be sent in-band with the document.[22]

Incident: Event that has the capacity to lead to human, intangible, or physical loss, or a disruption of an organization's operations, services, or functions—which, if not managed, can escalate into an emergency, crisis, or disaster.[89]

Independent practice association: *See* **IPA**.

Indicator: A measurable variable (or characteristic) that can be used to determine the degree of adherence to a standard or the level of quality achieved.[122]

Individual: Person who is the subject of information collected, used, or disclosed by the entity holding the information.[22]

Individually identifiable data: Data that can be readily associated with a specific individual. Examples would be a name, a personal identifier, or a full street address.[61]

Individually identifiable health information: Information that is a subset of health information, including demographic information collected from an individual, and: (1) Is created or received by a health care provider, health plan, employer, or health care clearinghouse; and (2) relates to the past, present, or future physical or mental health or condition of an individual; the provision of health care to an individual; or the past, present, or future payment for the provision of health care to an individual; and (i) that identifies the individual; or (ii) with respect to which there is a reasonable basis to believe the information can be used to identify the individual.[3]

Individually identifying information: Single item or compilation of information or data that indicates or reveals the identity of an individual, either specifically (such as the individual's name or Social Security number), or that does not specifically identify the individual but from which the individual's identity can reasonably be ascertained.[22]

Infiltration: Entry into the system via the communication lines of an inactive user that is still connected to the computer. Canceling a user's sign-off signal and then continuing to operate his or her password and authorization.[3] *See* **Piggyback**.

Infobutton: A simple alerting system that provides information on request. The information may be keyed to topic and/or user. May or may not be linked to decision support system.[194]

Infographics: A representation of information in a graphic format designed to make the data easily understandable at a glance.[2] People use infographics to quickly communicate a message, to simplify the presentation of large amounts of data, to see data patterns and relationships, and to monitor changes in variables over time.[195]

Informatics: 1. The discipline concerned with the study of information and manipulation of information via computer-based tools. **2.** Information science or informatics is the science of information. It is often, though not exclusively, studied as a branch of computer science and information technology and is related to database, ontology, and software engineering.[8,36]

Information: 1. Knowledge derived from study, experience, or instruction; a collection of facts or data; the act of informing or the condition of being informed. **2.** Data to which meaning is assigned, according to context and assumed conventions.[3,196]

Information access model: Depicts access to key processes and organization information for reporting and/or security purposes.[197]

Information asset: Refers to any information in any form (e.g., written, verbal, oral, or electronic) upon which the organization places a measurable value.

This includes information created by the entity holding the information, gathered for the entity, or stored by the entity for external parties.[22]

Information compromise: An intentional or accidental disclosure or surrender of clinical data to an unauthorized receiver.[3]

Information exchange initiative: Attempts by two or more independent healthcare organizations (HCOs) in a geographic area to collaborate to share common patient information for the improvement in community health status, patient care, or viability of the HCOs.[11]

Information flow model: Visually depicts information flows in the business-to-business functions, business organizations, and applications.[197]

Information infrastructure: 1. The combination of computers and an information system. **2.** The standards, laws, regulations, business practices, and technologies needed to facilitate unauthorized sharing of comparable data in a safe and secure manner.[45]

Information in identifiable form: *See* **IIF**.

Information interchange: (American Standard Code) A code for information exchange between computers made by different companies; a string of seven binary digits represents each character; used in most microcomputers.[75]

Information model: 1. A conceptual model of the information needed to support a business function or process. **2.** A representation of concepts, relationships, constraints, rules, and operations to specify data semantics for a chosen domain.[61,120]

Information modelling: The building of abstract models for the purpose of developing an abstract system.[36]

Information privacy: The contractual right of a person to know that his or her recorded personal medical information is accurate, pertinent, complete, up-to-date, and that effective steps have been taken to restrict access to mutually agreed-upon purposes by authorized data users.[3]

Information resource department: *See* **IRD**.

Information resource management: *See* **IRM**.

Information security: The result of effective protection measures that safeguard data or information from undesired occurrences and exposure to accidental or intentional disclosure to unauthorized persons, accidental or malicious alteration, unauthorized copying, loss by theft and/or destruction by hardware failures, software deficiencies, operating mistakes, or physical damage by fire, water, smoke, excessive temperature, electrical failure, or sabotage.[3]

Information system: A system that takes input data (data entered in, transferred from other systems, etc.), processes it, and provides information as output (reports, screen displays, etc.).[52]

Information system architecture: A framework from which applications, system software, and hardware can be developed in a coherent manner, and in which every part fits together without containing a mass of design details.[36]

Information systems: A general description that may include any combination of hardware, software, and network components that comprise the ability to store, process, and retrieve information.[3]

Information technology: The hardware, firmware, and software used as part of the information system to perform information functions. This definition includes computers, telecommunications, automated information systems, and automatic data processing equipment. Information technology (IT) includes any assembly of computer hardware, software, and/or firmware configured to collect, create, communicate, compute, disseminate, process, store, and/or control data or information.[23]

Information Technology Management Reform Act of 1996: *See* **ITMRA**.

Information technology security: *See* **ITSEC**.

Information warfare: Deliberate attacks on data confidentiality and possession, integrity and authenticity, and availability and utility.[3]

Infrared Data Association: *See* **IrDA**.

Infrastructure-centric: A security management approach that considers information systems and their computing environment as a single entity.[23]

Inheritance: In object-oriented programming, the concept that when a class of objects is defined, any subclass that is defined can inherit the definitions of one or more general classes. For the programmer this means that an object in a subclass need not carry its own definition of data and methods that are generic to the class (or classes) of which it is a part. This not only speeds up program development; it also ensures an inherent validity to the defined subclass object (what works and is consistent about the class will also work for the subclass).[2]

Initiator: An (authenticated) entity (e.g., human user or computer-based entity) that attempts to access other entities.[26] Also known as *claimant* or *principal*.

Injection laser diode: *See* **ILD**.

Inpatient: Patient who is admitted to a healthcare facility in order to receive healthcare.[36]

Inpatient record: Healthcare record of a hospitalized patient.[36]

Inputs: The resources needed to carry out a process or provide a service. Inputs required in healthcare are usually financial, physical structures, such as buildings, supplies and equipment, personnel, and clients.[101]

Integrated call management: An important strategy to improve speed and efficiency in many healthcare applications through the use of multiple automated system components for telecommunications support or medical information systems design.[3]

Integrated care: The systematic coordination of general and behavioral healthcare. Integrating mental health, substance abuse, and primary care services produces the best outcomes and proves the most effective approach to caring for people with multiple healthcare needs.[198]

Integrated circuit chip: *See* **ICC**.

Integrated client: Existing applications in hospitals and other medical facilities that will provide EHR functionality by integrating with the EHR using specified HL7 v3 messages.[59]

Integrated delivery network: *See* **IDN.**

Integrated delivery system: *See* **IDS.**

Integrated device electronics: *See* **IDE.**

Integrated networks: Proposal to provide seamless access to unified data across multiple care delivery sites to support patient care.[52]

Integrated service digital network: *See* **ISDN.**

Integrating the Healthcare Enterprise: *See* **IHE.**

Integration: 1. The process of bringing together related parts into a single system. To make various components function as a connected system. **2.** Combining separately developed parts into a whole, so that they work together. The means of integration may vary, from simply mating the parts together at an interface to radically altering the parts or providing something to mediate between them.[59]

Integration layer: Software component that presents a single, consolidated point of access to several systems and/or services.[59]

Integration profile: A precise description of how standards are to be implemented to address a specific clinical integration need. Each integration profile includes definition of the clinical use case, the clinical information and workflow involved, and the set of actors and transactions that address that need. Integration profiles reference the fully detailed integration specifications defined in the IHE technical framework in a form that is convenient to use in requests for proposals and product descriptions.[29]

Integration services: This group of services is made up of services that manage the integration, message brokering, and service catalog functions.[59]

Integration testing: A testing event that seeks to uncover errors in the interactions and interfaces among application software components when they are combined to form larger parts of a system.[52]

Integrity: 1. Quality of an IT system reflecting the logical correctness and reliability of the operating system; the logical completeness of the hardware and software implementing the protection mechanisms; and the consistency of the data structures and occurrence of the stored data. It is composed of data integrity and system integrity. **2.** Knowledge that a message has not been modified while in transit. May be done with digitally signed message digest codes. Data integrity, the accuracy and completeness of the data, program integrity, system integrity, and network integrity are all components of computer and system security.[3,23]

Intelligent agent: A program that can learn from its owner and complete a task according to the owner's personal preferences. These programs incorporate artificial intelligence technology, which allows them to be able to offer intuitive suggestions and make judgments.[3]

Intelligent call routing: *See* **ICR**.

Intelligent character recognition: *See* **ICR**.

Intelligent document recognition: *See* **IDR**.

Intended use/intended purpose: Use for which a product, process, or service is intended according to the specifications, instructions, and information provided by the manufacturer.[199]

Intentionally unsafe acts: Any events that result from a criminal act, a purposefully unsafe act, an act related to alcohol or substance abuse by an impaired provider and/or staff, or events involving alleged or suspected patient abuse of any kind.[33]

Interaction model: Logical diagram or narrative describing the exchange of data and sequence of method invocation between objects to perform a specific task within a use case.[59]

Interactive services: Services that allow customers to decide which information they will be presented with next, such as requesting a search, or conducting business-to-business or electronic commerce.[3]

Interactive voice response: *See* **IVR**.

Interface: Computer hardware or software that is designed to communicate information between devices, between programs, or between a computer and a user.[45]

Interface engine: Tool that translates functions from different systems and protocols into a common format to facilitate information sharing. It is a translator for data or files to pass between systems.[11]

Interface terminology: Support interactions between healthcare providers and computer-based applications. They aid practitioners in converting clinical "free text" thoughts into the structured, formal data representations, used internally by application programs.[118]

Interior gateway protocol: *See* **IGP**.

Internal protocol: Working protocol that executes in hosts and routers to interconnect a number of packet networks.[3]

International standard: Standard that is adopted by an international standardizing/standards organization and made available to the public.[36]

Internet: The global communication network that allows almost all computers worldwide to connect and exchange information.[46]

Internet access provider: *See* **IAP**.

Internet control message protocol: *See* **ICMP**.

Internet information server: *See* **IIS**.

Internet key exchange: *See* **IKE**.

Internet of Things: *See* **IoT**.

Internet Network Information Center: *See* **InterNIC**.

Internet protocol: *See* **IP**.

Internet protocol address: *See* **IP address**.

Internet protocol datagram: *See* **IPsec**.

Internet protocol security: *See* **IPsec**.

Internet relay chat: *See* **IRC.**

Internet service provider: *See* **ISP.**

Internet work packet exchange/sequence: A network of computer networks.[3]

InterNIC (Internet Network Information Center): Agency that provides and coordinates Internet services, such as IP addresses. In addition, the center also handles registration of IP addresses and domain names.[3] Also known as *NIC.*

Interoperability: There are three levels of health information technology interoperability: foundational, structural, and semantic. **1.** "Foundational" interoperability allows data exchange from one information technology system to be received by another and does not require the ability for the receiving information technology system to interpret the data. **2.** "Structural" interoperability is an intermediate level that defines the structure or format of data exchange (i.e., the message format standards) where there is uniform movement of health data from one system to another such that the clinical or operational purpose and meaning of the data is preserved and unaltered. Structural interoperability defines the syntax of the data exchange. It ensures that data exchanges between information technology systems can be interpreted at the data field level. **3.** "Semantic" interoperability provides interoperability at the highest level, which is the ability of two or more systems or elements to exchange information and to use the information that has been exchanged. Semantic interoperability takes advantage of both the structuring of the data exchange and the codification of the data including vocabulary so that the receiving information technology systems can interpret the data. This level of interoperability supports the electronic exchange of health-related financial data, patient-created wellness data, and patient summary information among caregivers and other authorized parties. This level of interoperability is possible via potentially disparate EHR systems, business-related information systems, medical devices, mobile technologies, and other systems to improve wellness, as well as the quality, safety, cost-effectiveness, and access to health-care delivery.[19,200]

Interoperability Standards Advisory: *See* **ISA.**

Interpreted language: Code that is not compiled. A line-by-line interpretation of code takes place each and every time an interpreted language program is run. Tends to run slowly.[3]

Interrupt: A request for service from an external device seeking attention. The external device requests service by asserting an interrupt request line connected to the processor.[3]

Interrupt request: *See* **IRQ.**

Intranet: Private computer network that uses Internet protocols and Internet-derived technologies, including web browsers, web servers, and web languages, to facilitate collaborative data sharing within an enterprise.[11]

Intrusion detection: The act of detecting actions that attempt to compromise the confidentiality, integrity, or availability of a resource.[11]

iOS (formerly iPhone OS): A mobile operating system created and developed by Apple Inc. exclusively for its hardware. It is the operating system that presently powers many of the company's mobile devices, including the iPhone, iPad, and iPod Touch and is the second most popular mobile operating system globally after Android by sales. The iOS user interface is based upon direct manipulation, using multi-touch gestures. Interface control elements consist of sliders, switches, and buttons. Interaction with the OS includes gestures such as swipe, tap, pinch, and reverse pinch, all of which have specific definitions within the context of the iOS operating system and its multi-touch interface. Internal accelerometers are used by some applications to respond to shaking the device (one common result is the undo command) or rotating it in three dimensions (one common result is switching between portrait and landscape mode). Major versions of iOS are released annually.[8]

IoT (Internet of Things): The ever-growing network of physical objects that feature an IP address for Internet connectivity, and the communication that occurs between these objects and other Internet-enabled devices and systems. IoT extends Internet connectivity beyond traditional devices like desktop and laptop computers, Smartphones and tablets to a diverse range of devices and everyday items with embedded technology to communicate and interact with the external environment via the Internet.[41] The Internet of Things (IoT) is a system of interrelated computing devices, mechanical and digital machines, objects, animals, or people that are provided with unique identifiers and the ability to transfer data over a network without requiring human-to-human or human-to-computer interaction.[2]

IP (Internet protocol): The method or protocol by which data is sent from one computer to another on the Internet.[3]

IP address: Internet protocol address. The equivalent of an Internet mailing address, which identifies the network, the subnet, and the host, such as 168.100.209.246. A specific 32-bit (4 octet) unique address assigned to each networked device.[3]

IP datagram: Internet protocol datagram. Basic unit of information that passes across the Internet. Contains data and source and destination address information.[3]

IPA (Independent practice association): 1. An organization for the maintenance of the solo private practitioner as a lobbying force and vocal springboard. **2.** Legal entity organized and operated on behalf of individual participating dental professionals for the primary purpose of collectively entering into contracts to provide dental services to enrolled populations. Dental professionals may practice in their own offices and may provide care to patients not covered by the contract as well as to IPA patients.[201]

iPhone operating system: *See* **iOS.**

IPsec (Internet protocol security): 1. A developing low-level protocol for encrypting the Internet protocol packet layer of a transmission instead of the application layer to provide improved confidentiality, authentication, and integrity. IPsec can be handled without requiring changes to individual user computers. **2.** IPSec virtual private network (VPN) is a compilation of standards created by the Internet Engineering Task Force to help the user filter the encrypted data packet.[11]

IRC (Internet relay chat): A program that allows "live" conversations between people all over the world by typing messages back and forth across the Internet.[3]

IRD (Information resource department): Department within a facility that provides data automation, hardware, software, and user support. Usually associated with U.S. Army facilities.[3]

IrDA (Infrared Data Association): A group of device manufacturers that worked on the development of a standard for transmitting data via infrared light waves, the IrDA port.[202]

IRM (Information resource management): A philosophical and practical approach to managing information. Information is regarded as a valuable resource that should be managed like other resources and should contribute directly to accomplishing organizational goals and objectives. IRM provides an integrated view for managing the entire life-cycle of information, from generation to dissemination to archiving and/or destruction, for maximizing the overall usefulness of information, and improving service delivery and program management. IRM views information and information technology as an integrating factor in the organization, that is, the various organizational positions that manage information are coordinated and work together toward common ends. Further, IRM looks for ways in which the management of information and the management of information technology are interrelated, and fosters that interrelationship and organizational integration. IRM includes the management of (1) the broad range of information resources, e.g., printed materials, electronic information, and microforms; (2) the various technologies and equipment that manipulate these resources; and (3) the people who generate, organize, and disseminate those resources.[46]

IRQ (Interrupt request): Standard interrupt assignment for the system timer.[3]

ISA (Industry standard architecture): Eight- and 16-bit internal bus, or used to identify an Internet server application.[3]

ISA (Interoperability Standards Advisory): The model by which the Office of the National Coordinator for Health Information Technology (ONC) coordinates the identification, assessment, and determination of "recognized" interoperability standards and implementation specifications for industry use to fulfill specific clinical health IT interoperability needs.[13]

ISBT 128: The global standard for the terminology, identification, coding, and labeling of medical products of human origin (including blood, cell, tissue, milk, and organ products). It is used in more than 77 countries across six continents and disparate healthcare systems. It is widely endorsed by the professional community. The standard has been designed to ensure the highest levels of accuracy, safety, and efficiency for the benefit of donors and patients worldwide. ISBT 128 provides international consistency to support the transfer, traceability, and transfusion/transplantation of blood, cells, tissues, and organs.[203]

ISDN (Integrated service digital network): A data transfer technology that can transfer data significantly faster than a dial-up modem. ISDN enables wide-bandwidth digital transmission over the public telephone network, which means more data can be sent at one time. A typical ISDN connection can support transfer rates of 64K or 128K of data per second.[11]

ISO/TC 215 International Organization for Standardization (ISO) Technical Committee for Health Informatics: Committee that focuses on standardization in the field of information for health, and Health Information and Communications Technology (ICT). Promotes interoperability between independent systems, to enable compatibility and consistency for health information and data, as well as to reduce duplication of effort and redundancies.[38]

Isolation: 1. A transaction's effect is not visible to other transactions until the transaction is committed. **2.** Transaction isolation levels specify what data are visible to statements within a transaction. These levels directly impact the level of concurrent access by defining what interaction is possible between transactions against the same target data source.[12,91] *See* **ACID.**

ISP (Internet service provider): Company that provides Internet connectivity and Internet-related services, online computer access, web site hosting, and domain name registration, for an added fee beyond their costs with the InterNIC or other registration retailers.[3]

ITIM Group: Group that administers user access to the Tivoli Identity Manager system. An ITIM group is a generic user group for the Tivoli Identity Manager Server; it is used to grant access to ITIM users through the use of Access Control Information (ACIs). You can structure the system access and administration with ITIM groups. Before a person entity can be assigned to an ITIM group as an ITIM user, the entity must be provisioned with a Tivoli Identity Manager account. ITIM groups have four basic properties: Name, Description, Access option, and User list.[204]

ITMRA (Information Technology Management Reform Act): Division E of the *1996 National Defense Authorization Act (NDAA)*. It repealed the Brooks Act, defined information technology and National Security Systems (NSS), established the requirement to designate a Chief Information Officer (CIO) for each major federal agency, assigned the responsibility for management of

IT to the Director, Office of Management and Budget (OMB), and moved procurement protest authority from the General Services Administration (GSA) to the Government Accountability Office (GAO). Frequently, but erroneously, referred to as the Clinger-Cohen Act (CCA).[205]

ITSEC (Information technology security): Protection of information technology against unauthorized access to or modification of information, whether in storage, processing, or transit, and against the denial of service to authorized users, including those measures necessary to detect, document, and counter such threats. Protection and maintenance of confidentiality, integrity, availability, and accountability.[23]

IVR (Interactive voice response): Ability to access information over the phone (claim payments, claim status, and a patient's eligibility).[48]

I

J

JAD (Joint application development): A development methodology that involves continuous interaction with users and designers of the system in development. JAD centers on workshop sessions that are structured and focused to improve the quality of the final product by focusing on the up-front portion of the development lifecycle, thus reducing the likelihood of errors that are expensive to correct later.[41]

JavaScript Object Notation: *See* **JSON**.

J-codes: A subset of the Healthcare Common Procedure Coding System (HCPCS) level II code set with a high-order value of "J" that has been used to identify certain drugs and other items. The final HIPAA transactions and code sets rule states that these J-codes will be dropped from the HCPCS and that NDC codes will be used to identify the associated pharmaceuticals and supplies.[116]

Joins: A data query operation performed on data tables in a relational database management system (DBMS), in which the data from two or more tables are combined using common data elements into a single table. Typically performed using Structured Query Language (SQL).[3]

Joint application development: *See* **JAD**.

Joint photographic experts group: *See* **JPEG**.

Journaling: Recording of all computer system activities and uses of a computer system. Used to identify access violations and the individual accountable for them, determine security exposures, track the activities of selected users, and adjust access control measures to changing conditions.[3]

JPEG (Joint photographic experts group): Standard for encoding, transmitting, and decoding full-color and grayscale still images. JPEG is a graphic file format that has a sophisticated technique for compressing full-color bit-mapped graphics, such as photographs.[3]

JPEG compression: A generic algorithm to compress still images.[3]

JSON (JavaScript Object Notation): A lightweight data-interchange format that is easy for humans to read and write and easy for machines to parse and generate. It is based on a subject of JavaScript Programming Language, Standard ECMA-262 3rd Edition. JSON is a text format that is completely language independent but uses conventions familiar to programmers of the C-family of languages, including C, C++, C#, Java, JavaScript, Perl, Python, and others. JSON is built on two structures: (1) a collection of name/value pairs, also known as an object; and (2) an ordered list of values, also known as an array.[206]

JTC (Joint Technical Committee): A standards body straddling the International Organization for Standardization (ISO) and International Electrotechnical Commission (IEC).[62]

JWG (Joint Working Group): A harmonization initiative of Health Informatics Standards organizations: CEN/TC251, ISO/TC215, and HL7 formed at an inaugural Joint Working Group meeting in Brisbane hosted by ISO/TC215 and Standards Australia.[10]

J

K

KB (Kilobyte): Equal to 1024 bytes of digital data.[3]

Kbps (Kilobits per second): Transmission of a thousand bits per second.[3]

Kennedy-Kassebaum Bill: Original name for the Health Insurance Portability and Accountability Act of 1996 (HIPAA).[3] *See* **HIPAA**.

Kerberos: Network security service for securing higher-level applications and providing confidentiality and authentication. Kerberos was developed in the Athena Project at the Massachusetts Institute of Technology. The name is taken from Greek mythology; Kerberos was a three-headed dog who guarded the gates of Hades.[3]

Kernel: The core components of most operating systems. It is the part of the system that manages files, peripherals, memory, and system resources. It runs the processes and provides communication between the processes.[3]

Key: 1. A value that particularizes the use of a cryptographic system. **2.** An input that controls the transformation of data by an encryption algorithm.[66]

Key image notes: *See* **KIN**.

Key management services: As data are brought in from various sources, there will be cases where certain primary source identity keys are not unique across source systems. The key management service will generate and manage keys during insert and update operations in the EHR repository.[59]

Keystroke verification: The determination of the accuracy of data entry by the re-entry of the same data through a keyboard.[38]

Keyword: Specified words used in text search engines. Through the use of multiple keywords, an organization increases its chances that search engines will locate its web page and serve it up to the requesting user.[3]

KHz (Kilohertz): One thousand cycles per second.[3]

KIN (Key image notes): Specifies transactions that allow a user to mark one or more images in a study as significant by attaching to them a note managed together with the study. This note includes a title stating the purpose of marking the images and a user comment field. Physicians may attach key image notes to images for a variety of purposes: referring physician access, teaching files selection, consultation with other departments, image quality issues, etc.[29] *See* **Profile**. **NOTE: KIN is an Integrating the Healthcare Enterprise (IHE) Profile.**

Knowledge: The distillation of information that has been collected, classified, organized, integrated, abstracted, and value-added. Knowledge is at the level of abstraction higher than the data and information on which it is based and can be used to deduce new information and new knowledge.[36]

Knowledge acquisition: The process of eliciting, analyzing, transforming, classifying, organizing, and integrating knowledge; and representing that knowledge in a form that can be used in a computer system.[36]

Knowledge base: Data tables, databases, and other tools designed to assist the process of care.[45]

Knowledge engineering: Converting knowledge, rules, relationships, heuristics, and decision-making strategies into a form understandable to the artificial software upon which an expert system is built.[52]

Knowledge representation: The process and results of formalization of knowledge in such a way that the knowledge can be used automatically for problem solving.[36]

L

Laboratory information management system: *See* **LIS.**

Laboratory information system: *See* **LIS.**

Laboratory scheduled workflow: *See* **LSWF.**

LAN (Local area network): A single network of physically interconnected computers that is localized within a small geographical area. Operates in a span of short distances (office, building, or complex of buildings).[11] *See* **MAN, WAN,** and **WLAN.**

LAN adapter: Allows access to a network, usually wireless network.[207]

LAT (Local Area Transport): A proprietary network protocol developed by Digital Equipment Corp. and used in local area networks and terminal server connections. LAT was created to provide connection between terminal servers and host computers via Ethernet cable, and enable communication between these hosts and serial devices such as video terminals and printers.[103]

Lattice Security Model: A security model with increasing degrees of security.[47]

Layered defense: Also called overlapping controls; employing more than one control against an attack on the computer or network where one control will compensate for a failure in another.[47]

Layered trust: Concept in design of a secure operating system utilizing a layered design, in which the trustworthiness and access rights of a process can be judged by the process's proximity to the center. The more trusted processes are closer to the center.[47]

Layering networks: Each layer in the OSI model reformats the transmission and exchanges information with its peer layer.[47]

LEAP (Lightweight and efficient application protocol): One of several protocols used with the International Electrical and Electronics Engineers (IEEE) 802.1 standard for local area network (LAN) port access control. In the IEEE framework, a LAN station cannot pass traffic through an Ethernet hub or wide local area network (WLAN) access point until it successfully authenticates itself. The station must identify itself and prove that it is an authorized user before it is actually allowed to use the LAN.[11]

Least privilege: Each user and each program should operate by using the fewest privileges possible. In this way, the damage from an inadvertent or malicious attack is minimized.[16]

Legacy systems: 1. Usually refers to computers that have been in use for a long period of time, that contain many years of data, and have been used over many years of software development. **2.** Data that were collected and maintained using a "previous" system, but are now preserved on a "current" system.[65]

Level Seven: The highest level of International Standards Organization's (ISO) communications model for Open Systems Interconnection (OSI)—the application level. Issues within the application level include definition of the data to be exchanged, the timing of the interchange, and communication of certain errors to the application.[10]

Lexicon: A group of related terms used in a particular profession, subject area, or style.[31]

Lexicon query service: *See* **LQS.**

License: Authorization to use a software product.[3]

Licensed software: A programmer develops and retains full ownership of the software. In return for a fee, the programmer grants to a company a license to use the program.[47]

Lifecycle: All phases in the life of a medical device or system, from the initial conception to final decommissioning and disposal.[199]

LIFO (Last in, first out): A queue that executes last-in requests before previously queued requests.[3] Also called a *stack*.

Lightweight and efficient application protocol: *See* **LEAP.**

Limited data set: Specifies health information from which identifiers have been removed. Information in a limited data set is protected but may be used for research, healthcare operations, and public health activities without the individual's authorization.[22]

Limited privilege: A program is allowed to access secure data, but the access is minimized and neither the access rights nor the data are passed along the other untrusted programs or back to an untrusted caller.[47]

Link: A connection between two network devices.[1] Also known as *anchors*, *hotlinks*, and *hyperlinks*.

Link encryption: Data are encrypted just before the system places them on the physical communications link. Encryption occurs at layer 1 or 2 in the OSI model.[47]

LINUX: A newer version of UNIX, a nonproprietary operating system, available free on the web. An operating system that runs many healthcare applications.[47]

LIS (Laboratory information system): An application to streamline the process management of the laboratory for basic clinical services, such as hematology and chemistry. This application may provide general functional support for microbiology reporting but does not generally support blood bank functions. Provides an automatic interface to laboratory analytical instruments to transfer verified results to nurse stations, chart carts, and remote physician offices. The module allows the user to receive orders from any designated location, process the order and report results, and maintain technical, statistical, and account information. It eliminates tedious paperwork, calculations, and written documentation, while allowing for easy retrieval of data and statistics.[11] Also known as *LIS, laboratory information management system (LIMS),* and *laboratory management system (LMS).*

LISTSERV: A distribution list management package whose primary function is to operate mailing lists. An e-mail program that allows multiple computer users to connect onto a single system, thus creating an online discussion.[3]

LLC (Logical link control): Upper part of the second layer of the OSI model. Oversees and controls the exchange of data between two network nodes.[3]

Local area network: *See* **LAN.**

Local area transport: *See* **LAT.**

Local codes: Generic term for code values that are defined for specific payers, providers, or political jurisdictions.[48]

Local name space: Collection of objects to which a process has access. The local name space or domain might include some programs, files, data segments, and I/O devices such as a printer and a terminal.[47]

Log: Record that is created by an event.[22]

Log analysis: Studying log entries to identify events of interest or suppress log entries for insignificant events.[22]

Log archival: Retaining logs for an extended period of time, typically on removable media, a storage area network (SAN), or a specialized log archival appliance or server.[22]

Log clearing: Removal of all entries from a log that precede a certain date and time.[22]

Log compression: Storing a log file in a way that reduces the amount of storage space needed for the file without altering the meaning of its contents.[22]

Log conversion: The process of parsing a log in one format and storing its entries in a second format.[22]

Log entry: Individual record within a log.[22]

Log management: Process for generating, transmitting, storing, analyzing, and disposing of log data.[22]

Logging: Activities involved in creating logs.[22]

Logic bombs: Malicious software that is triggered by a response to an event, such as launching an application or when a specific date/time is reached.[208]

Logical access control: An automated system that controls an individual's ability to access one or more computer system resources, such as a workstation, network, application, or database.[66]

Logical Data Model: Represents the structure of the relationship of data elements and entities within an information system. The logical model is crucial to the proper function of any system within an enterprise. The logical model allows for elegance in system design so that the system is adaptable to the changing information needs of the enterprise.[209]

Logical drive: Subdivision of a large physical drive into numerous smaller drives.[3]

Logical link control: *See* **LLC.**

Logical observation identifiers names and codes: *See* **LOINC.**

Logical separation: Users operate under the illusion that no other processes exist, as when an operating system constrains a program's accesses so that the program cannot access objects outside its permitted domain.[47]

Logical system design: Describes the functionality of the system and presents the vision of system performance and its features.[209]

Logical threat: A threat of the possibility of destruction or alteration of software or data. Would be realized by logical manipulation within the system, rather than by physical attack.[3]

Logical topology: Describes how data are transmitted through the physical devices.[210]

Logical unit: *See* **LU.**

Logoff/logout: Process of closing an open server session.[3] To formally exit from the computer's environment.[36]

Logon: Process of opening a server session through authentication.[3]

LOINC (Logical observation identifiers names and codes): Universal identifiers for laboratory and clinical observations, including such things as vital signs, hemodynamic measures, intake/output, EKG, obstetric ultrasound, cardiac echo, urologic imaging, gastro endoscopic procedures, pulmonary ventilator management, selected survey instruments, and other clinical observations.[211]

Long term care: *See* **LTC.**

Long term and post-acute care: *See* **LTPAC.**

Longitudinal lifetime patient record: The concept of access to health information across an individual's lifetime.[3] *See* **EHR.**

Loop: 1. A repeating structure or process. **2.** A collection of segments that can repeat.[61,117]

Loophole: An incompleteness or error in a computer program, or in the hardware that permits circumventing the access control mechanism.[3]

Loose lipped system: System provides too much information to an unknown user.[47]

Loosely coupled: Application roles with shared connection only exchange information with participating system components, thus limiting the scope of risks likely posed by unconnected systems.[87]

Loss reduction: A protection risk management strategy, loss reduction focuses on a single incident or claim and requires immediate response to any adverse occurrence.[209]

Lossless compression: Method of data compression that permits reconstruction of the original data exactly, bit-for-bit. The graphics interchange file (GIF) is an image format used on the web that provides lossless compression.[120]

Lossy compression: Method of data compression that permits reconstruction of the original data approximately, rather than exactly. JPEG is an example of lossy compression.[120]

LQS (Lexicon query service): Standardizes a set of read-only interfaces able to access medical terminology system definitions, ranging from sets of codes, to complex hierarchical classification and categorization schemes.[128]

LSWF (Laboratory scheduled workflow): Establishes the continuity and integrity of clinical laboratory testing and observation data throughout the healthcare enterprise. It involves a set of transactions to maintain the consistency of ordering and patient information, to control the conformity of specimens, and to deliver the results at various steps of validation.[29] *See* **Profile. NOTE: LSWF is an Integrating the Healthcare Enterprise (IHE) Profile.**

LTC (Long-term care): The segment of the healthcare continuum that consists of maintenance, custodial, and health services for the chronically ill or disabled; may be provided on an inpatient (rehabilitation facility, nursing home, mental hospital) or outpatient basis, or at home.[3]

LTPAC (Long term and post-acute care): Segment of the healthcare continuum that works to provide comprehensive longitudinal chronic care over a long period of time. Skilled nursing facilities, home care, hospice, long-term acute care, inpatient rehabilitation, assisted living, medication management, Program of All-Inclusive Care for the Elderly (PACE), and independent care fall within this spectrum of care.[212]

LU (Logical unit): Portion of the arithmetic logic unit (ALU) within the CPU that coordinates logical operations.[3]

Luminance brightness: The amount of light, in lumens, that is emitted by a pixel or an area of the computer screen.[120]

M

Machine code/machine language: The lowest-level programming language (except for computers that utilize programmable microcode), machine languages are the only languages understood by computers. While easily understood by computers, machine languages are almost impossible for humans to use because they consist entirely of numbers. Programmers, therefore, use either a high-level programming language or an assembly language. An assembly language contains the same instructions as a machine language, but the instructions and variables have names instead of being just numbers.[8]

Machine learning: A subset of artificial intelligence that permits computers to learn either inductively or deductively. Inductive machine learning is the process of reasoning and making generalizations or extracting patterns and rules from huge data sets; that is, reasoning from a large number of examples to a general rule. Deductive machine learning moves from premises that are assumed to be true to conclusions that must be true if the premises are true.[50]

MACRA (Medicare Access and CHIP Reauthorization Act 2015): Legislation that dictates three major changes to how Medicare reimburses those providers giving care to Medicare. These changes, which created the Quality Payment Program (QPP) under MACRA include (1) ending the Sustainable Growth Rate (SGR), a formula to determine Medicare payment for provider services, (2) creating a framework to reward providers for giving better care instead of more care, and (3) aligning existing quality programs into one single program to measure provider care quality. Eligible Professionals (EPs) will have two paths within the QPP; (1) the Merit-Based Incentive Payment System (MIPS), which includes the merging of existing quality programs or (2) Alternative Payment Models (APMs), which allow providers to explore new models to deliver care.[28] *See* **MIPS** and **APM.**

Macro: Small program that automates a function for an application program. Although many of these are supplied with the purchase of a program, in many applications, users can create their own by either recording keystrokes or writing the commands using the language that the application program provides. (This process is usually very similar to the Basic language.)[68]

Mail merge: The merging of database information, such as names and addresses, with a letter template in a word processor to create personalized letters.[3]

Mailing list: A list of e-mail users who are members of a group. A mailing list can be an informal group of people who share e-mail with one another, or it can be a more formal LISTSERV group that discusses a specific topic.[3]

Mailslots: Connection-oriented interprocess messaging interface between clients and servers in a Windows NT environment.[3]

Malicious code: Software that includes spyware, viruses, worms, and Trojan horses with the intent of destroying or overtaking computer processing.[50]

Malware: Malicious software, which is designed to damage or do other unwanted actions to another unsuspecting computer.[13]

MAN (Metropolitan-area network): 1. Provides high-speed data transfer regional connectivity through multiple physical networks. Operates over distances sufficient for a metropolitan area. An IEEE 802.6 standard. **2.** A backbone network that covers a metropolitan area and is regulated by state or local utility commissions. Suppliers that provide MAN services are telephone companies and cable services.[11] *See* **LAN, WAN,** and **WLAN.**

Manage consent directives: Ensure that protected health information is only accessed with a consumer's consent.[22]

Managed care: Use of a planned and coordinated approach to providing healthcare with the goal of quality care at a lower cost. Usually emphasizes preventive care, and often associated with a health management organization.[52]

Management information department: *See* **MID.**

Management information system (service): *See* **MIS.**

Management service organization: *See* **MSO.**

Mandatory access control: A system of access control that assigns security labels or classifications to system resources and allows access only to entities (people, processes, devices) with distinct levels of authorization or clearance.[3]

MAO (Maximum acceptable/ allowable outage): The maximum amount of time that an enterprise's key products or services can be unavailable or undeliverable after an event that causes disruption to operations, before its stakeholders perceive unacceptable consequences. Also known as *maximum tolerable period of disruption* or *MTPOD*.[8]

Map: A relationship between a concept in a terminology and a concept in the same or another terminology, according to a mapping scheme or rules.[77]

Mapping: 1. Assigning an element in one set to an element in another set through semantic correspondence. **2.** A rule of correspondence established between data sets that associates each element of a set with an element in the same or another set.[31,78] *See* **Data mapping** and **Crosswalk.**

Mapping services: The mapping service helps create a map file that translates a source document format to the destination format. This service can be used to map from XML to flat file and other formats, and vice versa.[59]

Marketing: Communications that encourage the purchase or use of a product or service. This does not include a covered entity's communications about its own products, services, or benefits, or communications for treatment, case management, care coordination, or referral for care.[22]

Mask: Method that a proxy server uses to protect the identity of a corporation's employees while they are surfing the Internet. The proxy server keeps track of which employees are using which masks and directs the traffic appropriately.[50]

Masquerading: Obtaining proper identification through improper means (such as wiretapping), and then accessing the system as a legitimate user.[3]

Massively parallel processing: *See* **MPP.**

Master browser: Computer on a network that maintains a list of all computers and services available on the network.[3]

Master data: 1. Core data is data that is essential to operations in a specific business or business unit and varies by industry and company. **2.** Often refers to data units that are nontransactional that an organization may reuse across a variety of software programs and technologies.[2,54] Also known as *reference data.*

Master data management: *See* **MDM.**

Master patient index: *See* **MPI.**

Master services agreement: *See* **MSA.**

Match/matching: The process of comparing biometric information against a previously stored biometric data, and scoring the level of similarity.[66]

Math co-processor: Accompanying integrated chip to the CPU that performs arithmetic functions, which allows the CPU to perform system functions.[3]

MAU (Media access unit): A token-ring network hub.[3]

Maximum acceptable/allowable outage: *See* **MAO.**

Maximum defined data set: All of the required data elements for a particular standard based on a specific implementation specification. An entity creating a transaction is free to include whatever data any receiver might want or need. The recipient is free to ignore any portion of the data that is not needed to conduct his or her port of the associated business transaction, unless the inessential data is needed for coordination of benefits.[116]

Maximum tolerable period of disruption or MTPOD: *See* **MAO.**

Mb (Megabit): 1,048,576 bits or 1024kb.[3]

MBDS (Minimum basic data set): A set of data that is the minimum required for a healthcare record to conform to a given standard.[36]

Mbps (Megabits per second): Transmission of a million bits per second.[3]

MDA (Model-driven architecture): A platform-independent model providing for separate business and application functionality from the technology-specific code, while enabling interoperability within and across platform boundaries.[169]

MDI (Medical device interface): Includes all points of interaction between the user and the device, including all elements of the device with which the user interacts. A device user interface might be used while the user sets up the device (e.g., unpacking, set up, calibration), uses the device, or performs maintenance on the device (e.g., cleaning, replacing a battery, repairing parts).[43]

MDI-X port: Hub port that can be configured to provide a crossover function that reverses the transmit and receive wire pairs. Used to connect hubs together with a standard drop cable. Alleviates creating a crossover cable to perform the same function.[3]

MDM (Master data management): A comprehensive method of enabling an enterprise to link all of its critical data to one file, called a master file, which provides a common point of reference. MDM can help streamline data sharing among departments and can facilitate computing in multiple system architectures, platforms, and applications.[2] MDM tools are used in healthcare by health information organizations to maintain a high degree of confidence that patient identity information is consistent, disambiguated, and de-duplicated across multiple disparate systems.[13]

MDM (Medical document management message): The HL7 MDM message helps manage medical records by transmitting new or updated documents, or by transmitting important status information and/or updates for the record. Trigger events and messages can be one of two categories: they can either describe the status of the document, or they can describe the status of the document AND contain the document contents. MDM messages can be created in relation to an order or independently of them.[213]

MDM (Mobile device management): Software dealing with deploying, securing, monitoring, integrating, and managing mobile devices, such as Smartphones, laptops, and tablets, in the workplace. The intent is to optimize the functionality and security of devices within the enterprise while protecting the corporate network.[2]

MDS (Minimum data set): A core of elements to use in performing comprehensive assessments in long-term care facilities.[28]

Mean time between failure: *See* **MTBF.**

Mean time to diagnose: *See* **MTTD.**

Mean time to repair: *See* **MTTR.**

Meaningful use: *See* **MU.**

Measure: A number assigned to an object or an event. Measures can be expressed as counts (45 visits), rates (10 visits/day), proportions (45 primary healthcare visits/380 total visits = .118), percentage (12 percent of the visits made), or ratios (45 visits four health workers = 11.25).[101]

MedDRA (Medical Dictionary for Regulatory Activities): 1. Used by regulatory agencies and drug manufacturers. **2.** A terminology developed under the auspices of the International Conference on Harmonization of Technical Requirements for Registration of Pharmaceuticals for Human Use. MedDRA is a standard international terminology for regulatory communication in the registration, documentation, and safety monitoring of medical products throughout all phases of their regulatory cycle. As a standard, MedDRA is expected to promote the harmonization of regulatory requirements and documentation for medical products in the United States, Japan, and the European Union.[45,97]

Media access control: Lower portion of the second layer of the open systems interconnection (OSI) model. Identifies the actual physical link between two nodes.[3]

Media access control address: 1. Synonym for unique hardware physical address of a network device identified at the media access control layer and stored in ROM. **2.** A hardware identification number that uniquely identifies each device on a network. The MAC address is manufactured into every network card, such as an Ethernet card or Wi-Fi card, and therefore cannot be changed.[3,54]

Media access unit: *See* **MAU.**

Medicaid information technology architecture: *See* **MITA.**

Medicaid management information system: *See* **MMIS.**

Medical code sets: Codes that characterize a medical condition to treatment. These code sets are usually maintained by professional societies and public health organizations.[116]

Medical device: Any instrument, apparatus, implement, machine, appliance, implant, in vitro reagent or calibrator, software, material, or other similar or related article, intended by the manufacturer to be used, alone or in combination, for human beings for one or more of the specific purposes of diagnosis, prevention, monitoring, treatment, or alleviation of disease; diagnosis, monitoring, treatment, alleviation of, or compensation for an injury; investigation, replacement, modification, or support of the anatomy or of a physiological process; supporting or sustaining life; control of conception; disinfection of medical devices; providing information for medical purposes by means of in vitro examination of specimens derived from the human body; and which does not achieve its primary intended action in or on the human body by pharmacological, immunological, or metabolic means, but which may be assisted in its function by such means.[199]

Medical error: 1. The failure of a planned action to be completed as intended, or the use of a wrong plan to achieve an aim in the healthcare delivery process. **2.** A mistake that harms a patient. Adverse drug events, hospital-acquired infections and wrong-site surgeries are examples of preventable medical errors.[84,114]

Medical home: 1. A model of delivering primary care that is accessible, continuous, comprehensive, family centered, coordinated, compassionate, and culturally effective. **2.** In a medical home model, primary care clinicians and allied professionals provide conventional diagnostic and therapeutic services, as well as coordination of care for patients who require services not available in primary care settings. The goal is to provide a patient with a broad spectrum of care, both preventive and curative, over a period of time and to coordinate all of the care the patient receives.[214,215]

Medical informatics: Scientific discipline concerned with the cognitive, information processing, and communication task of healthcare practice, education, and research, including the information science and technology to support healthcare tasks.[36]

Medical information BUS: *See* **MIB.**

Medical logic model: *See* **MLM.**

Medical record: *See* **EHR, EMR.**

Medical subject heading: *See* **MeSH.**

Medical terminology/controlled medical vocabulary: A vocabulary server application that normalizes various medication vocabularies used by system applications in a healthcare delivery environment.[11]

Medication error: Mishaps that occur during prescribing, transcribing, dispensing, administering, adherence, or monitoring a drug.[33]

MEDIX: A terminology developed for use in monitoring medical products throughout all phases of their regulatory cycle.[169]

MEDS (Minimum emergency data set): A standardized view of the critical components of a patient's past medical history.[3]

Megabyte: One million bytes of data used as a measure of computer processor storage and real and virtual memory. A megabyte is actually 2 to the 20th power of 1,048,576 bytes.[3]

Memorandum of understanding: *See* **MOU.**

Memory: 1. The part of a system which holds program instructions and information being processed. Sometimes referred to as RAM (random access memory). **2.** Area of a computer used to store data. Can be RAM or ROM. Another word for dynamic RAM, the chips where the computers store system software, programs, and data currently being used.[3] *See* **RAM** and **ROM.**

Memory ballooning: A management technique that allows a physical host to take advantage of unused memory on its guest virtual machines (VMs).[2]

Menu: A list of options listed on the screen from which to choose. Usually labeled, and the customer is asked to press the key corresponding to a choice.[36]

Merit based incentive payment system: *See* **MIPS.**

MeSH (Medical subject heading): A thesaurus of concepts and terms used for the indexing of biomedical literature.[36]

Message: An organized set of data exchanged between people or computer processes.[36]

Message authentication: Ensuring that a message is genuine, has arrived exactly as was sent, and comes from the stated source.[36]

Message authentication code: A digital code generated using a cryptographic algorithm, defined in an International Organization for Standardization

(ISO) standard that establishes that the contents of a message have not been altered or generated by an unauthorized party.[3]

Message format standards: Protocols that make communication between disparate systems possible. These message format standards should be universal enough that they do not require negotiation of an interface agreement between the two systems in order to make the two systems communicate.[45]

Message syntax: System of rules and definitions specifying the basic component types of messages, interrelationships, and arrangement.[36]

Message type: An identified, named, and structured set of functionally related information that fulfills a specific business purpose.[36]

Message, instant: A package of information communicated from one application to another.[59]

Messaging: Creating, storing, exchanging, and managing data messages across a communications network. The two main messaging architectures are publish-subscribe and point-to-point.[120]

Messaging services: A group of services that handle messages. Services in this group include parsing, serialization, encryption and decryption, encoding and decoding, transformation, and routing.[59]

Meta tag: A special HTML command that provides information about a web page. Unlike normal HTML tags, meta tags do not affect how the page is displayed.[3]

Metadata: Structured information that describes other data to help make such data easier to retrieve, use, or manage as an information resource. There are three main types of metadata: (1) descriptive metadata describes a resource for purposes of discovery and identification; (2) structural metadata indicates how compound objects are put together; and (3) administrative metadata provides information to help manage a resource, such as when or how it was created, file type, and other technical information.[156]

Metadata registry: A system that contains information that describes the origin, structure, format, and definitions of data. These registries provide an integrating resource for legacy data, acts as a lookup tool for designers of new databases, and documents each data element.[156]

Metadata stewards: Organizations that have the responsibility for the ongoing maintenance of a metadata item.[2]

Metathesaurus: The National Library of Medicine's Unified Medical Language System (UMLS) Metathesaurus cross-references national and international medical vocabularies.[45] *See* **UMLS**.

Metropolitan-area network: *See* **MAN**.

mHealth (Mobile health): The practice of medicine and public health, supported by mobile devices (written as *m-health* or *mobile health*).[8]

MHz (Megahertz): One million times, cycles, occurrences, alterations, or pulses per second. Used to describe a measurement of CPU or processor speed.[3]

MIB (Medical information BUS): 1. A hardware and software standard (IEEE P1073) that enables standardized connections between medical monitoring devices and clinical information systems. **2.** Institute of Electrical and Electronics Engineers (IEEE) P1073 (standard designation) standard for data exchange in a medical environment.[17,216]

Microcomputer: Desktop or laptop/notebook computer employing a microprocessor.[3]

Microprocessor: Central processing unit. A microprocessor is a computer processor on a microchip. It is the "engine" that goes into motion when you turn your computer on. Designed to perform arithmetic and logic operations that make use of small number-holding areas called *registers*.[3] *See* **CPU.**

MID (Management information department): Department within a facility that provides data automation, hardware, software, and user support.[3]

Middleware: Software systems that facilitate the interaction of disparate components through a set of commonly defined protocols. The purpose is to limit the number of interfaces required for interoperability by allowing all components to interact with the middleware using a common interface.[59]

Migration tool for NetWare: Utility included in Windows NT to migrate NetWare user accounts, group accounts, files, and directories from a NetWare server environment to a Windows NT server environment. Gateway services for NetWare (GSNW) and NWLink must be installed before a migration can take place.[3]

Millions of instructions per second: *See* **MIPS.**

MIME (Multipurpose Internet mail extensions): A format originally developed for attaching sounds, images, and other media files to electronic mail, but now also used with web applications.[3]

Minimum basic data set: *See* **MBDS.**

Minimum emergency data set: *See* **MEDS.**

Minimum necessary: Minimum amount of protected health information necessary to accomplish permitted use or disclosure for payment or healthcare operations.[22]

Minimum scope of disclosure: The principle that, to the extent practical, individually identifiable health information should only be disclosed to the extent needed to support the purpose of the disclosure.[116]

MIPS (Millions of instructions per second): Rate that a processor executes instructions. Used as a measurement of processing power and computer speed.[3]

MIPS (Merit based incentive payment system): A program created as a result of MACRA legislation passed in 2015 that combines components of existing quality and incentive programs outlined in the Physician Quality Reporting System (PQRS), the Value-based Payment Modifer (VM), and the Medicare Electronic Health Record Incentive Program (also known as Medicare's version of Meaningful Use). Under MIPS, eligible professionals (EPs) will be measured on quality, resource use, clinical practice improvement, and the meaningful use of certified EHR technology.[28] *See* **MACRA**.

Mirror set: Redundant array of independent disks (RAID) Level 1. Two-disk array where one disk shadows the contents of the original disk to maintain instant redundancy.[3]

Mirror site: A file transfer protocol (FTP) site that is created after the contents of an original FTP archive server are copied to it. Usually, mirror sites use larger and faster systems than the original, so it is easier to obtain material from the mirror.[3]

MIS (Management information system or service): A class of software that provides a manager with tools for organizing and evaluating his or her department, or the staff that supports information systems.[3]

Mission critical: Activities, processing, etc., which are deemed vital to the organization's business success, and possibly, its very existence.[22]

MITA (Medicaid information technology architecture): A national framework to support improved systems development and healthcare management for the Medicaid enterprise.[28]

MLM (Medical Logic Model): The logic model has proven to be a successful tool for program planning as well as implementation and performance management in numerous fields, including primary. A logic model is defined as a graphical/textual representation of how a program is intended to work and links outcomes with processes and the theoretical assumptions of the program. It is a depiction of a program or project showing what the program or project will do and what it is to accomplish. It is a series of "if–then" relationships that, if implemented as intended, lead to the desired outcomes. Stated another way, it is a framework for describing the relationships among resources, activities, and results as they related to a specific program or project goal. The logic model also helps to make underlying assumptions about the program or project explicit. It provides a common approach to integrating planning, implementation, and evaluation.[217]

MMIS (Medicaid management information system): An integrated group of procedures and computer processing operations (subsystems) developed at the general design level to meet the principal objectives of the Medicaid program.[28]

Mobile app: A software application developed specifically for use on small, wireless computing devices, such as Smartphones and tablets, rather than desktop or laptop computers. Mobile apps are sometimes categorized by whether they are web-based or native apps created specifically for a given platform. A third category, hybrid apps, combine elements of both web-based and native apps.[2]

Mobile computing: The use of portable computing devices, such as laptop or handheld computers, in conjunction with mobile communication technologies to enable users to access the Internet and data on their home or work computer from any location. Also known as nomadic computing.[2]

Mobile device management: *See* **MDM**.

Mobile devices: A portable device that uses wireless technologies to transmit and exchange data.[11]

Mobile health: *See* **mHealth**.

Model: A very detailed description or scaled representation of one component of a larger system that can be created, operated, and analyzed to predict actual operational characteristics of the final produced component.[66]

Model driven architecture: *See* **MDA**.

Modeling: The process of defining concepts to reflect their unique definition and meaning.[79] *See* **Data modeling**.

Modified frequency modulation: *See* **MFM**.

Modularity: The design goal of separating code into self-sufficient, highly cohesive, low coupling pieces resulting in little impact for modification.[3]

MOLAP (Multidimensional online analytical processing [OLAP]): A technical OLAP approach in which data are presummarized using specialized multidimensional DBMS technology in a very structured manner within predetermined dimensions, allowing for very high performance.[3]

Moore's Law: The empirical observation that at our rate of technological development, the complexity of an integrated circuit, with respect to minimum component cost, will double in about 18 months. It is attributed to Gordon E. Moore, a cofounder of Intel, and published in 1965.[8]

Motion picture expert group: *See* **MPEG**.

MOU (Memorandum of understanding): 1. A document providing a general description of the responsibilities that are to be assumed by two or more parties in their pursuit of some goals. More specific information may be provided in an associated statement of work (SOW). **2.** A document describing an agreement between parties that expresses a convergence of will and indicates an intended common line of action. Often used when parties do not wish to imply a legal commitment or in situations where the parties cannot create a legally enforceable agreement.[8]

MPEG (Motion picture expert group): Standard for digital encoding, transmitting, decoding, and presentation of video recorder quality motion video.[3]

MPI (Master patient index): 1. The unique numerical index identity of a patient that may contain the patient's Social Security number or any other locally derived or system-generated unique number. **2.** The MPI is important because it serves as the centerpiece for all subsequent functionality and software applications, such as links to the patient clinical record, the patient schedule for appointments, reporting results of lab, x-ray, pharmacy, patient-related images, etc. **3.** As part of HIPAA's unique identifier codes, a mandated standard was controversial due to patient concern about these numbers being accidentally made available providing potential means for, and thereby identifying, the confidential records to other persons.[3]

MPP (Massively parallel processing): A computing platform technology that clusters multiple independent servers, each managed by its own operating system.[3]

MSA (Master services agreement): A contract that spells out most but not all of the terms between the signing parties. Its purpose is to speed up and simplify future contracts. The initial time-consuming negotiation is done once, at the beginning. Future agreements need to spell out the differences from the contract and might require only a purchase order. MSAs are common in information technology, union negotiations, government contracts, and long-term client/vendor relationships. They can affect a wide area such as the county or a state, with subset terms negotiated at the local level.[218]

MSAU (Multiple station access unit): A central device/hub used in computer networking to connect network nodes or computer or devices with local area networks. MSAU provides a means of data sharing between different computing devices in an organization. The working mechanism of MSAU is based on token-ring network topology in which all computers and computing devices are connected with each other in a logical circle. In this system, connectivity with other computers remains stable and users continue to communicate with each other when one computer or computing device fails. Also known as a media access unit (MAU), which is often called an Ethernet transceiver. MSAU is a standalone device or connector that is used to connect devices attached to a network over a token-ring network.[103]

MSO (Management service organizations): These are entities designed to help with the administrative, or non-medical, work involved in running a practice. These organizations may be owned by non-healthcare provider investors, hospitals, groups of physicians, be a joint venture between a hospital and physicians, or even owned by health plans. MSOs can assist practices with operational issues, financial management, human resources, staff training, coding, billing and collection services, office space needs, discounts on EHRs and medical equipment, regulatory compliance, contract management, credentialing, group purchasing, and risk management.[219]

MTBF (Mean time between failure): The average device operating time, as measured between the last failure until the next failure occurs.[3]

MTTD (Mean time to diagnose): The time taken to diagnose a problem.[3]

MTTR (Mean time to repair): The time it takes to restore a device to service from a failure.[3]

MU (Meaningful use): The set of standards defined by the Centers for Medicare & Medicaid Services (CMS) Incentive Programs that governs the use of electronic health records and allows eligible providers and hospitals to earn incentive payments by meeting specific criteria. **MU Stage 1.** Data capture and sharing. **MU Stage 2**. Advance clinical processes. **MU Stage 3**. Improved outcomes.[13]

Multicast network transmission: Meant for multiple, but not all, network nodes. Technique that allows copies of a single packet to be passed to a select number of nodes within a subnet.[3]

Multidimensional online analytical processing: *See* **MOLAP**.

Multi-homed host: Computer that is physically connected to two networks. Has two IP addresses assigned to it, one for each network interface.[3]

Multimedia: Communications that combine voice, video, and graphics that require large amounts of disk space for storage and large amounts of bandwidth for transmission.[3]

Multiple station access unit: *See* **MSAU**.

Multiplex: The division of a single transmission medium into multiple logical channels, supporting many apparently simultaneous sessions.[3]

Multiplexer, multipleXer, or multipleXor: *See* **MUX**.

Multipurpose Internet mail extensions: *See* **MIME**.

Multi-site testing: A testing event that determines the ability of the application or its subsystems to function in multiple geographical settings.[52]

Mutual authentication: Occurs when parties at both ends of a communication activity authenticate each other.[22]

MUX (Multiplexer, multipleXer, or multipleXor): A network device in which multiple streams of information are combined from different sources onto a common medium for transmission.[3]

Mware vSphere Metro Storage Cluster (VMware vMSC): A configuration option that allows clustered servers to be spread across geographical locations. This configuration, which is referred to as stretched clustering or distributed clustering, allows an organization to perform load balancing and nondisruptive live migrations between active data centers.[2]

N

NAC (Network access control/network admission control): A method of bolstering the security of a proprietary network by restricting the availability of network resources to endpoint devices that comply with a defined security policy.[2]

Name: Designation of an object by a linguistic expression.[36]

Name resolution: The process of mapping a name into a corresponding address. The domain name system provides a mechanism for naming computers in which programs use remote name servers to resolve a machine name into an IP address.[3]

Named pipes: One- or two-way pipe used for connectionless interprocess messaging interface between clients and servers.[3]

NANDA taxonomy II: A taxonomy of nursing diagnostic concepts that identify and code a patient's responses to health problems or life processes.[5]

Narrowband: A telecommunications medium that uses (relatively) low-frequency signals, exceeding 1.544 Mbps.[172]

NAS (Network attached storage): A hard disk storage system that has its own network address rather than being attached to the department computer that is serving applications to a network's workstation users. By removing storage access and its management from the department server, both application programming and files can be served faster because they are not competing for the same processor resources.[11]

NAT (Network address translation): Involves rewriting the source and/or destination addresses of IP packets as they pass through a router or firewall. Most systems using NAT do so in order to enable multiple hosts on a private network to access the Internet using a single public IP address. According to specifications, routers should not act in this way, but many network administrators find NAT a convenient technique and use it widely. Nonetheless, NAT can introduce complications in communication between hosts. Also known as *network masquerading* or *IP-masquerading*.[8]

National Drug Code: *See* **NDC**.

National Emergency Medical System (EMS) Information System: *See* **NEMSIS**.

National employer ID: A system for uniquely identifying all sponsors of health-care benefits.[124]

National Health Information Infrastructure: *See* **NHII**.

National Health-Related Items Code: *See* **NHRIC**.

National member body: *See* **NMB**.

National patient identification (ID): A system for uniquely identifying all recipients of healthcare services.[3] Sometimes referred to as the *National Individual Identifier*, or as the *healthcare ID*.

National payer ID: A system for uniquely identifying all organizations that pay for healthcare services.[116]

National provider file: *See* **NPF.**

National provider identifier: *See* **NPI.**

National standard format: *See* **NSF.**

National standardization: Standardization that takes place at the level of a specific country.[36]

National standards body: Standards body recognized at the national level that is eligible to be the national member of the corresponding international and regional standards organization.[36]

National standards system network: *See* **NSSN.**

Nationwide Health Information Network: *See* **NHIN** or **NwHIN.**

Native format: Format generally readable only by that application, but other programs can sometimes translate it using filters.[3]

Natural language: Spoken or written human language in contrast to a computer language.[41]

Natural language processing: *See* **NLP.**

NAV (Notification of document availability): A mechanism allowing notifications to be sent point-to-point to systems and users within an affinity domain, eliminating the need for manual steps or polling mechanisms.[29] *See* **Profile. NOTE: NAV is an Integrating the Healthcare Enterprise (IHE) Profile.**

Navigation tools: Allows users to find their way around a web site or multimedia presentation. They can be hypertext links, clickable buttons, icons, or image maps.[3]

NCPDP batch standard: 1. A National Council for Prescription Drug Programs (NCPDP) standard designed for use by low-volume dispensers of pharmaceuticals, such as nursing homes. Use of Version 1 of this standard has been mandated under the Health Insurance Portability and Accountability Act (HIPAA). **2.** Created to use the functionality of the NCPDP Telecommunication Standard. Uses the same syntax, formatting, data set, and rules as the Telecommunication Standard. The Batch Standard wraps the Telecommunication Standard around a detail record; then adds a batch header and trailer. This allows implementers to code one. It was intended that once an NCPDP Data Record (containing the Telecommunication Standard transaction) was built, it could then be wrapped with the Detail Data Record. Then, the Transmission Header Record and the Transmission Trailer Record are created. The Batch consisting of Header, Detail Data Records, and Trailer are formed into a batch file.[116,220]

NCPDP Telecommunication Standard: 1. A National Council for Prescription Drug Programs (NCPDP) standard designed for use by high-volume dispensers of pharmaceuticals, such as retail pharmacies. Use of Version 5.1 of this standard has been mandated under HIPAA. **2.** Developed to provide a standard format for the electronic submission of third-party drug claims. The development of the standard was to accommodate the eligibility verification process at the point-of-sale and to provide a consistent format for electronic claims processing.[116,220]

NDC (National Drug Code): The Drug Listing Act of 1972 requires registered drug establishments to provide the Food and Drug Administration (FDA) with a current list of all drugs manufactured, prepared, propagated, compounded, or processed by it for commercial distribution. (*See* Section 510 of the Federal Food, Drug, and Cosmetic Act [Act] [21 U.S.C. § 360]). Drug products are identified and reported using a unique, three-segment number, called the National Drug Code (NDC), which is a universal product identifier for human drugs.[3]

NDIS (Network driver interface specification): For writing device drivers for network interface cards. Using the NDIS specification, multiple protocols can be bound to a single network adapter.[3]

NEDSS (National Electronic Disease Surveillance System): An initiative that promotes the use of data and information system standards to advance the development of efficient, integrated, and interoperable surveillance systems at federal, state, and local levels. It is a major component of the Public Health Information Network (PHIN).[22]

Needs assessment: The identification, definition, and description of the problems to be addressed for a selected system.[52]

Need-to-know: The explicit specification of the kind of data to be made available to a qualified, authorized user or an authorized computer system.[3]

NEMSIS (National EMS Information System): Framework for collecting, storing, and sharing standardized emergency medical system (EMS) data from states nationwide.[221]

Nesting: Placing documents within other documents. Nesting allows a user to access material in a nonlinear fashion. This is the primary factor needed for developing hypertext.[3]

NetBEUI (NetBIOS extended user interface): Fast, easy to install, nonconfigurable, nonroutable network protocol for use with up to 200 network nodes. Resides at the open systems interconnection (OSI) transport layer.[1]

NetBIOS (Network basic input output system): Standard interface to networks employing IBM and compatible PCs. Implemented at the application layer. NetBIOS names cannot exceed 15 characters.[3]

NetBIOS extended user interface: *See* **NetBEUI.**

Net-centric: The realization of a robust, globally interconnected, networked environment, in which data are shared timely and seamlessly among users, applications, and platforms.[3]

Network: A collection of hardware, such as printers, modems, servers, and terminals/personal computers, that enables users to store and retrieve information, share devices, and exchange information.[11]

Network access control: *See* **NAC.**

Network adapter card: Computer hardware adapter card that provides an interface between the computer and the network.[3]

Network address translation: *See* **NAT.**

Network administration: The process of managing all components of network operations. This may include WANs as well as LANs. Network administration includes the deployment, maintenance, and monitoring of active network gear: switches, routers, firewalls, etc. Network administration includes activities such as network address assignment, assignment of routing protocols, and routing table configuration as well as configuration of authentication and authorization-directory services.[11]

Network architecture: Specifies the function and data transmission needed to convey information across a network.[36]

Network attached storage: *See* **NAS.**

Network basic input output system: *See* **NetBIOS.**

Network computer: A computer with minimal memory, disk storage, and processor power designed to connect to a network, especially the Internet. The idea behind network computers is that many users who are connected to a network do not need all the computer power they get from a typical personal computer. Instead, they can rely on the power of the network servers.[41]

Network drive: A shared disk drive available to network users.[3]

Network driver interface specification: *See* **NDIS.**

Network file system: *See* **NFS.**

Network information center: *See* **NIC.**

Network layer: Third layer of the OSI model. Routes data from source to destination across networks, and handles addressing and switching.[3] Also known as the *Internet layer.*

Network operating system: *See* **NOS.**

Network operation center: *See* **NOC.**

Network printer: Shared printer available to network users. Can be connected to a print server, directly connected to the network, or shared from a workstation.[3]

Network protocol services: The network protocol service will provide communication capabilities over the physical network. The primary network protocol that will be supported is TCP/IP.[59]

Network redirector: Operating system feature that intercepts requests from the computer and directs them to the local or remote machine for processing. Resides at the OSI presentation layer.[3]

Network server: A network server supports the sharing of peripheral devices among the workstations in the network. Network servers provide printing, file sharing, and messaging services to end users' personal computers.[11]

Network service provider: *See* **NSP.**

Network topology: The pattern of links connecting pairs of nodes of a network. A given node has one or more links to others, and the links can appear in a variety of different shapes. The simplest connection is a one-way link between two devices. A second return link can be added for two-way communication. Modern communications cables usually include more than one wire in order to facilitate this, although very simple bus-based networks have two-way communication on a single wire. Network topology is determined only by the configuration of connections between nodes; it is, therefore, a part of graph theory. Distances between nodes, physical interconnections, transmission rates, and/or signal types are not a matter of network topology, although they may be affected by it in an actual physical network.[8]

Network traffic: Data transmitted on a network for the purpose of sending information from one node to another, or from one network to another.[3]

Network weaving: A penetration technique in which different communication networks are used to gain access to a data processing system to avoid detection and trace back.[38]

Neural network: A data mining predictive model-building algorithm that is composed of connected logical nodes with inputs, outputs, and processing at each node. The neural network is particularly useful for pattern recognition.[3]

New work item proposal: *See* **NWIP.**

NFS (Network file system): A protocol developed by Sun Microsystems that allows a computer system to access files over a network as if they were on its local disks.[3]

NHII (National Health Information Infrastructure): A healthcare standardization initiative for the development of an interoperable health information technology system. First proposed under President George W. Bush, the goal of NHII was to build an interoperable system of clinical, public health, and health information technology that encouraged public-private collaboration with the federal government in a leadership role. The NHII has evolved to become the Nationwide Health Information Network.[2]

NHIN or NwHIN (Nationwide Health Information Network): 1. A secure, nationwide, interoperable health information infrastructure to connect providers, consumers, and others involved in supporting health and healthcare. **2.** A web-services series of specifications designed to securely exchange healthcare-related data. The Nationwide Health Information Network, often abbreviated as NHIN or NwHIN. **3.** Provides for the exchange of health information across the nation, between and among various organizations and constituents, and is facilitated by nationally established standards for this exchange. NwHIN components include authentication, delivery protocols, security, directories, and vocabulary/documents/message standards.[8,11,13] **4.** A program under the Office of the National Coordinator for Health Information Technology (ONC) was established in 2004 to improve the quality and efficiency of healthcare by establishing a mechanism for nationwide health information exchange. The foundation includes technical, policy, data use and service level agreements and other requirements that enable data exchange, whether between two different organizations across the street or across the country.[13]

NHRIC (National Health-Related Items Code): A system for identification and numbering of marketed device packages that is compatible with other numbering systems such as the National Drug Code (NDC) or Universal Product Code (UPC). In the early 1970s, the Drug Listing Branch of the FDA set aside a block of numbers that could be assigned to medical device manufacturers and distributors. Those manufacturers who desire to use the NHRIC number for unique product identification may apply to the FDA for a labeler code.[43]

NIC (Network information center): 1. An organization that provides information, assistance, and services to network users. **2.** A computer circuit board or card that is installed in a computer so that it can be connected to a network.[3]

NIC (Network interface card): A card that allows one to access a network. *See* **LAN adapter**.

NIC (Nursing intervention classification): A comprehensive, research-based, standardized classification of interventions that nurses perform. NIC is useful for clinical documentation, communication of care across settings, integration of data across systems and settings, effectiveness research, productivity measurement, competency evaluation, reimbursement, and curricular design.[222]

NLP (Natural language processing): A subfield of artificial intelligence and linguistics. It studies the problems inherent in the processing and manipulation of natural language, and natural language understanding devoted to making computers "understand" statements written in human languages.[8]

NM (Nuclear medicine image integration): Specifies how nuclear medicine images should be stored by acquisition modalities and workstations, and how image displays should retrieve and make use of them. It defines the basic display capabilities that image displays are expected to provide, and also how result screens, both static and dynamic, such as those created by NM cardiac processing packages, should be stored using DICOM objects that can be displayed on general purpose image display systems.[29]

See **Profile. NOTE: NM is an Integrating the Healthcare Enterprise (IHE) Profile.**

NMB (National member body): The standards institute in each country that is a member of the International Organization for Standardization (ISO).[38]

NMDS (Nursing minimum data set): 1. The foundation for nursing languages development that identified nursing diagnosis, nursing intervention, nursing outcomes, and intensity of nursing care as unique nursing components of the Uniform Hospital Discharge Data Set (UHDDS). **2.** Essential set of information items that has uniform definitions and categories concerned with nursing. It is designed to be an abstraction tool or system for collecting uniform, standard, compatible, minimum nursing data.[5,52]

NMMDS (Nursing management minimum data set): A data set used to describe the environment at unit level of service related to nursing delivery (unit/service, patient/client population, care delivery method), as well as nursing care resources and financial resources.[5]

NOC (Network operation center): A location from which the operation of a network or Internet is monitored. Additionally, this center usually serves as a clearinghouse for connectivity problems and efforts to resolve those problems.[3]

NOC (Nursing outcome classification): A comprehensive, standardized classification of patient/client outcomes developed to evaluate the effects of nursing interventions. Standardized outcomes are necessary for documentation in electronic records, for use in clinical information systems, for the development of nursing knowledge, and the education of professional nurses.[222]

Node: 1. Originating or terminating point of information or signal flow in a telecommunications network. **2.** Computer or device connected to a network. Also known as a *host*.[3,22]

NOI (Notice of Intent): A document that describes a subject area for which the federal government is considering developing regulations. It may describe the presumably relevant considerations and invite comments from interested parties. These comments can then be used in developing a notice of proposed rulemaking (NPRM) or a final regulation.[116]

Nomenclature: A consistent method for assigning names to elements of a system.[52]

Nonconformity: Deviation from a specification, a standard, or an expectation.[8]

Nonoverwriting virus: A computer virus that appends the virus code to the physical end of a program, or moves the original code to another location.[3]

Nonrepudiation: Cryptographic receipts created so that an author of a message cannot falsely deny sending a message. Proof to a third party that only the signer could have created a signature. A basis of legal recognition of electronic signatures.[3]

Nonuniform memory architecture: *See* **NUMA.**

Nonvolatile memory: Memory that retains its content when power is removed.[3]

Normalization: 1. The process of creating a uniform and agreed-upon set of standards, policies, definitions, and technical procedures to allow for interoperability. **2.** The process of organizing the fields and tables of a relational database to minimize redundancy.[8,59]

Normalization services: This service will take various concepts from different sources, normalize, and store them in the EHR's internal form. This service could be extended to include normal values based on incoming and outgoing profiles.[59]

Normative document: Document that provides rules, guidelines, or characteristics for activities or results.[36]

NOS (Network operating system): Operating system that includes special functions for connecting computers and devices into a LAN. The term *network operating system* is generally reserved for software that enhances a basic operating system by adding networking features.[41]

Notice of Intent: *See* **NOI.**

Notification of document availability: *See* **NAV.**

NPF (National provider file): The database envisioned for use in maintaining a national provider registry.[116]

NPI (National provider identifier): 1. A system for uniquely identifying all providers of healthcare services, supplies, and equipment. 2. A Health Insurance Portability and Accountability Act (HIPAA) Administrative Simplification Standard. The NPI is a unique identification number for covered healthcare providers. Covered healthcare providers and all health plans and healthcare clearinghouses must use the NPIs in the administrative and financial transactions adopted under HIPAA. The NPI is a 10-position, intelligence-free numeric identifier (10-digit number). This means that the numbers do not carry other information about healthcare providers, such as the state in which they live or their medical specialty. The NPI must be used in lieu of legacy provider identifiers in the HIPAA standards transactions.[28,116]

NSF (National standard format): Generically, this applies to any nationally standardized data format, but it is often used in a more limited way to designate the professional flat file record format used to submit professional claims.[116]

NSP (Network service provider): A company providing consolidated service for some combination of e-mail, voice mail, phone, and fax configurations on broadband or wireless hand-held devices.[3] Also known as *unified messaging solutions.*

NSSN (National standards system network): A National Resource for Global Standards is a search engine that provides users with standards-related information from a wide range of developers, including organizations accredited by the American National Standards Institute (ANSI), other US private sector standards bodies, government agencies, and international organizations.[21]

Nuclear medicine image integration: *See* **NM.**

Null modem cable: Serial cable with transmit and receive pins crossed to simulate a modem for a direct connection between computers.[3]

NUMA (Nonuniform memory architecture): A computing platform technology that clusters multiple symmetrical multi-processing (SMP) nodes together, similar to massively parallel processing (MPP) technology.[3] *See* **SMP** and **MPP.**

Nursing informatics: The specialty that integrates nursing science with multiple information and analytical sciences to identify, define, manage, and communicate data, information, knowledge, and wisdom in nursing practice.[5]

Nursing information system: Part of the healthcare information system that deals with nursing documentation, particularly the maintenance of the nursing record.[36]

Nursing intervention classification: *See* **NIC.**

Nursing management minimum data set: *See* **NMMDS.**

Nursing minimum data set: *See* **NMDS.**

Nursing outcome classification: *See* **NOC.**

NwHIN Direct: The Direct Project was launched to specify a simple, secure, scalable, standards-based way for participants to send authenticated encrypted health information directly to known, trusted recipients over the Internet. The Direct Project expands existing Nationwide Health Information Network (NwHIN) standards and service descriptions to address the key Stage 1 requirements for Meaningful Use, and to provide an on-ramp to nationwide exchange for a wide set of providers and organizations.[3]

NWIP (New work item proposal): First balloting phase for draft standards and draft technical specifications. During this phase, at least five experts from five participating ISO/TC 215 countries are chosen to work on the document.[38]

N

O

OASIS (Outcome and Assessment Information Set): A group of data elements that represent core items of a comprehensive assessment for an adult home care patient, and form the basis for measuring patient outcomes for purposes of outcome-based quality improvement. This assessment is performed on every patient receiving services of home health agencies that are approved to participate in the Medicare and/or Medicaid programs.[28]

Object: A block of information that is self-contained and has additional information that describes the data, the application that created it, how to format it, and the location of related information stored in a separate disk file.[3]

Object identifier: *See* **OID**.

Object linking and embedding: *See* **OLE**.

Object model: Conceptual representation, typically in the form of a diagram, which describes a set of objects and their relationship.[59]

Object request broker: The common interface that permits object-to-object communication.[3]

Object reuse: Securing resources for the use of multiple users.[3]

Objective evidence: Data supporting the existence or verity of something.[105]

Object-oriented: Applied to analysis, design, and programming. The basic concept in this approach is that of objects, which consist of data structures encapsulated with a set of routines, often called "methods," which operate on the data. Operations on the data must be performed via these methods, which are common to all instances of objects of a particular class. Thus, the interface to objects is well-defined and allows the code implementing the methods to be changed, so long as the interface remains the same.[3]

Object-oriented programming: *See* **OOP**.

OC (Optical carrier): Used to specify the speed of fiber optic networks conforming to the Synchronous Optical Networking (SONET) standard.[11]

OCR (Optical character recognition): A technology that scans a printed page and converts it into an electronic document that can be edited on a computer.[3]

OCSP (Online certificate status protocol): An Internet protocol used for obtaining the revocation status of an X.509 digital certificate.[8]

Octal: Base eight numbering system where three bits are used to represent each digit. Uses the 0–7 digits for representations.[3]

Octet: Eight-bit or 1-byte unit of data. Four octets are used in an IP address.[3]

ODA (Open document architecture): A standard document file format created by the International Telecommunications Union-Telecommunication Standardization (ITU-T) to replace all proprietary document file formats.

It should not be confused with the OASIS Open Document Format for Office Applications.[8] Also known as *open document.*

Odd parity: 1. A technique of checking whether data have been lost or written over during transmission. **2.** In asynchronous communication systems, odd parity refers to parity checking modes, where each set of transmitted bits has an odd number of bits. If the total number of ones in the data plus the parity bit is an odd number of ones, it is called odd parity. If the data already has an odd number of ones, the value of the added parity bit is 0; otherwise it is 1.[54]

ODS (Operational data store): A subject-oriented, integrated, real-time, volatile store of detailed data, in support of operational and tactical decision making.[3]

OEID (Other entity identifier): Proposed data element for entities needing to be identified in standard transactions that are not health plans, healthcare providers, or individuals.[3]

Off-line: Device not available to be connected to or controlled by a computer.[3]

OID (Object identifier): An identifier used to name an object, usually strings of numbers. In computer programming, an object identifier generally takes the form of an implementation-specific integer or pointer that uniquely identifies an object.[8]

OLAP (Online analytical processing): A high-level concept that describes a category of tools that aid in the analysis of multidimensional queries.[54]

OLE (Object linking and embedding): 1. A document standard developed by Microsoft® that allows for the creation of objects within one application, and links them into a second application. **2.** OLE is used for compound document management, as well as application data transfer via drag-and-drop and clipboard operations.[54]

OLTP (Online transaction processing): A class of systems that supports or facilitates high transaction-oriented applications. OLTP's primary system features are immediate client feedback and high individual transaction volume.[54]

OM (Outbreak management): The capture and management of information associated with the investigation and containment of a disease outbreak or public health emergency.[82]

Omaha nursing diagnosis/intervention: *See* **Omaha system.**

Omaha system (Omaha nursing diagnosis/intervention): A research-based, comprehensive, and standardized taxonomy designed to enhance practice, documentation, and information management. It consists of three relational, reliable, and valid components: The Problem Classification Scheme, the Intervention Scheme, and the Problem Rating Scale for Outcomes. The components provide a structure to document client needs and strengths, describe multidisciplinary practitioner interventions, and measure client outcomes in a simple, yet comprehensive, manner.[223]

On-chip applications: Applications that reside on the integrated circuit chip.[3]

Online: Device available to be connected to, or controlled by, a computer. Actively connected to other computers or devices. A device is online when it is logged on to a network or service.[3]

Online analytical processing: *See* **OLAP.**

Online certificate status protocol: *See* **OCSP.**

Online service provider: An entity that provides a service online. It can include Internet service providers and web sites, such as message board operators. In its original, more limited definition, it referred only to a commercial computer communication service in which paid members could dial via a computer modem the service's private computer network and access various services and information resources, such as bulletin boards, downloadable files and programs, news articles, chat rooms, and electronic mail services. The term "online service" was also used in reference to these dial-up services.[8]

Online transaction processing: *See* **OLTP.**

Ontology: **1.** A specification of a conceptualization of a knowledge domain. An ontology is a controlled vocabulary that describes objects and the relations between them in a formal way, and has a grammar for using the vocabulary terms to express something meaningful within a specified domain of interest. The vocabulary is used to make queries and assertions. Ontological commitments are agreements to use the vocabulary in a consistent way for knowledge sharing. Ontologies can include glossaries, taxonomies, and thesauri, but normally have greater expressivity and stricter rules than these tools. A formal ontology is a controlled vocabulary expressed in an ontology representation language. **2.** An information model that provides the structure to enable all forms of available knowledge to be used in integrated applications with semantic understanding. A reference terminology is a form of ontology. **3.** Represents knowledge as a set of concepts within a domain and the relationships between those concepts.[8,45]

OOA (Out of area): Not within the market geographic bounds.[48]

OON (Out of network): In the geographic bounds, but not contracted.[8]

OOP (Object-oriented programming): **1.** An approach to software development that combines data and procedures into a single object. **2.** A computer program composed of a collection of individual units or objects, as opposed to a traditional view in which a program is a list of instructions to the computer. Each object is capable of receiving messages, processing data, and sending messages to other objects. **3.** Software programming model constructed around objects. This model compartmentalizes data into objects (data fields) and describes object contents and behavior through the declaration of classes (methods).[3,54] *See* **SOA.**[8]

OOP (Out of pocket): Expenses for medical care that aren't reimbursed by insurance. Out-of-pocket costs include deductibles, coinsurance, and copayments for covered services plus all costs for services that aren't covered.[224]

OpArc (Operational architecture): Describes the mission, functions, information requirements, and business rules (operational requirements) for healthcare delivery. Further defined in the Department of Defense Architecture Framework (DoDAF).[225] *See* **Architecture.**

Open access: The free, immediate, online availability of research outputs with the rights to use these articles fully in the digital environment, though there may be some restrictions on use in terms of licensing and copyrights.[226]

Open card system: An electronic system that contains a single certificate from a third party used to certify a consumer's identity, thus enabling the consumer to use the certificate for transactions with numerous merchants.[3]

Open source: Software in which the source code is available free to users, who can read and modify the code.[84]

Open systems architecture: In telecommunications, the layered hierarchical structure, configuration, or model of a communications or distributed data processing system that (1) enables system description, design, development, installation, operation, improvement, and maintenance to be performed at a given layer or layers in the hierarchical structure; (2) allows each layer to provide a set of accessible functions that can be controlled and used by the functions in the layer above it; (3) enables each layer to be implemented without affecting the implementation of other layers; and (4) allows the alteration of system performance by the modification of one or more layers without altering the existing equipment, procedures, and protocols at the remaining layers.[8]

Open systems environment: Software systems that can operate on different hardware platforms because they use components that follow the same standards for user interfaces, applications, and network protocols.[3]

Open systems interconnection: *See* **OSI.**

Operating system: *See* **OS.**

Operating system (O/S) interface layer: The layer that allows for the interconnection and interrelationship among the various operating systems in the form of two or more devices, applications, and the user interfacing with an application or device.[3]

Operation system certification: A guarantee based on an objective and closed process or assessment that no design and/or implementation flaw is present, and that the occurrence of a random hardware and/or software error is below a specified value.[3]

Operational architecture: *See* **OpArc.**

Operational data store: Repository of clinical data used by client applications to create, update, and process encounter specific information at the points of service.[59]

Optical card: An optical memory card with laser-recorded and laser-read information that can be edited or updated.[3]

Optical carrier: *See* **OC.**

Optical character recognition: *See* **OCR.**

Optical disc: 1. An electronic data storage medium that is read or recorded using a low-powered laser beam. There has been a constant succession of optical disc formats, first in CD formats, followed by a number of DVD formats. Optical disc offers a number of advantages over magnetic storage media. An optical disc holds much more data. **2.** A disk read or written by light, generally laser light; such a disk may store video, audio, or digital data.[11,146]

Optical resolution: The built-in resolution of a scanning device. Contrast with "interpolated resolution" or "digital resolution" which enhances an image by software. Both resolutions are given as dots per inch (dpi), thus a 2400 dpi scanner can be the true resolution of the machine or a computed resolution.[35]

Opt-in: Mechanism that states data collection and/or use methods, and provides user choice to accept such collection and/or use.[227]

Opt-out: Mechanism that states data collection and/or use methods, and provides user choice to decline such collection and/or use.[227]

OR gate: Logic gate that implements logical disjunction. A HIGH output (1) results if one or both the inputs to the gate are HIGH (1). If neither input is high, a LOW output (0) results.[228]

Order: Request for a certain procedure or activity to be performed.[36]

Order entry system: System for recording and processing orders.[36] *See* **CPOE.**

Organized healthcare arrangement: Organized system of healthcare in which more than one covered entity participates, and in which the participating covered entities hold themselves out to the public as participating in a joint arrangement; and participate in joint utilization review, quality assurance, or financial risk for healthcare services.[22]

OS (Operating system): Software that manages the computer's memory and processes, as well as all of its software and hardware. It also allows for communication with the computer without knowing how to speak the computer's language. A computer would not be functional without an operating system.[229]

OS/2 (Operating system/2): IBM's 32-bit GUI multitasking operating system with the ability to run DOS, Win16, Win 32, OS/2 16, and OS/2 32 applications, for 80286 and 80386 computers.[3]

OSI (Open systems interconnection): A reference model to the protocols in the seven-layer data communications networking standards model and services performed at each level. The OSI standard is defined by the International Organization for Standardization (ISO). The seven layers from the bottom are physical, data link, network, transport, session, presentation, and application.[3]

Out of area: *See* **OOA.**

Out of network: *See* **OON.**

Out of pocket: *See* **OOP.**

Outbreak management: *See* **OM**.

Outcome and Assessment Information Set: *See* **OASIS**.

Outcome measure: A parameter for evaluating the success of a system, treatment, or process; the parameter reflects the top-level of goals of the system.[36]

Outcomes-based practice: Multidisciplinary clinical practice, based on evidence that specific treatments will improve patient outcomes.[230]

Out-of-band: Communications that occur outside of a communications method or channel (e.g., the communication of security policies that will be applied to data in the future are communicated out-of-band; they are communicated prior to, not at the same time as, the data).[22]

Outpatient: Patient who does not reside in a healthcare facility.[36]

Outpatient record: Healthcare record of an outpatient.[36]

Output: The direct result of the interaction of inputs and processes in the system; the types and qualities of goods and services produced by an activity, project, or program.[101]

Overwriting virus: A virus that reproduces by overwriting the first parts of the program with itself. Because important parts of the program are effectively destroyed, it will not ever run, but the virus code will. These viruses are dangerous and can cause damage to computers.[86]

OWL (Web ontology language): Designed for use by applications that need to process the content of information instead of just presenting information to humans. OWL facilitates greater machine interpretability of web content than that supported by extensible markup language (XML), resource description framework (RDF), and RDF Schema (RDF-S) by providing additional vocabulary along with formal semantics.[63]

P

P2P (Peer-to-peer): 1. A network structure in which the computers share processing and storage tasks as equivalent members of the network. Different from a client/server network, in which computers are assigned specific roles. **2.** A general term for popular file-sharing systems like Gnutella, in which there is no central repository of files. Instead, files can be stored on, and retrieved from, any user's computer.[84]

Packet: 1. The unit of data that is routed between an origin and a destination on the Internet or any other packet-switched network. Packets have no set size. **2.** A typical packet contains 1000 or 1500 bytes.[171]

Packet-filtering firewall: A computer that decides packet-by-packet whether a packet should be copied from one network to another.[3]

Packet format: Contains three sections: the header, data, and trailer.[3]

Packet header: First three octets of an X.25 packet that specifies packet destination, source, and contains an alert.[3]

Packet Internet Groper: *See* **PING**.

Packet sniffing: A technique in which attackers surreptitiously insert a software program at remote network switches or host computers. The program monitors information packets as they are sent through networks, and sends a copy of the information retrieved to the hacker.[3]

Packet switched: Transmission technique in which data are broken up into packets and sent along multiple destination paths using store and forward techniques. Once all the packets forming a message arrive at the destination, they are recompiled into the original message.[3] *See* **Circuit switched**.

Packet switching: Data are coded into small units and sent over an electronic communication network. Most traffic over the Internet uses packet switching, and the Internet is basically a connectionless network.[3]

PACS (Picture archiving and communication system): A system that begins by converting the standard storage of x-ray films into digitized electronic media that can later be retrieved by radiologists, clinicians, and other staff to view exam data and medical images. Computers or networks are dedicated to the storage, retrieval, distribution, and presentation of images. Full PACS handle images from various modalities, such as ultrasonography, magnetic resonance imaging, positron emission tomography, computed tomography, and radiography (plain x-rays).[3] Small-scale systems that handle images from a single modality (usually connected to a single acquisition device) are also known as *mini-PACS*.

PAN (Personal-area network): Personal wireless devices, such as mobile phones, headsets, and notebook PCs, connected together wirelessly via protocol such as Bluetooth.[146]

PAP (Password authentication protocol): Allows the use of clear text passwords at its lowest level.[3]

Parallel branching: Specifies that two or more tasks are executed independently of each other.[169] *See* **Exclusive branching**.

Parallel split: The divergence of a branch into two or more parallel branches, each of which execute concurrently.[170]

Parameter: A word, number, or symbol that is typed after a command to further specify how the command should function.[3]

Parameter RAM: *See* **PRAM**.

Parity: **1.** Parity is used to check a unit of data for errors during transmission through phone lines or modem cables. **2.** Refers to a technique of checking whether data have been lost or written over when they are moved from one place in storage to another or when transmitted between computers.[2]

Parser: **1.** A function that recognizes valid sentences of a language by analyzing the syntax structure of a set of tokens passed to it from a lexical analyzer. **2.** A software tool that parses programs or other text, often as the first step of assembly, compilation, interpretation, or analysis.[59]

Parser services: This service will parse the messages that come in through the protocol layer. The parser will provide support for input formats such as XML, flat files positional, flat file fixed field length, etc.[59]

Partitioning code: Applications can be broken into three logical parts: presentation, logic, and data. These are areas in which the program can be separated to facilitate execution of each logical piece on a different machine. Each segment is known as a partition. For example, the thin-client web model requires that interface presentation be handled by the browser, application logic by the web server and other application servers, and data by a database server. Developers are responsible for determining where the separation occurs.[146]

PAS (Publicly available specification): Standards from the International Organization for Standardization (ISO) which are freely available for standardization purposes. PAS is protected by ISO copyright.[38]

Passive threat: A potential breach of security, the occurrence of which would not change the state of the system. Such threat could arise from unauthorized reading of files or use of the computer system for an unauthorized application.[3]

Password: A special code word, or a string of characters, that a user must present before gaining access to a data system's resources. A sequence that an individual presents to a system for purposes of authentication.[3]

Password authentication protocol: *See* **PAP**.

P

Password cracking: A technique in which attackers try to guess or steal passwords to obtain access to computer systems.[3]

Patch: Vendors, in response to the discovery of security vulnerabilities, provide sets of files that have to be installed on computer systems. These files "fix" or "patch" the computer system or programs and remove the security vulnerability.[14]

Patient administration system: Information system or subsystem used for patient administration, billing, and reimbursement purposes.[36]

Patient care data set: *See* **PCDS**.

Patient-centric: A design goal or characteristic that establishes that all information in an application system shall be grouped and/or indexed according to the patient/person.[59]

Patient classification: A classification of patients based on specific criteria or data elements.[36]

Patient demographic query: *See* **PDQ**.

Patient identifier domain: A single system or a set of interconnected systems that all share a common identification scheme for patients. Such a scheme includes (1) a single identifier-issuing authority; (2) an assignment process of an identifier to a patient; (3) a permanent record of issued patient identifiers with associated traits; and (4) a maintenance process over time. The goal of patient identification is to reduce errors.[29]

Patient information reconciliation: *See* **PIR**.

Patient portal: A web application that provides access to various interactive service functions such as medical content for patients/consumers in a healthcare delivery organization. The portal may provide functions such as preregistration, prescheduling of procedures or outpatient services, bill payment services, access to diagnostic results, or access to a personal health record.[11]

Patient Protection and Affordable Care Act: *See* **PPACA** and **ACA**.

Patient record: Systematic record of the history of the health of a patient kept by a physician, nurse, or other healthcare practitioner.[36]

Patient record system: The set of components that form the mechanism by which patient records are created, used, stored, and retrieved; a patient record system is usually located within a healthcare provider setting. Includes people, dates, rules and procedures, processing and storage devices, and communication and support facilities.[3]

Patient registry: 1. A patient database maintained by a hospital, provider's office, or health plan that allows the identification of patients according to a condition, diagnosis, demographic characteristics, and other factors. Patient registries can help providers better coordinate care for their patients, monitor treatment and progress, and improve overall quality of care. 2. Patient registries are also maintained by local and state governments (e.g., immunization registry), specialty societies (cardiovascular disease registry of American College of Cardiology), and some patient support organizations.[114,231]

Patient-specific data: All data captured and stored in the system pertaining to a patient, such as clinical assessments, medications, insurance information, etc.[52]

Patient synchronized applications: *See* **PSA**.

Payer: Indicates a third-party entity that pays for or underwrites coverage for healthcare expenses. A payer may be an insurance company, a health maintenance organization (HMO), a preferred provider organization (PPO), a government agency, or an agency such as a third-party administrator (TPA).[10]

PC (Personal computer): A small computer designed for an individual user. All personal computers are based on the microprocessor technology that enables manufacturers to put an entire CPU on one chip.[41]

PCB (Printed circuit board): Used to mechanically support and electrically connect electronic components using conductive pathways, tracks, or signal traces etched from copper sheets laminated onto a non-conductive substrate. Printed circuit boards are used in virtually all but the simplest commercially produced electronic devices.[8] Also known as a *printed wiring board (PWB)* or *electronic wiring board*.

PCDS (Patient care data set): A compilation of precoordinated terms used in patient records to record patients' problems, therapeutic goals, and care actions.[45]

PCMCIA (Personal computer memory card international): Association that has worked to standardize and promote PC card technology.[3]

PDC (Primary domain controller): First operational computer in a Windows NT domain, and only PDC in a domain. Authenticates all users, and maintains the master security accounts database.[3]

PDF (Portable document format): A PDF file is an electronic facsimile of a printed document; the filename extension for a packed data file.[3]

PDF 417: A 2-dimensional bar code symbology, enabling error-free transmission of larger blocks of data than is feasible with a 1-dimensional bar code.[112]

PDI (Portable data for imaging): Specifies actors and transactions that provide the distribution of diagnostic and therapeutic imaging information on interchange media. The goal of this profile is to provide reliable interchange of evidence objects and diagnostic reports for import, display, or print by a receiving actor.[29] *See* **Profile. NOTE: PDI is an Integrating the Healthcare Enterprise (IHE) Profile**.

PDP (Policy decision point): The system entity that evaluates applicable policy and renders an authorization decision.[26] *See* **ACS**.

PDQ (Patient demographic query): Provides ways for multiple distributed applications to query a central patient information server for a list of patients, based on user-defined search criteria. Patient demographics data can be entered directly into the application from which the user is querying by picking the appropriate record from a list of possible matches called a patient pick list.[29] *See* **Profile. NOTE: PDQ is an Integrating the Healthcare Enterprise (IHE) Profile**.

Peer-to-peer network: LAN with no central computer where 10 or fewer user computers are connected together. This network setup allows every computer to both offer and access network resources, such as shared files.[3] Also known as a *work group*.

Penetration: A successful and repeatable extraction and identification of recognizable privileged (i.e., clinical) data from a protected resource of a data system.[3]

PEP (Policy enforcement point): The system entity that performs access control, by making decision requests and enforcing authorization decisions.[26] *See* **ACS**.

Perioperative nursing data set: *See* **PNDS**.

Peripheral: A piece of hardware that is outside the main computer. It usually refers to external hardware, such as disk drives, printers, and scanners.[3]

Permanent virtual circuit: *See* **PVC**.

Persistent data: Data that are stored on a permanent basis.[65]

Person identification service: *See* **PIDS**.

Personal computer: *See* **PC**.

Personal computer memory card international: *See* **PCMCIA**.

Personal health information: *See* **PHI**.

Personal health management tool: *See* **PHMT**.

Personal health record: *See* **PHR** and **ePHR**.

Personal identification number: *See* **PIN**.

Personal identification verification: *See* **PIV**.

Personal-area network: *See* **PAN**.

Personally identifiable health information: Health information that contains an individual's identifiers (e.g., name, Social Security number, birth date) or contains a sufficient number of variables to allow identification of an individual.[3]

Personnel White Pages: *See* **PWP**.

Pervasive computing: One of the goals of ubiquitous computing is to enable devices to sense changes in their environment, and to automatically adapt and act based on these changes, based on user needs and preferences. Some simple examples of this type of behavior include GPS-equipped automobiles that give interactive driving directions, and RFID store checkout systems.[8] *See* **Ubiquitous computing**.

PGP (Presentation of grouped procedures): Addresses what is sometimes referred to as the linked studies problem: viewing image subsets resulting from a single acquisition with each image subset related to a different requested procedure (e.g., CT chest, abdomen, and pelvis). It provides a mechanism for facilitating workflow when viewing images and reporting on individual requested procedures that an operator has grouped (often for the sake of acquisition efficiency and patient comfort). A single acquired image set is produced, but the combined use of the scheduled workflow transactions and the consistent presentation of images allow separate viewing and interpretation of the image subsets related to each of the requested procedures.[29] *See* **Profile. NOTE: PGP is an Integrating the Healthcare Enterprise (IHE) Profile.**

PGP (Pretty good privacy): A public key encryption program used to encrypt and decrypt e-mail over the Internet. Also, PGP may be used for digital signatures to let the receiver know the sender's identity and that the transmission was not changed en route.[3]

Pharmacy informatics: The scientific field that focuses on medication-related data and knowledge within the continuum of healthcare systems, including its acquisition, storage, analysis, use, and dissemination, in the delivery of optimal medication-related patient care and health outcomes.[55]

Pharmacy information systems: Health information system that deals with the pharmacy. Such systems can be linked to prescribing system for electronic processing of requests for medications and can provide inventory control.[36]

Pharmacy management system: 1. An application used by a pharmacy to manage fulfillment of prescriptions, claims processing, and other administrative functions. **2.** An application that provides support to the pharmacy department from an operational, clinical, and management perspective, helping to optimize patient safety, streamline workflow, and reduce operational costs.[11,59]

PHI (Protected/personal health information): Any individually identifiable health information, whether oral or recorded in any form or medium that is created or received by a healthcare provider, health plan, public health authority, employer, life insurer, school or university, or healthcare clearinghouse; and relates to the past, present, or future physical or mental health or condition of an individual; the provision of healthcare to an individual; or the past, present, or future payment for the provision of healthcare to an individual. Any data transmitted or maintained in any other form or medium by covered entities, including paper records, fax documents, and all oral communications, or any other form (i.e., screen prints of eligibility information, printed e-mails that have identified individual's health information, claim, or billing information, hard copy birth or death certificate). Protected health information excludes school records that are subject to the Family Educational Rights and Privacy Act, and employment records held in the Department of Homeland Security's role as an employer.[14]

PHIN (Public health information network): The Centers for Disease Control and Prevention (CDC) vision for advancing fully capable and interoperable information systems in the many organizations that participate in public health. PHIN is a national initiative to implement a multi-organizational business and technical architecture for public health information systems.[82]

PHIN-MS (Public health information network-messaging system): A protocol for secure transmission of data, based on the ebXML model. Developed and supported by Centers for Disease Control and Prevention (CDC), the protocol allows for rapid and secure messages to send sensitive health information over the Internet to other local, state, and federal organizations, as well as the CDC.[82]

Phishing: Form of fraud in which the attacker tries to learn information such as login credentials or account information by masquerading as a reputable entity or person via communication channels such as email or instant messaging.[2] Links within these messages can direct you to spoof sites— sites that look real but whose purpose is to steal information.[232]

PHMT (Personal health management tool): A set of functions that assist a consumer in managing his or her health status or healthcare.[3]

PHR (Personal health record): 1. An electronic personal health record ("ePHR") is a universally accessible, layperson comprehensible, lifelong tool for managing relevant health information, promoting health maintenance, and assisting with chronic disease management via an interactive, common data set of electronic health information and e-health tools. The ePHR is owned, managed, and shared by the individual or his or her legal proxy(s) and must be secure to protect the privacy and confidentiality of the health information it contains. It is not a legal record unless so defined and is subject to various legal limitations. **2.** Usually used when referring to the version of the health/medical record owned by the consumer/patient. **3.** An electronic record of health-related information on an individual that conforms to nationally recognized interoperability standards and that can be drawn from multiple sources while being managed, shared, and controlled by the individual.[13,48,55]

Physical access control: An automated system that controls an individual's ability to access a physical location, such as a building, parking lot, office, or other designated physical space. A physical access control system requires validation of an individual's identity through some mechanism, such as a personal identification number (PIN), card, biometric, or other token prior to providing access. It has the capability to assign different access privileges to different persons, depending on their roles and responsibilities in an organization.[66]

Physical layer: First layer in the OSI model. Defines the physical characteristics of a link between communicating devices.[3]

Physical safeguards: The physical measures, policies, and procedures to protect a covered entity's electronic information system and related buildings and equipment from natural and environmental hazards and unauthorized intrusion.[14]

Physical security: The measures taken against all physical threats to a clinical data system, including its remote facilities and operational area; including control of access and exit, protection against fire, explosion, natural disaster, sabotage, social protests, and power problems, and protection of all the stored clinical data from malicious destruction or theft.[3]

Picosecond: One trillionth of a second.[3]

Picture archiving and communication system: *See* **PACS** and **Radiology PACS**.

PIDS (Person identification service): Specification defined by Object Management Group that organized person ID management functionality to meet healthcare needs. PIDS is designed to support the assignment of IDs within a particular ID domain and the correlation of IDs among multiple ID domains. It supports the searching and matching of people, independent of a matching algorithm.[121]

Piggyback: Interception of messages between a user and the computer system and then releasing them, modifying them, or returning error messages.[3]

PIM (Platform independent model): A model of a software or business system that is independent of the specific technological platform used to implement it. For example, HTML defines a model for hypertext that includes concepts such as title, headings, paragraphs, etc. This model is not linked to a specific operating system or web browser and is, therefore, being successfully implemented on a variety of different computing systems. The term *platform-independent model* is most frequently used in the context of model-driven architectures.[233]

PIN (Personal identification number): Used to authenticate or identify a user.[3]

PING (Packet Internet Groper): Utility used to test destination reachability. Sends an Internet control message protocol (ICMP) echo request to the destination and waits for a reply.[3]

PIP (Policy information point): Point that can provide external information to a policy decision point.[26] *See* **ACS**.

PIR (Patient information reconciliation): Extends the scheduled workflow integration profile by offering the means to match images, diagnostic reports, and other evidence objects acquired for a misidentified or unidentified patient (e.g., during a trauma case) with the patient's record.[29] *See* **Profile**. **NOTE: PIR is an Integrating the Healthcare Enterprise (IHE) Profile.**

PIV (Personal identification verification): A physical artifact (e.g., identity card, "smart" card) issued to an individual that contains stored identity credentials (e.g., photograph, cryptographic keys, digitized fingerprint representation) so that the claimed identity of the cardholder can be verified against the stored credentials by another person (human readable and verifiable) or an automated process (computer readable and verifiable).[17]

PIX (Patient identifier cross-referencing): Provides cross-referencing of patient identifiers from multiple patient identifier domains. These patient identifiers can then be used by identity consumer systems to correlate information about a single patient from sources that know the patient by different identifiers.[29] *See* **Profile. NOTE: PIX is an Integrating the Healthcare Enterprise (IHE) Profile.**

Pixel: The smallest unit of data for defining an image in the computer. The computer reduces a picture to a grid of pixels.[3]

Pixel skipping: A means of reducing image resolution by simply deleting pixels throughout the image.[3]

PKC (Public key certificate): X.509 public key certificates (PKCs), which bind an identity and a public key; the identity may be used to support identity-based access control decisions after the client proves that it has access to the private key that corresponds to the public key contained in the PKC.[74]

PKI (Public key infrastructure): 1. Technology, facilities, people, operational procedures, and policy to support public key-based security mechanisms. It is an enabler for these encryption and digital signatures. **2.** Infrastructure used in the relation between a key holder and a relying party that allows a relying party to use a certificate relating to the key holder for at least one application using a public key dependent security service, and that includes a certification authority, a certificate data structure, means for the relying party to obtain current information on the revocation status of the certificate, a certification policy, and methods to validate the certification practice.[74]

Plain text: Any string (i.e., finite sequence of characters) that consists entirely of printable characters (i.e., human-readable characters) and, optionally, a very few specific types of control characters (e.g., characters indicating a tab or the start of a new line). Plain text usually refers to text that consists entirely of the ASCII printable characters and a few of its control characters. ASCII, an acronym for American standard code for information interchange, is based on the characters used to write the English language as it is used in the United States. It is the de facto standard for the character encoding (i.e., representing characters by numbers) that is utilized by computers and communications equipment to represent text, and it (or some compatible extension of it) is used on most computers, including nearly all personal computers and workstations.[234]

Plan of care (Also interdisciplinary plan of care): A plan, based on data gathered during patient assessment, that identifies the participant's care needs, describes the strategy for providing services to meet those needs, documents treatment goals and objectives, outlines the criteria for terminating specified interventions, and documents the participant's progress in meeting goals and objectives. Patient-specific policies and procedures, protocols, clinical practice guidelines, clinical paths, care maps, or a combination thereof, may guide the format of the plan in some organizations. The care plan may include care, treatment, habilitation, and rehabilitation.[235]

Platform independent model: *See* **PIM.**

Plenum cable: Fire-resistant cable that is installed in false ceilings. Uses a coating that will not emit toxic fumes in the event of a fire.[3]

Plotter: Output device that produces graphs and diagrams.[3]

Plug-and-play: Software that can be plugged into the operating system, or other software, and used immediately, without any adaptation or reconfiguration on the part of the user.[3]

Plug-in: A software tool that extends the capabilities of a web browser, allowing the browser to run multimedia files.[3]

PNDS (Perioperative nursing data set): A standardized nursing vocabulary of nursing diagnoses, nursing interventions, and nurse-sensitive patient outcomes, which addresses the perioperative patient experience from pre-admission to discharge.[5]

PNG (Portable network graphics): A bitmapped image format that employs lossless data compression. PNG was created to improve upon and replace graphic interchange format (GIF) as an image-file format not requiring a patent license.[3]

Point-of-care system: Hospital information system that includes bedside workstations or other devices for capturing and entering data at the locations where patients receive care.[36]

Point-to-multipoint connection: A communications architecture in which multiple devices are connected to a link that branches from a single point called an intelligent controller, which manages the flow of information.[3]

Point-to-point connection: A communications link between two specific end devices, such as two computers or two modems.[3]

Point-to-point protocol: *See* **PPP.**

Point-to-point tunneling protocol: *See* **PPTP.**

Policy: Overall intention and direction as formally expressed by management.[128]

Policy decision point: *See* **PDP.**

Policy enforcement point: *See* **PEP.**

Policy information point: *See* **PIP.**

Pop: To remove data from the top of a stack.[3]

POP (Post office protocol): A server using this protocol to hold users' incoming e-mail until they read or download it.[3]

Pop-down list box: In a graphical user interface (GUI) environment, the list box that appears when the user selects an icon that represents a box with various choices.[3]

POP server (Point-of-presence server): A description for a server supporting POP, serving as a dial-up modem for an Internet service provider (ISP) or e-mail service provider.[3] *See* **ISP.**

P

Portability: 1. The capability of a program to be executed on various types of data processing systems with little or no modification, and without converting the program to a different language.[59] **2.** The ability of a program to run on systems with different architectures.[36]

Portable data for imaging: *See* **PDI.**

Portable document format: *See* **PDF.**

Portable network graphics: *See* **PNG.**

Portable open systems interface: *See* **POSIX.**

Portal: *See* **Web portal.**[8]

Porting: Moving software and data files to other computer systems.[36]

POS: Physician office system.[59]

POSIX (Portable open systems interface): IEEE standard for UNIX-like program implementation. Capable of case-sensitive file naming, last-access time stamping, and hard links. A standard, not an operating system. Windows NT supports POSIX.[3]

Post office protocol: *See* **POP.**

Postcoordination: 1. Describes representation of a concept using a combination of two or more codes. **2.** Using more than one concept from one or many formal systems, combined using mechanisms within or outside the formal systems.[79,117]

Postprocessing workflow: *See* **PWF.**

Postproduction: Part of the lifecycle of the product after the design has been completed and the medical device has been manufactured and released.[199]

Power PC: RISC microprocessor developed by IBM with built-in features that allow the personal computer to emulate other microprocessors.[3]

PPACA (Patient Protection and Affordable Care Act) (Public Law 111-148): Focuses on provisions to expand healthcare coverage, control healthcare costs, and improve the healthcare delivery system.[236] *See* **ACA.**

PPP (Point-to-point protocol): Protocol that links two networks for serial data transfer. Supports multiple network protocols (TCP/IP, IPX/SPX, and NetBEUI) compression and encryption.[3]

PPTP (Point-to-point tunneling protocol): Protocol for data transfer over the Internet supporting secure communication through encryption.[3]

Practice management system: Generic term used to reference a management system.[3] *See* **Pharmacy management system.**

PRAM (Parameter RAM): A small portion of the RAM set aside to hold basic information, such as the date and time, speaker volume, desktop pattern, and keyboard and mouse settings.[3]

Precision medicine: An emerging approach for disease treatment and prevention that takes into account individual variability in genes, environment, and lifestyle for each person. The National Institutes of Health began work on a Precision Medicine Initiative Cohort Program in January 2015 to pioneer research on this approach. The research phases emphasize engaged research participants, responsible data sharing, and privacy protections.[237]

Predicate migration: Steps taken to enable pre-existing data retrieval predicates (including queries, standard reports, and decision support protocols) to be converted or utilized in a system using a mappable vocabulary.[79]

Predictive modeling: A statistical technique to predict future behavior. Predictive modeling solutions are a form of data-mining technology that works by analyzing historical and current data and generating a model to help predict future outcomes.[146]

Preferred term: The term that is deemed to be the most clinically appropriate way of expressing a concept in a clinical record. Preferred term is one of the three types of terms that can be indicated by the description type field.[79]

Preparedness: Activities, programs, and systems developed and implemented prior to an incident that may be used to support and enhance mitigation of, response to, and recovery from disruptions, disasters, or emergencies.[89] Also known as *readiness*.

Prescribing system: An information system used in healthcare for processing the prescription of medication by a physician; such a system links the physician with pharmacies and others engaged in prescription of medication.[36] *See* **e-Prescribing.**

Presentation layer: Sixth layer of the open systems interconnection (OSI) model. Provides services to interface applications to the communications system in the form of encryption, compression, translation, and conversion. The network redirector resides here.[3]

Presentation of grouped procedures: *See* **PGP.**

Presentation services: 1. Service that provides user interface capabilities and deals with formatting and presenting data to the user. May use user profiles/preferences, personalization, style sheets, etc. **2.** Client application systems that allow authorized users to access and view patient EHR data in an easily customizable manner.[59] Also known as *presentation systems* or *EHR portal*.

Pretty good privacy: *See* **PGP.**

Prevention: Measures that enable an organization to avoid, preclude, or limit the impact of a disruption.[89]

Preventive action: Action to eliminate the cause of a potential nonconformity.[89]

PRG (Procedure-related group): A classification system that groups patients based on the procedure rather than the diagnosis. This classification is based on the main procedures performed in the course of a patient's treatment. A potential benefit from this classification system includes incentives for the use of advanced technology. A drawback that currently exists in current models is that noninterventional procedures are still reimbursed on a per diem basis.[238]

Primary domain controller: *See* **PDC**.

Primary key: A data element or combination of data elements in a table whose values uniquely identify a row or record. The primary key must have a unique value for each record or row in the table.[3]

Primary patient record: Primary record of care. The primary legal record documenting the healthcare services provided to a person in any aspect of healthcare delivery. This term is synonymous with medical record, electronic health record, client record, and resident record.[3]

Print server: A computer that manages print requests from many different users by holding them in a queue until they can be printed. It sends print requests to the appropriate printer in a multi-printer environment.[3]

Printed circuit board: *See* **PCB**.

Privacy: 1. An individual's right to have all records and information pertaining to healthcare treated as confidential. **2.** Freedom from intrusion into the private life or affairs of an individual, when that intrusion results from undue or illegal gathering and use of data about that individual.[38,52]

Privacy consent policy: One of the acceptable-use privacy consent policies that are agreed to and understood in the affinity domain.[29]

Privacy consent policy identifier: An affinity domain assigned object identifier (OID) that uniquely identifies the affinity domain, privacy consent policy. There is one unique OID for each privacy consent policy within the affinity domain.[29]

Privacy impact assessment: Tells the "story" of a project or policy initiative from a privacy perspective, and helps to manage privacy impacts.[239]

Privacy officer: Appointed by a covered entity to be responsible for developing and implementing policies and procedures for complying with the health information privacy requirements of the Health Insurance Portability and Accountability Act.[22]

Privacy rights: Specific actions that an individual can take, or request to be taken, with regard to the uses and disclosures of their information.[22]

Private key: A key in an asymmetric algorithm; the possession of this key is restricted, usually to one entity. Used for signing one's signature to a block of data, which is an HTML document, an e-mail message, or a photograph.[3] *See* **Digital signature**.

Private key cryptography: Encryption methodology in which the encryptor and decryptor use the same key, which must be kept secret.[3]

Privilege: An individual's right to hold private and confidential the information given to a healthcare provider in the context of a professional relationship. The individual may, by overt act of consent or by other means, waive the right to privilege.[3]

Privileged information: A datum or data combination for which adequate technological and administrative safeguards for handling, disclosure, storage, and disposal are required by law or by administrative policy.[3]

Problem-oriented medical record: Healthcare record in which all data may be linked to a list of health problems of an individual patient.[36]

Procedure-related group: *See* **PRG.**

Process: Set of interrelated or interacting activities which transform inputs into outputs.[199]

Process model: A number of tasks that have to be carried out, and a set of conditions that determine the order of the tasks.[169]

Process standard: Standard that specifies requirements to be fulfilled by a process, to establish fitness for purpose.[36]

Processor: The logic circuitry that responds to and processes the basic instructions that drive a computer. The term *processor* has generally replaced the term *central processing unit.*[3]

Product standard: Standard that specifies requirements to be fulfilled by a product or groups of products to establish fitness for purpose.[36]

Profile: A set of selected parameters that describes a particular reimplementation of a standard.[36]

Program: A set of instructions that can be recognized by a computer system and used to carry out a set of processes.[36]

Program manager: The person ultimately responsible for the overall procurement, development, integration, modification, or operation and maintenance of an IT system.[23]

Program security controls: Controls designed to prevent unauthorized changes to programs in systems that are already in production.[3]

Programmable read-only memory: *See* **PROM.**

Programmers: Highly trained technical specialists who write computer software instructions.[3]

Project management: A set of principles, methods, tools, and techniques for effective planning of work, thereby establishing a sound basis for effective scheduling, controlling, and preplanning in the implementation and management of programs and products.[52]

Project Sentinel: A project of the National Biosurveillance Testbed. Project Sentinel takes de-identified HIPAA compliance data from participating emergency departments, aggregates it for a specific area, and allows for regional and national comparison for identification of emerging diseases and bioterrorism threats.[3]

PROM (Programmable read-only memory): Subclass of ROM, nonvolatile memory chip used in control devices because it can be programmed once.[3]

Prompt: A message displayed on the monitor screen, which asks the customer to perform some action and shows that the computer is ready to accept a command or instruction.[36]

Properties: Information about an object or file, including settings or options for that object. For example, user looks at properties of a file for information, such as the date created, file size, file type, and file attributes.[3]

Proprietary: Privately owned and controlled, typically by a single party. In the computer industry, proprietary is the opposite of open. A proprietary design or technique is one that is owned by a company. It also implies that the company has not divulged specifications that would allow other companies to duplicate the product.[3]

Protected/personal health information: *See* **PHI.**

Protocol: A special set of rules using end points in a telecommunication connection for communication. Protocols exist at several levels.[97]

Protocol stack: Set of combined protocols that accomplish the communications process.[3]

Proximity: Refers to a technology used to provide physical access control. This technology uses a contactless interface with a card reader.[66]

Proxy server: Hardware security tool to help protect an organization against security breaches.[50]

PSA (Patient synchronized applications): A means for viewing data for a single patient using independent and unlinked applications on a user's workstation, reducing the repetitive tasks of selecting the same patient in multiple applications. Data can be viewed from different identifier domains when used with the Patient Identifier Cross-referencing Integration Profile to resolve multiple identifications for the same patient. This profile leverages the HL7 CCOW standard specifically for patient subject context management.[29] *See* **Profile. NOTE: PSA is an Integrating the Healthcare Enterprise (IHE) Profile.**

Psychotherapy notes: Recorded in any medium by a healthcare provider who is a mental health professional, documenting or analyzing the contents of conversation during a private counseling session, or a group, joint, or family counseling session, when notes are separated from the rest of the individual's record.[22]

Public health agency: An agency that performs or conducts one or more of the following essential functions that characterize public health programs, services, or activities: **(a)** monitor health status to identify community health problems; **(b)** diagnose and investigate health problems and health hazards in the community; **(c)** inform, educate, and empower people about health issues; **(d)** mobilize community partnerships to identify and solve health problems; **(e)** develop policies and plans that support individual and community health efforts; **(f)** enforce laws and regulations that protect health and ensure safety; **(g)** link people to needed personal health services and ensure the provision of healthcare when otherwise unavailable; **(h)** ensure a competent public health and personal healthcare workforce; **(i)** evaluate effectiveness, accessibility, and quality of personal and population-based health services; and **(j)** research for new insights and innovation solutions to health problems.[14]

Public health information network: *See* **PHIN.**

Public information: Data which, by their nature, require nonspecific handling, limited disclosure, protected storage, and disposal.[3]

Public key: A key in an asymmetric algorithm that is publicly available. Used for verifying a signature after it has been signed. *See also* **Digital signature**.[3]

Public key algorithms: A method of cryptography in which one key is used to encrypt a message and another key is used to decrypt it.[3]

Public key certificate: *See* **PKC.**

Public key cryptography: Encryption system that uses a linked pair of keys; one key encrypts, the other key decrypts.[3]

Public key infrastructure: *See* **PKI.**

Publicly available specification: *See* **PAS.**

Push: Putting data on a stack.[3]

PVC (Permanent virtual circuit): A fixed circuit between two users in a packet-switched network. PVCs are more efficient for connections between hosts that communicate frequently.[3] *See* **SVC.**

PWF (Postprocessing workflow): Addresses the need to schedule, distribute, and track the status of typical postprocessing workflow steps, such as computer-aided detection or image processing. Work lists for each of these tasks are generated and can be queried, work items can be selected, and the status returned from the system performing the work to the system managing the work.[29] *See* **Profile. NOTE: PWF is an Integrating the Healthcare Enterprise (IHE) Profile.**

PWP (Personnel White Pages): Provides access to basic human workforce user directory information. This information has broad use among many clinical and nonclinical applications across the healthcare enterprise. The information can be used to enhance the clinical workflow (contact information), enhance the user interface (user friendly names and titles), and ensure identity (digital certificates). This Personnel White Pages directory will be related to the user identity provided by the Enterprise User Authentication (EUA) Integration Profile previously defined by IHE.[29] *See* **Profile. NOTE: PWP is an Integrating the Healthcare Enterprise (IHE) Profile.**

P

Q

QA (Quality assurance): An ongoing planned and systematic effort to ensure confidence that processes and products meet established goals.[240]

QDM (Quality data model): An information model that defines concepts used in quality care and is intended to enable automation of EHR use.[187]

QMF (Query management facility): Ad hoc query tool to extract data from some mainframe systems.[48]

QMR (Quick medical reference): Search system for the National Library of Medicine.[241]

QoS (Quality of service): 1. A negotiated contract between a user and a network provider that renders some degree of reliable capacity in the shared network.[146] 2. The ability to provide different priority to different applications, users, or data flows, or to guarantee a certain level of performance to a data flow.[8]

QR codes (Quick response codes): High-density, two-dimensional bar codes that are readable by mobile phones and computer cameras with the correct software.[146]

Qualified certificate: In public key infrastructure security information technology, a qualified certificate is used to describe a certificate with a certain qualified status within applicable governing law.[74]

Quality: The totality of features and other characteristics of a product or service that bear on its ability to satisfy stated or implied needs.[101]

Quality control: A process to control the quality of care and services.[36]

Quality data model: *See* **QDM**.

Quality design: Systematic approach to service design that identifies the key features needed or desired by both external and internal clients, creates design options for the desired features, and then selects the combination of options that will maximize satisfaction within available resources.[101]

Quality indicator: An agreed-upon process to outcome measurement that is used to determine the level of quality achieved. A measurable variable, or characteristic, that can be used to determine the degree of adherence to a standard or achievement of quality goals.[101]

Quality management: An ongoing effort to provide services that meet or exceed customer expectations through a structured, systematic process for creating organizational participation in planning and implementing quality improvements.[101]

Quality measures: Mechanisms used to assign a quantity to quality of care by comparison to a criterion.[114]

Quality monitoring: The collection and analysis of data for selected indicators that enable managers to determine whether key standards are being achieved as planned, and are having the expected effect on the target population.[101]

Quality of care: Degrees of excellence of care in relation to actual medical knowledge, identified by quality tracers based on outcomes of care, as well as on structure and process.[36]

Quality of Service: *See* **QoS**.

Quantity: Attribute of a phenomenon, body, or substance that may be distinguished qualitatively and determined quantitatively (e.g., length).[36]

Query: 1. The process by which a web client requests specific information from a web server, based on a character string that is passed along. **2.** A request for information that results in the aggregation and retrieval of data.[41]

Query management facility: *See* **QMF**.

Queue: A storage concept in which data are ordered in such a manner that the next data item to be retrieved is the one stored first. This concept is also characterized as "first in, first out" (FIFO).[59]

Queuing services: This service provides store and forward capabilities. It can use message queues, as well as other persistence mechanisms, to store information. This service can be used for asynchronous types of operations.[59]

Quick response codes: *See* **QR codes**.

R

RA (Registration authority): 1. Body responsible for assigning healthcare coding scheme designators and for maintaining the Register of Health Care Coding Schemes as described in a standard. **2.** Entity that is responsible for identification and authentication of certificate subjects, but that does not sign or issue certificates (i.e., an RA is delegated certain tasks on behalf of a CA).[36,74]

RAD (Rapid application development): An application development approach that includes small teams—typically two to six people using joint application development (JAD) and iterative-prototyping techniques to construct interactive systems of low to medium complexity within a timeframe of 60 to 120 days.[146]

Radio frequency identification: *See* **RFID.**

Radio frequency interference: Disruption caused by radio and television. A subset of electromagnetic interference.[3]

Radiology information system: *See* **RIS.**

Radiology PACS: Radiology picture archiving communications system. Rather than using film, computed radiography uses an imaging plate. This plate contains photostimulable storage phosphors, which retain the latent image. When the imaging plate is scanned with a laser beam in the digitizer, the latent image information is released as visible light. This light is captured and converted into a digital stream to compute the digital image.[11]

RAID (Redundant array of independent disks): A method of storing data on multiple hard disks. When disks are arranged in a RAID configuration, the computer sees them all as one large disk. However, they operate much more efficiently than a single hard drive. Since the data are spread out over multiple disks, the reading and writing operations can take place on multiple disks at once, which can speed up hard-drive access time significantly.[11]

RAM (Random access memory): 1. Primary storage of data or program instructions that can directly access any randomly chosen location in the same amount of time. **2.** The data in RAM stay there only as long as your computer is running. When you turn the computer off, RAM loses its data.[3]

Random access memory: *See* **RAM.**

Ransomware: A form of malware with the defining characteristic being that it attempts to deny access to a user's data by encrypting the data and demanding a ransom payment for the decryption key. Ransomware spreads through email attachments, infected programs, and compromised websites. Hackers may also deploy ransomware that also destroys or exfiltrates data or in conjunction with other malware that does so.[37]

Rapid application development: *See* **RAD**.

RARP (Reverse address resolution protocol): Discovers the IP address of a device by broadcasting a request on a network. Hardware address to IP address resolution.[3]

RAS (Remote access server): Dial-in capability of Windows NT® providing remote access to the server or the entire network from a remote location. Allows the use of modems, ISDN, and X.25 adapters for connectivity.[3]

Raster: A synonym for grid. Sometimes used to refer to the grid of addressable positions in an output device.[3]

Raster graphics: Digital images created or captured as a set of samples of a given space. A raster is a grid of x and y coordinates on a display space. Examples of raster image file types are BMP, TIFF, GIF, and JPEG files.[3]

Rate: 1. A fixed ratio between two things. **2.** A quantity, amount, or degree of something measured per unit of something else.[31]

Ratio: The relationship between two numbers.[101]

RBAC (Role-based access control): An approach to restricting system access to authorized users.[8]

RDBMS (Relational database management system): A type of database management system that stores data in the form of related tables. Relational databases are powerful because they require few assumptions about how data are related or how they will be extracted from the database. As a result, the same database can be viewed in many different ways.[3] *See* **DBMS**.

RDF (Resource description framework): A family of World Wide Web Consortium (W3C) specifications originally designed as a metadata model. Used as a general method for conceptual description or modeling of information that is implemented in web resources, using a variety of syntax formats.[8]

Read codes: Clinical terminology system used in the United Kingdom, now National Health Service (NHS) Clinical Terms, Version 3.[242]

Reader/writer: A smartcard reader/writer device provides a means for passing information from the smartcard to a larger computer, and for writing information from the larger computer onto the smartcard.[3]

Reader/writer driver layer: The layer in various reader and writer devices that pulls information from, writes to, or erases segments and/or zones of a smartcard.[3]

Readiness: *See* **Preparedness**.

Read-only memory: *See* **ROM**.

Realm: A sphere of authority, expertise, or preference that influences the range of concepts and descriptions required, or the frequency with which they are used. A realm may be a nation, an organization, a professional discipline, a specialty, or an individual user.[79]

Real-time location service: *See* **RTLS**.

Real-time system: Online computer that generates a nearly simultaneous output from the inputs received.[3]

REC (Regional extension center): Organizations established by the Office of the National Coordinator (ONC) to serve local communities as a support and resource center to assist providers in EHR implementation and health IT needs. RECs aim to bridge the technology gap by helping to navigate the EHR adoption process from vendor selection and workflow analysis to implementation and meaningful use.[13]

Record: 1. Document stating results achieved or providing evidence of activities performed. 2. A collection of fields that are related to, or associated with, a focal point.[52,199]

Records management: *See* **RM**.

Recovery time objective: *See* **RTO**.

Red, green, blue color model: *See* **RGB**.

Redaction tools: Software used to edit content, i.e., selectively and reliably remove information from documents or web sites before sharing the remaining content with someone who is not authorized to see the entire original document.[146]

Reduced instruction set computer: *See* **RISC**.

Redundant array of independent disks: *See* **RAID**.

Reference architecture: Generalized architecture of several end systems that share one or more common domains. The reference architecture defines the infrastructure common to the end systems and the interfaces of components that will be included in the end systems. The reference architecture is then instantiated to create a software architecture of a specific system.[59]

Reference information model: *See* **RIM**.

Reference model: An abstract framework for understanding significant relationships among the entities of some environments, and for the development of consistent standards or specifications supporting that environment. It is based on a small number of unifying concepts and may be used as a basis for education and explaining standards to a nonspecialist.[243]

Reference model for open distributed processing: *See* **RM-ODP**.

Reference terminology: 1. Standardized terminology that comprises a set of terms to which the terminology in the interface terminologies is mapped, enabling comparisons to be made even when different terminologies are used. 2. Relates terms to one another (with a set of relationships) and qualifies them (with a set of attributes) to promote precise and accurate interpretation.[11,150]

Reference terminology model: *See* **RTM**.

Regional extension center: *See* **REC**.

Regional health information organization: *See* **RHIO**.

Registration authority: *See* **RA**.

Registry: Directory-like system that focuses solely on managing data pertaining to one conceptual entity. In an EHR, registries store, maintain, and provide access to peripheral information not categorized as clinical in nature, but required to operationalize an EHR. The primary purpose of a registry is to respond to searches using one or more predefined parameters in order to find and retrieve a unique occurrence of an entity.[59] *See also* **Disease registry**.

Regression model: Regression models are used to predict one variable from one or more other variables. Regression models provide the scientist with a powerful tool, allowing predictions about past, present, or future events to be made with information about past or present events.[244]

Regression testing: 1. A hypothesis testing event that attempts to determine whether a recent change in one part of the application affects another specific event. **2.** A type of software testing that seeks to uncover new software bugs, or regressions, in existing functional and nonfunctional areas of a system after changes, such as enhancements, patches, or configuration changes have been made to them. The intent of regression testing is to ensure that a change, such as a bug fix, did not introduce new faults.[8,52]

Relational data model: A logical database model that treats data as if they were stored in two-dimensional tables. It can relate data stored in one table to data in another, as long as the two tables share a common data element.[3]

Relational database: A flexible collection of data stored in various locations that are held together by common elements.[52]

Relational database management system: *See* **RDBMS**.

Relational online analytical processing: *See* **ROLAP**.

Relationship: Link between two or more concepts.[36]

Relationships table: A data table consisting of rows, each of which represents a relationship.[79]

Relative value unit: *See* **RVU**.

Release of information: *See* **ROI**.

Reliability: A measure of consistency of data items based on their reproducibility and an estimation of their error of measurement.[3]

Relying party: Recipient of a certificate who acts in reliance on that certificate and/or digital signature verified using that certificate.[74]

Remote access: Access to a system or to information therein, typically by telephone or communication network, by a customer who is physically removed from the system.[36]

Remote access server: *See* **RAS**.

Remote access software: The software that enables remote access to a network and/or its resources.[3]

Remote hosting: A form of outsourcing where a client's personal computers are networked into a vendor's remote data processing center via high-speed phone lines. Rapid response times allow the client to access software at the vendor's site. Thus, a client avoids hardware costs, and shares processing and software costs with the vendor's other remote processing clients. If this is done with a web-based architecture, it is referred to as application service provisioning (ASP).[11]

Remote method invocation: *See* **RMI.**

Remote network monitor: *See* **RMON.**

Remote service: A support service (e.g., testing, diagnostics, software upgrades) that is not physically or directly connected to the device (e.g., remote access via modem, network, Internet).[55]

Removable media: *See* **Electronic media.**

Rendering: Process of formatting a machine-readable document by a dedicated software package or system to a final product that is human-readable, such as printed content or clinical documents.[3]

Repeater: Device that extends a LAN by increasing the signal of a LAN segment and joining it with another. The repeater forwards every packet appearing on one network to another.[3]

Repetition separator: Used in some data fields to separate multiple occurrences of a field. It is used only where specifically authorized in the descriptions of the relevant data fields.[10]

Replication: Periodic push duplication of specific data over the network from one server (export) to another (import).[3]

Reporting workflow: *See* **RWF.**

Repository: **1.** A central place where data are stored and maintained. A repository can be a place where multiple databases or files are located for distribution over a network, or a repository can be a location that is directly accessible to the user without having to travel across a network. **2.** An implementation of a collection of information along with data access and control mechanisms, such as search, indexing, storage, retrieval, and security.[8,59]

Representational state transfer: *See* **REST.**

Repudiation: Denial by one of the entities involved in a communication of having participated in all, or part of, the communication.[3]

Request for information: *See* **RFI.**

Request for proposal: *See* **RFP.**

Request to send: *See* **RTS.**

Requirements: A set of needs, functions, and demands which need to be satisfied by a particular software implementation or specification.[36]

Research: Systematic investigation, including research development, testing, and evaluation, designed to develop or contribute to generalized knowledge.[22]

Resident virus: A computer virus that installs itself as part of the operating system to infect all suitable hosts that are accessed.[3]

Residual risk: Risk remaining after risk control measures have been taken.[199]

Resolution: Measure of graphical image dot density sharpness on a monitor. The higher the density, the sharper the display.[3]

Resource description framework: *See* **RDF.**

Response plan: The documented collection of procedures and information developed, compiled, and maintained in readiness for use in an emergency.[89]

Response team: Group of individuals responsible for developing, executing, rehearsing, and maintaining the response plan, including the processes and procedures.[89]

Response time: The time period between a terminal operator's completion of an inquiry and the receipt of a response. Response time includes the time taken to transmit the inquiry, process it by the computer, and transmit the response back to the terminal. Response time is frequently used as a measure of the performance of an interactive system.[146]

REST (Representational state transfer): Architectural style and approach to communications that is often used in the development of web services. REST does not leverage as much bandwidth as SOAP's style, making it a better fit for use over the Internet. REST has been identified as a logical choice for building APIs that allow end users to connect and interact with cloud services. RESTful API breaks down a transaction to create a series of small modules, each of which addresses an underlying part of the transaction.[2]

Retention: The maintenance and preservation of information in some form (e.g., paper, microfilm, or electronic storage) for a given period of time. There are no federal laws outlining timeframes for the retention of health information.[3]

Retrieve information for display: *See* **RID**.

Return on investment: *See* **ROI**.

Reverse address resolution protocol: *See* **RARP**.

Revocation: The process of permanently ending the operational period of a certificate from a specified time forward. Generally, revocation is performed when a private key has been compromised.[66]

RFI (Request for information): A standard business process, the purpose of which is to collect written information about the capabilities of various suppliers. Normally it follows a format that can be used for comparative purposes.[8]

RFID (Radio frequency identification): The tag attached to the patient, medications, or supplies. The tag consists of a microchip with an antenna, and an interrogator or reader with an antenna. The reader sends out electromagnetic waves. The tag antenna is tuned to receive these waves. A passive RFID tag draws power from the field created by the reader and uses it to power the microchip's circuits. The chip then modulates the waves that the tag sends back to the reader, and the reader converts the new waves into digital data.[11]

RFP (Request for proposal): A standard business process that typically asks for more than a price, including basic corporate information and history, financial information, and product information, such as stock availability and estimated completion period. The bidder returns a quote or proposal by a set date and time, known as a tender closing. The proposals are used to evaluate the suitability as a supplier, vendor, or institutional partner.[8]

RGB (Red, green, blue color model): A device-dependent color model. Different devices detect or reproduce a given RGB value differently since the color elements (such as phosphors or dyes) and response to the individual R, G, and B levels vary from manufacturer to manufacturer, or even in the same device over time. The name of the model comes from the initials of the three additive primary colors, red, green, and blue. The RGB color model is used in color image-producing technology for sensing, representation, and display of images in electronic systems, such as televisions and computers.[8]

RHIN (Regional health information network): *See* **RHIO**.

RHIO (Regional health information organization): 1. A network of stakeholders within a defined region who are committed to improving the quality, safety, access, and efficiency of healthcare through the use of health IT. No two RHIOs look alike, and each reflects the unique nature and interests of its region and resources. **2.** A group of organizations with a business stake in improving the quality, safety, and efficiency of healthcare. **3.** A health information organization that brings together healthcare stakeholders within a defined geographic area and governance health information exchange among them for the purpose of improving health and care in that community.[13,55]

Rich text format: *See* **RTF**.

RID (Retrieve information for display): A simple and rapid read-only access to patient information necessary for provision of better care. It supports access to existing persistent documents in well-known presentation formats, such as CDA, PDF, JPEG, etc. It also supports access to specific key patient-centric information, such as allergies, current medications, summary of reports, etc., for presentation to a clinician.[29] *See* **Profile**. **NOTE: RID is an Integrating the Healthcare Enterprise (IHE) Profile**.

RIM (Reference information model): A static model of health and healthcare information as viewed within the scope of HL7 standards development activities. It is the combined consensus view of information from the perspective of the HL7 working group and the HL7 international affiliates. The RIM is the ultimate source from which all HL7 Version 3.0 protocol specification standards draw their information-related content.[10]

Ring network: Network topology in which all computers are linked by a closed loop in a manner that passes data in one direction, from one computer to another.[3]

RIP (Routing information protocol): Used to advertise and exchange information between routers within an autonomous system.[3]

RIS (Radiology information system): 1. The components of radiology software, hardware, and network infrastructure to support patient documentation, retrieval, and analysis. **2.** An automated RIS manages the operations and services of the radiology department. The functionality includes scheduling, patient and image tracking, and rapid retrieval of diagnostic reports.[11] *See also* **PACS.**

RISC (Reduced instruction set computer): A type of microprocessor architecture that utilizes a small, highly optimized set of instructions, rather than a more specialized set of instructions often found in other types of architectures.[245]

Risk: Combination of the probability of an event and its consequences.[128]

Risk analysis: A method for assessing risk. This may be used to subsequently compare the cost of achieving something (such as hospital system security) against the risk of losing something.[36]

Risk assessment: 1. Process of analyzing threats to, and vulnerabilities of, an IT system, and the potential impact that the loss of information or capabilities of a system would have on national security. The resulting analysis is used as a basis for identifying appropriate and effective measures. **2.** Overall process of risk analysis and risk evolution.[23,128]

Risk control: Process in which decisions are made and measures implemented by which risks are reduced to, or maintained within, specified levels.[199]

Risk estimation: Process used to assign values to the probability of occurrence of harm and the severity of that harm.[199]

Risk evaluation: Process of comparing the estimated risk against given risk criteria to determine the significance of the risk.[128]

Risk management: 1. Systematic application of management policies, procedures, and practices to the tasks of analyzing, evaluating, controlling, and monitoring risk. **2.** Coordinated activities to direct and control an organization with regard to risk.[128,199]

Risk tolerance: Organization's readiness to bear the risk after risk treatments in order to achieve its objectives.[89]

Risk treatment: Process of selection and implementation of measures to modify risk.[128]

RM (Records management): Technologies that enable organizations to enforce policies and rules for the retention and disposition of required business transaction content. RM strategies and policies are an essential part of the organization-wide lifecycle management of records. RM principles and technologies apply to both physical and electronic content. The US National Archives and Records Administration (NARA) is the nation's RM agency for RM training to federal employees and contractors on RM topics from archive schedules to emergency preparedness.[146]

RMI (Remote method invocation): An adaptation of the remote procedure call paradigm for object-oriented environments.[31]

RM-ODP (Reference model for open distributed processing): The RM-ODP efforts began in 1987 as part of the International Organization for

Standardization (ISO) Object Management Group (OMG), to enable the inter-working of applications and sharing of data across computer networks spanning organizational and national boundaries. As it relates to the healthcare domain, the uppermost two of five layers deal with the information viewpoint (such as HL7, X12, DICOM, CPT) and the enterprise viewpoint (such as patient registration, order communications, results retrieval).[3]

RMON (Remote network monitor): Device that collects network traffic information for use by remote monitoring stations.[3]

Roadmap: Technology road mapping is a management tool that attempts to plan and forecast the necessary steps toward achieving one or more technology goals. Technology roadmaps are different from project plans, in that roadmaps attempt to emphasize the uncertainty in the forecast rather than create a linked set of tasks. The value of a technology roadmap includes communicating vision, encouraging collaborative thinking, garnering necessary resources to solve technology challenges, creating contingency approaches, and consensus view for decision making. One of the most common extensions of the technology roadmap is to link it to product roadmaps and market roadmaps to provide the complete picture of "what, why, and how" in relation to the achievement and delivery of a particular technology goal.[8] *See* **Transition plan**.

Robotics: A branch of engineering that involves the conception, design, manufacture, and operation of robots. This field overlaps with electronics, computer science, artificial intelligence, mechatronics, nanotechnology, and bioengineering.[2]

ROI (Release of information): Formal process to request to release health information to other healthcare providers and authorized users, ensuring that the information is timely, accurate, complete, and confidential.[30]

ROI (Return on investment): A calculation used to determine whether a proposed investment is wise and how well it will repay the investor. It is calculated as the ratio of the amount gained (taken as positive) or lost (taken as negative), relative to the basis.[8]

ROLAP (Relational online analytical processing [OLAP]): A technical OLAP approach where data are presented dimensionally, but stored and accessed using traditional 2-dimensional relational DBMS technology allowing for very high flexibility.[3] *See* **OLAP**.

Role: 1. Roles are attributes. These terms are synonymous. **2.** Set of behaviors that are associated with a task.[74,79]

Role-based access control: *See* **RBAC**.

ROM (Read-only memory): Nonvolatile permanent memory written in firmware. Contents usually cannot be changed.[3]

Root directory: System base directory. All other directories and files are found under the root directory.[3]

Router: 1. Device that attaches multiple networks, LANs, and WANs, and routes packets between the networks through the use of software. **2.** Allows two devices connected to LANs or WLANs (wireless local area networks) of different types to access each other. Router's function is similar to a bridge, but it must be able to communicate between different LAN/WLAN protocols and choose the best path where multiple paths exist between nodes on the network.[11] *See* **Routing switch**.

Routing information protocol: *See* **RIP**.

Routing services: This service will route messages to the various internal integration channels, based on a publish/subscribe model.[59]

Routing switch: Device that attaches multiple networks, LANs, and WANs, and routes packets between the networks through the use of hardware. Ten times faster than a conventional router.[3]

Routing table: Lists maintained by routers that include the most recent information on routes advertised by other routers for different destinations.[3]

RSA: A public key crypto-system, invented and patented by Ronald Rivest, Ade Shamir, and Leonard Adelman, based on large prime numbers. RSA is the best-known asymmetric algorithm.[3]

RTF (Rich text format): A minimum file format for text files that includes formatting instructions, the text itself, and very little additional information.[3] Also known as *interchange format*.

RTLS (Real-time location service): Provides actionable information regarding the location, status, and movement of equipment and people. Advanced RTLS search capabilities allow searching by specific location (floor, area, room) or unique asset identifiers (department owner, type, manufacturer, model number, asset control number, or employee ID number). The detailed asset information and reporting capabilities of RTLS allow further analysis to support a variety of uses including equipment utilization data to identify inefficiencies that have required excess equipment inventory purchases.[11]

RTM (Reference terminology model): A framework of categories or attributes of terms and the relationships among these attributes that provide a structure for the organization of terms to represent concepts. Includes not only the sets of terms to describe relevant concepts, but also specifies the way in which individual concepts may be linked to create compositional expressions.[246]

RTO (Recovery time objective): Time goal for the restoration and recovery of functions or resources based on the acceptable down time and acceptable level of performance in case of a disruption of operations.[89]

RTS (Request to send): Modem control operation from data terminal equipment requesting clearance to transmit.[3]

Rule: A formal way of specifying a recommendation, directive, or strategy, expressed as "IF premise THEN conclusion" or "IF condition THEN action."[36]

Run chart: A visual display of data that enables monitoring of a process to determine whether there is a systematic change in that process over time.[101]

RVU (Relative value unit): A comparable service measure used by hospitals to permit comparison of the amount of resource required to perform various services within a single department or between departments. It is determined by assigning weight to such factors as personnel time, level of skill, and sophistication of equipment required to render patient services. RVUs are a common method of physician bonus plans based partially on productivity.[3]

RWF (Reporting workflow): Addresses the need to schedule, distribute, and track the status of the reporting workflow tasks, such as interpretation, transcription, and verification. Work lists for each of these tasks are generated and can be queried; work items can be selected, and the resulting status returned from the system performing the work to the system managing the work.[29] *See* **Profile. NOTE: RWF is an Integrating the Healthcare Enterprise (IHE) Profile.**

S

S/MIME (Secure MIME): Extends the Multipurpose Internet Mail Extensions (MIME) standard to allow for encrypted e-mail.[3]

SaaS (Software as a Service): 1. A software delivery model in which software and associated data are centrally hosted on the cloud. Typically accessed using a thin client via a web browser. **2.** Software that is owned, delivered, and managed remotely by one or more providers. The provider delivers software based on one set of common code and data definitions, which are consumed in a one-to-many model by all contracted customers at any time on a pay-for-use basis or as a subscription based on metrics.[8,146] Also known as *on-demand software.*

Safeguard: A protective measure to mitigate against the effect of system vulnerability.[3]

Salami: A technique by which criminals steal resources a little at a time. Programs may adjust payroll deductions by just a few cents in each transaction and then collect the funds. This type of transaction is very difficult to detect.[3]

SAML (Security assertion markup language): An XML standard for exchanging authentication and authorization data between security domains; that is, between an identity provider and a service provider.[161]

Sample: One or more parts taken, or to be taken from a system, and intended to provide information on that system or a subsystem, or to provide a basis for decision on either.[36]

SAN (Storage area network): A high-speed special purpose network (or sub-network) that interconnects different kinds of data storage devices with associated data servers on behalf of a larger network of users. Typically, a storage area network is part of the overall network of computing resources for an enterprise.[11]

Sanitization: Erasing all identifiers from certain files (i.e., clinical files).[3]

SATA (Serial advanced technology attachment [ATA]): De facto standard for internal PC storage, SATA is the evolutionary replacement for the Parallel ATA storage interface. A serial interface that can operate at speeds up to 6 Gb/s.[247]

SATAN (Security administrator tool for analyzing networks): A testing and reporting toolbox that collects a variety of information about networked hosts.[159]

SBAR (Situation–background–assessment–recommendation): Institute for Healthcare Improvement (IHI) technique that provides a framework for communication between members of the healthcare team about a patient's condition.[3]

Scalability: The ability to support the required quality of service as load increases.[59]

Scanner: 1. A device used to digitize a picture of a document so that it can be stored in memory and on a disk. Fax machines use this process to transmit documents to other fax machines. **2.** An electronic device that generates a digital representation of an image for data input to a computer.[11]

Scatter diagram: A graphic display of data plotted along two dimensions.[101]

Scenario: Formal description of a class of business activities, including the semantics of business agreements, conventions, and information content.[36]

Scheduled workflow: See **SWF.**

Scheduler: Portion of the operating system that moves programs from input to ready.[3]

Schema: In general, a schema is an abstract representation of an object's characteristics and relationship to other objects. An XML schema represents the interrelationship between the attributes and elements of an XML object (e.g., a document or a portion of a document). To create a schema for a document, one would analyze its structure, defining each structural element as it is encountered (e.g., within a schema for a document describing a web site, one would define a web site element, a web page element, and other elements that describe possible content divisions within any page on that site). Just as in XML and HTML, elements are defined within a set of tags.[2,63]

Science of clinical informatics: The transformation of clinical data into information, then knowledge, which supports clinical decision making. This transformation requires an understanding of how clinicians structure decision making and what data are required to support this process.[52]

SCOS (Smartcard operating system): Organizes data on the integrated circuit chip into files and protects them from unauthorized access.[3]

Screen saver: A moving picture or pattern that is displayed on the screen when no activity takes place for a specified period of time.[3] Also called a *time out.*

Script: A type of code or program that consists of a set of instructions for another application or utility to use.[3]

SCSI (Small computer system interface): Set of standards for physically connecting and transferring data between computers and peripheral devices.[8]

SCUI (Smartcard user interface): Provides a standard interface between applications and the data on the chip. Multiple applications can reside on the chip, and the SCUI allows an application to access its own data without affecting another application's data.[3]

SDLC (System design lifecycle): The process used by a systems analyst to develop an information system, including requirements, validation, training, and user ownership through investigation, analysis, design, implementation, and maintenance. An SDLC should result in a high-quality system that meets or exceeds customer expectations, within time and cost estimates, works effectively and efficiently in the current and planned information technology infrastructure, and is inexpensive to maintain and cost-effective to enhance.[8] Also known as *information systems development* or *application development.*

SDO (Standards development organization): An organization dedicated to standardization in the field of information for health, and health information and communications technology, to achieve compatibility and interoperability between independent systems. Also, to ensure compatibility of data for comparative statistical purposes (e.g., classifications) and to reduce duplication of effort and redundancies.[38]

SDOH (Social determinants of health): Conditions in the places where people live, learn, work, and play affect a wide range of health risks and outcomes.[82]

SDXC (Secure digital extended capacity): A flash memory card that resembles a secure digital (SD) card with greater storage capacity. SD and SDXC cards make storage portable among devices such as Smartphones, eBooks, digital cameras, camcorders, music players, and computers.[2]

Search/resolution services: This service is used to interface with resolution services present in registries, such as client, provider, and other registries. It is also used to resolve situations where clinical data about a client resides in different locations and systems across an interoperated network of EHRs.[59]

Searchable identifiers: Characteristics that uniquely identify an information object, support persistent access to that object, and support access to information about the object (i.e., metadata).[162]

Seat license: The fee is paid per user or "per seat," or per concurrent user, through negotiations with a vendor to allow a fixed number of copies of copyrighted software.[3] *See* **Site license**.

SEC (Security): Establishes basic security measures that can, as part of an institution's overall security policies and procedures in the enterprise, help protect the confidentiality of patient information. It also provides institutions with a mechanism to consolidate audit trail events on user activity across several systems interconnected in a secure manner.[29] *See* **Profile. NOTE: SEC is an Integrating the Healthcare Enterprise (IHE) Profile.**

Secondary data use: Use of data for additional purposes than the primary reason for their collection, adding value to this data.[107]

Secondary record: A record that is derived from the primary record and contains selected data elements.[3]

Secrecy: The intentional concealment or withholding of information.[3]

Secret key: A key in a symmetric algorithm; the possession of this key is restricted, usually to two entities.[3]

Secure communications channel: Ensure the authenticity, the integrity, and the confidentiality of transactions, and the mutual trust between communicating parties.[22]

Secure digital extended capacity: *See* **SDXC**.

S

Secure electronic transmission: *See* **SET**.

Secure file transport protocol: *See* **SFTP**.

Secure HTTP: *See* **S-HTTP**.

Secure MIME: *See* **S/MIME**.

Secure shell: *See* **SSH**.

Secure socket layer: *See* **SSL**.

Secure web server: A program that implements certain cryptographic protocols to prevent eavesdropping on information transferred between a web server and a web browser. A server resistant to a determined attack over the Internet or from corporate insiders.[3]

Security: Measures and controls that ensure confidentiality, integrity, availability, and accountability of the information processed and stored by a computer.[23]

Security administration control: Includes all management control measures and appropriate policies necessary to provide an acceptable level of protection of data stored in the data system.[3]

Security administrator: A member of the data system management team trained in data security matters, authorized to enforce the data security measures, and to create a confidentiality/privacy-conscious working environment.[3]

Security and control testing: A testing event that examines the presence and appropriate functioning of the application's security and controls to ensure integrity and confidentiality of data.[52]

Security architecture: A plan and set of principles for an administrative domain and its security domains that describe the security services that a system is required to provide to meet the needs of its users, the system elements required to implement the services, and the performance levels required in the elements to deal with the threat environment.[59]

Security assertion markup language: *See* **SAML**.

Security audit: A security audit is a systematic evaluation of the security of a company's information system by measuring how well it conforms to a set of established criteria. A thorough audit typically assesses the security of the system's physical configuration and environment, software, information handling processes, and user practices. Security audits are often used to determine regulatory compliance, in the wake of legislation (such as HIPAA, the Sarbanes-Oxley Act, and the California Security Breach Information Act) that specifies how organizations must deal with information.[2]

Security compromise: A specific loss of a component of the security system, due to an unauthorized person obtaining classified information.[3]

Security design-in: The provision of hardware and software features for security from the inception of the system.[3]

Security incident: The attempted or successful unauthorized access, use, disclosure, modification, or destruction of information or interference with system operations in an information system.[14]

Security level: Categorization of a controlled resource or defined data user.[3]

Security manager: The person assigned responsibility for management of the organization's security program.[3]

Security overhead: The total cost, in dollars, of the added hardware features and software drafting/running to serve the safeguarding purposes.[3]

Security policy: The framework within which an organization establishes needed levels of information security to achieve the desired confidentiality goals.[3]

Security process: The series of activities that monitor, evaluate, test, certify, accredit, and maintain the system accreditation throughout the system lifecycle.[23]

Security requirements: Types and levels of protection necessary for equipment, data, information, applications, and facilities to meet security policy.[23]

Security service: A processing or communication service that is provided by a system to give a specific kind of protection to resources, where said resources may reside with said system or reside with other systems (e.g., an authentication service, or a public key infrastructure-based document attribution and authentication service).[59]

Security system of a data system: The integrated combination of technological means, security administrator's activities, and the related statutory laws intended to prevent accidental or unauthorized disclosure of clinical data, modification, or destruction of stored clinical data, or damage to the clinical data system, or at least to reduce the risk to an acceptable level.[3]

Security tool: A program run to evaluate or enhance the security of a site.[3]

Segment: A logical grouping of data fields. Segments of a message may be required or optional. They may occur only once in a message or they may be allowed to repeat. Each segment is identified by a unique character code known as the segment identifier.[10]

Semantic: Pertains to the meaning or interpretation of a word, sign, or other representation.[45]

Semantic correspondence: Measure of similarity between concepts.[78]

Semantic interoperability: 1. Ability for data shared by systems to be understood at the level of fully defined domain concepts. **2.** The ability to preserve the meaning of exchanged information.[128]

Semantic link: Formal representation of a directed associative relation or partitive relation between two concepts.[78]

Semantic network: A formalism (often expressed graphically) for representing relational information, the arcs of the network representing the relationships, and the nodes of objects in the network.[36]

Semantic web: A project that intends to create a universal medium for information exchange by giving meaning (semantics), in a manner understandable by machines, to the content of documents on the web. The semantic web extends the ability of the web through the use of standards, markup languages, and related processing tools.[8]

Semantics: Meaning of symbols and codes.[36]

Sensitivity label: A security level associated with the content of the information. Society has historically considered as sensitive that information which has a heightened potential for causing harm to the patient or data subject, or to others, such as the subject's spouse, children, friends, or sexual partners.[3]

Sequence: A task in a process is enabled after the completion of a preceding task in the same process.[170]

Serial ATA: *See* **SATA.**

Serial line Internet protocol: *See* **SLIP.**

Serial transmission: Sequential transmission of the signal elements of a group representing a character or other entity of data. The characters are transmitted in a sequence over a single line, rather than simultaneously over two or more lines, as in parallel transmission.[120]

Server: Centralized network computer that provides an array of resources and services to network users. Also, a program that responds to a request from a client.[3]

Service: Discrete units of application logic that expose loosely coupled message-based interfaces suitable for being accessed across a network.[59]

Service event: The act of providing a health-related service.[59]

Service-oriented architecture: *See* **SOA.**

Session: A period of interaction. **1.** In computer science, in particular, networking. A session is either a lasting connection using the session layer of a network protocol or a lasting connection between a user (or user agent) and a peer, typically a server. **2.** In healthcare, a period of treatment; e.g., a "therapy session." **3.** Government: legislative, judicial, or executive session.[59]

Session layer: Fifth layer of the open systems interconnection (OSI) model. Provides file management needed to support intersystem communication through the use of synchronization and data stream checkpoints. Also responsible for the establishment, management, and termination of sessions.[3]

Session management service: This service manages user sessions. A user session will contain information such as ticket number, function and role information, authorization information, and other information that the system may choose to store to provide efficient access to information.[59]

SET (Secure electronic transmission): A cryptographic protocol designed for sending encrypted credit card numbers over the Internet.[3]

Severity system: Expected likelihood of disease progression independent of treatment. Systems attempting to measure severity may use diagnostic codes, such as ICD, and/or additional clinical information.[248]

SFTP (Secure file transport protocol): Standard for secure transfer of packets of information from one computer system to another. Commonly used in the transport of files of information containing confidential information.[112]

SGML (Standard generalized markup language): A metalanguage in which one can define markup languages for documents. SGML should not be confused with the Geography Markup Language (GML) developed by the Open Geographic Information System (Open GIS) Consortium, cf, or the Game Maker scripting language, GML. SGML provides a variety of markup syntaxes that can be used for many applications.[38]

SGMP (Simple gateway monitoring protocol): Allows commands to be issued to application protocol entities to set or retrieve values (integer or octet string types), for use in monitoring the gateways on which the application protocol entities reside. SGMP was replaced by SNMP (simple network management protocol).[8]

Shared environment: A computing environment in which computers at a remote location provide the information systems processing for several clients.[11]

Shared service: An approach to computerization provided by a service organization that offers remote computer services with supporting software functions for the full range of hospital business and clinical applications.[11]

Shared space: A mechanism that provides storage of, and access to, data for users with bounded network space. Enterprise-shared space refers to a store of data that is accessible within or across security domains on the global information grid. A shared space provides virtual access to any number of data assets (catalogs, web sites, registries, document storage database). Any user, system, or application that posts data uses shared space.[249]

Shareware: Software that can be tried before purchase. It is distributed through online services and user groups.[3]

Shielded twisted pair: *See* **STP.**

Short Message Service: *See* **SMS.**

S-HTTP (Secure HTTP): A system for signing and encrypting information sent over the web's HTTP protocol.[3] *See* **HTTP.**

SIG (Special interest group): Subset of professional computer organizations that concentrates on a specific technical computing area.[3]

SIMM (Single in-line memory module): A type of RAM chip.[3]

Simple gateway monitoring protocol: *See* **SGMP.**

Simple image and numeric report: *See* **SINR.**

Simple mail transfer protocol: *See* **SMTP.**

Simple merge: The convergence of two or more branches into a single subsequent branch, such that each enablement of an incoming branch results in the thread of control being passed to the subsequent branch.[170] *See* **Exclusive choice.**

Simple network monitoring protocol: *See* **SNMP.**

Simplex: Communication channel/circuit that allows data transmission in one direction only.[3]

Simulation: Resembles a real-life situation that the learner might encounter; learners can engage in safe decision making.[52]

Simulation exercise: Test performed under conditions as close as practicable to real-world conditions.[250]

Simultaneous peripheral operation online: *See* **SPOOL**.

Single in-line memory module: *See* **SIMM**.

Single sign-on: *See* **SSO**.

SINR (Simple image and numeric report): Facilitates the growing use of digital dictation, voice recognition, and specialized reporting packages by separating the functions of reporting into discrete actors for creation, management, storage, and viewing. Separating these functions while defining transactions to exchange the reports between them enables a vendor to include one or more of these functions in an actual system.[29] *See* **Profile**. NOTE: SINR is an Integrating the Healthcare Enterprise (IHE) Profile.

Site license: A renewable fee that has been paid through negotiations with a vendor to allow a fixed number of copies of copyrighted software at one site.[3] *See* **Seat license**.

Situation–background–assessment–recommendation: *See* **SBAR**.

SLIP (Serial line Internet protocol): Minimal overhead protocol for TCP/IP-only data transfer over serial links, such as telephone circuits or RS-232 cables. Does not support multiple protocols, encryption, or compression. The precursor to point-to-point protocol.[3]

Slow-scan video: A device that transmits and receives still video pictures over a narrow telecommunications channel.[172]

Smartcard: An integrated circuit card that incorporates a processor unit. The processor may be used for security algorithms, data access, or for other functions according to the nature and purpose of the card.[36]

Smartcard operating system: *See* **SCOS**.

Smartcard user interface: *See* **SCUI**.

Smartphone: A device licensed to be a telephone using U.S. Federal Communications Commission (FCC) authorized frequencies, which has Internet browser capabilities; web-enabled applications, the ability to view e-mail file attachments that include documents and images, file storage capability to support calendaring, e-mail, and texting.[11]

SME (Subject-matter expert): An individual who has expertise on a particular topic.[8]

SMP (Symmetrical multiprocessing): A computing platform technology in which a single server uses multiple CPUs in a parallel fashion managed by a single operating system.[3]

SMS (Short message service): 1. A mechanism of delivery of short messages over the mobile networks. **2.** Part of the Global System for Mobile Communications (GSM) standard developed by the European Telecommunications Standards Institute that enables a mobile device to send, receive, and display messages of up to 160 characters in Roman text and variations for non-Roman character sets. Messages received are stored in the network if the subscriber device is inactive and are relayed when it becomes active. SMS has become available increasingly in Code Division Multiple Access (CDMA) technology networks.[8,146]

SMTP (Simple mail transfer protocol): Protocol used to transfer mail between systems and from one computer to another. SMTP specifies how two mail systems interact, and the format of control messages they exchange to transfer mail.[3]

SNA (System network architecture): Network architecture developed by IBM for mainframe networking. Does not interoperate with TCP/IP.[3]

Sniffer: Network tool that collects network traffic packets to provide analysis on network and protocol usage, and generates statistics to assist in monitoring and optimizing networks.[3]

Sniffers: Programs used to intercept clear text data in packets transmitted through local area networks. A method of eavesdropping on communications.[3]

SNMP (Simple network monitoring protocol): Used to monitor hosts, routers, and networks. Enables a monitoring management station to configure, monitor, and receive alarms from network devices.[3]

SNMP (System network management protocol): Forms part of the Internet protocol suite as defined by the Internet Engineering Task Force. The protocol can support monitoring of network-attached devices for any conditions that warrant administrative attention.[8]

SNOMED–CT (Systematized nomenclature of medicine–clinical terms): A controlled healthcare terminology developed by the College of American Pathologists in collaboration with the United Kingdom's National Health Service. SNOMED–CT includes comprehensive coverage of diseases, clinical findings, therapies, procedures, and outcomes.[79]

SOA (Service-oriented architecture): 1. An infrastructure where many N-tier applications are deployed, sharing common software services that are accessible from any user interface. In this environment, any application can access any service, provided the application has the proper security permissions. **2.** A software architectural concept that defines the use of services to support the requirements of software users. In an SOA environment, nodes on a network make resources available to other participants in the network as independent services that the participants access in a standardized way.[8,59]

SOAP (Simple object access protocol): A third-generation programmable web service built on top of standards-based Internet protocols that can be implemented on any platform, in any language.[3]

Social determinants of health: *See* **SDOH.**

Socket: The logical address of a communications access point to a specific device or program on a host. A socket is defined as the endpoint in a connection. Also, the communication between a client program and a server program in a network.[3] *See* **API** and **SSL.**

Soft copy: File maintained on disk in electronic storage format.[3]

Software: A computer program encoded in such a fashion that the program (the instruction set) contents can be changed with minimal effort. Computer software can have various functions, such as controlling hardware, performing computations, communication with other software, human interaction, etc., all of which are prescribed in the program.[8]

Software access: The ability and the means to communicate with the operating system or any file/database controlled by the operating system of a clinical data sytem.[3]

Software architecture: The software architecture of a program or computing system is the structure or structures of the system, which comprise software components, the externally visible properties of those components, and the relationships among them.[59]

Software as a Service: *See* **SaaS.**

Software asset management: A management process for making software acquisition and disposal decisions. It includes strategies that identify and eliminate unused or infrequently used software, consolidating software licenses, or moving toward new licensing models.[3]

Software security system: A computer operating system certified as incorporating those hardware and software functions and features that are necessary to prohibit accidental or malicious access.[3]

SONET (Synchronous optical network): American National Standard Institute (ANSI) standard for connecting high-speed, high-quality, digital fiber-optic transmission systems. The international equivalent of SONET is synchronous digital hierarchy.[3] *See* **ATM** and **Frame relay.**

SOP (Standard operating procedure): Formalized way of uniformly carrying out a process.[48]

Source systems: Application systems where service encounter data are collected (e.g., laboratory information systems, pharmaceutical information systems, immunization systems). These clinical data are extracted from the source system and transformed prior to being used in the electronic health record.[59] *See* **Feeder systems.**

SOW (Statement of work): A document describing the specific tasks and methodologies that will be followed to satisfy the requirements of an associated contract or memorandum of understanding.[116]

SP (Subportal): Provides highly targeted aggregate content and interactive capabilities that focus on a specific vertical healthcare market segment, as opposed to overall portals, such as Yahoo or Microsoft Network.[3]

Spam: Trash e-mail. The practice of blindly or intentionally posting commercial messages or advertisements to a large number of unrelated and uninterested newsgroups.[3]

SPD (Summary plan description): Document that explains the product and services a subscriber purchased.[48]

Special interest group: *See* **SIG**.

Specification: An explicit statement of the required characteristics for an input used in the healthcare system. The requirements are usually related to supplies, equipment, and physical structures used in the delivery of health services.[101]

Spider: *See* **Web crawler**.[8]

SPIN (Standard Prescriber Identification Number): National Council for Prescription Drug Programs (NCPDP) sponsored the Standard Prescriber Identification Number from the early to mid-1990s in an effort to address the need for a unique prescriber identifier for the retail pharmacy industry. However, the Health Insurance Portability and Accountability Act of 1996 (HIPAA) contained a provision for a National Provider Identifier (NPI). Years passed with no National Provider Identifier (NPI). Unfortunately, the need that NCPDP and others had identified in the early to mid-1990s did not diminish, but steadily grew over these years. By early 2001, NCPDP launched the HCIdea™ project, a prescriber and provider database to assist in streamlining the claims process by validating providers. On January 23, 2004, HHS published the Final Rule for the HIPAA NPI in the *Federal Register*.[3]

SPOOL (Simultaneous peripheral operation online): It refers to putting jobs in a buffer, a special area in memory, or on a disk where a device can access them when it is ready. This is similar to a sewing machine spool, which a person puts thread onto, and a machine pulls at its convenience. Spooling is useful because devices access data at different rates. The buffer provides a waiting station where data can reside while the slower device catches up. Material is only added and deleted at the ends of the area; there is no random access or editing. This also allows the CPU to work on other tasks, while waiting for the slower device to do its task.[8]

Spooler: Service that buffers data for low-speed output devices.[3]

Spreadsheet: A rectangular table (or grid) of information, often financial information. (It is, therefore, a kind of matrix.) Spreadsheet programs can be used to tabulate many kinds of information, not just financial records; so the term "spreadsheet" has developed a more general meaning as information (= data = facts) presented in a rectangular table, usually generated by a computer.[8]

Sprite: An element that can be manipulated in an animation. Each different object in an animation is called a sprite.[120]

SQL (Structured query language): A syntax used by many database programs to retrieve and modify information (pronounced either *see-kwell* or as separate letters). SQL is a standardized query language for requesting information from a database.[3]

SRAM (Static random access memory): A type of memory that is faster and more reliable than the more common dynamic RAM or DRAM. The term *static* is derived from the fact that it does not need to be refreshed like dynamic RAM.[3]

SSH (Secure shell): Encrypted remote terminal that provides confidentiality and authentication.[3]

SSL (Secure socket layer): Secure method and protocol for managing the secure transfer of data between a web browser and a web server.[3] *See* **Socket** and **API**.

SSO (Single sign-on): A specialized form of software authentication that enables a user to authenticate once and gain access to the resources of multiple software systems.[11]

Standard: 1. A prescribed set of rules, conditions, or requirements established by consensus and approved by a recognized body that provides, for common and repeated use, rules, guidelines, or characteristics for activities or their results, aimed at the achievement of the optimum degree of order in a given context. **2.** A definition or format that has been approved by a recognized standards organization, or is accepted as a de facto standard by the industry. Standards exist for programming languages, operating systems, data formats, communications protocols, and electrical interfaces.[8,45]

Standard operating procedure: *See* **SOP**.

Standard prescriber identification number: *See* **SPIN**.

Standards body: Entity that is recognized at national, regional, or international level that has as a principle function, by virtue of statutes, for the preparation, approval, consensus, and adoption of standards that are made generally available.[36]

Standards development organization: *See* **SDO**.

Standardization: Activity of establishing, with regard to actual or potential problems, provisions for common and repeated use, aimed at the achievement of the optimum degree of order in a given content.[36]

Standardization of terminology: Official recognition of a terminology by an authoritative body.[36]

Standardized generalized markup language: *See* **SGML**.

Standardized taxonomy: Use of common standardized definitions, criteria, terminology, and data elements for treatment processes, outcomes, data collection, and electronic transmission, with the goal of saving much time, effort, and misunderstanding in communicating these elements.[3]

Standing orders: Physicians' orders pre-established and approved for use by nurses and other professionals under specific conditions, in the absence of a physician.[101]

Star network: Type of LAN topology in which networked nodes are connected to a hub at a central point.[3]

Star schema: A data-modeling technique and relational database management system extension that is optimized for ad hoc, unpredictable, and denormalized data queries. It facilitates simple and speedy access to information by decision support users.[3] *See* **OLTP**.

Start of care: *See* **Admission date**.

Statement of work: *See* **SOW**.

Static audit tool: System scanner that looks for and reports weaknesses.[3]

Static memory: Memory that does not need to be refreshed while power is maintained. Faster than dynamic memory.[3]

Static random access memory: *See* **SRAM**.

Stealth virus: A type of resident virus that attempts to evade detection by concealing its presence in infected files. To achieve this, the virus intercepts system calls, which examine the contents and attributes of infected files.[3]

Steganography: Hiding information in innocuous files and documents (e.g., insertion of instructions that modify portions of a program's output to carry information).[3]

Stemming: A process that determines the morphological root of a given inflected (or, sometimes, derived) word form. A stemmer for English, for example, should identify the string "cats" (and possibly "catlike," "catty," etc.) as based on the root "cat," and "stemmer," "stemming," and "stemmed," as based on "stem." Used by search engines and for natural language processing.[8]

Storage: The function of storing records for future retrieval and use.[251]

Storage area network: *See* **SAN**.

Store-and-forward: Transmission of static images or audio-video clips to a remote data storage device, from which they can be retrieved by a medical practitioner for review and consultation at any time, obviating the need for the simultaneous availability of the consulting parties and reducing transmission costs due to low bandwidth requirements.[172]

Storyboard: Originally developed by Disney Studios in the 1930s, storyboards allow action elements to be identified and organized into various sequences to form a story. Storyboards are used to brainstorm and capture all the ideas before taking action. The process of visual thinking and planning allows a group of people to brainstorm together, placing their ideas on storyboards, and then arranging the storyboards on the wall. This fosters more ideas and generates consensus inside the group.[8]

STP (Shielded twisted pair): Type of cabling 1.5 inches in diameter, in which the wire pairs are twisted together in a shielded protective jacket to reduce the effects of electromagnetic interference. Used to implement 10BaseT–100BaseT networks.[3]

Stream algorithms: Algorithms that encrypt data byte by byte.[3]

Streaming: A technique for delivering data used with audio and video in which the recipient is able to hear or see part of the file before the entire file is delivered. Involves a method for the recipient computer to be able to do a smooth delivery, despite the uneven arrival of data.[68]

S

Stress testing: A type of performance testing focused on determining an application's robustness, availability, and reliability under extreme conditions. The goal of stress testing is to identify application issues that arise or become apparent only under extreme conditions. These conditions can include heavy loads, high concurrency, or limited computational resources.[70]

Structured data: Coded, semantically interoperable data that are based on a reference information model. The consent directive may be captured as a scanned image, which is not semantically interoperable and would preclude the ability of the consent repository to analyze the data for conflicts with previously persisted consent directives.[22]

Subject field: Domain field of special knowledge.[77]

Subject-matter expert: *See* **SME**.

Subject of care identifier: A unique number or code issued for the purpose of identifying a subject of (health)care.[251]

Subset: Represents groups of components that share specified characteristics that affect the way they are displayed or otherwise accessible within a particular realm, specialty, application, or context.[79]

Substitution: A method of cryptography based on the principle of replacing each letter in the message with another one. A cipher that replaces the characters of the original plain text. The characters retain their original position, but are altered.[3]

SVC (Switched virtual circuit): A temporary virtual circuit that is set up and used only as long as data are being transmitted. Once the communication between the two hosts is complete, the SVC disappears. In contrast, a permanent virtual circuit (PVC) remains available at all times.[3]

SWF (Scheduled workflow): Establishes the continuity and integrity of basic departmental imaging data acquired in an environment where examinations are generally being ordered. It specifies a number of transactions that maintain the consistency of patient and ordering information, as well as defining the scheduling and imaging acquisition procedure steps. This profile also makes it possible to determine whether images and other evidence objects associated with a particular performed procedure step have been stored (archived) and are available to enable subsequent workflow steps, such as reporting. It may also provide central coordination of the completion of processing and reporting steps.[29] *See* **Profile. NOTE: SWF is an Integrating the Healthcare Enterprise (IHE) Profile.**

System: The combination of hardware and software which processes information for the customer.[36]

System administrator: A person who is responsible for managing a multi-user computing environment, such as a local area network. The responsibilities typically include installing and configuring system hardware and software, establishing and managing user accounts, upgrading software, and backup and recovery tasks.[2] Also known as *sysadmin* or *systems administrator*.

System analysis: The process of determining how a set of interconnected components whose individual characteristics are known will behave in response to a given input of a set of inputs. Closely related to requirements analysis and operations research.[86]

System design: A specification of human factors, and hardware and software requirements, for an information system.[52]

System integration: 1. The composition of a capability by assembling elements in a way that allows them to work together to achieve an intended purpose. **2.** The process of creating a complex information system that may include designing or building a customized architecture or application, integrating it with new or existing hardware, packaged and custom software, and communications.[146,252] *See* **EAI.**

System integrator: A firm or process that delivers the various services of systems integration.[3]

System network management protocol: *See* **SNMP.**

System security: The result of all safeguards, including hardware, software, personnel policies, information practice policies, disaster preparedness, and oversight of these components.[3]

System security administrator: The person who controls access to computer systems by entering commands to perform such functions, such as assigning user access codes and privileges, revoking user access privileges, and setting file protection parameters.[3]

System testing: A multifaceted testing event that evaluates the functionality, performance, and fit of the whole application. System testing encompasses usability, final requirements, volume and stress, security and controls, recovery, documentation and procedures, and multisite testing.[52]

Systematized nomenclature of medicine–clinical terms: *See* **SNOMED–CT.**

S

T

Table: Database object with a unique name, and structured in columns and rows.[3]

TC (Technical committee): A term, often used by consensus standards organizations, including Health Level Seven (HL7), European Committee for Standardization (CEN), and International Organization for Standardization (ISO) to describe a formal group of subject matter experts who work together in a committee structure to solve problems.[22,38]

TCO (Total cost of ownership): A document that describes the cost of a project or initiative that usually includes hardware, software, development, and ongoing expenses.[48]

TCP/IP (Transmission control protocol/Internet protocol): 1. Routable protocol required for Internet access. TCP portion is associated with data. IP is associated with source to destination packet delivery. **2.** A set of communication protocols encompassing media access, packet transport, session communications, file transfer, electronic mail, and terminal emulation. It is supported by a large number of hardware and software vendors and is the basis for Internet transactions.[3,11]

TDR (Time-domain reflectometer): Testing device that sends sound waves along cabling to detect shorts or breaks in the cable.[3]

Technical specification: A second level International Organization for Standardization (ISO) deliverable. Contains both normative and informative knowledge.[38]

Telehealth: A broad variety of technologies and tactics to deliver virtual medical, health, and education services. A collection of means to enhance care and education delivery. This term encompasses the concept of "telemedicine," which refers to traditional clinical diagnosis and monitoring delivered by technology. The term "telehealth" covers a wide range of diagnosis, management, education, and other related healthcare fields including but not limited to dentistry, counseling, physical and occupational therapy, home health, chronic disease monitoring and management, and consumer and professional education.[253]

Telemedicine: *See* **Telehealth.**

TELNET (TELecommunications NETwork): Protocol for remote terminal service connectivity. Connectivity from one site to interact with a remote system. A method of logging one computer onto another. A program that allows users to remotely use computers across networks.[3]

Terabyte: Approximately one trillion bytes; unit of computer storage capacity.[3]

Term: 1. Verbal designation of a concept in a specific subject field. **2.** The word or phrase in a particular language used to represent a concept (e.g., the concept *doctor* is represented in English by the term "doctor" or "physician," and in Italian by the term "*il medico*").[36,77]

Terminal: Any computer display or workstation that connects with limited capabilities to a network.[2] *See* **Workstation.**

Terminal printing suppression: Suppressing the printing of passwords or other access control information.[3]

Terminal server: Network communications device that allows one or more serial devices to connect to an Ethernet LAN.[3]

Terminology: A system of words used to name things in a particular discipline.[31]

Terminology identifier: Unique permanent identifier of a healthcare terminology for use in information interchange.[77]

Test log: A thorough record of testing, results, and follow-up.[52]

Test objectives: Descriptions of what a specific testing event seeks to validate. The objectives state each feature of function to be tested and described, at a high level, the expected results.[52]

TFTP (Trivial file transfer protocol): Minimal overhead file transfer used to upload or download bootstrap files to diskless workstations through the use of UDP.[3]

Thesaurus: The vocabulary of a controlled indexing language, formally organized so that the *a priori* relationships between concepts (e.g., broader and narrower) are made explicit.[38]

Thin client/dumb terminal: A computer or computer program that depends heavily on some other computer (such as an application or network server) to fulfill its traditional computational roles. A thin client is used to access data; does not process data.[11]

Third party: Party, other than data originator or data recipient, required to perform a function as part of a communication protocol.[74]

Third-party administrator: *See* **TPA.**

Third-party vendor: *See* **TPV.**

Thread: A collection of any number of online posts defined by a title. A thread is a component of an Internet forum.[8]

Threat: 1. Any circumstance or event with the potential to cause harm to an IT system in the form of destruction, disclosure, adverse modification of data, and/or denial of service. **2.** Exploitation or compromise of a security of systems or networks.[22,23]

Threshold: A level of achievement that determines the difference between what is deemed to be acceptable quality or not.[101]

Thunking: Process of converting 32-bit code to 16-bit code in systems that are not supporting 32-bit memory address.[3]

TIFF (Tag image file format): A common format for exchanging raster graphics (bitmap) images between application programs, including those used for scanner images.[120]

Tightly coupled: These types of application roles assume that common information about the subject classes participating in a message is available to system components outside of the specific message.[59]

Time bomb: A subclass of logic bombs that explode at a certain event, such as a certain date. Can be used to damage disk directories on a certain date.[3]

Time-domain reflectometer: *See* **TDR.**

Time to live: *See* **TTL.**

TKIP (Temporal key integrity protocol): Security protocol used in the IEEE 802.11 wireless networking standard.[11]

TLAlgia: Term composed of "TLA" for three-letter acronym and "-algia" meaning "pain"; thus, pain induced by excessive use of three-letter acronyms.[112]

Token: 1. A physical authentication device that the user carries (e.g., smartcard, SecureID™). Often combined with a PIN to provide a two-factor authentication method that is generally thought of as superior to simple password authentication. **2.** Packet used for LAN access in a token-based network. The node that possesses the token controls the transmission medium, and is allowed to transmit on the network.[3,55]

Token-bus network: Type of LAN topology in which networked nodes are connected to the main cable of the network and uses a token for transmission access.[3]

Token-ring network: Type of proprietary LAN topology in which network nodes are connected at points to form a ring in which data packets travel. Uses a token for transmission access.[11]

Top-level concept: A concept that is directly related to the root concept by a single relationship of the relationship type "ISA." All other concepts are descended from one top-level concept via at least one series of relationships of the relationship type "ISA" (i.e., all other concepts are subtypes of one top-level concept).[79]

Topology: Physical layout or architecture of a network. Bus, star, ring, and hybrid are network topologies.[3]

Total cost of ownership: *See* **TCO.**

Touch screen: Input technology that permits the entering or selecting of commands and data by touching the surface of a sensitized video display monitor with a finger or pointer.[3]

TPA (Third-party administrator): A company that provides claim processing and administrative services for hospital or physicians groups.[48]

TPV (Third-party vendor): A company designated to support specific services for healthcare.[48]

Traceroute: A command causing the utility to initiate the sending of a packet, including in the packet a time limit that is designed to be exceeded by the first router that receives it, which will return a "time exceeded" message.[3]

Trading partner agreement: Related to the exchange of information in electronic transactions, specifically the communications protocols and transaction standards to be used.[22]

Train the trainer: A core group of individuals are trained and then used to train other individuals who will be using the system. This is a common strategy when there are hundreds of users to be trained in a matter of weeks.[52] Also known as *super-user.*

Transaction: 1. The exchange of information between two parties to carry out clinical, financial, and administrative activities related to healthcare. **2.** An exchange of information between actors. For each transaction, the technical framework describes how to use an established standard, such as HL7, DICOM, or W3C.[29,116]

Transaction standard: A standard specifying the format of messages being sent from or received by a system, rather than for how the information is stored in the system.[116]

Transactional data: A transaction, in this context, is a sequence of information exchange and related work (such as database updating) that is treated as a unit for the purposes of satisfying a request. Transactional data can be financial, logistical, or work-related, involving everything from a purchase order to shipping status to employee hours worked to insurance costs and claims.[2]

Transition plan: A strategy/map to guide the adoption of systems or technologies. A written plan for a transition from the current organization structure to a design that will minimize disruption, adverse impacts, capitalization, and startup requirements.[254]

Transitions of care: The movement of a patient from one setting of care (hospital, ambulatory primary care practice, ambulatory specialty care practice, long-term care, home health, rehabilitation facility) to another.[28]

Transmission: The exchange of data between person and system, or system and system, when the sender and receiver are remote from each other.[3]

Transmission confidentiality: Process to ensure that information in transit is not disclosed to unauthorized individuals, entities, or processes.[22]

Transmission control protocol/Internet protocol: See **TCP/IP.**

Transmission integrity: Process to guard against improper information modification or destruction while in transit.[22]

Transparent background: Transparent GIF images can have one color designed to be transparent. Since all graphic images are stored as either square or rectangular shapes, even the background color will show up on a web page.[3] *See* **GIF.**

Transport layer: Fourth layer of the OSI model. Handles the interface between hardware levels and software levels. Provides for end-to-end flow control and ensures that messages are delivered error-free.[3]

Transposition: A method of cryptography based on the principle of scrambling the characters that are in the message.[3]

Transposition cipher: A cipher in cryptography that rearranges the characters of the original plain message. Thus, the characters are unchanged but their position is altered, making the text unintelligible.[3]

Trap doors: Hardware features, software limitations, or specially planted entry points that can provide an unauthorized source with access to the system.[3] *See* **Back door.**

Trial implementation supplement: A specification candidate for addition to an IHE Domain Technical Framework (e.g., a new profile) that is issued for early implementation by any interested party. The authoring technical committee expects developers' feedback.[127]

Trigger event: An event, such as the reception of a message or completion of a process, which causes another action to occur.[29]

Trivial file transfer protocol: *See* **TFTP.**

Trojan horse: A program that appears to have one ubiquitous function, but actually has a hidden malicious function. A program that performs a desired task, but also includes unexpected and usually undesirable functions. Does not replicate.[3]

Trunk: Single circuit between two switching center points. Handles many channels simultaneously.[3]

Trust-based security: Security management and access provision based on trusted domains or facilities.[59]

Trusted system: A system delivered to enforce a given set of attributes to a stated degree of assurance or confidence.[3]

Trusted third party: *See* **TTP.**

Trusted user access level: A system user who needs access to sensitive information.[3]

TTL (Time to live): Length of active Internet time technique used to avoid endless loop packets. Every packet is assigned a decrementing TTL. Packets with expired TTLs are discarded by routers.[3]

TTP (Trusted third party): Third party that is considered trusted for purposes of a security protocol. (ENV 13608-1). **Note:** This term is used in many ISO/IEC International Standards and other documents describing mainly the services of a certification authority (CA). The concept is, however, broader and includes services such as time-stamping and possibly escrowing.[74]

Tunneling: *See* **Virtual private network.**[59]

Tutorial: A method of transferring knowledge that may be used as a part of a learning process. More interactive and specific than a book or a lecture; a tutorial seeks to teach by example and supply the information to complete a certain task.[62]

Twisted-pair cable: Cable consisting of copper core wires surrounded by an insulator. A pair, consisting of two wires twisted together, forms a circuit that can transmit data. The twisting helps to prevent interference.[3]

U

UART (Universal asynchronous receiver transmitter): The microchip with programming that controls a computer's interface to its attached serial devices.[2]

Ubiquitous computing: The growing trend toward embedding microprocessors in everyday objects so they can communicate information. The words pervasive and ubiquitous mean "existing everywhere." Ubiquitous computing devices are completely connected and constantly available. *See* **pervasive computing**.[2]

UCC (Uniform Code Council): In 2005, the organization changed its name to GS1. An administrative and educational organization whose mission is to promote multi-industry standards for product identification and related electronic communications. The Universal Product Code (UPC) is a bar code symbol used by companies in North America to uniquely identify themselves and their products worldwide.[8]

UDDI (Universal description, discover, and integration): A web-based distributed directory that enables businesses to list themselves on the Internet and discover each other, similar to a traditional phone book's yellow and white pages.[41]

UDI (Unique device identifier): A unique numeric or alphanumeric code that consists of two parts: a device identifier (DI), a mandatory, fixed portion of a UDI that identifies the labeler and the specific version or model of a device, and a production identifier (PI), a conditional, variable portion of a UDI that identifies one or more of the following when included on the label of a device: the lot or batch number within which a device was manufactured; the serial number of a specific device; the expiration date of a specific device; the date a specific device was manufactured; the distinct identification code required by §1271.290(c) for a human cell, tissue, or cellular and tissue-based product (HCT/P) regulated as a device.[43]

UDK (User-defined keys): Used to store frequently used commands through the F6 to F20 keys on a video terminal keyboard.[3]

UDP (User datagram protocol): A connectionless protocol that resides at the same level on the OSI model as TCP. Since it is connectionless, there is no handshaking or authentication.[3]

UI (User interface): 1. The part of the application that allows the user to access the application and manipulate its functionality. It can include menus, forms, command buttons, etc. **2.** The part of the information system through which the end user interacts with the system; type of hardware and the series of on-screen commands and responses required for a user to work with the system.[3]

UM (Utilization management): The evaluation of the necessity, appropriateness, and efficiency of the use of healthcare services, procedures, and facilities.[48]

UMDNS (Universal medical device nomenclature system): The purpose of UMDNS is to facilitate identifying, processing, filing, storing, retrieving, transferring, and communicating data about medical devices. The nomenclature is used in applications ranging from hospital inventory and work order controls to national agency medical device regulatory systems, and from eCommerce and procurement to medical device databases.[255]

UML (Unified Modeling Language): A language for specifying, visualizing, constructing, and documenting the artifacts of software systems. UML is a standard notation for the modeling of real-world objects.[146]

UMLS (Unified Medical Language System): The National Library of Medicine (NLM) produces the Unified Medical Language System® (UMLS®) to facilitate the development of computer systems that behave as if they "understand" the meaning of the language of biomedicine and health. As part of the UMLS, NLM produces and distributes the UMLS Knowledge Sources (databases) and associated software tools (programs) for use by system developers in building or enhancing electronic information systems that create, process, retrieve, integrate, and/or aggregate biomedical and health data and information, as well as in informatics research.[256]

UMS (Unified messaging system): The handling of voice, fax, and regular text messages as objects in a single mailbox that a user can access either with a regular e-mail client or by telephone.[3]

UNC (Universal naming convention): Text-based method to identify the path to a remote device, server, directory, or file. Implemented as: \\computername \sharename\directoryname\filename.[3]

Underuse: Refers to the failure to provide a healthcare service when it would have produced a favorable outcome for a patient. Standard examples include failures to provide appropriate preventive services to eligible patients (e.g., Pap smears, flu shots for elderly patients, screening for hypertension) and proven medications for chronic illnesses (e.g., steroid inhalers for asthmatics, aspirin, beta-blockers, and lipid-lowering agents for patients who have suffered a recent myocardial infarction).[97]

Undirected information: Information that is broadcast without regard to who reads it. Usenet and mailing lists are undirected.[3]

Unfreezing: Requires the process that involves finding a method of making it possible for people to let go of an old pattern that was somehow counterproductive. It is necessary to overcome the strains of individual resistance and group conformity. There are three methods that can lead to the achievement of unfreezing. The first is to increase the driving forces that direct behavior away from the existing situation or status quo. Second, decrease the restraining forces that negatively affect the movement from the existing equilibrium. Third, find a combination of the first two methods.[257]

Unicode: A standard character set that represents most of the characters used in the world using a 16-bit encoding. Unicode can be encoded in using UTF-8 (USC Transformation Format) to more efficiently store the most common ASCII characters.[79]

Unified messaging system: *See* **UMS**.

Unified modeling language: *See* **UML**.

Uniform Code Council: *See* **UCC**.

Uniform data standards: Methods, protocols, or terminologies agreed to by an industry to allow disparate information systems to operate successfully with one another.[45]

Uniform resource locator: *See* **URL**.

Uninterruptible power supply: *See* **UPS**.

Unique device identifier: *See* **UDI**.

Unique health plan identifier: *See* **HPID**.

Unique patient identifier: *See* **UPI**.

Unit testing: A software development process in which the smallest testable parts of an application, called units, are individually and independently scrutinized for proper operation. Unit testing is often automated but it can also be done manually.[2]

Universal asynchronous receiver transmitter: *See* **UART**.

Universal identifier: A means to provide positive recognition of a particular individual for all people in a population. A universal healthcare or patient identifier provides the identifier for use in healthcare transactions.[3]

Universal medical device nomenclature system: *See* **UMDNS**.

Universal naming convention: *See* **UNC**.

Universal product code: *See* **UPC**.

Universal product number: *See* **UPN**.

Universal serial bus: *See* **USB**.

Unstructured data: Data that are not contained in a database. Data residing in text files which can represent more than 75% of an organization's data. Data that are not organized or that lack structure.[50]

UPC (Universal product code): A unique 12-digit number assigned to retail merchandise that identifies both the product and the vendor that sells the product. The UPC on a product typically appears adjacent to its bar code, the machine-readable representation of the UPC. The first six digits of the UPC are the vendor's unique identification number. All of the products that one vendor sells will have the same first six digits in their UPCs. The next five digits are the product's unique reference number that identifies the product within any one vendor's line of products. The last number is called the check digit that is used to verify that the UPC for that specific product is correct.[41]

UPI (Unique patient identifier): 1. The identity of an individual consists of a set of personal characters by which that individual can be recognized. Identification is the proof of one's identity. Identifier verifies the sameness of one's identity. Patient identifier is the value assigned to an individual to facilitate positive identification of that individual for healthcare purposes. Unique patient identifier is the value permanently assigned to an individual for identification purposes and is unique across the entire national healthcare system. Unique patient identifier is not shared with any other individual. **2.** A form of identification and access control that identifies humans by their characteristics or traits. Biometric identifiers (or biometric authentication) are the distinctive, measurable characteristics used to label and describe individuals. Two categories of biometric identifiers include physiological and behavioral characteristics.[8]

Upload: To send a file to another machine.[3]

UPN (Universal product number): *See* **UPC.**

UPS (Uninterruptible power supply): Device that keeps a computer running by protecting against power outages and power sags by maintaining constant power via battery. Provides the opportunity for a graceful shutdown in a commercial power-out condition.[3]

URI (Uniform resource identifiers): The way you identify any of those points of content, whether it be a page of text, a video or sound clip, a still or animated image, or a program. The most common form of URI is the web page address, which is a particular form or subset of URI called a Uniform Resource Locator (URL).[2]

URL (Uniform resource locator): The global address of documents and other resources on the World Wide Web.[41] Also, a standardized address name layout for resources, such as documents or images, on the Internet or elsewhere.[8]

Usability: The measure of a product's potential to accomplish the goals of the user. In information technology, the term is often used in relation to software applications and web sites, but it can be used in relation to any product that is employed to accomplish a task (for example, a toaster, a car dashboard, or an alarm clock). Some factors used in determining product usability are ease-of-use, visual consistency, and a clear, defined process for evolution.[2]

Usability testing: Evaluating a product or service by testing it with representative users. Typically, during a test, participants will try to complete typical tasks while observers watch, listen, and takes notes. The goal is to identify any usability problems, collect qualitative and quantitative data, and determine the participant's satisfaction with the product.[258]

USB (Universal serial bus): 1. A plug-and-play interface between a computer and add-on devices, such as media players, keyboards, etc. **2.** A commercial desktop standard input/output (I/O) bus that provides a single peripheral connection and vastly increases bus speed. It simplifies peripheral connections via a "daisy chaining" scheme whereby the desktop system has only one I/O port to which all peripherals are connected in a series. Up to 120 peripherals can be connected to a single system.[2,146]

Use: Sharing, employment, application, utilization, examination, or analysis of information within the entity that maintains such information.[22]

Use case: A methodology used in system analysis to identify, clarify, and organize system requirements. The use case is made up of a set of possible sequences of interactions between systems and users in a particular environment and related to a particular goal. It consists of a group of elements (for example, classes and interfaces) that can be used together in a way that will have an effect larger than the sum of the separate elements combined. The use case should contain all system activities that have significance to the users. A use case can be thought of as a collection of possible scenarios related to a particular goal, indeed, the use case and goal are sometimes considered to be synonymous.[2]

User access: A person or a group/organization in need of data for legitimate service function, teaching, or research, authorized to have access.[3]

User authentication: 1. The provision of assurance of the claimed identity of an individual or entity. **2.** A means of identifying the user and verifying that the user is allowed access to a restricted service.[3,11]

User datagram protocol: *See* **UDP**.

User-defined keys: *See* **UDK**.

User-friendly: Refers to anything that makes it easier for novices to use a computer.[41]

User ID: The string of characters that identifies a computer/system user. The user name by which the user is known to the network.[3] Also known as *username*.

User interface: *See* **UI**.

User profile: 1. Information about an individual user. Along with name, address, phone number, etc., it may include personal information, especially if it is part of a social networking site. **2.** The preferences and current desktop configuration of a user's machine. User profiles enable several users to work on the same computer with their own desktop setup. When stored in a server, user profiles enable users to obtain their desktop configuration when working at a different machine.[35]

USHIK (United States Health Information Knowledgebase): A metadata registry of healthcare-related data elements from Standard Development Organizations supported by the Agency for Healthcare Research and Quality (AHRQ).[259]

Utility program: System software consisting of programs for routine, repetitive tasks, which can be shared by many users.[4]

Utilization management: *See* **UM**.

UTP (Unshielded twisted pair): A popular type of cable that consists of two unshielded wires twisted around each other. Due to its low cost, UTP cabling is used extensively for local-area networks (LANs) and telephone connections. UTP cabling does not offer as high bandwidth or as good protection from interference as coaxial or fiber optic cables, but it is less expensive and easier to work with.[41]

V

Validation: Determination of the correct implementation in the completed IT system, with the security requirements and approach agreed-upon by the users and the acquisition authority.[23]

Value-added network: *See* **VAN**.

Value stream: The specific activities within a supply chain required to design, order, and provide a specific product or service.[146]

Value stream map: Visual representation of a value stream.[146]

VAN (Value-added network): A network that provides services in addition to a standard telephone system, such as fax, data transmission, or email.[260]

Vanilla: In information technology, an adjective meaning plain or basic. The unfeatured version of a product is sometimes referred to as the vanilla version. The term is based on the fact that vanilla is the most commonly served flavor of ice cream. Or, as Eric Raymond, editor of *The New Hacker's Dictionary*, puts it, the default ice cream.[2]

Vaporware: Software that does not currently exist, but may be introduced sometime in the future.[3]

Variance analysis: Process aimed at computing variance between actual and budgeted or targeted levels of performance, and identification of their causes.[4]

Variant virus: A type of virus generated by modifying a known virus. These modifications may add functionality or ways to evade detection.[3]

VAX (Virtual address extension): An established line of mid-range server computers from the Digital Equipment Corporation (DEC, now a part of Hewlett-Packard).[2]

Vendor: A company/consortium that provides products and/or services.[59]

Verification confirmation: Process used to determine whether the product or functionality fulfills the intended use and user requirements.[199]

Veterans Health Information Systems Technology Architecture: *See* **VistA**.

Video RAM or video random access memory: *See* **VRAM**.

Virtual address extension: *See* **VAX**.

Virtual appliance: A virtual machine image file consisting of a preconfigured operating system environment and a single application.[2]

Virtual community: A community of people sharing common interests, ideas, and feelings over the Internet of collaborative networks.[8]

Virtual CPU: A virtual CPU (vCPU), also known as a virtual processor, is a physical central processing unit that is assigned to a virtual machine.[2]

Virtual machine: *See* **VM**.

Virtual private network: *See* **VPN**.

Virtual reality: The computer-generated simulation of a three-dimensional image or environment that can be interacted with in a seemingly real or physical way by a person using special electronic equipment, such as a helmet with a screen inside or gloves fitted with sensors.[260]

Virtual reality modeling language: *See* **VRML**.

Virtual SAN appliance: A virtual SAN appliance, also called a virtual storage appliance (VSA), is a software bundle that allows a storage manager to turn the unused storage capacity in his or her network's virtual servers into a storage area network (SAN). The SAN provides a pool of shared storage that can be accessed by the virtual servers as needed.[2]

Virtual server farm: A networking environment that employs multiple application and infrastructure servers running on two or more physical servers using a server virtualization program such as VMware or Microsoft Virtual Server®.[2]

Virtual to virtual (V2V): A term that refers to the migration of an operating system (OS), application programs, and data from a virtual machine or disk partition to another virtual machine or disk partition. The target can be a single system or multiple systems. To streamline the operation, part or all of the migration can be carried out automatically by means of specialized programs known as migration tools.[2]

Virtualization: The creation of a virtual (rather than actual) version of something, such as an operating system, a server, a storage device, or network resources. Virtualization can be viewed as part of an overall trend in enterprise IT that includes autonomic computing, a scenario in which the IT environment will be able to manage itself based on perceived activity, and utility computing, in which computer processing power is seen as a utility that clients can pay for only as needed. The usual goal of virtualization is to centralize administrative tasks while improving scalability and work loads.[2]

Virtualization software: Virtualization software acts as a layer between a computer's primary OS and the virtual OS. It allows the virtual system to access the computer's hardware, such as the RAM, CPU, and video card, just like the primary OS. This is different than emulation, which actually translates each command into a form that the system's processor can understand. Since Macintosh and Windows computers now both use the "x86" processor architecture, it is possible to run both OSes on the same machine via virtualization, rather than emulation.[75]

Virus: 1. A type of programmed threat—a code fragment (not an independent program) that reproduces by attaching to another program. It may damage data directly, or it may degrade system performance by taking over system resources, which are then not available to authorized users. It is designed to spread from one computer to another and interferes with computer operation. **2.** Code embedded within a program that causes a copy of itself to be inserted in one or more other programs; in addition to propagation, the virus usually performs some unwanted function and, therefore, interferes with computer operation.[14,261]

Virus scanner: A type of antivirus program that searches a system for virus signatures that have attached to executable programs and applications such as e-mail clients. A virus scanner can either search all executables when a system is booted or scan a file only when a change is made to the file as viruses will change the data in a file.[41]

Vishing (voice or VoIP phishing): An electronic fraud tactic in which individuals are tricked into revealing critical financial or personal information to unauthorized entities. Vishing works like phishing but does not always occur over the Internet and is carried out using voice technology. A vishing attack can be conducted by voice email, VoIP (voice over IP), or landline or cellular telephone.[2]

VistA (Veterans Health Information Systems Technology Architecture): A Health Information Technology (HIT) system created and used by the Veterans Health Administration (VHA) of the U.S. Department of Veterans Affairs (VA) in serving America's veterans through the provision of exceptional-quality health care which enhances our veterans' health and well-being.[262]

VM (Virtual machine): 1. The name given to various programming language interpreters. **2.** One instance of an operating system along with one or more applications running in an isolated partition within the computer. It enables different operating systems to run in the same computer at the same time. Virtual machines (VMs) are also widely used to run multiple instances of the same operating system, each running the same set or a different set of applications. Each virtual machine functions as if it owned the entire computer. The operating systems in each VM partition are called "guest operating systems," and they communicate with the hardware via the virtual machine monitor (VMM) control program. The VMM "virtualizes" the hardware for each VM (for details, *see* Virtual machine monitor).[154]

VMM (Virtual machine monitor): A host program that allows a single computer to support multiple, identical execution environments. All the users see their systems as self-contained computers isolated from other users, even though every user is served by the same machine. In this context, a virtual machine is an operating system (OS) that is managed by an underlying control program.[263]

Vocabulary: 1. The body of words used in a particular language. **2.** Words used on a particular occasion or in a particular sphere. **3.** A list of difficult or unfamiliar words with an explanation of their meanings, accompanying a piece of specialist or foreign-language text.[260]

Voice ID (voice authentication): A type of user authentication that uses voice print biometrics, voice ID relies on the fact that vocal characteristics, like fingerprints and the patterns of people's irises, are unique for each individual.[2]

Voice over Internet protocol: *See* **VoIP.**

Voice recognition: Computer analysis of the human voice, especially for the purposes of interpreting words and phrases or identifying an individual voice.[260]

Voice response system: Specialized technologies designed for providing callers with verbal and faxed answers to inquiries without assistance from a person. They provide account information, fulfill requests for mailable items, prescreen callers for script customization, interact with host systems (read and write), and produce reports.[146]

Voice response unit: *See* **VRU.**

VoIP (Voice over Internet protocol): 1. A technology that allows telephone calls using a broadband Internet connection instead of a regular (or analog) phone line. Some services using VoIP may only allow you to call other people using the same service, but others may allow you to call anyone who has a telephone number—including local, long distance, mobile, and international numbers. **2.** Refers to the use of the Internet protocol (IP) to transfer voice communications in much the same way that web pages and e-mail are transferred. Each piece of voice data is digitized into chunks and then sent across the Internet (in the case of public VoIP) to a destination server where the chunks are reassembled. This process happens in real-time so that two or more people can carry on a conversation.[11,264,265]

Volume and stress testing: Stress testing evaluates the behavior of a system that is pushed beyond its specified operational limits (this may be beyond the stated requirements). IT evaluates responses to bursts of peak activity that exceed system limitations. Volume testing, also known as load testing, evaluates system performance with predefined load levels. Load testing measures how long it takes a system to perform various program tasks and functions under normal or predetermined conditions.[266]

von Neumann bottleneck: The term is named for John von Neumann, who developed the theory behind the architecture of modern computers. Earlier computers were fed programs and data for processing while they were running. von Neumann came up with the idea behind the stored program computer, our standard model, which is also known as the von Neumann architecture. In the von Neumann architecture, programs and data are held in memory; the processor and memory are separate and data moves between the two. In that configuration, latency is unavoidable.[2]

VoxML™ (Voice markup language): A technology from Motorola for creating a voice dialog with a web site in which a user can call a web site by phone and interact with it through speech recognition and web site responses. VoxML allows a developer to create a script of the conversation a user can have with an application program run by a web server. The user calling in is connected to a client program called a voice browser. The voice browser in turn passes requests on to the web server. The markup defined in VoxML is consistent with the Extensible Markup Language (XML), the strategic data definition language for the Internet. Using VoxML is intended to be no more difficult than writing a web page using the Hypertext Markup Language (HTML).[2]

VPN (Virtual private network): 1. Refers to a network in which some of the parts are connected using the public Internet, but the data sent across the Internet are encrypted, so the entire network is "virtually" private. Secure and encrypted connection between two points across the Internet. **2.** VPNs transfer information by encrypting and encapsulating traffic in IP packets and sending the packets over the Internet. That practice is called "tunneling." Most VPNs are built and run by Internet service providers, and secure protocols like Point-to-Point Tunneling Protocol (PPTP) to ensure that data transmissions are not intercepted by unauthorized parties.[32,59,260] *See* **Tunneling**.

VRAM (Video RAM or video random access memory): Refers to all forms of random access memory used to store image data in computer display cards. VRAM is a type of buffer between a computer and the display.[260]

VRML (Virtual reality modeling language): An open-standard programming language created to design three-dimensional (3-D) and web-based models, textures, and illusions. VRML is used to illustrate 3-D objects, buildings, landscapes, or other items requiring 3-D structure and is very similar to Hypertext Markup Language (HTML). VRML also uses textual representation to define 3-D illusion presentation methods.[54]

VRU (Voice response unit): An automated telephone answering system consisting of hardware and software that allows the caller to navigate through a series of prerecorded messages and use a menu of options through the buttons on a touch-tone telephone or through voice recognition.[146]

Vulnerability: A cybersecurity term that refers to a flaw in a system that can leave it open to attack. A vulnerability may also refer to any type of weakness in a computer system itself, in a set of procedures, or in anything that leaves information security exposed to a threat.[54]

Vulnerability assessment: 1. Systematic examination of an information system or product to determine the adequacy of security measures, identify security deficiencies, provide data from which to predict the effectiveness of proposed security measures, and confirm the adequacy of such measures after implementation. **2.** The process of identifying and quantifying vulnerabilities and prioritizing (or ranking) the vulnerabilities in a system.[23,89]

V

W

WAI (Web Accessibility Initiative): An initiative of the World Wide Web Consortium launched in 1997 to ensure that as the Internet grows in usage, web sites are designed to accommodate people with disabilities. The WAI was implemented to ensure that web site design addresses the needs of people with these disabilities.[41]

WAIS (Wide-area information server): An Internet system that specializes in searches for various sources of academic information that have been indexed based on content. Its indices consist of every word in a document, and each word carries the same weight in a search.[3]

WAN (Wide area network): A collection of long-distance telecommunication links and networks used to connect local area networks and end stations across regional, national, or international distances.[11] *See* **LAN, MAN,** and **WLAN.**

WAP (Wireless application protocol): A secure specification that allows users to access information instantly via handheld wireless devices such as mobile phones, pagers, two-way radios, Smartphones, and communicators.[41]

WASP (Wireless application service provider): Provides the same service of a regular ASP but to wireless clients. WASPs are typically used in enterprises to connect a mobile workforce to company data, including e-mail, Internet access, CRM, ERP, and company financials.[41]

Waterfall model: A systems development life cycle model for software engineering. Often considered the classic approach to the systems development life cycle, the waterfall model describes a development method that is linear and sequential with distinct goals for each phase of development.[2]

WAV or WAVE (Waveform audio format [.wav]): A commonly used term in the telecommunications industry. Waveform is a graphical representation of a signal as a plot of amplitude versus time, i.e., the shape of a wave.[41]

Waveform audio format (.wav): *See* **WAV** or **WAVE.**

Wavelet: A mathematical function useful in digital signal processing and image compression. Wavelet compression works by analyzing an image and converting it into a set of mathematical expressions that can then be decoded by the receiver.[2]

Wearable technology: Also known as Wearables. Technology, worn in clothing or accessories, which records and reports information about behaviors such as physical activity or sleep patterns. This technology aims to educate and motivate individuals toward better habits and better health.[267]

Web address: 1. Identifies a node on the Internet. **2.** The web address may also refer to the name or IP number of a web site Uniform Resource Locator (URL).

The URL is a string of characters that represents the location or address of a resource on the Internet. **3.** The term Internet address can also represent someone's e-mail address.[41]

Web crawler: A program that browses the web in a methodical, automated manner. Web crawlers are mainly used to create a copy of all the visited pages for later processing by a search engine, which will index the downloaded pages to provide fast searches.[8] A web crawler (also known as a web spider or web robot) is a program or automated script that browses the World Wide Web in a methodical, automated manner. Many legitimate sites, in particular search engines, use spidering as a means of providing up-to-date data. Web crawlers are mainly used to create a copy of all the visited pages for later processing by a search engine, which will index the downloaded pages to provide fast searches.[268]

Web master: An individual who manages and ensures that a website effectively and efficiently meets its deliverables.[41]

Web portal: 1. A web site that provides a starting point, a gateway, or portal, to other resources on the Internet or an intranet.[8] **2.** A web portal or public portal refers to a web site or service that offers a broad array of resources and services, such as e-mail, forums, search engines, and online shopping malls. The first web portals were online services, such as AOL, which provided access to the web. **3.** An enterprise portal is a web-based interface for users of enterprise applications. Enterprise portals also provide access to enterprise information such as corporate databases, applications (including web applications), and systems.[41]

Web security: WS-Security (Web Services Security) is a proposed IT industry standard that addresses security when data is exchanged as part of a web service. WS-Security is one of a series of specifications from an industry group that includes IBM, Microsoft, and Verisign. Related specifications include the Business Process Execution Language (BPEL), WS-Coordination, and WS-Transaction.[2]

Web server: 1. More often refers to software than the physical hardware. A web server is a program that uses the client/server model and the WWW HTTP to serve the files that form web pages to web users (whose computers contain hypertext transfer protocol [HTTP] clients that forward their requests). **2.** Every computer on the Internet that contains a web site must have a web server program. References may be made to hardware, or the dedicated computers on which server software resides.[3] *See* **HTTP** and **S-HTTP**.[3]

Web services: A standardized way of integrating Web-based applications using the XML, SOAP, WSDL, and UDDI open standards over an Internet protocol backbone.[41] Services that are made available from a business's web server for web users or other web-connected programs. Web services range from such major services as storage management and customer relationship management (CRM) down to more limited services.[2]

Web services description language: *See* **WSDL.**

Web stack: The collection of software required for web development. At a minimum, a web stack contains an operating system (OS), a programming language, database software, and a web server.[2]

WEP (Wired equivalent privacy): A security protocol, specified in the IEEE Wireless Fidelity (Wi-Fi) standard, 802.11b, that is designed to provide a wireless local area network (WLAN) with a level of security and privacy comparable to what is usually expected of a wired LAN.[11]

Wet signature: Created when a person physically marks a document. Ink on paper signature.[269]

WG (Work group): A collection of individuals (peer to peer) working together on a task. Workgroup computing occurs when all the individuals have computers connected to a network that allows them to send e-mail to one another, share data files, and schedule meetings. Sophisticated workgroup systems allow users to define workflows so that data are automatically forwarded to appropriate people at each stage of a process.[41]

Whois: Search provides domain name registration information by domain names, IP addresses, and/or network information center handle.[75]

Wide-area information server: *See* **WAIS.**

Wide area network: *See* **WAN.**

Wide SCSI (Wide small computer system interface): 20–40 Mbps high-speed interface for connecting devices to the computer bus.[3]

Wide small computer system interface: *See* **Wide SCSI.**

Wi-Fi (Wireless Fidelity): Wireless network components that are based on one of the Wi-Fi Alliance's 802.11 standards. The Wi-Fi Alliance created the 802.11 standards so that manufacturers can make wireless products that work with other manufacturers' equipment.[11]

Wi-Fi protected access: *See* **WPA.**

Wiki: Piece of server software that allows users to freely create and edit web page content using any web browser.[31]

Wildcard: Used when searching for files, a wildcard is a character (usually * or ?) that can stand for one or more unknown characters during a search, and cause the search results to yield all files within a general description or type of software.[3]

Window: An object on the screen that presents information, such as a document or message.[70]

Wired equivalent privacy: *See* **WEP.**

Wireless application protocol: *See* **WAP.**

Wireless application service provider: *See* **WASP.**

Wireless e-mail device: A hand-held mobile device providing e-mail, telephone, text messaging, web browsing, and other wireless data access.[3]

Wireless Fidelity: *See* **Wi-Fi.**

Wireless local area network: *See* **WLAN.**

Wireless technology: Radio frequency architecture that transmits signals from remote, lightweight workstations to the wireless local area network (LAN) in such a way that health-related work processes can be re-engineered toward greater mobility with an improved focus on the patient, such as bedside patient registration.[3] *See* **LAN, MAN,** and **WAN.**

WLAN (Wireless local area network): A communication system that transmits and receives data using wireless technology and implemented as an extension to or as an alternative for a hard-wired LAN.[11]

Woot: A term used mainly by computer enthusiasts to express excitement or joy. Also spelled w00t.[41]

Work group: *See* **WG.**

Workflow: 1. A process description of how tasks are done, by whom, in what order, and how quickly. Workflow can be used in the context of electronic systems or people (i.e., an electronic workflow system can help automate a physician's personal workflow). **2.** A graphic representation of the flow of work in a process and its related subprocesses, including specific activities, information dependencies, and the sequence of decisions and activities.[11]

Workflow management: An approach that allows for the definition and control of business processes that span applications.[146]

Workflow services: The workflow service is responsible for maintaining lists of active components and the workflow schedules/process. It assembles the components and uses an executable engine to execute the workflow.[59]

Workstation: 1. Node, terminal, or computer, attached to a network that runs local applications, or connects to servers to access shared server resources. Usually a microcomputer.[3] *See* **Terminal.**[3,11] **2.** Workstations generally come with a large, high-resolution graphics screen, at least 64 MB (megabytes) of RAM, accesses shared network resources, and runs local applications. Most workstations also have a mass storage device such as a disk drive, but a special type of workstation, called a diskless workstation, comes without a disk drive. The most common operating systems for workstations are UNIX and Windows NT.[41]

Workstation on wheels: *See* **WOW.** *See also* **COW.**

World Wide Web: *See* **WWW.**

WORM (Write once, read many times): 1. An acronym for Write Once, Read Many, an optical disk technology that allows you to write data onto a disk just once. After that, the data is permanent and can be read any number of times.[41] **2.** A program or algorithm that replicates itself over a computer network and usually performs malicious actions, such as using up the computer's resources and possibly shutting the system down.[41]

WOW (Workstation on wheels): Carts with mounted computer monitors (typically laptops or other computer systems) that connect to a network in a wireless manner and are wheeled easily from room to room.[11]

WPA (Wi-Fi protected access): A security scheme for wireless networks, developed by the networking industry in response to the shortcomings of Wired Equivalent Privacy (WEP). WPA uses Temporal Key Integrity Protocol (TKIP) encryption and provides built-in authentication, giving security comparable to VPN tunneling with WEP, with the benefit of easier administration and use.[9]

Write back: A storage method in which data are written into the cache every time a change occurs, but is written into the corresponding location in main memory only at specified intervals or under certain conditions.[2]

Write once, read many times: *See* **WORM**.

WSDL (Web services description language): An XML-formatted language used to describe a web service's capabilities as collections of communication endpoints capable of exchanging messages. WSDL is an integral part of UDDI, an XML-based worldwide business registry. WSDL is the language that UDDI uses. WSDL was developed jointly by Microsoft and IBM.[41]

WWW (World Wide Web): The web, or World Wide Web, is basically a system of Internet servers that support specially formatted documents. The documents are formatted in a markup language called HTML (HyperText Markup Language) that supports links to other documents, as well as graphics, audio, and video files.[41]

WYSIWYG (What you see is what you get): Some early systems yielded a screen image that was unlike a printed document or file. This term is used to confirm that the system presents a screen image that matches what prints on paper. Pronounced "wizzy-wig."[3]

WYSIWYP (What you see is what you print): Pronounced wizzy-whip, refers to the ability of a computer system to print colors exactly as they appear on a monitor. WYSIWYP printing requires a special program, called a color management system (CMS), to calibrate the monitor and printer.[41] Interactive whiteboard display in which multiple computer users in different geographical locations can write or draw while others watch. They are often used in teleconferencing.[68]

X

X.25: 1. Standard protocol for packet switched wide area network (WAN) communication developed by the International Telecommunication Union-Telecommunication (ITU-T) Standard Sector. **2.** Interface between Data Terminal Equipment (DTE) and Data Circuit-terminating Equipment (DCE) for terminals operating in the packet mode and connected to public data networks by dedicated circuit.[270]

X12 standard SC X12: Chartered by the American National Standards Institute, develops and maintains EDI (Electronic Data Interchange) and CICA (Context Inspired Component Architecture) standards along with XML schemas which drive business processes globally. The ASC X12 organization meets to develop and maintain EDI standards that facilitate electronic interchange relating to business transactions such as order placement and processing, shipping and receiving information, invoicing, payment and cash application data, and data to and from entities involved in finance, insurance, transportation, supply chains, and state and federal governments. Committee members jointly develop and promote EDI standards that streamline business transactions, using a common, uniform business language.[271]

XDS (Cross-enterprise document sharing): Focused on providing a standards-based specification for managing the sharing of documents that healthcare enterprises (anywhere from a private physician, to a clinic, to an acute care inpatient facility) have decided to explicitly share. This contributes to the foundation of a shared electronic health record.[29] *See* **Profile. NOTE: XDS is an Integrating the Healthcare Enterprise (IHE) Profile.**

XML (Extensible markup language): 1. General-purpose markup language for creating special-purpose markup languages. It is a simplified subset of standard generalized markup language, capable of describing many different kinds of data. Its primary purpose is to facilitate the sharing of data across different systems, particularly systems connected via the Internet. **2.** Describes a class of data objects, called XML documents, and partially describes the behavior of computer programs that process them. XML is an application profile or restricted form of SGML, the Standard Generalized Markup Language (ISO 8879). By construction, XML documents are conforming SGML documents.[8] Extensible Markup Language, a specification developed by the W3C. XML is a pared-down version of SGML (Standard Generalized Markup Language) (ISO 8879), designed especially for web documents. It allows designers to create their own customized tags, enabling the definition, transmission, validation, and interpretation of data between applications and between organizations.[41]

XSL (Extensible Stylesheet Language): A standard developed by the World Wide Web Consortium defining a language for transforming and formatting XML (eXtensible Markup Language) documents. An XSL stylesheet is written in XML and consists of instructions for tree transformation and formatting. The tree transformations describe how each XML tag relates to other data and the formatting instructions describe how to output the various types of data.[46]

X

Z

.zip: The filename extension used by files compressed into the ZIP format common on PCs.[3]

Zero day attack: Exploitation by a hacker of a software vulnerability that is initially unknown to the manufacturer. Once the attack is discovered, the software developer works to close the vulnerability.[50]

Zero latency enterprise: The immediate exchange of information across geographical, technical, and organizational boundaries so that all departments, customers, and related parties can work together in real time.[146]

Zigbee: A specification for a suite of high-level communication protocols using small, low-power digital radios based on an IEEE 802 standard for personal area networks.[272]

Zip or zipping: A popular data compression format. Files that have been compressed with the ZIP format are called ZIP files and usually end with a .ZIP extension.[41]

Zombie process: 1. UNIX process that does not terminate. Must be removed by the kill command. **2.** A compromised web server that is used as an attack launch point to launch an overwhelming number of requests toward an attacked web site, which will soon be unable to service legitimate requests from its users.[3]

Z

Appendix A: Healthcare Organizations

Academy of Nutrition and Dietetics
> Organization representing food and nutrition professionals with over 75,000 members. The Academy is committed to improving the nation's health and advancing the profession of dietetics through research, education, and advocacy.
> *120 South Riverside Plaza, Suite 2000*
> *Chicago, IL 60606-6995*
> *Tel: 800-877-1600*
> *www.eatrightpro.org*

AAAAI (American Academy of Allergy, Asthma & Immunology)
> Physician membership organization focused on advancing the knowledge and practice of allergies, asthma, and immunology.
> *555 East Wells Street*
> *Suite 1100*
> *Milwaukee, WI 53202-3823*
> *Tel: 414-272-6071*
> *www.aaaai.org*

AAACN (American Association of Ambulatory Care Nursing)
> The association of professional nurses and associates who identify ambulatory care practice as essential to the continuum of high-quality, cost-effective healthcare.
> *East Holly Avenue*
> *Box 56*
> *Pitman, NJ 08071-0056*
> *Tel: 800-262-6877*
> *www.aaacn.org*

AACN (American Association of Colleges of Nursing)
The national voice for America's baccalaureate and higher-degree nursing education programs.
One Dupont Circle, NW
Suite 530
Washington, DC 20036
Tel: 202-463-6930
Fax: 202-785-8320
www.aacn.nche.edu

AACN (American Association of Critical-Care Nurses)
Acute and critical care nurses rely on AACN for expert knowledge and the influence to fulfill their promise to patients and their families.
101 Columbia
Aliso Viejo, CA 92656-4109
Tel: 949-362-2000
Toll free: 800-899-2226
Fax: 949-362-2020
www.aacn.org

AAD (American Academy of Dermatology)
Physician membership organization for dermatologists inside or outside the United States.
P.O. Box 4014
Schaumburg, IL 60168
Toll free: 866-503-SKIN (7546)
International: 847-240-1280
Fax: 847-240-1859
www.aad.org

AADE (American Association of Diabetic Educators)
A professional association dedicated to promoting the expertise of the diabetes educator.
200 W. Madison Street
Suite 800
Chicago, IL 60606
Toll free: 800-338-3633
www.diabeteseducator.org

AAFP (American Academy of Family Physicians)
Membership organization for physicians and physicians in training engaged in family medicine, the teaching of family medicine, or medical administration inside or outside the United States.
P.O. Box 11210
Shawnee Mission, KS 66207-1210
Tel: 913-906-6000
Toll free: 800-274-2237
Fax: 913-906-6075
www.aafp.org

AAHAM (American Association of Healthcare Administrative Management)
National membership association that represents a broad-based constituency of healthcare professionals.
11240 Waples Mill Road
Suite 200
Fairfax, VA 22030
Tel: 703-281-4043
Fax: 703-359-7562
www.aaham.org

AAHC (American Association for Homecare)
Membership association of companies in the homecare community.
1707 L Street, NW
Suite 350
Washington, DC 20036
Tel: 202-372-0107
Fax: 202-835-8306
www.aahomecare.org

AAHC (Association of Academic Health Centers)
Nonprofit organization to improve the healthcare system by mobilizing and enhancing the strengths and resources of the academic health centers.
1400 Sixteenth Street, NW
Suite 720
Washington, DC 20036
Tel: 202-265-9600
Fax: 202-265-7514
www.aahcdc.org

AAHN (American Association for the History of Nursing)
Membership network to advance historical scholarship in nursing and healthcare.
10200 W. 44th Avenue
Suite 304
Wheat Ridge, CO 80033
Tel: 303-422-2685
www.aahn.org

AAHP (American Association of Health Plans)
See **AHIP**. (AAHP is now AHIP.)

AAIHDS (American Association of Integrated Healthcare Delivery Systems)
A nonprofit dedicated to the educational advancement of provider-based managed care professionals involved in integrated healthcare delivery.
4435 Waterfront Drive
Suite 101
Glen Allen, VA 23060
Tel: 804-747-5823
Fax: 804-747-5316
www.aaihds.org

AALNA (American Assisted Living Nurses Association)
Nationwide network of assisted living nurses.
P.O. Box 10469
Napa, CA 94581
Tel: 707-253-7299
www.alnursing.org

AALNC (American Association Legal Nurse Consultants)
A not-for-profit membership organization dedicated to the professional enhancement and growth of registered nurses practicing in the specialty area of legal nurse consulting and to advancing this nursing specialty.
330 N. Wabash Avenue
Chicago, IL 60611
Tel: 877-402-2562
Fax: 312-673-6655
www.aalnc.org

AAMA (American Academy of Medical Administrators)
Membership association of multispecialty healthcare administrators in federal and public and private sectors.
330 N. Wabash Avenue
Suite 2000
Chicago, IL 60611
www.linkedin.com/company/american-academy-of-medical-administrators

AAMA (American Association of Medical Assistants)
Membership organization for medical assistants.
20 N. Wacker Drive
Suite 1575
Chicago, IL 60606
Tel: 312-899-1500
Fax: 312-899-1259
www.aama-ntl.org

AAMC (Association of American Medical Colleges)
Membership association of medical schools accredited by the Liaison Committee on Medical Education (LCME), not-for-profit teaching hospitals and academic society 501(c)3 organizations with primary missions that include advancing medical education and/or biomedical research in the United States and Canada.
655 K Street NW
Suite 100
Washington, DC 20001-2399
Tel: 202-828-0400
www.aamc.org

AAMCN (American Association of Managed Care Nurses)
Membership community of nurses working in managed care throughout the country.
4435 Waterfront Drive
Suite 101
Glen Allen, VA 23060
Tel: 804-707-9698
Fax: 804-747-5316
www.aamcn.org

AAMI (Association for Advancement of Medical Instrumentation)
A unique alliance of over 6000 members united by the common goal of increasing the understanding and beneficial use of medical instrumentation.
4301 N. Fairfax Drive
Suite 301
Arlington, VA 22203-1633
Tel: 703-525-4890
Fax: 703-276-0793
www.aami.org

AAN (American Academy of Neurology)
Membership academy for physicians, medical students, and nonphysician neurology professionals.
201 Chicago Avenue South
Minneapolis, MN 55415
Tel: 612-928-6000
Toll free: 800-879-1960
Fax: 612-454-2746
www.aan.com

AAN (American Academy of Nursing)
Membership academy for nursing professionals.
1000 Vermont Avenue, NW, St 910
Washington, DC 20005
Tel: 202-777-1170
www.aanet.org

AANA (American Association of Nurse Anesthetists)
Membership association of national and international nurse anesthetists.
222 S. Prospect Avenue
Park Ridge, IL 60068-4037
Tel: 847-692-7050
Fax: 847-692-6968
www.aana.com

AANN (American Association of Neuroscience Nurses)
Membership organization of nurses passionate about neuroscience.
8735 W. Higgins Road
Suite 300
Chicago, IL 60631
Tel: 847-375-4733
Toll free: 888-557-2266 (US only)
Fax: 847-375-6430
International fax: 732-460-7313
www.aann.org

AANP (American Academy of Nurse Practitioners)
Membership-focused organization for nurse practitioners and others interested in fostering the objectives of the NP profession.
National Administrative Office
P.O. Box 12846
Austin, TX 78711
Tel: 512-442-4262
Fax: 512-442-6469
www.aanp.org

AAOHN (American Association of Occupational Health Nurses)
Membership association of nurses engaged in occupational and environmental health nursing.
National Office
7794 Grow Drive
Pensacola, FL 32514
Tel: 850-474-6963
Toll free: 800-241-8014
Fax: 850-484-8762
www.aaohn.org

AAOS (American Academy of Orthopedic Surgeons/American Association of Orthopedic Surgeons)
Physician membership organization for physicians in the exclusive practice of orthopedic surgery in the United States and physicians enrolled in approved orthopedic residency programs inside and outside the United States.
9400 W. Higgins Road
Rosemont, IL 60018
Tel: 847-823-7186
Fax: 847-823-8125
www.aaos.org

AAP (American Academy of Pediatrics)
Physician membership organization for pediatricians, pediatric medical subspecialists, pediatric surgical specialists, and physicians in approved pediatric residency programs inside or outside the United States.
141 Northwest Point Boulevard
Elk Grove Village, IL 60007-1098
Tel: 847-434-4000
Toll free: 800-433-9016
Fax: 847-434-8000
www.aap.org

AAPA (American Academy of Physician Assistants)
Membership organization for ARC-PA or NCCPA-certified physician assistants, PA affiliates, physicians, and related businesses.
2318 Mill Road
Suite 1300
Alexandria, VA 22314
Tel: 703-836-2272
www.aapa.org

AAPL (American Association for Physician Leadership)
U.S. organization for physician leaders. Members of the association include chief executive officers, chief medical officers, vice presidents of medical affairs, medical directors, and other physician leaders inside or outside the United States.
400 North Ashley Drive
Suite 400
Tampa, FL 33602
Tel: 813-287-2000
Toll free: 800-562-8088
Fax: 813-287-8993
http://www.physicianleaders.org/

AAPM&R (American Academy of Physical Medicine and Rehabilitation)
Physician membership organization for Diplomates of the American Board of Physical Medicine and Rehabilitation and physicians in an approved PM&R residency program inside or outside the United States.
9700 W. Bryn Mawr Avenue
Suite 200
Rosemont, IL 60018
Tel: 847-737-6000
Toll free: 877-227-6799
Fax: 847-754-4368
www.aapmr.org

AAPPO (American Association of Preferred Provider Organizations)
Membership association of preferred provider organizations, including specialty networks, pharmaceutical manufacturers, provider organizations, consultants, benefit administrators, hospitals, and others.
974 Breckenridge Lane
#162
Louisville, KY 40207
Tel: 502-403-1122
Fax: 502-403-1129
www.aappo.org

AARC (American Association for Respiratory Care)
Membership association for credentialed respiratory care professionals, individuals with a position related to respiratory care, and students in a respiratory care program.
9425 N. MacArthur Boulevard
Suite 100
Irving, TX 75063-4706
Tel: 972-243-2272
www.aarc.org

AASCIN (American Association of Spinal Cord Injury Nurses)
See **ASCIP.** (AASCIN is now ASCIP.)

ABA (American Board of Anesthesiology)
Physician certification organization to qualify and examine anesthesiology candidates who have successfully completed an accredited program of anesthesiology training in the United States.
4208 Six Forks Road
Suite 1500
Raleigh, NC 27609-5765
Tel: 866-999-7501
Fax: 866-999-7503
www.theABA.org

ABAI (American Board of Allergy and Immunology)
Physician certification organization to qualify and examine allergists/immunologists who have successfully completed an accredited educational program.
1835 Market Street
Suite 1210
Philadelphia, PA 19103
Tel: 215-592-9466
Toll free: 866-264-5568
Fax: 215-592-9411
www.abai.org

ABCGN (American Board of Certification for Gastroenterology Nurses)
A volunteer nonprofit organization to maintain and improve the knowledge, understanding, and skill of nurses in the fields of gastroenterology and gastroenterology endoscopy by developing and administering a certification program.
330 N. Wabash Avenue
Suite 2000
Chicago, IL 60611
Tel: 855-25-ABCGN and 855-252-2246
Fax: 312-673-6723
www.abcgn.org

ABCRS (American Board of Colon and Rectal Surgery)
Physician certification organization to qualify and examine colon and rectal surgery candidates who have successfully completed an accredited educational program.
20600 Eureka Road
Suite 600
Taylor, MI 48180
Tel: 734-282-9400
Fax: 734-282-9402
www.abcrs.org

ABD (American Board of Dermatology)
Physician certification organization to qualify and examine dermatologist and dermatology subspecialist candidates who have successfully completed an accredited educational program.
2 Wells Avenue
Newton, MA 02459
Tel: 617-910-6400
www.abderm.org

ABEM (American Board of Emergency Medicine)
Physician certification organization to qualify and examine emergency medicine and seven subspecialty candidates who successfully meet certification requirements.
3000 Coolidge Road
East Lansing, MI 48823-6319
Tel: 517-332-4800
Fax: 517-332-2234
www.abem.org

ABFM (American Board of Family Medicine)
Physician certification organization to qualify and examine family medicine and subspecialty candidates who have successfully completed an accredited program and meet certification requirements.
1648 McGrathiana Parkway
Suite 550
Lexington, KY 40511-1247
Tel: 859-269-5626
Toll free: 888-995-5700
Fax: 859-335-7501 and 859-335-7509
www.theabfm.org

ABIM (American Board of Internal Medicine)
A nonprofit independent evaluation organization for physicians in internal medicine and its 19 subspecialties.
510 Walnut Street
Suite 1700
Philadelphia, PA 19106-3699
Toll free: 800-441-2246
Fax: 215-446-3590
www.abim.org

ABMG (American Board Medical Genetics)
Physician/PhD certification organization to qualify and examine medical genetic and subspecialty candidates who successfully meet certification requirements.
9650 Rockville Pike
Bethesda, MD 20814-3998
Tel: 301-634-7315
Fax: 301-634-7320
www.abmg.org

ABNM (American Board of Nuclear Medicine)
The primary certifying organization for nuclear medicine physicians in the United States.
4555 Forest Park Boulevard
Suite 119
St. Louis, MO 63108-2173
Tel: 314-367-2225
www.abnm.org

ABNS (American Board of Neurological Surgery)
Physician certification organization to qualify and examine neurological surgery candidates who have successfully completed an accredited educational program.
245 Amity Road
Suite 208
Woodbridge, CT 06525
Tel: 203-397-2267
Fax: 203-392-0400
www.abns.org

ABOG (American Board of Obstetrics and Gynecology)
Independent, nonprofit organization that certifies obstetricians and gynecologists in the United States.
2915 Vine Street
Dallas, TX 75204
Tel: 214-871-1619
Fax: 214-871-1943
www.abog.org

ABOHN (American Board for Occupational Health Nurses)
Nursing certification organization to qualify and examine occupational health and subspecialty candidates who successfully meet certification requirements.
201 East Ogden Avenue
Suite 114
Hinsdale, IL 60521-3652
Tel: 630-789-5799
Toll free: 888-842-2646
Fax: 630-789-8901
www.abohn.org

ABOP (American Board of Ophthalmology)
Physician certification organization to qualify and examine ophthalmologist candidates who have successfully completed an accredited educational program and meet certification requirements.
111 Presidential Boulevard
Suite 241
Bala Cynwyd, PA 19004-1075
Tel: 610-664-1175
Fax: 610-664-6503
www.abop.org

ABOS (American Board of Orthopedic Surgery)
Physician certification organization to qualify and examine orthopedic surgery candidates who have successfully completed an accredited educational program and meet certification requirements.
400 Silver Cedar Court
Chapel Hill, NC 27514
Tel: 919-929-7103
Fax: 919-942-8988
www.abos.org

ABOto (American Board of Otolaryngology)
  Physician certification organization to qualify and examine otolaryngology
  candidates who have successfully completed an accredited educational pro-
  gram and meet certification requirements.
  5615 Kirby Drive
  Suite 600
  Houston, TX 77005
  Tel: 713-850-0399
  Fax: 713-850-1104
  www.aboto.org

ABP (American Board of Pathology)
  Physician certification organization to qualify and examine anatomic pathology, clinical pathology, and subspecialties candidates who have successfully completed an accredited educational program and meet certification
  requirements.
  4830 W Kennedy Boulevard
  Suite 690
  Tampa, FL 33609
  Tel: 813-286-2444
  Fax: 813-289-5279
  www.abpath.org

ABP (American Board of Pediatrics)
  Physician certification organization to qualify and examine pediatric and
  pediatric subspecialty candidates who have successfully completed an accredited educational program and meet certification requirements.
  111 Silver Cedar Court
  Chapel Hill, NC 27514
  Tel: 919-929-0461
  Fax: 919-929-9255
  www.abp.org

ABPM (American Board of Preventive Medicine)
  Physician certification organization to qualify and examine physicians in
  aerospace medicine, occupational medicine, public health, and general preventive medicine to candidates who have successfully completed an accredited program and meet certification requirements.
  Tel: 312-939-2276
  www.theabpm.org

ABPMR (American Board of Physical Medicine and Rehabilitation)
Physician certification organization to qualify and examine physical medicine and rehabilitation candidates who have successfully completed an accredited educational program and meet certification requirements.
3015 Allegro Park Lane SW
Rochester, MN 55902-4139
Tel: 507-282-1776
Fax: 507-282-9242
www.abpmr.org

ABPN (American Board of Psychiatry and Neurology)
Physician certification organization to qualify and examine psychiatry and neurology candidates who have successfully completed an accredited program and meet certification requirements.
2150 E. Lake Cook Road
Suite 900
Buffalo Grove, IL 60089
Tel: 847-229-6500
Fax: 847-229-6600
www.abpn.com

ABPS (American Board of Plastic Surgery)
Physician certification organization to qualify and examine plastic surgery specialists and subspecialty candidates who have successfully completed an accredited program and meet certification requirements.
Seven Penn Center
Suite 400
1635 Market Street
Philadelphia, PA 19103-2204
Tel: 215-587-9322
Fax: 215-587-9622
www.abplasticsurgery.org

ABR (American Board of Radiology)
Physician certification organization to qualify and examine diagnostic radiology, radiation oncology, and medical physics candidates who have successfully completed an accredited program and meet certification requirements.
5441 E. Williams Circle
Tucson, AZ 85711-7412
Tel: 520-790-2900
Fax: 520-790-3200
www.theabr.org

ABS (American Board of Surgery)
An independent, nonprofit organization certifying surgeons who have met a defined standard of education, training, and knowledge.
1617 John F. Kennedy Boulevard
Suite 860
Philadelphia, PA 19103
Tel: 215-568-4000
Fax: 215-563-5718
www.absurgery.org

ABTS (American Board of Thoracic Surgery)
Physician certification organization to qualify and examine thoracic candidates who have successfully met certification requirements.
633 North St. Clair Street
Suite 2320
Chicago, IL 60611
Tel: 312-202-5900
Fax: 312-202-5960
www.abts.org

ABU (American Board of Urology)
Physician certification organization to examine urology candidates who meet certification requirements.
600 Peter Jefferson Parkway
Suite 150
Charlottesville, VA 22911
Tel: 434-979-0059
Fax: 434-979-0266
www.abu.org

ABUCM (American Board for Urgent Care Medicine)
An independent certifying body for urgent care medicine.
2813 S. Hiawassee Rd., Suite 206
Orlando, FL 32835
Tel: 407-521-5789
Fax: 407-521-5790
www.abucm.org

ACAAI (American College of Allergy, Asthma & Immunology)
Membership organization for allergists/immunologists, and allied health professionals inside or outside the United States who meet eligibility requirements.
85 West Algonquin Road
Suite 550
Arlington Heights, IL 60005
Tel: 847-427-1200
Fax: 847-427-1294
www.acaai.org

AcademyHealth
National organization serving the fields of health services and policy research and the professionals who produce and use this important work.
1666 K Street NW
Washington, DC 20006
Tel: 202-292-6700
www.academyhealth.org

ACAHO (Association of Canadian Academic Healthcare Organizations)
See **HealthCareCAN**. (ACAHO is now part of HealthCareCAN.)

ACAP (Alliance of Claims Assistance Professionals)
A national, nonprofit organization dedicated to the growth and development of the claims assistance industry.
1127 High Ridge Road, #216
Stamford, CT 06905
or
9600 Escarpment, Suite 745-65
Austin, TX 78749
Toll free: 888-394-5163
www.claims.org

ACC (American College of Cardiology)
Membership organization for physicians, nurses, nurse practitioners, physician assistants, pharmacists, and practice managers inside and outside the United States.
Heart House
2400 N Street, NW
Washington, DC 20037
Tel: 202-375-6000, ext. 5603
Toll free: 800-253-4636, ext. 5603
Fax: 202-375-7000
www.acc.org

ACCE (American College of Clinical Engineering)
Membership organization for engineers in a clinical environment.
5200 Butler Pike
Plymouth Meeting, PA 19462-1298
Tel: 610-825-6067
Fax: 480-247-5040
www.accenet.org

ACCP (American College of Chest Physicians)
Physician education and board review organization for chest physicians and subspecialty candidates.
2595 Patriot Boulevard
Glenview, IL 60026
Tel: 224-521-9800
Toll free: 800-343-2227
Fax: 224-521-9801
www.chestnet.org

ACEHSA (Accrediting Commission on Education for Health Services Administration)
See **CAHME**. (ACEHSA is now CAHME.)

ACEP (American College of Emergency Physicians)
Physician membership organization for emergency physician specialists.
1125 Executive Circle
Irving, TX 75038-2522
Mailing:
P.O. Box 619911
Dallas, TX 75261-9911
Tel: 972-550-0911
Toll free: 800-798-1822
Fax: 972-580-2816
www.acep.org

ACGME (Accreditation Council for Graduate Medical Education)
A private professional organization responsible for the accreditation of residency education programs.
515 North State Street
Suite 2000
Chicago, IL 60654
Tel: 312-755-5000
Fax: 312-755-7498
www.acgme.org

ACHA (American College of Healthcare Architects)
Professional education and board review organization for architects in the field of healthcare architecture.
P.O. Box 14548
Lenexa, KS 66285-4548
18000 W. 105th Street
Olathe, KS 66061-7543
Tel: 913-895-4604
Fax: 913-895-4652
www.healtharchitects.org

ACHCA (American College of Health Care Administrators)
Membership organization for administrators, those with substantial interest in health/residential care administration, allied health professionals, and individual providers of healthcare products/services.
1101 Connecticut Avenue NW
Suite 450
Washington, DC 20036
Tel: 202-536-5120
Fax: 866-874-1585
www.achca.org

ACHE (American College of Healthcare Executives)
Membership organization for healthcare executives who lead hospitals, healthcare systems, and other healthcare organizations.
One N. Franklin Street
Suite 1700
Chicago, IL 60606-3529
Tel: 312-424-2800
Fax: 312-424-0023
www.ache.org

ACHP (Alliance of Community Health Plans)
National membership advocacy organization for health plans and provider groups.
1825 Eye Street, NW
Suite 401
Washington, DC 20006
Tel: 202-785-2247
Fax: 202-785-4060
www.achp.org

ACM (Association for Computing Machinery)
Professional organization of computing professionals. The special interest group (SIGHIT) emphasizes the computing and information science-related aspects of health informatics.
2 Penn Plaza
Suite 701
New York, NY 10121-0701
Tel: 212-626-0500
Toll free: 800-342-6626
Fax: 212-944-1318
www.acm.org

ACMA (American Case Management Association)
Certification organization to qualify and examine hospital/health system case management professionals who successfully meet certification requirements.
11701 W. 36th Street
Little Rock, AR 72211
Tel: 501-907-ACMA (2262)
Fax: 501-227-4247
www.acmaweb.org

ACNM (American College of Nurse-Midwives)
Membership organization for certified nurse-midwives and certified mid-wives who meet eligibility requirements in the United States.
8403 Colesville Road
Suite 1550
Silver Spring, MD 20910
Tel: 240-485-1800
Fax: 240-485-1818
www.midwife.org

ACOG (American Congress of Obstetricians and Gynecologists)
Physician certification organization for obstetrics and/or gynecology candidates.
P.O. Box 70620
Washington, DC 20024-9998
409 12th Street, SW
Washington, DC 20024-2188
Tel: 202-638-5577
Toll free: 800-673-8444
www.acog.org

ACP (American College of Physicians)
Physician membership organization for internists, internal medicine sub-specialists, medical students, residents, and fellows and physicians in an approved pediatric residency program inside or outside the United States.
190 North Independence Mall West
Philadelphia, PA 19106-1572
Tel: 215-351-2400
Toll free: 800-523-1546
www.acponline.org

ACPE (American College of Physician Executives)
See **AAPL**. (ACPE is now AAPL.)

ACPeds (American College of Pediatricians)
National organization of pediatricians and other healthcare professionals dedicated to the health and well-being of children.
P.O. Box 357190
Gainesville, FL 32635
Tel: 352-376-1877
Fax: 352-415-0922
www.acpeds.org

ACR (American College of Radiology)
Physician membership organization for radiologists, radiation specialists, and physicians in an approved residency program who meet eligibility requirements.
1891 Preston White Drive
Reston, VA 20191
Tel: 703-648-8900
www.acr.org

ACS (American College of Surgeons)
Physician membership organization for surgeons, subspecialists, physicians in approved residency programs, and members of the surgical team inside or outside the United States who meet eligibility requirements.
633 North St. Clair Street
Chicago, IL 60611-3211
Tel: 312-202-5000
Toll free: 800-621-4111
Fax: 312-202-5001
www.facs.org

ACT (Association for Competitive Technology | The App Association)
Advocacy organization for small and mid-size application developers and information technology firms.
1401 K Street NW
Suite 501
Washington, DC 20005
Tel: 202-331-2130
Fax: 202-331-2139
www.actonline.org

ACU (Association of Clinicians for the Underserved)
Transdisciplinary organization of clinicians, advocates, and healthcare organizations that provide healthcare for the underserved.
1420 Spring Hill Road, Suite 600
Tysons Corner, VA 22102
Tel: 844-422-8247
www.clinicians.org

ADA (American Dental Association)
Membership organization for dentists, students, or charitable practitioners inside or outside the United States.
211 E. Chicago Avenue
Chicago, IL 60611-2678
Tel: 312-440-2500
www.ada.org

ADA (American Diabetes Association)
General membership organization designed for people with diabetes, their families, friends, and caregivers.
1701 North Beauregard Street
Alexandria, VA 22311
Tel: 703-549-1500, ext. 5203
Toll free: 800-342-2383
www.diabetes.org

AdvaMed (Advanced Medical Technology Association)
Membership organization open to medical technology firms worldwide.
701 Pennsylvania Ave, NW
Suite 800
Washington, DC 20004-2654
Tel: 202-783-8700
Fax: 202-783-8750
www.advamed.org

AeA (Advancing the Business of Technology)
See **TechAmerica**. (In 2008, AeA merged with the Information Technology
Association of America [ITAA] to form TechAmerica.)

AEHIA (Association for Executives in Healthcare Information Applications)
An association within CHIME launched to provide an education and net-
working platform to healthcare's senior IT applications leaders.
710 Avis Drive
Suite 200
Ann Arbor, MI 48108
Tel: 734-665-0000
Fax: 734-665-4922
http://aehia.org/

AEHIS (Association for Executives in Healthcare Information Security)
An association within CHIME launched to provide an education and net-
working platform to healthcare's senior IT security leaders.
710 Avis Drive
Suite 200
Ann Arbor, MI 48108
Tel: 734-665-0000
Fax: 734-665-4922
http://aehis.org/

AEHIT (Association for Executives in Healthcare Information Technology)
An association within CHIME launched to provide an education and net-
working platform to healthcare's senior IT technology leaders.
710 Avis Drive
Suite 200
Ann Arbor, MI 48108
Tel: 734-665-0000
Fax: 734-665-4922
http://aehit.org/

AEP (Association of Emergency Physicians)
Physician membership organization for emergency physicians from across the
United States.
911 Whitewater Drive
Mars, PA 16046-4221
Toll free: 866-772-1818
Fax: 866-422-7794
www.aep.org

AFEHCT (Association for Electronic Health Care Transactions)
See **HIMSS**. (In 2006, AFEHCT merged with HIMSS.)
Tel: 312-664-4467
Fax: 312-664-6143

AfPP (Association for Perioperative Practice)
Membership organization for all who work in or around the perioperative environment.
Daisy Ayris House
42 Freemans Way
Harrogate, North Yorkshire, HG3 1DH
Tel: 01423 881300
Fax: 01423 880997
www.afpp.org.uk

AGMA (American Medical Group Association)
Physician membership organization for group practices, independent practice associations, academic/faculty practices, integrated delivery systems, and other organized systems of care including groups with three or more licensed physicians organized to deliver healthcare services.
One Prince Street
Alexandria, VA 22314-3318
Tel: 703-838-0033
Fax: 703-548-1890
www.amga.org

AHA (American Heart Association)
Volunteer organization dedicated to building healthier lives free of cardiovascular (heart) diseases and stroke.
National Center
7272 Greenville Avenue
Dallas, TX 75231
Toll free: 800-AHA-USA-1 and 800-242-8721
www.heart.org

AHA (American Hospital Association)
Membership organization for hospitals, healthcare systems, pre-acute/post-acute patient care facilities, and hospital-affiliated educational programs (e.g., hospital school of nursing, program in health administration).
155 N. Wacker Drive
Chicago, IL 60606
Tel: 312-422-3000
800 10th Street, N.W.
Two City Center, Suite 400
Washington, DC 20001-4956
Tel: 202.638.1100
Toll free: 800.424.4301
www.aha.org

AHCA (American Health Care Association)
Nonprofit federation of affiliate state health organizations, together representing more than 11,000 nonprofit and for-profit nursing facility, assisted living, developmentally disabled, and subacute care providers that care for approximately one million elderly and disabled individuals each day.
1201 L Street NW
Washington, DC 20005
Tel: 202-842-4444
www.ahcancal.org

AHCJ (Association of Health Care Journalists)
An independent, nonprofit organization dedicated to advancing public understanding of healthcare issues. Its mission is to improve the quality, accuracy, and visibility of healthcare reporting, writing, and editing.
Missouri School of Journalism
10 Neff Hall
Columbia, MO 65211
Tel: 573-884-5606
Fax: 573-884-5609
www.healthjournalism.org

AHDI (Association for Healthcare Documentation Integrity)
Membership organization for individuals enrolled in a medical transcription program, individual professionals working or involved in healthcare documentation and data capture, healthcare delivery facilities, companies or manufacturers that employ healthcare documentation specialists or provide services or products to the profession, and educational facilities that train medical transcriptionists.
4120 Dale Road
Suite J8-233
Modesto, CA 95356
Tel: 209-527-9620
Toll free: 800-982-2182
Fax: 209-527-9633
www.ahdionline.org

AHHE (Association of Hispanic Healthcare Executives)
Membership organization for individuals in healthcare administration or persons on a career path to healthcare management, including healthcare consultants and full-time academicians who support AHHE's mission and objectives.
153 West 78th Street
Suite 1
New York, NY 10024
Tel: 212-877-1615
www.ahhe.org

AHIMA (American Health Information Management Association)
Membership organization for health information management (HIM) professionals interested in the AHIMA purpose.
233 N. Michigan Avenue
21st Floor
Chicago, IL 60601-5809
Tel: 312-233-1100
Toll free: 800-335-5535
Fax: 312-233-1090
www.ahima.org

AHIP (America's Health Insurance Plans)
National trade association for the health insurance industry.
601 Pennsylvania Avenue, NW
South Building
Suite 500
Washington, DC 20004
Tel: 202-778-3200
Fax: 202-331-7487
www.ahip.org

AHLA (American Health Lawyers Association)
Nonpartisan, 501(c)(3) educational organization devoted to legal issues in the healthcare field.
1620 Eye Street NW, 6th Floor
Washington, DC 20006-4010
Tel: 202-833-1100
Fax: 202-833-1105
www.healthlawyers.org

AHNA (American Holistic Nurses Association)
Membership organization open to everyone (nurses, other healthcare professionals, and the public) interested in all aspects of holistic caring and healing.
2900 SW Plass Court
Topeka, KS 66611-1980
Tel: 785-234-1712
Toll free: 800-278-2462
Fax: 785-234-1713
www.ahna.org

AHQA (American Health Quality Association)
Membership organization of State Health Care Quality Associations.
7918 Jones Branch Drive
Suite 300
McLean, VA 22102
Tel: 202-331-5790
www.ahqa.org

AHRMM (Association for Healthcare Resource & Materials Management)
Membership organization of supply chain provider and suppliers for professionals, students, and retirees.
155 N. Wacker Drive
Suite 400
Chicago, IL 60606
Tel: 312-422-3840
Fax: 312-422-4573
www.ahrmm.org

AHRQ (Agency for Healthcare Research and Quality)
Federal agency within the Department of Health and Human Services focused on the national mission to improve the quality, safety, efficiency, and effectiveness of healthcare for Americans.
5600 Fishers Lane
7th Floor
Rockville, MD 20857
Tel: 301-427-1364
www.ahrq.gov

AIM (Association for Automatic Identification and Mobility)
An international trade association representing automatic identification and mobility technology solution providers.
20399 Route 19
Suite 203
Cranberry Township, PA 16066
Tel: 724-742-4470
Fax: 724-742-4476
www.aimglobal.org

ALA (American Lung Association)
Volunteer organization to prevent lung disease and promote lung health.
55 W. Wacker Drive
Suite 1150
Chicago, IL 60601
Toll free: 1-800-LUNGUSA (1-800-548-8252)
www.lungusa.org

Alliance HPSR (Alliance for Health Policy and Systems Research)
Academic organization to promote health policy and systems research in developing countries.
20 Avenue Appia
1211 Geneva
Switzerland
Tel: +41 22 791 2973
Fax: +41 22 791 4817
www.who.int/alliance-hpsr

AMA (American Medical Association)
Association of physicians and physicians in training committed to ethics in medicine.
330 N. Wabash Avenue
Chicago, IL 60611-5885
Tel: 800-621-8335
www.ama-assn.org

AMCP (Academy of Managed Care Pharmacy)
National professional association of pharmacists and other healthcare practitioners organizations.
100 North Pitt Street
Suite 400
Alexandria, VA 22314
Tel: 703-683-8416
Toll free: 800-827-2627
Fax: 703-683-8417
www.amcp.org

AMDA (American Medical Directors Association—The Society for Post-Acute and Long-Term Care Medicine)
Professional association of medical directors and physicians practicing in the long-term care continuum.
11000 Broken Land Parkway
Suite 400
Columbia, MD 21044
Tel: 410-740-9743
Toll free: 800-876-2632
Fax: 410-740-4572
www.paltc.org

AMDIS (Association of Medical Directors of Information Systems)
Membership organization for medical directors of information systems.
682 Peninsula Drive
Lake Almanor, CA 96137
Tel: 719-548-9360
www.amdis.org

AMIA (American Medical Informatics Association)
Membership organization open to individuals interested in biomedical and health informatics.
4720 Montgomery Lane
Suite 500
Bethesda, MD 20814
Tel: 301-657-1291
Fax: 301-657-1296
www.amia.org

AMP (Applied Measurement Professionals, Inc.)
Certification organization for psychometric consultation, testing, and measurement services.
18000 W. 105th Street
Olathe, KS 66061
Tel: 913-895-4600
Fax: 913-895-4650
www.goamp.com

AMSA (American Medical Student Association)
Student-governed, national organization committed to representing the concerns of physicians-in-training. AMSA members are medical students, premedical students, interns, residents, and practicing physicians.
45610 Woodland Road
Sterling, Virginia 20166
Tel: 703-620-6600
www.amsa.org

AMSN (Academy of Medical-Surgical Nurses)
Membership organization for nurses and licensed healthcare professionals interested in the care of adults.
East Holly Avenue
Box 56
Pitman, NJ 08071-0056
Toll free: 866-877-2676
www.amsn.org

ANA (American Nurses Association)
Professional membership organization representing the interests of the registered nurses through its constituent and state nurses associations and organizational affiliates.
8515 Georgia Avenue
Suite 400
Silver Spring, MD 20910-3492
Toll free: 800-274-4ANA (4262)
Fax: 301-628-5001
www.nursingworld.org

ANASA (Association of Nursing Agencies of South Africa)
Membership association representing nursing agencies in South Africa.
P.O. Box 10101
Edenglen 1613
South Africa
Tel: +083-444-9227
Fax: +086-535-1794
e-mail (Inquiries): office@anasa.org.za
www.anasa.org.za

ANCC (American Nurses Credentialing Center)
Nursing certification organization to qualify and examine nurse candidates
who have successfully completed an accredited program and meet certification requirements.
8515 Georgia Avenue
Suite 400
Silver Spring, MD 20910-3492
Toll free: 800-284-2378
www.nursecredentialing.org

ANI (Alliance for Nursing Informatics)
Membership organization of nursing informatics associations and groups.
33 West Monroe Street
Suite 1700
Chicago, IL 60603-5616
Tel: 312-664-4467
Fax: 312-664-6143
www.allianceni.org

ANIA (American Nursing Informatics Association)
Membership organization to advance the field of nursing informatics.
200 East Holly Avenue
Sewell, NJ 08080
Toll free: 866-552-6404
www.ania.org

ANNA (American Nephrology Nurses Association)
Membership organization for nurses, allied health professionals, and others inside and outside the United States involved in the care of nephrology patients.
East Holly Avenue
Box 56
Pitman, NJ 08071
Tel: 856-256-2320
Toll free: 888-600-2662
Fax: 856-589-7463
www.annanurse.org

ANSI (American National Standards Institute)
National voice of the U.S. standards and conformity assessment system, the American National Standards Institute is a membership organization for government agencies, organizations, companies, academic and international bodies, and individuals.
25 West 43rd Street
4th Floor
New York, NY 10036
Tel: 212-642-4900
Fax: 212-398-0023
www.ansi.org

AOA (American Osteopathic Association)
Membership organization for osteopathic physicians, associates, and allied healthcare providers inside and outside the United States.
142 E. Ontario Street
Chicago, IL 60611-2864
Tel: 312-202-8000
Toll free: 800-621-1773
Fax: 312-202-2000
www.osteopathic.org

AONE (American Organization of Nurse Executives)
Membership organization for nurses in leadership positions, students, and individuals interested in supporting the AONE mission and vision.
200 10th Street, NW
Two City Center
Suite 400
Washington, DC 20001-4956
Tel: 202-626-2240
Fax: 202-638-5499
155 N. Wacker Drive
Suite 400
Chicago, IL 60606
Tel: 312-422-2800
Fax: 312-278-0861
www.aone.org

AORN (Association of periOperative Registered Nurses)
Membership organization of perioperative nurses, nursing students, and industry professionals who provide direct or indirect perioperative services.
2170 South Parker Road
Suite 400
Denver, CO 80231
Tel: 303-755-6304
Toll free: 800-755-2676
Fax: 800-847-0045
www.aorn.org

APhA (American Pharmacists Association)
Membership organization for pharmacists, students, spouses, technicians, and retirees inside or outside the United States.
2215 Constitution Avenue, NW
Washington, DC 20037
Tel: 202-628-4410
Toll free: 800-237-APhA (2742)
Fax: 202-783-2351
www.pharmacist.com

APHA (American Public Health Association)
Membership organization open to health professionals, other career workers
in the health field, and persons interested in public health.
800 I Street, NW
Washington, DC 20001
Tel: 202-777-2742
Fax: 202-777-2534
www.apha.org

API (Association for Pathology Informatics)
Membership organization for individuals, trainees (e.g., residents, fellows,
students, and post-docs), teaching institutions, commercial entities, and
other organizations interested in pathology informatics.
5607 Baum Boulevard
Room 518A
Pittsburgh, PA 15206
Tel: 412-648-9552
Fax: 412-624-5100
www.pathologyinformatics.org

APNA (American Psychiatric Nurses Association)
Membership organization for nurses and affiliated mental health professionals inside and outside the United States who are committed to the specialty
practice of psychiatric-mental health (PMH) nursing, wellness promotion,
prevention of mental health problems, and the care and treatment of persons
with psychiatric disorders.
3141 Fairview Park Drive
Suite 625
Falls Church, VA 22042
Tel: 571-533-1919
Toll free: 855-863-2762
Fax: 855-883-2762
www.apna.org

APTA (American Physical Therapy Association)
Membership organization for physical therapists (PT) and assistants (PTA)
inside and outside the United States.
1111 North Fairfax Street
Alexandria, VA 22314-1488
Tel: 703-684-APTA (2782)
Toll free: 800-999-2782
Fax: 703-684-7343
www.apta.org

AQIPS (Alliance for Quality Improvement and Patient Safety)
Professional association for patient safety organizations and their healthcare provider members.
5114 Cherokee Avenue
Alexandria, Virginia 22312
Tel: 703-581-9285
www.allianceforqualityimprovement.org

ARN (Association of Rehabilitation Nurses)
To promote and advance professional rehabilitation nursing practice through education, advocacy, collaboration, and research to enhance the quality of life for those affected by disability and chronic illness.
8735 W. Higgins Road
Suite 300
Chicago, IL 60631-2738
Toll free: 800-229-7530
e-mail: info@rehabnurse.org
www.rehabnurse.org

ASAE (American Society of Association Executives)
Membership organization for professional staff, students, consultants, executives of a nonprofit association or association management companies.
1575 I Street, NW
Washington, DC 20005
Tel (Main): 202-626-2723
Tel (Member Services): 202-371-0940
Toll free: 888-950-2723
Fax: 202-371-8315
www.asaecenter.org

ASC X12 (Accredited Standards Committee X12)
Membership organization chartered by Accredited Standards Committee (ASC) under the American National Standards Institute (ANSI) to support business and technical professionals in a cross-industry forum to enhance business processes.
8300 Greensboro Drive
Suite 800
McLean, VA 22102
Tel: 703-970-4480
Fax: 703.970.4488
www.x12.org

ASCIP (Academy of Spinal Cord Injury Professionals)
Membership association of physicians, nurses, psychologists, social workers, counselors, therapists, and researchers engaged in education, research, advocacy, and policy for spinal cord injuries inside and outside the United States.
206 South Sixth Street
Springfield, IL 62701
Tel: 217-753-1190
Fax: 217-525-1271
www.academyscipro.org

ASCO (American Society of Clinical Oncology)
Membership organization for oncology professionals.
2318 Mill Road
Suite 800
Alexandria, VA 22314
Tel: 703-299-0158
Toll free: 888-282-2552
Fax: 703-299-0255
www.asco.org

ASCP (American Society for Clinical Pathology)
Membership organization for pathologists and laboratory professionals.
33 West Monroe Street
Suite 1600
Chicago, IL 60603
Tel: 312-541-4999
Fax: 312-541-4998
www.ascp.org

ASHE (American Society for Healthcare Engineering)
Membership organization for individuals devoted to optimizing the healthcare physical environment in a healthcare facility, company, or organization other than healthcare, educators, and students.
155 N. Wacker Drive
Suite 400
Chicago, Illinois 60606
Tel: 312-422-3800
Fax: 312-422-4571
www.ashe.org

ASHP (American Society of Health-System Pharmacists)
Membership organization for pharmacists, students, spouses, technicians, and retirees inside or outside the United States.
7272 Wisconsin Avenue
Bethesda, MD 20814
Toll free: 866-279-0681
International Tel: 0-01-301-664-8700
www.ashp.org

ASHRM (American Society for Healthcare Risk Management)
Membership organization for anyone who is actively involved or interested in healthcare risk management or whose primary job responsibility includes healthcare risk management.
155 N. Wacker Drive
Suite 400
Chicago, IL 60606
Tel: 312-422-3980
Fax: 312-422-4580
www.ashrm.org

ASN (American Society of Nephrology)
Organization working to fight against kidney disease by educating health professionals, advancing research, and advocating the highest quality care for patients.
1510 H Street, NW
Suite 800
Washington, DC 20005
Tel: 202-640-4660
www.asn-online.org

ASNC (American Society of Nuclear Cardiology)
Membership organization for physicians, scientists, technologists, biomedical engineers, computer specialists, and other healthcare personnel involved in nuclear cardiology as well as industry representatives who actively work in this field of medicine.
4340 East-West Highway
Suite 1120
Bethesda, MD 20814
Tel: 301-215-7575
Fax: 301-215-7113
www.asnc.org

ASPAN (American Society of PeriAnesthesia Nurses)
   Membership organization for nurses involved in all phases of preanesthesia and postanesthesia care, ambulatory surgery, and pain management or in the management, teaching, or research of the same, students, and licensed healthcare professionals interested in perianesthesia inside or outside the United States.
   90 Frontage Road
   Cherry Hill, NJ 08034-1424
   Tel: 856-616-9600
   Toll free: 877-737-9696
   Fax: 856-616-9601
   www.aspan.org

ASQ (American Society for Quality)
   Global membership community of people passionate about quality who use the tools, their ideas and expertise to make our world work better.
   P.O. Box 3005
   Milwaukee, WI 53201-3005
   600 North Plankinton Avenue
   Milwaukee, WI 53203
   Tel: 800-248-1946
   Mexico: 001-800-514-1564
   All other locations: +1-414-272-8575
   Fax: 414-272-1734
   www.asq.org

ASSE (American Society of Safety Engineers)
   Membership organization for the safety, health, and environmental (SH&E) profession with an interest in the healthcare practice specialty.
   520 N. Northwest Highway
   Park Ridge, IL 60068
   Tel: 847-699-2929
   www.asse.org

ASTHO (Association of State and Territorial Health Officials)
   All state and territorial health agency staff members are eligible to participate in open meetings.
   2231 Crystal Drive
   Suite 450
   Arlington, VA 22202
   Tel: 202-371-9090
   Fax: 571-527-3189
   www.astho.org

ASTM International (American Society for Testing and Materials)
Membership organization chartered by ASTM under the American National Standards Institute (ANSI) to support the development of test methods, specifications, guides, and practice standards that support industries and governments worldwide.
100 Barr Harbor Drive
P.O. Box C700
West Conshohocken, PA 19428-2959
Toll free: 877-909-ASTM
International: 610-832-9585
www.astm.org

ATA (American Telemedicine Association)
Membership is open to all individuals and organizations interested in providing distance healthcare through technology.
1100 Connecticut Avenue, NW
Suite 540
Washington, DC 20036
Tel: 202-223-3333
Fax: 202-223-2787
www.americantelemed.org

AUPHA (Association of University Programs in Health Administration)
Membership organization of healthcare management/administration education programs in North America includes non-academic institutions and individuals inside and outside the United States.
2000 14th Street North
Suite 780
Arlington, VA 22201
Tel: 703-894-0940
Fax: 703-894-0941
www.aupha.org

AWHONN (Association of Women's Health, Obstetric and Neonatal Nurses)
Membership organization for nurses and other healthcare professionals interested in improving the health of women and newborns.
1800 M Street
Suite 740S
Washington, DC 20036
Tel: 202-261-2400
Toll free US: 800-673-8499
Toll free Canada: 800-245-0231
Fax: 202-728-0575
www.awhonn.org

BACCN (British Association of Critical Care Nurses)
Membership organization open to any professional with an interest in critical care.
BACCN Administration
14 Blandford Square
Newcastle Upon Tyne
NE1 4HZ
Tel: 0844 800 8843
www.baccn.org.uk

BCI (Business Continuity Institute)
Membership organization open to business continuity management practitioners at all levels of experience worldwide.
10-11 Southview Park
Marsack Street
Caversham,
Berkshire
RG4 5AF
United Kingdom
Tel: +44 (0) 118-947-8215
Fax: +44 (0) 118-947-6237
www.thebci.org

CAC (Citizen Advocacy Center)
Membership organization for state health professional licensing boards and other interested organizations and individuals.
1400 16th Street, NW
Suite 101
Washington, DC 20036
Tel: 202-462-1174
Fax: 202-354-5372
www.cacenter.org

CACCN (Canadian Association of Critical Care Nurses)
Canadian nursing membership organization for any registered nurse with an interest in critical care who possesses a current and valid license or certificate.
P.O. Box 25322
London, Ontario
N6B 6B1 Canada
Tel: 519-649-5284
Toll free: 866-477-9077
Fax: 519-649-1458
www.caccn.ca

CADTH (Canadian Agency for Drugs and Technologies)
An independent, not-for-profit agency funded by Canadian federal, provincial, and territorial governments to provide credible, impartial advice and evidence-based information about the effectiveness of drugs and other health technologies to Canadian healthcare decision makers.
865 Carling Avenue
Suite 600
Ottawa, Ontario
K1S 5S8 Canada
Tel: 613-226-2553
Toll free: 866-988-1444
Fax: 613-226-5392
www.cadth.ca

CAHME (Commission on Accreditation of Healthcare Management Education)
Any interested healthcare organization or corporation may become a corporate member.
6110 Executive Boulevard
Suite 614
Rockville, MD 20852
Tel: 301-298-1820
www.cahme.org

CAHTA (Catalan Agency for Health Technology Assessment and Research)
See **HEN**. (CAHTA is now HEN.)

CAP (College of American Pathologists)
Membership organization exclusively for pathology residents.
325 Waukegan Road
Northfield, IL 60093-2750
Toll free: 800-323-4040
Fax: 847-832-8000
International fax: 001-847-832-7000
www.cap.org

CAQH (Council for Affordable Quality Healthcare)
Membership alliance of nonprofit health plans and trade associations.
601 Pennsylvania Avenue, NW
South Building
Suite 500
Washington, DC 20004
Tel: 202-861-1492
Fax: 202-861-1454
www.caqh.org

CARING (Capital Area Roundtable on Informatics in Nursing)
See **ANIA**. (In 2011, CARING merged with ANIA.)

CCA (Care Continuum Alliance)
Membership organization of corporate and individual members from health plans and disease management organizations; health information technology innovators and manufacturers; pharmaceutical manufacturers and pharmacy benefit managers; employers and other purchasers, physicians, researchers, and nurses.
701 Pennsylvania Avenue, NW
Suite 700
Washington, DC 20004-2694
Tel: 202-737-5980
Fax: 202-478-5113
www.carecontinuumalliance.org

CCC (Computing Community Consortium)
Cooperative consortium formed by the Computing Research Association (CRA) and the U.S. National Science Foundation, CCC is broadly inclusive, and is open to any computing researcher who wishes to become involved.
1828 L Street, NW
Suite 800
Washington, DC 20036-4632
Tel: 202-234-2111
Fax: 202-667-1066
www.cra.org/ccc

CDC (Centers for Disease Control and Prevention)
Federal agency within the Department of Health and Human Services focused on the national mission to improve the quality, safety, efficiency, and effectiveness of healthcare for Americans.
1600 Clifton Road
Atlanta, GA 30333-4027
Toll free: 800-CDC-INFO (800-232-4636)
www.cdc.gov

CDISC (Clinical Data Interchange Standards Consortium)
Membership organization open to any organization of any size interested in information system interoperability to improve medical research and related areas of healthcare.
401 West 15th Street
Suite 975
Austin, TX 78701
www.cdisc.org

CEN (European Committee for Standardization)
Membership is the 27 European Union National Standards Bodies (NSBs), Croatia, the Former Yugoslav Republic of Macedonia, Turkey, and three countries of the European Free Trade Association (Iceland, Norway, and Switzerland).
CEN-CENELEC Management Centre
Avenue Marnix 17
B-1000 Brussels
Tel: +32 2 550 08 11
Fax: +32 2 550 08 19
www.cen.eu

CHA (Children's Hospital Association)
CHA advances child health through innovation in the quality, cost, and delivery of care with our children's hospitals.
6803 West 64th Street
Overland Park, KS 66202
Tel: (913) 262-1436
Fax: (913) 262-1575

600 13th Street, NW Suite 500
Washington, DC 20005
Tel: (202) 753-5500
Fax: (202) 347-5147
www.childrenshospitals.org

CHCA (Child Health Corporation of America)
See **CHA.** (In 2011, CHCA, the National Association of Children's Hospitals and Related Institutions [NACHRI] and its public policy affiliate National Association of Children's Hospitals [N.A.C.H.] merged to create CHA, the Children's Hospital Association.)

CHI (Canada Health Infoway)
Organization accountable to Canada's 14 federal, provincial, and territorial governments represented by their Deputy Ministers of Health to foster development and adoption of information technology to transform healthcare in Canada.
www.infoway-inforoute.ca

CHI (Center for Healthcare Innovation)
Organization encouraging and enabling meaningful and executable innovation that aims to address existing and ensuing healthcare dynamics through communication, education, training, symposia, reports, and research.
222 Riverside Plaza
Chicago, IL 60606
Tel: 312-906-6153
www.chisite.org

CHIME (College of Healthcare Information Management Executives)
  Membership open to CIOs and senior IT leaders at healthcare-related
  organizations.
  710 Avis Drive
  Suite 200
  Ann Arbor, MI 48108
  Tel: 734-665-0000
  Fax: 734-665-4922
  www.chimecentral.org

CHT (Center for Health and Technology)
  Private, academic research organization.
  Center for Health and Technology
  4610 X Street
  Sacramento, CA 95817
  Tel: 916-734-5675
  Fax: 916-734-3580
  www.ucdmc.ucdavis.edu/cht/

CIAQ (Center for Innovation Access & Quality)
  Organization promoting the creation and implementation of innovative
  approaches to improving quality care at safety net systems.
  1001 Potrero Ave
  San Francisco, CA 94110
  Tel: 415-206-4523
  www.ciaqsf.org

CIHI (Canadian Institute for Health Information)
  An independent, not-for-profit organization that provides essential data and
  analysis on Canada's health system and the health of Canadians.
  495 Richmond Road
  Suite 600
  Ottawa, Ontario
  K2A 4H6 Canada
  Tel: 613-241-7860
  Fax: 613-241-8120
  www.cihi.ca

CIHR (Canadian Institutes of Health Research)
Agency responsible for funding health research in Canada.
160 Elgin Street
9th Floor
Address Locator 4809A
Ottawa, Ontario
K19 0W9 Canada
Tel: 613-954-1968
Toll free: 888-603-4178
Fax: 613-954-1800
www.cihr-irsc.gc.ca

CITL (Center for Information Technology Leadership)
Independent information technology and health technologies research organization.
www.citl.org

CITPH (Center for Innovation and Technology in Public Health)
A research group engaged in public policy development, public health (PH) practices, and the direct provision of services related to enabling technologies. *See* **Public Health Institute**.
www.citph.org

CLMA (Clinical Laboratory Management Association)
Membership organization for individuals who hold, have held, or aspire to hold an administrative, managerial, or supervisory position in the clinical laboratory or whose administrative responsibilities include diagnostic services.
330 N. Wabash Avenue
Suite 2000
Chicago, IL 60611
Tel: 312-321-5111
www.clma.org

CLSI (Clinical and Laboratory Standards Institute)
Membership organization for IVD manufacturers and suppliers, LIS/HIS companies, pharmaceutical and biotechnology companies, consulting firms, professional societies, trade associations, and government agencies.
950 West Valley Road
Suite 2500
Wayne, PA 19087 USA
Tel: 610-688-0100
Fax: 610-688-0700
www.clsi.org

CMS (Centers for Medicare & Medicaid Services)
Federal agency within the Department of Health and Human Services focused on the national mission to improve the quality, safety, efficiency, and effectiveness of healthcare for Americans.
7500 Security Boulevard
Baltimore, MD 21244
Tel: 410-786-3000
Toll free: 877-267-2323
TTY: 410-786-0727
TTY: 866-226-1819
www.cms.gov

CMSA (Case Management Society of America)
Membership organization for individuals engaged in the field of case management inside and outside the United States.
6301 Ranch Drive
Little Rock, AR 72223
Tel: 501-225-2229
Toll free: 800-216-2672
Fax: 501-221-9068 or 501-227-5444
Secure Fax: 501-421-2135
www.cmsa.org

CMSS (Council of Medical Specialty Societies)
Non-profit organization representing 44 medical specialty societies.
35 E. Wacker Drive
Chicago, IL 60601
Tel: 312-224-2585
www.cmss.org

CNA (Canadian Nurses Association)
National professional membership organization for registered nurses in Canada.
50 Driveway
Ottawa, Ontario
K2P 1E2 Canada
Tel: 613-237-2133
Toll free: 800-361-8404
Fax: 613-237-3520
www.cna-aiic.ca

CNC (Center for Nursing Classification and Clinical Effectiveness)
Academia research center at the University of Iowa School of Nursing.
University of Iowa College of Nursing
101 College of Nursing Building
50 Newton Road
Iowa City, IA 52242-1121
Tel: 319-335-7018
Fax: 319-335-9990
www.nursing.uiowa.edu/center-for-nursing-classification-and-clinical
-effectiveness

COACH (Canada's Health Informatics Association)
Open to all individuals with an interest in health informatics, health information management, or related healthcare issues and practices.
151 Yonge Street
11th Floor
Toronto, Ontario
M5C 2W7 Canada
Tel: 647-775-8555
Toll free: 888-253-8554
www.coachorg.com

COC (AHIMA's Commission on Certification)
Certification organization for the AHIMA mission of quality healthcare through quality information.
233 N. Michigan Avenue
21st Floor
Chicago, IL 60601-5800
Tel: 312-233-1100
Fax: 312-233-1090
www.ahima.org/certification

CommonWell Health Alliance
Membership is open to all organizations that share CommonWell's vision that health IT must be inherently interoperable, including health IT suppliers, healthcare providers, and other health-focused organizations such as nonprofit and for-profit institutes.
info@commonwellalliance.org
http://www.commonwellalliance.org/

CompTIA (The Computing Technology Industry Association Trade Association)
Nonprofit trade association for IT professionals and companies inside and outside the United States.
3500 Lacey Road
Suite 100
Downers Grove, IL 60515
Tel: 630-678-8300
Toll free: 866-835-8020
www.comptia.org

CVAA (Canadian Vascular Access Association)
Membership organization open to corporations and all nurses registered with their provincial governing body, extended to the United States and Bermuda, engaged in the field of intravenous or vascular access therapy.
753 Main Street East
P.O. Box 68030
Hamilton, Ontario
L8M 3M7 Canada
Toll Free Telephone and Fax: 888-243-9307
www.cvaa.info

DAHTA (German Agency for Health Technology Assessment)
German Institute of Medical Documentation and Information (DIMDI) agency responsible for granting research assignments for the assessment of procedures and technology relevant to health in the form of Health Technology Assessment (HTA) reports and for the maintenance of a database-supported information system for the assessment of the effectiveness and cost of medical procedures and technologies.
Tel: +49 221 4724-1
Fax: +49 221 4724-444
www.dimdi.de

DAMA (Data Management Association International)
Chapter-based, as well as global, membership organization for those who engage in information and data management.
www.dama.org

Danish Health Authority
Government agency for the regulation of health and medicines in Denmark.
Islands Brygge 67
2300 København S
Denmark
Tel: +45 72 22 74 00
sundhedsstyrelsen.dk/

DARPA (Defense Advanced Research Projects Agency)
U.S. Military research agency.
675 North Randolph Street
Arlington, VA 22203-2114
Tel: 703-526-6630
www.darpa.mil

DHHS (Department of Health and Human Services)
The U.S. government's principal agency for protecting the health of all Americans and providing essential human services, especially for those who are least able to help themselves.
200 Independence Avenue, SW
Washington, DC 20201
Toll free: 877-696-6775
www.hhs.gov

DICOM (Digital Imaging and Communications in Medicine)
Membership organization chartered by Digital Imaging and Communications in Medicine (DICOM) under the American National Standards Institute (ANSI) to develop health information standards.
NEMA
1300 N. 17th Street
Rosslyn, VA 22209
Tel: 703-475-9217
http://dicom.nema.org/

DIHTA (Danish Institute for Health Technology Assessment)
See **Danish Health Authority**. (DIHTA is now Danish Health and Medicines Authority.)

DirectTrust
Nonprofit entity created by and for participants in the Direct community. DirectTrust serves as a forum and governance body for persons and entities engaged in Directed exchange of electronic health information as part of the Nationwide Health Information Network (NwHIN).
www.directtrust.org

DISA (Data Interchange Standards Association)
See **ASCX12**

DMAA (Disease Management Association of America)
See **CCA**. (DMAA is now the Care Continuum Alliance.)

DNA (Dermatology Nurses' Association)
Professional membership organization for nurses, individuals in related healthcare fields, and corporations interested in or involved in the care of dermatology patients.
435 N. Bennett Street
Southern Pines, NC 28387
Tel: 800-454-4362
Fax: 910-246-2361
www.dnanurse.org

DoD (Department of Defense) (Health Affairs)
U.S. Military department responsible for the health benefits and healthcare operations of those entrusted to our care.
http://prhome.defense.gov/HA

ECRI Institute
A nonprofit organization dedicated to bringing the discipline of applied scientific research to discover which medical procedures, devices, drugs, and processes are best, all to enable you to improve patient care.
5200 Butler Pike
Plymouth Meeting, PA 19462-1298
Tel: 610-825-6000 ext. 5891
Fax: 610-834-1275
www.ecri.org

eHI (eHealth Initiative)
Membership is open to all organizations in the healthcare industry.
818 Connecticut Avenue, NW
Suite 500
Washington, DC 20006
Tel: 202-624-3270
www.ehidc.org

EHRA HIMSS (Electronic Health Record Association)
A trade association of Electronic Health Record (EHR) companies addressing national efforts to create interoperable EHRs in hospital and ambulatory care settings. The EHR Association operates on the premise that the rapid, widespread adoption of EHRs will help improve the quality of patient care, as well as the productivity and sustainability of the healthcare system.
33 West Monroe Street
Suite 1700
Chicago, IL 60603-5616
Tel: 312-664-4467
Fax: 312-664-6143
www.himssehrva.org

EMEA (European Medicines Agency)
Decentralized agency of the European Union responsible for the scientific evaluation of medicines developed by pharmaceutical companies for use in the European Union.
30 Churchill Place
Canary Wharf
London E14 5EU
United Kingdom
Tel: +44 (0) 20 3660 600
Fax: +44 (0) 20 3660 5555
www.ema.europa.eu/ema

ENA (Emergency Nurses Association)
Membership organization for nurses in emergency nursing practice.
915 Lee Street
Des Plaines, IL 60016-6569
Tel: 800-900-9659
www.ena.org

ESQH (European Society for Quality in Healthcare)
A not-for-profit organization dedicated to the improvement of quality in European healthcare.
St. Camillus Hospital
Shelbourne Road
Limerick
Ireland
Tel: 00353 61 483315
e-mail: info@esqh.net
www.esqh.net

ETSI (European Telecommunications Standards Institute)
Membership organization for individuals, nonprofit associations, universities, public research bodies, governmental organizations, and observers interested in globally applicable standards for Information and Communications Technologies (ICT), including fixed, mobile, radio, converged, broadcast, and Internet technologies.
650, Route des Lucioles
06921 Sophia-Antipolis Cedex
France
Tel: +33 (0)4 92 94 42 00
Fax: +33 (0)4 93 65 47 16
www.etsi.org

EUnetHTA (European Network for Health Technology Assessment)
Organization supporting collaboration between European Health Technology
Applications (HTA).
Hosted by Danish Health and Medicines Authority
Axel Heides Gade 1
2300 Copenhagen S
Denmark
Tel: +45 7222 7727
Fax: +45 2075 9647
www.eunethta.net

FAH (Federation of American Hospitals)
Membership organization for investor-owned community hospitals and health
systems including institutions, associations (hospital associations, medical societies, law firms and foundations, suppliers of services and products to the healthcare
industry, management companies) and individual student members enrolled in a
course in hospital administration or other career study in the healthcare industry.
750 9th Street, NW
Suite 600
Washington, DC 20001-4524
Tel: 202-624-1500
Fax: 202-737-6462
www.fah.org

FCC (Federal Communications Commission)
An independent U.S. government agency directly responsible to Congress
charged with regulating interstate and international communications by
radio, television, wire, satellite, and cable.
445 12th Street SW
Washington, DC 20554
Toll free: 888-225-5322
TTY: 888-835-5322
Fax: 866-418-0232
www.fcc.gov

FDA (U.S. Food and Drug Administration)
Federal agency responsible for protecting the public health by assuring the safety,
efficacy, and security of human and veterinary drugs, biological products, medical devices, our nation's food supply, cosmetics, and products that emit radiation.
10903 New Hampshire Avenue
Silver Spring, MD 20993
Tel: 888-463-6332
www.fda.gov

FDRHPO (Fort Drum Regional Health Planning Organization)
An agency that strengthens the North Country Healthcare System for Fort Drum Soldiers, their families, and the surrounding civilian community. *www.fdrhpo.org*

George Institute for Global Health
Global research and health policy center.
50 Bridge St
Level 3
Sydney, NSW
Australia 2000
Tel: +61 2 8052 4300
Fax: +61 2 8052 4301
www.thegeorgeinstitute.org

GHC (Global Health Care, LLC)
GHC seeks to illuminate complex issues of healthcare practice and policy by bringing together leading-edge doers and thinkers. Since 1997, it has offered conferences and symposia sponsored by over 250 healthcare associations, organizations, and publications and attended by approximately 25,000 registrants.
37 Tatoosh Key
Bellevue, WA 98006
Tel: (206) 757-8053
Fax: (206) 757-7053
www.globalhealthcarellc.com/

GS1 (U.S. Global Standards-1)
Authorized provider of globally unique GS1 company prefixes for businesses and the design and implementation of supply chain standards and solutions.
Local GS1 offices by country: USA
Princeton Pike Corporate Center
1009 Lenox Drive
Suite 202
Lawrenceville, NJ 08648
Tel: 609-620-0200
www.gs1.org

HCCA (Health Care Compliance Association)
Membership organization for all compliance professionals, corporations, and students.
6500 Barrie Road
Suite 250
Minneapolis, MN 55435
Tel: 952-988-0141
Toll free: 888-580-8373
Fax: 952-988-0146
www.hcca-info.org

HCCA (Health Care Conference Administrators, LLC)
See **GHC** (Global Health Care, LLC). (HCCA is now GHC.)

HCEA (Healthcare Convention and Exhibitors Association)
Trade association for healthcare organizations involved as exhibitors at healthcare conventions and exhibitions. Membership includes healthcare associations and companies that provide products and services to the healthcare convention and exhibition industry.
7918 Jones Branch Drive
Suite 300
McLean, VA 22102
Tel: 703.935.1961
Fax: 703.506.3266
www.hcea.org

HCTAA (Home Care Technology Association of America)
Association representing home care and hospice providers and technology companies that support health information technology, health information exchange, and telehealth in the home.
228 7th Street SE
Washington, DC 20003
Tel: 202-547-2871
www.hctaa.org

HDWA (Healthcare Data Warehousing Association)
Membership is open to employees of healthcare payor and provider organizations. Memberships are held by organizations, not members.
www.hdwa.org

Health Tech (Health Technology Center)
(In 2009, Health Tech merged with the Public Health Institute and established the Center for Innovation and Technology in Public Health.)

HealthCare*CAN*
The national voice of healthcare organizations and hospitals across Canada.
17 York Street
Suite 100, 3rd floor
Ottawa, Ontario K15 5S7
Canada
www.healthcarecan.ca

Healthwise
Nonprofit organization with a mission to help people make better health decisions.
2601 N. Bogus Baisin Road
Boise, ID 83720
Tel: 1-800-706-9646
www.healthwise.org

HEN World Health Organization (Health Evidence Network)
Network of organizations and institutions promoting the use of evidence in health policy or health technology assessment.
WHO Regional Office for Europe
UN City
Marmorvej 51DK-2100 Copenhagen Ø Denmark
Tel: +45 45 33 70 00
Fax: +45 45 33 70 01
http://www.euro.who.int/en/data-and-evidence/evidence-informed-policy
-making/health-evidence-network-hen

HFES (Human Factors and Ergonomics Society)
Association representing human factors/ergonomics professionals. Members include psychologists and other scientists, designers, and engineers, all of whom have a common interest in designing systems and equipment to be safe and effective for the people who operate and maintain them.
1124 Montana Avenue, Suite B
Santa Monica, CA 90403-1617
www.hfes.org

HFMA (Healthcare Financial Management Association)
Membership organization for healthcare financial management executives and leaders.
3 Westbrook Corporate Center
Suite 600
Westchester, IL 60154
Tel: 708-531-9600
Toll free: 800-252-4362
Fax: 708-531-0032
www.hfma.org

HHS (Department of Health and Human Services)
See **DHHS**.

HIAA (Health Insurance Association of America)
See **AHIP**. (HIAA is now AHIP.)

HIBCC (Health Industry Business Communications Council)
An industry-sponsored and supported nonprofit organization. As an ANSI-accredited organization, our primary function is to facilitate electronic communications by developing appropriate standards for information exchange among all healthcare trading partners.
2525 E. Arizona Biltmore Circle
Suite 127
Phoenix, AZ 85016
Tel: 602-381-1091
Fax: 602-381-1093
www.hibcc.org

HIMA (Health Industry Manufacturers Association)
See **AdvaMed**.

HIMSS (Healthcare Information and Management Systems Society)
As a cause-based nonprofit, HIMSS North America provides thought leadership, community building, professional development, public policy, and events.
33 West Monroe Street
Suite 1700
Chicago, IL 60603-5616
Tel: 312-664-4467
Fax: 312-664-6143
www.himss.org

HL7 (Health Level Seven)
A not-for-profit, ANSI-accredited standards developing organization dedicated to providing a comprehensive framework and related standards for the exchange, integration, sharing, and retrieval of electronic health information that supports clinical practice and the management, delivery, and evaluation of health services.
3300 Washtenaw Avenue
Suite 227
Ann Arbor, MI 48104
Tel: +1 734-677-7777
Fax: +1 734-677-6622
www.hl7.org

HLC (Healthcare Leadership Council)
A coalition of chief executives from all disciplines within the healthcare system.
750 9th Street, NW
Suite 500
Washington, DC 20001
Tel: 202-452-8700
Fax: 202-296-9561
www.hlc.org

HPNA (Hospice and Palliative Nurses Association)
Membership organization for all members of the nursing team—nurses, nursing assistants, students, and non-nurses—engaged in hospice and pallia-tive end-of-life care.
One Penn Center West
Suite 425
Pittsburgh, PA 15276
Tel: 412-787-9301
www.hpna.org

HSC (Center for Studying Health System Change)
(On December 31, 2013, HSC merged with Mathematica Policy Research [MPR] and ceased operations as an independent organization.)

HTAi (Health Technology Assessment International)
Membership organization embracing all stakeholders, including research-ers, agencies, policymakers, industry, academia, health service providers, and patients/consumers interested in the field of scientific research to inform policy and clinical decision-making around the introduction and diffusion of health technologies.
HTAi Secretariat
1200, 10405 Jasper Avenue
Edmonton, Alberta
T5J 3N4 Canada
Tel: 780-448-4881
Fax: 780-448-0018
www.htai.org

IAPP (International Association of Privacy Professionals)
Membership organization for privacy professionals, corporations, govern-ment agencies, and nonprofit groups from around the world.
Pease International Tradeport
75 Rochester Avenue
Suite 4
Portsmouth, NH 03801 USA
Tel: +1 603-427-9200
Toll free: 800-266-6501
Fax: +1 603-427-9249
www.privacyassociation.org

ICCBBA (International Council for Commonality in Blood Bank Automation)
Registration and licensing organization for the ISBT 128 global standard for the identification, labeling, and information processing of human blood, cell, tissue, and organ products across international borders and disparate health-care systems.
P.O. Box 11309
San Bernardino, CA 92423-1309
Tel: 909-793-6516
Fax: 909-793-6214
www.iccbba.org

ICE (Institute for Credentialing Excellence)
Developer of standards for certification and certificate programs. Organizations may join at any time whether the organization has any programs accredited by the National Commission for Certifying Agencies (NCCA).
2025 M Street, NW
Suite 800
Washington, DC 20036
Tel: 202-367-1165
Fax: 202-367-2165
www.credentialingexcellence.org

ICN (International Council of Nurses)
A federation of more than 130 national nurses associations representing more than 13 million nurses worldwide.
3, Place Jean Marteau
1201 - Geneva
Switzerland
Tel: +41-22-908-01-00
Fax: +41-22-908-01-01
www.icn.ch

ICOR (International Consortium of Organizational Resilience)
Membership organization for professionals from a wide variety of public and private sectors including international organizations, government, consultant, or vendor with demonstrated experience in organizational resilience.
P.O. Box 1171
Lombard, IL 60148
Tel: 630-705-0910
Toll free: 866-765-8321
www.theicor.org

IDF (Immune Deficiency Foundation)
Patient organization dedicated to improving the diagnosis, treatment, and quality of life of persons with primary immunodeficiency diseases (PI) through advocacy, education, and research.
110 West Road, Suite 300
Towson, MD 21204
Tel: 800-296-4433
www.primaryimmune.org

IEC (International Electrotechnical Commission)
A not-for-profit, nongovernmental organization. Members are national committees and their appointed experts and delegates coming from industry, government bodies, associations, and academia to participate in technical and conformity assessments.
3, rue de Varembé
P.O. Box 131
CH - 1211 Geneva 20 Switzerland
Tel: +41 22 919 02 11
Fax: +41 22 919 03 00
www.iec.ch

IEEE (Institute of Electrical & Electronics Engineers, Inc.)
Membership organization for individuals and students who are contributing or working in a technology or engineering field.
2001 L Street, NW
Suite 700
Washington, DC 20036-4910
Tel: 202-785-0017
Fax: 202-785-0835
www.ieee.org

IEFT (Internet Engineering Task Force)
An open international community of network designers, operators, vendors, and researchers concerned with the evolution of the Internet architecture and the smooth operation of the Internet. Membership is open to any interested individual.
c/o Association Management Solutions, LLC (AMS)
48377 Fremont Boulevard
Suite 117
Fremont, California 94538
Tel: 510-492-4080
Fax: 510-492-4001
www.ietf.org

IHA (Intelligent Health Association)
Nonprofit organization with the mission to raise the level of awareness through educational programs, empower the health community with vendor neutral information, and encourage the adoption and implementation of technology.
www.ihassociation.org

IHE (Integrating the Healthcare Enterprise)
A nonprofit organization that promotes the coordinated use of established standards such as DICOM and HL7 to address specific clinical needs in support of optimal patient care.
820 Jorie Boulevard
Oak Brook, IL 60523-2251 USA
Tel: 630-481-1004
www.ihe.net

IHF (International Hospital Federation)
Global association of healthcare organizations, which includes in particular, but not exclusively, hospital associations and representative bodies, as well as their members and other healthcare related organizations.
P.A. Hôpital de Loëx
Route de Loëx 151
1233 Bernex
Switzerland
Tel: +41 (0) 22 850 94 20
Fax: +41 (0) 22 757 10 16
www.ihf-fih.org

IHI (Institute for Healthcare Improvement)
An independent, not-for-profit organization, serving as a leading innovator, convener, partner and driver of results in health and health care improvement worldwide.
20 University Road
7th Floor
Cambridge, MA 02138
Tel: 617-301-4800
Toll-Free: 866-787-0831
Fax: 617-301-4830
www.ihi.org

IHTSDO (International Health Terminology Standards Development Organization)
Members of IHTSDO can be either an agency of a national government or other bodies (such as corporations or regional government agencies) endorsed by an appropriate national government authority within the country it represents. The IHTSDO welcomes new members.
Vester Farimagsgade 23,
1606 Copenhagen V
Denmark
Tel: +45 (0)203-755-0974
www.ihtsdo.org

IIE (International Institute of Education)
An international education and training organization providing global fellowships and scholarships in applied research and policy analysis.
Midwest Office:
25 E. Washington Street
Suite 1735
Chicago, IL 60602
Tel: 312-346-0026
Fax: 312-346-2574
e-mail: midwest@iie.org
www.iie.org

IIR (Institute for International Research)
Providers of trade conferences and expositions, seminars, training events, and specialized business information and networking experiences in America.
708 3rd Avenue
4th Floor
New York, NY 10017
Toll free: 800-345-8016
Tel: 212-661-3500
Fax: 212-599-2192
www.iirusa.com

IMDMC (Indiana Medical Device Manufacturers Council)
IMDMC serves the interests of its member companies in the delivery of innovative, life-changing technologies to patients by increasing public awareness of the economic and health benefits, providing training and educational opportunities to industry employees and advocating on behalf of the medical device industry at both the state and federal level.
P.O. Box 441385
Indianapolis, IN 46244
Tel: 260-609-2802
www.Imdmc.org

IMIA (International Medical Informatics Association)
Membership is limited to organizations, societies, and corporations interested in promoting informatics in healthcare.
c/o Health On the Net
Chemin du Petit-Bel-Air 2
CH-1225 Chêne-Bourg, Geneva
Switzerland
Tel: +41-22-3727249
www.imia.org

INAHTA (International Network of Agencies for Health Technology Assessment)
An organization of nonprofit making organizations producing health technology assessments (HTA) and linked to regional or national governments.
NAHTA Secretariat
c/o Institute of Health Economics
#1200
10405 Jasper Avenue
Edmonton, Alberta
Canada T5J 3N4
Tel: 780 401 1770
Fax: 780 448 0018
www.inahta.net

INS (International Neuropsychological Society)
Membership organization for persons with a significant proportion of activities devoted to neuropsychology or related fields.
2319 South Foothill Drive
Suite 260
Salt Lake City, Utah 84109
Tel: 801-487-0475
www.the-ins.org

INS (Infusion Nurses Society)
Membership is open to healthcare professionals from all practice settings who are involved in or interested in the specialty practice of infusion therapy.
315 Norwood Park South
Norwood, MA 02062
Tel: 781-440-9408
Fax: 781-440-9409
www.ins1.org

Institute for e-Health Policy
Nonprofit organization providing research and educational opportunities for public- and private-sector stakeholders—two key constituents that make and are most directly impacted by e-health policy decisions.
4300 Wilson Boulevard
Arlington, VA 22203
www.e-healthpolicy.org

INCITS (InterNational Committee for Information Technology Standards)
Membership is open to organizations directly and materially affected by standardization in the field of Information and Communications Technologies (ICT), encompassing storage, processing, transfer, display, management, organization, and retrieval of information.
1101 K Street, NW
Suite 610
Washington, DC 20005
Tel: 202-737-8888
www.incits.org

IOM (Institute of Medicine of the National Academies)
An honorific organization. The full membership annually elects up to 70 new members and 10 foreign associates for their excellence and professional achievement in a field relevant to the IOM's mission. These individuals represent the healthcare professions as well as the natural, social, and behavioral sciences.
500 Fifth Street, NW
Washington, DC 20001
Tel: 202-334-2352
www.iom.edu

IOMSN (International Organization for Multiple Sclerosis Nurses)
Membership organization for licensed nursing professional whose professional interest and activities are devoted to the care of patients with multiple sclerosis either through direct practice, research, or education who reside throughout the world.
359 Main Street
Suite A
Hackensack, NJ 07601
Tel: 201-487-1050
Fax: 862-771-7275
www.iomsn.org

ISNCC (International Society of Nurses in Cancer Care)
Membership is open to cancer nursing associations, institutions, and individual cancer nursing professionals worldwide.
570 West 7th Avenue
Suite 400
Vancouver, British Columbia
V5Z 1B3 Canada
Tel: +1-604-630-5516
Fax: +1-604-874-4378
www.isncc.org

ISO (International Organization for Standardization)
A network of national standards bodies that develop and publish International Standards. The national standards bodies represent ISO in their country.
International Organization for Standardization
ISO Central Secretariat
BIBC II
Chemin de Blandonnet 8
CP 401
1214 Vernier, Geneva Switzerland
Tel: +41 22 749 01 11
www.iso.org

ISPN (International Society of Psychiatric-Mental Health Nurses)
An international membership organization for all advanced practice psychiatric nurses.
2424 American Lane
Madison, WI 53704-3102
Tel: 608-443-2463
Toll free: 866-330-7227
Fax: 608-443-2474 or 2478
www.ispn-psych.org

ISQUA (International Society for Quality in Health Care)
Membership organization with individual, institutional, and affiliated categories for those engaged in quality improvement.
Joyce House
8-11 Lombard Street East
Dublin D02 Y729
Ireland
Tel: +353 (0)1 6706750
Fax: +353 (0)1 671039
www.isqua.org

ISSA (Information Systems Security Association)
Volunteer organization for information security professionals and practitioners.
12100 Sunset Hills Road, Suite 130
Reston, VA 20190
Tel: 703-234-4077
Toll free: 866-349-5818
Fax: 703-435-4390
www.issa.org

ITAC (Information Technology Association of Canada)

A membership organization of for-profit companies with a presence in Canada, for whom the provision of information technology products or services is a significant component of revenue and of strategic importance, or one which increases the efficiency of electronic markets by facilitating the meeting and interaction of buyers and sellers over the Internet.

5090 Explorer Drive
Suite 801
Mississauga, Ontario
L4W 4T9 Canada
Tel: 905-602-8345
www.itac.ca

ITIF (Information Technology and Innovation Foundation)

An independent, nonpartisan research and educational institute focusing on the intersection of technological innovation and public policy.

1101 K Street NW, Suite 610
Washington, DC 20005
Tel: 202-449-1351
www.Itif.org

ITU (International Telecommunication Union)

Membership organization representing a cross-section of the global Information and Communication Technologies (ICT) sector along with leading research and development (R&D) institutions and academia. ITU is the United Nations specialized agency for Information and Communication Technologies (ICT).

Place des Nations
1211 Geneva 20
Switzerland
Tel: +41 22 730 5111
Fax: +41 22 733 72 56
www.itu.int

JCAHO (The Joint Commission on Accreditation of Healthcare Organizations)
See **Joint Commission**. (JCAHO is now The Joint Commission.)

JCR (Joint Commission Resources)

Publication subsidiary of The Joint Commission offering products, publications, educational conferences, consulting, and distance learning services.

1515 W. 22nd Street
Suite 1300W
Oak Brook, IL 60523
Tel: 630-268-7400
International Tel: +1-770-238-0454
www.jcrinc.com

The Joint Commission
Accreditation organization to support performance improvement in health-care organizations.
Tel: 630-792-5800
www.jointcommission.org

JPHIT (Joint Public Health Informatics Taskforce)
Coalition of nine national associations that help U.S. governmental agencies build modern information systems across a spectrum of public health programs.
www.jphit.org

Kantara Initiative
Organization providing strategic vision and real world innovation for the digital identity transformation. Developing initiatives including: Identity Relationship Management, User Managed Access, Identities of Things, and Minimum Viable Consent Receipt, Kantara Initiative connects a global, open, and transparent leadership community.
401 Edgewater Place
Wakefield, MA 01880
www.kantarainitiative.org

Leapfrog Group
Voluntary program aimed at mobilizing employer purchasing power to alert America's health industry that big leaps in healthcare safety, quality, and customer value will be recognized and rewarded.
1660 L Street, NW
Suite 308
Washington, DC 20036
Tel: 202-292-6713
Fax: 202-292-6813
www.leapfroggroup.org

LOINC (Logical Observation Identifiers Names and Codes)
LOINC is a database and universal standard for identifying medical laboratory observations developed and maintained by the Regenstrief Institute, an international nonprofit medical research organization, associated with Indiana University. The scope of the LOINC effort includes laboratory and other clinical observations.
LOINC c/o Regenstrief Center for Biomedical Informatics
410 W. 10th Street
Suite 2000
Indianapolis, IN 46202-3012
www.loinc.org

MATRC (Mid-Atlantic Telehealth Resource Center)
Telehealth Resource Center (TRC) providing technical assistance to Delaware, Washington, D.C., Kentucky, Maryland, New Jersey (Central & South), North Carolina, Pennsylvania, Virginia, and West Virginia to advance the adoption and utilization of telehealth. TRCs are funded by the U.S. Department of Health and Human Service's Health Resources and Services Administration (HRSA) Office for the Advancement of Telehealth, which is part of the Office of Rural Health Policy. Nationally there are 12 regional and 2 national TRCs.
P.O. Box 800711
Charlottesville, VA 22908
www.matrc.org

MDISS (Medical Device Innovation, Safety and Security Consortium)
Nonprofit professional organization committed to advancing quality healthcare with a focus on the safety and security of medical devices. Serves providers, payers, manufacturers, universities, government agencies, technology companies, individuals, patients, patient advocates, and associations.
3620 Oxford Avenue
Bronx, NY 10463
www.mdiss.org

MGMA (Medical Group Management Association)
Membership organization for individuals, teaching faculty, students, and uniformed services interested in practice management.
104 Inverness Terrace East
Englewood, CO 80112-5306
Tel: 303-799-1111
Toll free: 877-275-6462
www.mgma.com

MITA (Medical Imaging and Technology Alliance)
The leading organization and collective voice of medical imaging equipment manufacturers, innovators, and product developers, a division of the National Electrical Manufacturers Association (NEMA).
1300 North 17th Street
Suite 900
Arlington, VA 22209
Tel: 703-841-3200
Fax: 703-841-3392
www.medicalimaging.org

MLA (Medical Library Association)
Membership organization for individuals with an interest in the health sciences information field.
65 East Wacker Place
Suite 1900
Chicago, IL 60601-7246
Tel: 312-419-9094
Fax: 312-419-8950
www.mlanet.org

MS-HUG (Microsoft Healthcare Users Group)
Membership organization for members in the global community with healthcare IT expertise.
www.mshug.org

MSIG (MEMS & Sensors Industry Group)
Nonprofit organization linking the MEMS and sensors supply chain to diverse markets, MSIG helps companies in and around the MEMS and sensors industry to make meaningful business connections and informed decisions.
1620 Murray Avenue
Pittsburgh, PA 15217
Tel: 412-390-1644
www.memsindustrygroup.org

MTPPI (Medical Technology & Practice Patterns Institute)
A nonprofit organization conducting research on the clinical and economic implications of healthcare technologies. MTPPI research is directed toward the formulation and implementation of local and national healthcare policies.
5272 River Road
Suite 500
Bethesda, MD 20816
Tel: 301-652-4005
Fax: 301-652-8335
www.mtppi.org

NACCHO (National Association of County and City Health Officials)
Organization dedicated to serving every local health department in the nation. NACCHO serves over 13,000 individual members serving in about 1500 local health departments and is the leader in providing cutting-edge, skill-building, professional resources and programs, seeking health equity, and supporting effective local public health practice and systems.
1100 17th Street, NW, Seventh Floor
Washington, DC 20036
Tel: 202-783-5550
Fax: 202-783-1583
www.naccho.org/

NACHC (National Association of Community Health Center)
Serves as the national healthcare advocacy organization for America's medically underserved and uninsured and the community health centers that serve as their healthcare home.
7501 Wisconsin Ave, Suite 1100W
Bethesda, MD 20814
Tel: 301-347-0400
www.nachc.org/

NAEMT (National Association of Emergency Medical Technicians)
National association representing the professional interests of all emergency and mobile healthcare practitioners. NAEMT members work in all sectors of EMS, including government agencies, fire departments, hospital-based ambulance services, private companies, industrial and special operations settings, and in the military.
P.O. Box 1400
Clinton, MS 39060
Tel: 601-924-7744
www.naemt.org

NAHC (National Association for Home Care & Hospice)
A membership organization for agencies delivering hands-on care to patients at home, corporate (multi-entity) providers delivering care at home, businesses that provide products or services to home care agencies, state home care and hospice associations that are organized into the National Association for Home Care's Forum of State Associations, and nonprofit groups, universities, libraries, schools of nursing, and international groups with an interest in home care and/or hospice.
228 Seventh Street, SE
Washington, DC 20003
Tel: 202-547-7424
Fax: 202-547-3540
www.nahc.org

NAHDO (National Association of Health Data Organizations)
A national, not-for-profit membership organization dedicated to improving healthcare through the collection, analysis, dissemination, public availability, and use of health data.
124 South 400 East
Suite 220
Salt Lake City, UT 84111-5312
Tel: 801-532-2299
Fax: 801-532-2228
www.nahdo.org

NAHQ (National Association for Healthcare Quality)
Membership organization open to anyone involved in the healthcare quality field and any healthcare organization with four or more individuals is eligible for membership.
8735 W. Higgins Road
Suite 300
Chicago, IL 60631
Tel: 847-375-4720
Toll free: 800-966-9392
Fax: 847-375-6320
www.nahq.org

NAHSE (National Association of Health Services Executives)
Nonprofit association of Black healthcare executives for the purpose of promoting the advancement and development of Black healthcare leaders, and elevating the quality of healthcare services rendered to minority and underserved communities.
1050 Connecticut Avenue NW
Washington, DC 20036
Tel: 202-772-1030
www.nahse.org

NANDA International
Membership organization open to those who meet their country's requirements for professional nursing licensure and to matriculating undergraduate students.
P.O. Box 157
Kaukauna, WI 54130-0157
www.nanda.org

NAPHSIS (National Association for Public Health Statistics and Information Systems)
Membership association of state vital records and public health statistics offices in the United States.
962 Wayne Avenue
Suite 701
Silver Spring, MD 20910
Tel: 301-563-6001
e-mail: hq@naphsis.org
www.naphsis.org

NASCIO (National Association of State Chief Information Officers)
Membership organization of state chief information and information technology executives from the states, territories, and the District of Columbia. Leading advocate for technology policy at all levels of government. Other public sector and nonprofit organizations may join.
c/o AMR Management Services
201 East Main Street
Suite 1405
Lexington, KY 40507
Tel: 859-514-9156
www.nascio.org

NASEMSO (National Association of State EMS Officials)
Membership organization for individuals in state Emergency Medical Service (EMS) office, federal agencies, and individuals with an interest in emergency care, education, professional standards, trauma systems, and data systems.
201 Park Washington Court
Falls Church, VA 22046-4527
Tel: 703-538-1799
Fax: 703-241-5603
www.nasemso.org

NASN (National Association of School Nurses)
Membership organization for registered professional nurses having as their primary assignment the administration, education, or the provision of school health services.
1100 Wayne Avenue
Suite 925
Silver Spring, MD 20910
Tel: 240-821-1130
Fax: 301-585-1791
www.nasn.org

NASPA (National Alliance of State Pharmacy Associations)
Association dedicated to enhancing the success of state pharmacy associations in their efforts to advance the profession of pharmacy. NASPA's membership is comprised of state pharmacy associations and over 70 other stakeholder organizations. NASPA promotes leadership, sharing, learning, and policy exchange among its members and pharmacy leaders nationwide.
2530 Professional Road, Suite 202
Richmond, VA 23235
Tel: 804-285-4431
www.Naspa.us

NATE (National Association for Trusted Exchange)
Nonprofit association bringing the expertise of its membership and other stakeholders together to find common solutions that optimize the appropriate exchange of health information for greater gains in adoption and outcomes.
www.nate-trust.org

NBDHMT (National Board of Diving & Hyperbaric Medical Technology)
Certification organization for hyperbaric technologists, nurses, and diving medical technicians to ensure that the fields of hyperbaric medicine, hyperbaric chamber operation, and diving medicine are filled with highly qualified personnel.
9 Medical Park
Suite 330
Columbia, SC 29203
Tel: 803-434-7802
Fax: 866-451-7231
www.nbdhmt.org

NCCA (National Commission for Certifying Agencies)
See **Institute for Credentialing Excellence**. (NCCA merged with NOCA.)

NCCLS (National Committee for Clinical Laboratory Standards)
See **CLSI**.

NCEMI (National Center for Emergency Medicine Informatics)
Website designed for qualified physicians and other medical professionals.
www.ncemi.org

NCHN (National Cooperative of Health Networks)
National association of health networks and strategic partners.
400 S Main Street
Hardinsburg, KY 40143
www.nchn.org

NCHS (National Center for Health Statistics)
Centers for Disease Control and Prevention (CDC) center for statistical information.
1600 Clifton Road
Atlanta, GA 30333
Toll free: 800-232-4636
www.cdc.gov/nchs

NCPDP (National Council for Prescription Drug Program)
Membership organization producers/providers, payers/processors, and general vendors interested in ANSI-accredited standards, and guidance for promoting information exchanges related to medications, supplies, and services within the healthcare system.
9240 East Raintree Drive
Scottsdale, AZ 85260-7518
Tel: 480-477-1000
Fax: 480-767-1042
www.ncpdp.org

NCQA (National Committee for Quality Assurance)
Certification organization to improve the quality of healthcare.
1100 13th Street, NW
Suite 1000
Washington, DC 20005
Tel: 202-955-3500
Fax: 202-955-3599
www.ncqa.org

NCSA (National Cyber Security Alliance)
Organization building strong public/private partnerships to create and implement broad-reaching education and awareness efforts to empower users at home, work, and school with the information they need to keep themselves, their organizations, their systems, and their sensitive information safe and secure online and encourage a culture of cybersecurity.
www.staysafeonline.org

NCSBN (National Council of State Boards of Nursing)
Nursing examination organization to qualify and examine nurses who have successfully completed an accredited program and meet examination requirements for the National Council Licensure Examination for Registered Nurses (NCLEX-RN) and the National Council Licensure Examination for Practical Nurses (NCLEX-PN) that are used by boards of nursing to assist in making state licensure decisions.
111 East Wacker Drive
Suite 2900
Chicago, IL 60601-4277
Tel: 312-525-3600
Fax: 312-279-1032
International Tel: 001 1 312 525 3600
www.ncsbn.org

NCSL (National Convention of State Legislatures)
The strength of NCSL is bipartisanship and commitment to serving both Republicans and Democrats. It is recognized in their comprehensive, unbiased research. NCSL serves both legislators and staff.
444 North Capitol Street, N.W., Suite 515
Washington, DC 20001
Tel: 202-624-5400
Fax: 202-737-1069
www.ncsl.org

NCVHS (National Committee on Vital and Health Statistics)
Established by Congress to serve as an advisory body to the Department of Health and Human Services on health data, statistics, and national health information policy.
www.ncvhs.hhs.gov

NeHC (National eHealth Collaborative)
See **HIMSS**. (HIMSS merged with NeHC as of December 23, 2013.)

NEHI (Network for Excellence in Health Innovation)
Dedicated to identifying innovations that improve the quality and lower the costs of healthcare. NEHI's network of nearly 100 healthcare organizations is a hotbed for consensus solutions that cut across traditional silos and drive policy change.
One Broadway
Cambridge, MA 02142
Tel: 617-225-0857
www.NEHI.net

NEHTA (National E-Health Transition Authority)
Established by the Australian State and Territory governments to develop better ways of electronically collecting and securely exchanging health information.
Level 25, 56 Pitt Street
Sydney NSW 2000
Australia
Tel: (02) 8298 2600
Fax: (02) 8298 2666
www.nehta.gov.au

NHCAA (National Health Care Anti-Fraud Association)
Member organization open to private for-profit and not-for-profit healthcare reimbursement organizations (health insurers, managed care organizations, self-insured/self-administered organizations, third-party administrators, Medicare Program Safeguard Contractors [PSC]) interested in fighting against healthcare fraud.
1200 L Street, NW
Suite 600
Washington, DC 20005
Tel: 202-659-5955
Fax: 202-785-6764
www.nhcaa.org

NHIC (National Health Information Center)
A health information referral service sponsored by the Office of Disease Prevention and Health Promotion, Office of Public Health and Science, Office of the Secretary, and U.S. Department of Health and Human Services (HHS). NHIC links people to organizations that provide reliable health information.
U.S. Department of Health and Human Services
1101 Wootton Parkway, Suite LL100
Rockville, MD 20852
Fax: 240-453-8282
www.health.gov/nhic

NHIT (National Health IT Collaborative for the Underserved)
Nonprofit organization working to ensure that underserved populations are not left behind as health information technologies are developed and employed.
1629 K Street
Washington, DC 20006
www.nhitunderserved.org

NHLBI (National Heart, Lung, and Blood Institute)
The Institute, part of the National Institutes of Health, promotes the prevention and treatment of diseases of the heart, lungs, and blood.
Building 31, Room 5A52
31 Center Drive MSC 2486
Bethesda, MD 20892
Tel: 301-592-8573
www.nhlbi.nih.gov

NIH (National Institutes of Health)
A part of the U.S. Department of Health & Human Services, NIH is the nation's medical research agency.
9000 Rockville Pike
Bethesda, MD 20892
www.nih.gov

NIHR (National Institute of Health Research)
An independent research center producing information about the effectiveness, costs, and broader impact of healthcare treatments and tests for those who plan, provide, or receive care in the National Health Service, U.K.
National Institute for Health Research
Room 132
Richmond House
79 Whitehall
London SW1A 2NS
www.nihr.ac.uk

NINR (National Institute of Nursing Research)
Institute, part of the National Institutes of Health, supports and conducts nursing and clinical research and research training on health and illness across the lifespan.
31 Center Drive
Room 5B10
Bethesda, MD 20892-2178
Tel: 301-496-0207
Fax: 301-480-8845
www.ninr.nih.gov

NIST (National Institute of Standards and Technology)
Federal agency responsible for advancing measurement science, standards, and technology to improve quality of life. Manages the Malcolm Baldrige National Quality Award.
100 Bureau Drive
Stop 1070
Gaithersburg, MD 20899-1070
Tel: 301-975-6478
TTY: 800-877-8339
www.nist.gov

NITRD (The Networking and Information Technology Research and Development Program)
National program that provides a framework in which many federal agencies coordinate networking and information technology (IT) research and development (R&D) efforts. Operates under the aegis of the NITRD Subcommittee of the National Science and Technology Council's (NSTC) Committee on Technology.
4201 Wilson Boulevard
Suite II-405 ᐟ
Arlington, VA 22230
Tel: 703-292-4873
Fax: 703-292-9097
www.nitrd.gov

NKCHS (Norwegian Knowledge Centre for Health Services)
See **NOKC**. (NKCHS is now NOKC.)

NKF (National Kidney Foundation)
A major health organization. NKF seeks to prevent kidney and urinary tract diseases, improve the health and well-being of individuals and families affected by these diseases, and increase the availability of all organs for transplantation.
30 East 33rd Street
New York, NY 10016
Toll free: 800-622-9010
www.kidney.org

NLM (National Library of Medicine)
NLM is the world's largest medical library. The library collects materials in all areas of biomedicine and healthcare, as well as works on biomedical aspects of technology, the humanities, and the physical, life, and social sciences. The collections stand at more than 9 million items—books, journals, technical reports, manuscripts, microfilms, photographs, and images. NLM is a national resource for all U.S. health science libraries through a National Network of Libraries of Medicine®.
8600 Rockville Pike
Bethesda, MD 20894
Tel: 301-594-5983
TTD: 800-735-2258
Fax: 301-496-2809
www.nlm.nih.gov

NLN (National League for Nursing)
A membership organization for nurse faculty and leaders in nursing education dedicated to excellence in nursing. Members include nurse educators, healthcare agencies, and interested members of the public.
2600 Virginia Avenue, NW
8th Floor
Washington, DC 20037
Toll free: 800-669-1656
www.nln.org

NOA (Nursing Organizations Alliance)
Membership is open to any nursing organization whose focus is to address current and emerging nursing and healthcare issues. Structural nursing components of a multidisciplinary organization are also welcome.
Tel: 859-514-9157
Fax: 859-514-9166
www.nursing-alliance.org

NOCA (National Organization for Competency Assurance)
See **ICE**. (NOCA is now the Institute for Credentialing Excellence [ICE].)

NOKC (Norwegian Knowledge Centre for Health Services)
Organized under the Norwegian Directorate of Health, product and services include systematic reviews, health economic evaluations, patient and user experience surveys, and other quality measurements to support the development of quality in the health services by summarizing research, promoting the use of research results, measuring the quality of health services, and working to improve patient safety.
Norwegian Institute of Public Health
P.O. Box 4404 Nydalen
0403 Oslo
N-0130 Oslo, Norway
Tel: +47 21 07 70 00
Fax: +47 22 35 36 05
www.kunnskapssenteret.no

NPSF (National Patient Safety Foundation)
Membership association committed to working with all stakeholders to advance patient safety worldwide. NPSF membership programs bring together like-minded individuals and organizations to work together toward the central mission of improving patient safety.
280 Summer Street · 9th Floor
Boston, MA 02210 USA
Tel: (617) 391-9900
Fax: (617) 391-9999
www.npsf.org

NQF (National Quality Forum)
Private sector standard-setting organization whose efforts center on the evaluation and endorsement of standardized performance measurement.
1030 15th Street, NW
Suite 800
Washington, DC 20005
Tel: 202-783-1300
Fax: 202-783-3434
www.qualityforum.org

NRHA (National Rural Health Association)
National nonprofit membership organization with the mission to provide leadership on rural health issues through advocacy, education, and research. NRHA membership consists of a diverse collection of individuals and organizations, all of whom share the common bond of an interest in rural health.
4501 College Boulevard
Leawood, KS 66211
Tel: 816-756-3140
www.ruralhealthweb.org

NRHRC (National Rural Health Resource Center)
Nonprofit organization that provides technical assistance, information, tools, and resources for the improvement of rural healthcare. It serves as a national rural health knowledge center and strives to build state and local capacity.
525 S. Lake Avenue
Duluth, MN 55802
Tel: 800-997-6685
www.ruralcenter.org

NSF (National Science Foundation)
An independent federal agency funding approximately 20 percent of all federally supported basic research conducted by America's colleges and universities. In many fields, such as mathematics, computer science, and the social sciences, NSF is the major source of federal backing.
4201 Wilson Boulevard
Arlington, VA 22230
Tel: 703-292-5111
FIRS: 800-877-8339
TDD: 800-281-8749
www.nsf.gov

NUBC (National Uniform Billing Committee)
Membership includes national provider and payer organizations. Recently, the NUBC increased its membership to include the public health sector as well as the electronic standard development organization. NUBC maintains the integrity of the UB-92 data set.
c/o American Hospital Association
155 North Wacker Drive, Suite 400
Chicago, IL 60606
Tel: 312-422-3000
Fax: 312-422-4500
www.nubc.org

NUCC (National Uniform Claim Committee)
A voluntary organization comprised of key parties affected by healthcare electronic data interchange (EDI), generally payers and providers. Criteria for membership include a national scope and representation of a unique constituency affected by healthcare EDI, with an emphasis on maintaining or enhancing the provider/payer balance.
American Medical Association
AMA Plaza
330 North Wabash Avenue, Suite 39300
Chicago, IL 60611-5885
Tel: 800-626-3211
Email: nuccinfo@nucc.org
www.nucc.org

NZHTA (New Zealand Health Technology Assessment)
Clearinghouse for health outcomes and health technology assessment, operating from 1997 to June 2007. Publications can still be accessed.
University of Otago, Christchurch
2 Riccarton Avenue
Christchurch 8140
New Zealand
Tel: +64 3 364 0530
Fax: +64 3 364 0525
www.otago.ac.nz/christchurch/research/nzhta

OASIS (Advancing Open Standards for the Information Society)
Open membership to ensure that all those affected by open standards have a voice in their creation.
35 Corporate Drive Suite 150
Burlington, MA 01803-4238
Tel: 781-425-5073
Fax: 781-425-5072
www.oasis-open.org

OMG (Object Management Group)

An international, open membership, not-for-profit computer industry consortium of government agencies, small and large information technology users, vendors, and research institutions. Any organization may join OMG and participate in the standards-setting process. OMG Task Forces develop enterprise integration standards for a wide range of technologies.

109 Highland Avenue
Needham, MA 02494
Tel: 781-444 0404
Fax: 781-444-0320
www.omg.org

ONC (Office of the National Coordinator for Health Information Technology)

The Office of the National Coordinator for Health Information Technology is the principal federal entity charged with coordination of nationwide efforts to implement and use the most advanced health information technology and the electronic exchange of health information. ONC is organizationally located within the Office of the Secretary for the U.S. Department of Health & Human Services.

U.S. Department of Health and Human Services
330 C Street SW
Floor 7
Washington, DC 20024
Tel: 202-690-7151
Fax: 202-690-6079
e-mail: onc.request@hhs.gov
www.healthit.gov

ONS (Oncology Nursing Society)

A professional membership organization for registered nurses and other healthcare providers dedicated to excellence in patient care, education, research, and administration in oncology nursing.

125 Enterprise Drive
Pittsburgh, PA 15275
Tel: 412-859-6100
Toll free: 866-257-4ONS
Fax: 412-859-6162
Toll free Fax: 877-369-5497
www.ons.org

OSHA (Occupational Safety & Health Administration)
Part of the U.S. Department of Labor with responsibility to assure the safety
and health of America's workers by setting and enforcing standards; providing training, outreach, and education; establishing partnerships; and encouraging continual improvement in workplace safety and health.
200 Constitution Avenue, NW
Washington, DC 20210
Toll free: 800-321-6742
TTY: 877-889-5627
www.osha.gov

Patient Safety Movement
Nonprofit organization working to confront the large-scale problem of more
than 200,000 preventable patient deaths in U.S. hospitals each year by providing actionable ideas and innovations that can transform the process of
care, dramatically improve patient safety, and help eliminate patient preventable deaths.
www.patientsafetymovement.org

PCHA (Personal Connected Health Alliance)
A collaboration between Continua, mHealth Summit, and HIMSS, focused
on engaging consumers with their health via personalized health solutions
designed for user-friendly connectivity (interoperability) that meet their lifestyle needs.
www.pchalliance.org

PCORI (Patient-Centered Outcomes Research Institute)
An independent nonprofit, nongovernmental organization located in
Washington, DC, authorized by Congress in 2010, focused on improving
the quality and relevance of evidence available to help patients, caregivers,
clinicians, employers, insurers, and policy makers make informed health
decisions.
1828 L Street, NW, Suite 900
Washington, DC 20036
Tel: (202) 827-7700
Fax: (202) 355-9558
www.pcori.org

PCPCC (Patient-Centered Primary Care Collaborative)
Organization dedicated to advancing primary care and the patient-centered medical home (PCMH) though activities to ensure innovations in care delivery, payment reform, benefit design, and patient engagement. General public membership is free of charge.
601 Thirteenth Street, NW
Suite 430 North
Washington, DC 20005
Tel: 202-417-2081
Fax: 202-417-2082
www.pcpcc.net

PEHRC (Physicians' EHR Coalition)
Coalition assisting physicians—particularly those in small- and medium-sized ambulatory care medical practice—acquire and use affordable, standards-based electronic health records (EHRs) and other health IT to improve quality, enhance patient safety, and increase efficiency.
www.pehrc.org

Perio American Academy of Peridontology
Membership organization of periodontists and general dentists inside the United States and around the world.
737 N. Michigan Avenue
Suite 800
Chicago, IL 60611-6660
Tel: 312-787-5518
Fax: 312-787-3670
www.perio.org

Pharmacy HIT (Health Information Technology) Collaborative
Formed by 9 pharmacy professional associations representing over 250,000 members, the Pharmacy HIT Collaborative's vision and mission is for the U.S. healthcare system to be supported by the integration of pharmacists for the provision of quality patient care.
www.pharmacyhit.org

PHDSC (Public Health Data Standards Consortium)
A nonprofit membership-based organization representing stakeholders including federal, state, and local health agencies; professional associations; academia; public and private sector organizations; international members; and individuals with an interest in health information technology and population health.
111 South Calvert Street
Suite 2700
Baltimore, MD 21202
Tel: 410-385-5272
Fax: 866-637-6526
www.phdsc.org

PHI (Public Health Institute)
An independent, nonprofit organization that partners with foundations, federal and state agencies, and other nonprofit organizations to support a diverse array of research products and public health interventions.
555 12th Street
10th Floor
Oakland, CA 946075
Tel: 510-285-5500
Fax: 510-285-5501
www.phi.org

PHII (Public Health Informatics Institute)
A program of the Task Force for Global Health at the Centers for Disease Control and Prevention that works to improve health outcomes worldwide by transforming health practitioners' ability to apply information effectively. The Institute works with public health organizations, both domestically and internationally, through a variety of projects funded by government agencies and private foundations.
325 Swanton Way
Decatur, Georgia 30030
Toll free: 866-815-9704
Toll free fax: 800-765-7520
www.phii.org

PMI (Project Management Institute)
Individual membership is open to anyone interested in project management.
14 Campus Boulevard
Newtown Square, PA 19073-3299
Tel: 610-356-4600
Toll free: 855-746-4849
Fax: 610-482-9971
www.pmi.org

RCN (Royal College of Nursing)
Professional nursing body and union for nurses in the United Kingdom (UK).
20 Cavendish Square
London W1G 0RN
United Kingdom
Tel: +020 7409 3333
www.rcn.org.uk

Regenstrief Institute
An internationally recognized informatics and healthcare research organization. It is closely affiliated with the Indiana University School of Medicine, Roudebush VA Medical Center, and Wishard Health Services to improve health through research that enhances the quality and cost-effectiveness of healthcare.
1101 West 10th Street
Indianapolis, IN 46202
Tel: 317-270-9000
Fax: 317-274-9302
www.regenstrief.org

RSNA (Radiological Society of North America)
International physician membership organization of radiologists, medical physicists, and other medical professionals.
820 Jorie Boulevard
Oak Brook, IL 60523-2251
Tel: 630-571-2670
Toll free US and Canada: 1-800-381-6660
Fax: 630-590-7712
www.rsna.org

SBU (Swedish Agency for Health Technology Assessment and Assessment of Social Services)
Mandated by the Swedish government to comprehensively assess healthcare technology from medical, economic, ethical, and social standpoints.
P.O. Box 6183,
SE-102 33 Stockholm, Sweden
S:t Eriksgatan 117
Tel: +46 8 412 32 00
Fax: +46 8 411 32 60
www.sbu.se/en

Scottsdale Institute

Not-for-profit organization facilitating collaboration, education, and networking on information topics including strategy, deployment, adoption, national direction and trends, benchmarking, and benefits realization for executives in health systems who wish to share experiences in information technology management.

Membership Services Office
7767 Elm Creek Boulevard North
Suite 208
Maple Grove, MN 55369
Tel: 763-710-7089
Fax: 763-432-5635
www.scottsdaleinstitute.org

Sequoia Project

Independent advocate for nationwide health information exchange. Rallying the healthcare community to get to the root of health IT interoperability.

8300 Boone Boulevard, Suite 500
Vienna, VA, 22182
Tel: 571.327.3640
Fax: 571.327.3640
www.sequoiaproject.org

SGNA (Society of Gastroenterology Nurses and Associates)

A professional organization of nurses and associates dedicated to the safe and effective practice of gastroenterology and endoscopy nursing. SGNA carries out its mission by advancing the science and practice of gastroenterology and endoscopy nursing through education, research, advocacy, and collaboration, and by promoting the professional development of its members in an atmosphere of mutual support.

330 North Wabash Avenue
Suite 200
Chicago, IL 60611-7621
Tel: 312-321-5165
Toll free: 800-245-7462
Fax: 312-673-6694
www.sgna.org

SHARE for Cures

Nonprofit organization dedicated to empowering you to use your health data to advance medical research and save lives.

www.shareforcures.org

SHIEC (Strategic Health Information Exchange Collaborative)
Organization representing regional, statewide, and community HIEs that occupy a unique position in many key healthcare markets across the county. *www.strategichie.com*

SHS (The Society for Health Systems)
Membership association for productivity and efficiency professionals specializing in industrial engineering, healthcare, ergonomics, and other related professions.
3577 Parkway Lane
Suite 200
Norcross, GA 30092
Tel: 770-449-0460
Toll free: 800-494-0460
Fax: 770-441-3295
www.iienet2.org/SHS

SIIM (The Society for Imaging Informatics in Medicine)
Membership open to anyone with an interest in the vital and growing field of medical imaging informatics and image management.
19440 Golf Vista Plaza
Suite 330
Leesburg, VA 20176-8264
Tel: 703-723-0432
www.siimweb.org

SIMGHOSTS
Nonprofit organization dedicated to supporting individuals and institutions operating medical simulation technology and spaces through hands-on training events, online resources, and professional development.
3870 E Flamingo Road
Las Vegas, NV 89121
Tel: 702-763-3457
www.simghosts.org

SIR (Society of Interventional Radiology)
Membership organization for individuals who have a special interest in interventional radiology inside and outside the United States.
3975 Fair Ridge Drive
Suite 400 North
Fairfax, VA 22033
Tel: 703-691-1805
Toll free: 800-488-7284
Fax: 703-691-1855
www.sirweb.org

SNRS (Southern Nursing Research Society)
Membership organization for registered professional nurses, non-nurses, corporations, and institutions interested in promoting nursing research.
10200 W. 44th Avenue
Suite 304
Wheat Ridge, CO 80033
Tel: 303-327-7548
Toll free: 877-314-SNRS
www.snrs.org

TAANA (The American Association of Nurse Attorneys)
Membership association of nurse attorneys.
3416 Primm Lane
Birmingham, AL 35216
Tel: 205-824-7615,
Toll free: 877-538-2262
Fax: 205-823-2760
www.taana.org

TechAmerica
See **CompTIA**. (TechAmerica merged with CompTIA in 2014.)

TIGER Initiative (Technology Informatics Guiding Education Reform)
An initiative focused on education reform and interprofessional community development to maximize the integration of technology and informatics into seamless practice, education, and research resource development.
33 West Monroe Street
Suite 1700
Chicago, IL 60603-5616
Tel: 312-664-4467
www.himss.org/professional-development/tiger-initiative

TNA (Transplant Nurses' Association)
Membership organization to advance the education of nurses and allied health professionals involved in the transplant process.
P.O. Box M94
Missenden Road
NSW 2050
Australia
Tel: 08 9336 3178
Fax: 08 8204 6959
www.tna.asn.au

UCC (Uniform Code Council)
See **GS1 US**. (UCC is now GS1, 2006.)

UHIN (Utah Health Information Network)
Health Information Network dedicated to reducing healthcare costs and improving care quality and access.
6056 Fashion Square Drive
Murray, UT 84107
www.uhin.org

UNECE (United Nations Economic Commission for Europe)
The United Nations Economic Commission for Europe (UNECE) internships are open to graduate or postgraduate students who have specialized in a field related to UNECE programs of work, namely environment, transport, statistics, sustainable energy, trade, timber and forests, housing and land management, population, economic cooperation and integration, and gender.
Palais des Nations, Office 363
CH - 1211
Geneva 10
Switzerland
Tel: +41 (0) 22 917 12 34
Fax: +41 (0) 22 917 05 05
http://www.unece.org/info/ece-homepage.html

VA (Department of Veterans Affairs); Veterans Health Administration
Comprehensive system of assistance to serve our nation's veterans and their families.
810 Vermont Avenue, NW
Washington, DC 20420
Toll free: 800-827-1000
www.va.gov

VNAA (Visiting Nurse Associations of America)
Membership organization for nonprofit, free-standing home health and/or hospice providers, organizations that provide or promote home healthcare and/or hospice-related services, and individuals who wish to stay connected and advance nonprofit home healthcare and hospice.
2121 Crystal Drive
Suite 750
Arlington, VA 22202
Tel: 571-527-1520
Toll free: 888-866-8773
Fax: 571-527-1521
www.vnaa.org

W3C (World Wide Web Consortium)
An international community where member organizations, a full-time staff, and the public work together to develop Web standards. The W3C mission is to lead the World Wide Web to its full potential by developing protocols and guidelines that ensure the long-term growth of the Web.
W3C/MIT
32 Vassar Street
Room 32-G515
Cambridge, MA 02139 USA
Contact Information for non-US locations on website
www.w3.org

WEDI (Workgroup for Electronic Data Interchange)
Membership organization actively seeking membership of all key parties in healthcare to ensure broad representation from throughout the healthcare community including individuals, providers, health plans, hybrid organizations (formerly mixed provider/health plan), government organizations, standards organizations, vendors, not-for-profit, and affiliates/regional entities.
1984 Isaac Newton Square
Suite 304
Reston, VA 20190
Tel: 202-618-8792
Fax: 202-684-7794
www.wedi.org

WHO (World Health Organization)
The directing and coordinating authority for health within the United Nations system. It is responsible for providing leadership on global health matters, shaping the health research agenda, setting norms and standards, articulating evidence-based policy options, providing technical support to countries, and monitoring and assessing health trends.
Avenue Appia 20
1211 Geneva 27
Switzerland
Tel: +41 22 791 21 11
Fax: +41 22 791 31 11
www.who.int

Appendix B: Healthcare Related Credentials

Certifications, Healthcare and Related Degrees, Professional Fellowships, Honors Designations

I. Certifications

Credential	Full Name	Organization Acronym	Organization Full Name
AACRN	Advanced HIV/AIDS Certified Registered Nurse	HANCB	HIV/AIDS Nursing Certification Board
ACCNS-AG	(Adult-Gerontology) Clinical Nurse Specialist; Wellness through Acute Care	AACN	American Association of Critical-Care Nurses Certification Corporation
ACCNS-N	(Neonatal) Clinical Nurse Specialist; Wellness through Acute Care	AACN	American Association of Critical-Care Nurses Certification Corporation
ACCNS-P	(Pediatric) Clinical Nurse Specialist; Wellness through Acute Care	AACN	American Association of Critical-Care Nurses Certification Corporation
ACHPN	Advanced Certified Hospice and Palliative Nurse	HPCC	Hospice and Palliative Credentialing Center

(Continued)

Credential	Full Name	Organization Acronym	Organization Full Name
ACNP	Acute Care Nurse Practitioner	ANCC	American Nurses Credentialing Center
ACNPC	(Adult) Acute Care Nurse Practitioner	AACN	American Association of Critical-Care Nurses Certification Corporation
ACNPC-AG	(Adult-Gerontology) Acute Care Nurse Practitioner	AACN	American Association of Critical-Care Nurses Certification Corporation
ACNS	Adult Health Clinical Nurse Specialist	ANCC	American Nurses Credentialing Center
ACRN	AIDS Certified Registered Nurse	HANCB	HIV/AIDS Nursing Certification Board
AE-C	Certified Asthma Educator	NAECB	National Asthma Education Certification Board
AFN-BC	Advanced Forensic Nursing	ANCC IAFN	American Nurses Credentialing Center, International Association of Forensic Nurses
AGACNP	Adult-Gerontology Acute Care Nurse Practitioner	ANCC	American Nurses Credentialing Center
AGCNS-BC	Adult Gerontology Clinical Nurse Specialist	ANCC	American Nurses Credentialing Center
AGN-BC	Advanced Genetics Nursing	ANCC	American Nurses Credentialing Center

(*Continued*)

Credential	Full Name	Organization Acronym	Organization Full Name
A-GNP	Adult-Gerontology Primary Care Nurse Practitioner	AANPCP	American Academy of Nurse Practitioners Certification Program
AGPCNP	Adult-Gerontology Primary Care Nurse Practitioner	ANCC	American Nurses Credentialing Center
AHN-BC	AHN-BC—Advanced Holistic Nurse, Board Certified	AHNCC	American Holistic Nurses Credentialing Corporation
ALS	Andrology Laboratory Scientist	ABOR	American Association of Bioanalysts (AAB) Board of Registry
ANP	Adult Nurse Practitioner	ANCC AANPCP	American Nurses Credentialing Center, American Academy of Nurse Practitioners Certification Program
AOCN	Advanced Oncology Certified Nurse	ONCC	Oncology Nursing Certification Corporation
AOCNP	Advanced Oncology Certified Nurse Practitioner	ONCC	Oncology Nursing Certification Corporation
AOCNS	Advanced Oncology Certified Clinical Nurse Specialist	ONCC	Oncology Nursing Certification Corporation
APHN	Advanced Public Health Nurse	ANCC	American Nurses Credentialing Center

(*Continued*)

Credential	Full Name	Organization Acronym	Organization Full Name
APHN-BC	Advanced Practice Holistic Nurse, Board Certified	AHNCC	American Holistic Nurses Credentialing Corporation
APRN	Advanced Practice Registered Nurse	ANCC	American Nurses Credentialing Center
BB	Technologist in Blood Banking	ASCP BOC	American Society for Clinical Pathology Board of Certification
BC	Board Certified	ANCC	American Nurses Credentialing Center
BC-ADM	Board Certified Advanced Diabetes Management	AADE	American Association of Diabetes Educators
BMTCN	Bone and Marrow Transplant Certified Nurse	ONCC	Oncology Nursing Certification Corporation
C	Technologist in Chemistry	ASCP BOC	American Society for Clinical Pathology Board of Certification
CAAMA	Credentialed Member of the American Academy of Medical Administrators	AAMA	American Academy of Medical Administrators
CAHIMS	Certified Associate in Healthcare Information and Management Systems	HIMSS	Healthcare Information and Management Systems Society
CANS	Certified Aesthetic Nurse Specialist	PSNCB	Plastic Surgical Nurses Certification Board

(Continued)

Credential	Full Name	Organization Acronym	Organization Full Name
CAP	Certification and Accreditation Professional	(ISC)^2	International Information Systems Security Certification Consortium
CAPA	Certified Ambulatory Perianesthesia Nurse	ABPANC	American Board of Perianesthesia Nursing Certification
CAPM	Certified Associate in Project Management	PMI	Project Management Institute
CARN	Certified Addictions Registered Nurse Examination	ANCB	Addictions Nursing Certification Board
CARN-AP	Certified Addictions Registered Nurse– Advanced Practice Examination	ANCB	Addictions Nursing Certification Board
CBCN	Certified Breast Care Nurse	ONCC	Oncology Nursing Certification Corporation
CBN	Certified Bariatric Nurse	ASMBS	American Society for Metabolic and Bariatric Surgery
CCA	Certified Coding Associate	AHIMA	American Health Information Management Association
CCC-A	Certificate of Clinical Competence– Audiology	ASHA	American Speech-Language-Hearing Association
CCCN	Certified Continence Care Nurse	WOCNCB	Wound, Ostomy, Continence Nursing Certification Board
CCCN-AP	Certified Continence Care Nurse– Advanced Practice	WOCNCB	Wound, Ostomy, Continence Nursing Certification Board

(Continued)

Credential	Full Name	Organization Acronym	Organization Full Name
CCC-SLP	Certificate of Clinical Competence–Speech-Language Pathology	ASHA	American Speech-Language-Hearing Association
CCCTM	Certified in Care Coordination and Transition Management	MSNCB	Medical-Surgical Nursing Certification Board
CCHT	Certified Clinical Hemodialysis Technician	NNCC	Nephrology Nursing Certification Commission
CCHT-A	Certified Clinical Hemodialysis Technician–Advanced	NNCC	Nephrology Nursing Certification Commission
CCM	Certified Case Manager	CCMC	Commission for Case Manager Certification
CCMHP	Certified Clinical Mental Health Counselor	NBCC	National Board for Certified Counselors
CCNS	Critical Care Nurse Specialist	AACN	American Association of Critical-Care Nurses Certification Corporation
CCRA	Certified Clinical Research Associate	ACRP	Association of Clinical Research Professionals
CCRC	Certified Clinical Research Coordinator	ACRP	Association of Clinical Research Professionals
CCRN	Critical Care Registered Nurse	AACN	American Association of Critical-Care Nurses

(*Continued*)

Credential	Full Name	Organization Acronym	Organization Full Name
CCRN-E	Adult Tele-ICU Acute/ Critical Care Nursing	AACN	American Association of Critical-Care Nurses Certification Corporation
CCRN-K	Acute/Critical Care Knowledge Professional	AACN	American Association of Critical-Care Nurses Certification Corporation
CCRP	Certified Cardiac Rehab Professional	AACVPR	American Association of Cardiovascular and Pulmonary Rehabilitation
CCRP	Certified Clinical Research Professional	SOCRA	Society of Clinical Research Associates
CCS	Certified Coding Specialist	AHIMA	American Health Information Management Association
CCS-P	Certified Coding Specialist— Physician-Based	AHIMA	American Health Information Management Association
CDE	Certified Diabetes Educator	NCBDE	National Certification Board for Diabetes Educators
CDIP	Certified Documentation Improvement Practitioner	AHIMA	American Health Information Management Association
CD-LPN	Certified Dialysis Licensed Practical Nurse	NNCC	Nephrology Nursing Certification Commission
CD-LVN	Certified Dialysis Licensed Vocational Nurse	NNCC	Nephrology Nursing Certification Commission

(*Continued*)

Credential	Full Name	Organization Acronym	Organization Full Name
CDM	Certified Dietary Manager	ANFP	Association of Nutrition and Foodservice Professionals
CDMS	Certified Disability Management Specialist	CDMSC	Certification of Disability Management Specialists Commission
CDN	Certified Dialysis Nurse	NNCC	Nephrology Nursing Certification Commission
C-EFM	Certificate of Added Qualification in Electronic Fetal Monitoring	NCC	National Certification Corporation
CEN	Certified Emergency Nurse	BCEN	Board of Certification for Emergency Nursing
CENP	Certified in Executive Nursing Practice	AONE-CC	American Organization of Nurse Executives Credentialing Center
CERT	Community Emergency Response Team	FEMA	Federal Emergency Management Agency
CFCN	Certified Foot Care Nurse	WOCNCB	Wound, Ostomy, Continence Nursing Certification Board
CFN	Certified Forensic Nurse	ACFEI	American College of Forensic Examiners Institute

(Continued)

Credential	Full Name	Organization Acronym	Organization Full Name
CFPP	Certified Food Protection Professional	ANFP	Association of Nutrition and Foodservice Professionals
CFRN	Certified Flight Registered Nurse (CFRN)	BCEN	Board of Certification for Emergency Nursing
CG	Technologist in Cytogenetics	ASCP BOC, NAACLS	American Society for Clinical Pathology Board of Certification, National Accrediting Agency for Clinical Laboratory Sciences
CGRN	Certified Gastroenterology Registered Nurse	ABCGN	American Board of Certification for Gastroenterology Nurses
CHC	Certified Healthcare Constructor	AHA-CC	American Hospital Association Credentialing Center
CHCIO	Certified Healthcare CIO	CHIME	College of Healthcare Information Management Executives
CHDA	Certified Health Data Analyst	AHIMA	American Health Information Management Association
CHE	Certified Healthcare Executive	ACHE	American College of Healthcare Executives

(Continued)

Credential	Full Name	Organization Acronym	Organization Full Name
CHESP	Certified Healthcare Environmental Services Professional	AHA-CC	American Hospital Association Credentialing Center
CHFM	Certified Healthcare Facility Manager	AHA-CC	American Hospital Association Credentialing Center
CHFN	Certified Heart Failure Nurse	AAHFN-CB	American Association of Heart Failure Nurses Certification Board
CHFN-K	Non-Clinical Certified Heart Failure Nurse	AAHFN-CB	American Association of Heart Failure Nurses Certification Board
CHFP	Certified Healthcare Financial Professional	HFMA	Healthcare Financial Management Association
CHHR	Certified in Healthcare Human Resources	AHA-CC	American Hospital Association Credentialing Center
CHPCA	Certified Hospice and Palliative Care Administrator	HPCC	Hospice and Palliative Credentialing Center
CHPLN	Certified Hospice and Palliative Licensed Nurse	HPCC	Hospice and Palliative Credentialing Center
CHPN	Certified Hospice and Palliative Nurse	HPCC	Hospice and Palliative Credentialing Center
CHPNA	Certified Hospice and Palliative Nursing Assistant	HPCC	Hospice and Palliative Credentialing Center

(*Continued*)

Credential	Full Name	Organization Acronym	Organization Full Name
CHPPN	Certified Hospice and Palliative Pediatric Nurse	HPCC	Hospice and Palliative Credentialing Center
CHPS	Certified in Healthcare Privacy and Security	AHIMA	American Health Information Management Association
CHTS	Certified Healthcare Technology Specialist	AHIMA	American Health Information Management Association
CIC	Certification in Infection Control	CBIC	Certification Board of Infection Control and Epidemiology
CIIP	Certified Imaging Informatics Professional	SIIM	Society for Imaging Informatics in Medicine
CISA	Certified Information Systems Auditor	ISACA	Information Systems Audit and Control Association
CISM	Certified Information Security Manager	ISACA	Information Systems Audit and Control Association
CISSP	Certified Information Systems Security Professional	(ISC)^2	International Information Systems Security Certification Consortium
CJCP	Certified Joint Commission Professional	JC/JCR	Joint Commission/ Joint Commission Resources
CLC	Certified Laboratory Consultant	AMT	American Medical Technologists
CLNC	Certified Legal Nurse Consultant	NACLNC	National Alliance of Certified Legal Nurse Consultants

(Continued)

Credential	Full Name	Organization Acronym	Organization Full Name
CLSSBB	Certified Lean Six Sigma Black Belt	ASQ	American Society for Quality or other certified credentialing body
CLSSGB	Certified Lean Six Sigma Green Belt	ASQ	American Society for Quality or other certified credentialing body
CM	Case Manager	ABOHN	American Board for Occupational Health Nurses
CM	Certified Midwife	AMCB	American Midwifery Certification Board
CMA	Certified Management Accountant	IMA	Institute of Management Accountants
CMAS	Certification of Medical Auditors	CCMA	Council for Certification of Medical Auditors, Inc.
CMAS	Certified Medical Administrative Specialist	AMT	American Medical Technologists
CMC	(Adult) Cardiac Medicine	AACN	American Association of Critical-Care Nurses Certification Corporation
CMCN	Certification in Managed Care Nursing	ABMCN	American Board of Managed Care Nursing
CMLA	Medical Laboratory Assistant	AMT	American Medical Technologists
CMRP	Certified Materials and Resource Professional	AHA-CC	American Hospital Association Credentialing Center

(*Continued*)

Credential	Full Name	Organization Acronym	Organization Full Name
CMSRN	Certified Medical-Surgical Registered Nurse	AMSN MSNCB	Academy of Medical-Surgical Nurses, Medical-Surgical Nursing Certification Board
CNE	Certified Nurse Educator	NLN	National League for Nursing
CNL	Clinical Nurse Leader	CNC	Commission on Nurse Certification
CNLCP	Certified Nurse Life Care Planner	CNLCP	Certified Nurse Life Care Planner Certification Board
CNM	Certified Nurse Midwife	AMCB	American Midwifery Certification Board
CNML	Certified Nurse Manager and Leader	AONE/AACN	American Organization of Nurse Executives Credentialing Center/American Association of Critical-Care Nurses Certification Corporation
CNMT	Certified Nuclear Medicine Technologist	NMTCB	Nuclear Medicine Technology Certification Board
CNN	Certified Nephrology Nurse	NNCC	Nephrology Nursing Certification Commission
CNN-NP	Certified Nephrology Nurse–Nurse Practitioner	NNCC	Nephrology Nursing Certification Commission
CNOR	Certified Nurse, Operating Room	CCI	Competency and Credentialing Institute

(Continued)

Credential	Full Name	Organization Acronym	Organization Full Name
CNOR	Certified in Operating Room Nursing	CCI	Competency and Credentialing Institute of the Association of Perioperative Nurses
C-NPT	Certificate of Added Qualification in Neonatal Pediatric Transport	NCC	National Certification Corporation
CNRN	Certified Neuroscience Registered Nurse	ABNN	American Board of Neuroscience Nursing
CNS	Clinical Nurse Specialist	AACN	American Association of Critical-Care Nurses Certification Corporation
CNS-CP	Certified Perioperative Clinical Nurse Specialist	CCI	Competency and Credentialing Institute
COCN	Certified Ostomy Care Nurse	WOCNCB	Wound, Ostomy, Continence Nursing Certification Board
COCN-AP	Certified Ostomy Care Nurse-Advanced Practice	WOCNCB	Wound, Ostomy, Continence Nursing Certification Board
COHN	Certified Occupational Health Nurse	ABOHN	American Board for Occupational Health Nurses, Inc.
COHN-S	Certified Occupational Health Nurse—Specialist	ABOHN	American Board for Occupational Health Nurses
CORLN	Certified Otorhinolaryngology Nurse	NCBOHN	National Certifying Board for Otorhinolaryngology and Head-Neck Nurses

(*Continued*)

Credential	Full Name	Organization Acronym	Organization Full Name
COTA	Certified Occupational Therapy Assistant	NBCOT	National Board for Certification in Occupational Therapy
CPA	Certified Public Accountant	AICPA	American Institute of Certified Public Accountants
CPAN	Certified Post Anesthesia Nurse	ABPANC	American Board of Perianesthesia Nursing Certification
CPAS	Certified PACS Associate	PARCA	PACS Administrators Registry and Certification Association
CPIA	Certified PACS Interface Analyst	PARCA	PACS Administrators Registry and Certification Association
CPEMS	Certified Professional EMR Specialist	PARCA	PACS Administrators Registry and Certification Association
CHEA	Certified Healthcare Enterprise Architect	PARCA	PACS Administrators Registry and Certification Association
CPC	Certified Professional Coder	AAPC	American Academy of Professional Coders
CPE	Certified Physician Executive	CCMM	Certifying Commission in Medical Management
CPEHR*	Certified Professional in Electronic Health Records	HITC	Health IT Certification

(*Continued*)

Credential	Full Name	Organization Acronym	Organization Full Name
CPEN	Certified Pediatric Emergency Nurse	PNCB BCEN	Pediatric Nurse Certification Board, Board of Certification for Emergency Nursing
CPFT	Certified Pulmonary Function Technologist	NBRC	National Board for Respiratory Care
CPHIE*	Certified Professional in Health Information Exchange	HITC	Health IT Certification
CPHIMS	Certified Professional in Healthcare Information and Management Systems	HIMSS	Healthcare Information and Management Systems Society
CPHIT*	Certified Professional in Health Information Technology	HITC	Health IT Certification
CPHON	Certified Pediatric Hematology Oncology Nurse	ONCC	Oncology Nursing Certification Corporation
CPHQ	Certified Professional in Healthcare Quality	HQCB NAHQ	Healthcare Quality Certification Board, National Association for Healthcare Quality
CPHRM	Certified Professional in Healthcare Risk Management	AHA-CC	American Hospital Association Credentialing Center
CPhT	Certified Pharmacy Technician	PTCB	Pharmacy Technician Certification Board
CPLC	Certified in Perinatal Loss Care	HPCC	Hospice and Palliative Credentialing Center

(Continued)

Credential	Full Name	Organization Acronym	Organization Full Name
CPN	Certified Pediatric Nurse	PNCB	Pediatric Nurse Certification Board
CPNP	Certified Pediatric Nurse Practitioner	PNCB	Pediatric Nurse Certification Board
CPNP-AC	Certified Pediatric Nurse Practitioner– Acute Care	PNCB	Pediatric Nursing Certification Board
CPON	Certified Pediatric Oncology Nurse	ONCC	Oncology Nursing Certification Corporation
CPORA*	Certified Professional in Operating Rules Administration	HITC	Health IT Certification
CPP-AC	Certified Pediatric Nurse Practitioner– Acute Care	PNCB	Pediatric Nursing Certification Board
CPSA	Certified PACS System Analyst	PARCA	PACS Administrators Registry and Certification Association
CPSN	Certified Plastic Surgical Nurse	PSNCB	Plastic Surgical Nursing Certification Board
CRN	Certified Radiology Nurse	RNCB	Radiologic Nursing Certification Board
CRNA	Certified Registered Nurse Anesthetist	AANA	American Association of Nurse Anesthetists
CRNFA	Certified Registered Nurse First Assistant	CCI	Competency and Credentialing Institute of the Association of Perioperative Nurses

(Continued)

Credential	Full Name	Organization Acronym	Organization Full Name
CRNI	Certified Registered Nurse Infusion	INCC	Infusion Nurses Certification Corporation
CRNO	Certification for Registered Nurses of Ophthalmology	NCBORN	National Certifying Board for Ophthalmic Registered Nurses
CRRN	Certified Rehabilitation Registered Nurse	RNCB	Rehabilitation Nursing Certification Board
CRT	Certified Respiratory Therapist	NBRC	National Board for Respiratory Care
CSC	(Adult) Cardiac Surgery	AACN	American Association of Critical-Care Nurses Certification Corporation
CSP	Certified Specialty Pharmacist	SPCB	Specialty Pharmacy Certification Board
CSSD	Board Certified Specialist in Sports Dietetics	CDR	Commission on Dietetic Registration
CSSLP	Certified Secure Software Lifecycle Professional	(ISC)^2	International Information Systems Security Certification Consortium
CSSM	Certified Surgical Services Manager	CCI	Competency and Credentialing Institute
C-SWCM	Certified Social Work Case Manager	NASW	National Association of Social Workers
CT	Cytotechnologist	ASCP BOC	American Society for Clinical Pathology Board of Certification

(Continued)

Credential	Full Name	Organization Acronym	Organization Full Name
CTRN	Certified Transport Registered Nurse	BCEN	Board of Certification for Emergency Nursing
CUA	Urologic Associate	CBUNA	Certification Board for Urologic Nurses and Associates
CUNP	Certified Urologic Nurse Practitioner	CBUNA	Certification Board for Urologic Nurses and Associates
CURN	Certified Urologic Registered Nurse	CBUNA	Certification Board for Urologic Nurses and Associates
CWCA	Certified Wound Care Associate	ABWM	American Board of Wound Management
CWCN	Certified Wound Care Nurse	WOCNCB	Wound, Ostomy, Continence Nursing Certification Board
CWCN-AP	Certified Wound Care Nurse–Advanced Practice	WOCNCB	Wound, Ostomy, Continence Nursing Certification Board
CWOCN	Certified Wound Ostomy Continence Nurse	WOCNCB	Wound, Ostomy, Continence Nursing Certification Board
CWOCN-AP	Certified Wound Ostomy Continence Nurse–Advanced Practice	WOCNCB	Wound, Ostomy, Continence Nursing Certification Board
CWON	Certified Wound Ostomy Nurse	WOCNCB	Wound, Ostomy, Continence Nursing Certification Board
CWS	Certified Wound Specialist	ABWM	American Board of Wound Management
DCC	Diplomate of Comprehensive Care	ABCC	American Board of Comprehensive Care

(Continued)

Credential	Full Name	Organization Acronym	Organization Full Name
DCNP	Dermatology Certified Nurse Practitioner	DNCB	Dermatology Nurse Certification Board
DLM	Diplomat in Laboratory Management	ASCP BOC	American Society for Clinical Pathology Board of Certification
DMS	Diagnostic Molecular Scientist	NAACLS	National Accrediting Agency for Clinical Laboratory Sciences
DNC	Dermatology Nurse Certified	DNCB	Dermatology Nurse Certification Board
DPT	Donor Phlebotomy Technician	ASCP BOC	American Society for Clinical Pathology Board of Certification
DTR	Dietetic Technician, Registered	CDR	Commission on Dietetic Registration
DWC	Diabetic Wound Certified	NAWCO	National Alliance of Wound Care and Ostomy
ELS	Embryology Laboratory Scientist	ABOR	American Association of Bioanalysts (AAB) Board of Registry
ENP-BC	Emergency Nurse Practitioner	ANCC	American Nurses Credentialing Center
FACHE	Fellow of the American College of Healthcare Executives	ACHE	American College of Healthcare Executives
FNP	Family Nurse Practitioner	ANCC AANPCP	American Nurses Credentialing Center, American Academy of Nurse Practitioners Certification Program

(Continued)

Credential	Full Name	Organization Acronym	Organization Full Name
GCNS	Gerontological Nurse Practitioner	ANCC	American Nurses Credentialing Center
GCPP	General Credential Pain Practitioner	AAPM	American Academy of Pain Management
GNP	Gerontological Clinical Nurse Specialist	ANCC	American Nurses Credentialing Center
H	Technologist in Hematology	ASCP BOC	American Society for Clinical Pathology Board of Certification
HCISPP	Healthcare Certified Information Security Privacy Practitioner	(ICS)²	International Information Systems Security Certification Consortium, Inc.
HCQM	Health Care Quality Management	ABQAURP	American Board of Quality Assurance and Utilization Review Physicians
HHCNS-BC	Home Health Clinical Nurse Specialist	ANCC	American Nurses Credentialing Center
HNB-BC	Holistic Baccalaureate Nurse, Board Certified	AHNCC	American Holistic Nurses Credentialing Corporation
HN-BC	Holistic Nurse–Board Certified	AHNCC	American Holistic Nurses Credentialing Corporation
HT	Histotechnician	ASCP BOC NAACLS	American Society for Clinical Pathology Board of Certification, National Accrediting Agency for Clinical Laboratory Sciences

(Continued)

Credential	Full Name	Organization Acronym	Organization Full Name
HTL	Histotechnologist	ASCP BOC NAACLS	American Society for Clinical Pathology Board of Certification, National Accrediting Agency for Clinical Laboratory Sciences
HWNC-BC	Health and Wellness Nurse Coach, Board Certified	AHNCC	American Holistic Nurses Credentialing Corporation
IIP	Imaging Informatics Professional	SIIM	Society for Imaging Informatics in Medicine
INPT-BC	Women's Health Care Nurse Practitioner	NCC	National Certification Corporation
ISSAP	Information Systems Security Architecture Professional	(ISC)^2	International Information Systems Security Certification Consortium
ISSEP	Information Systems Security Engineering Professional	(ISC)^2	International Information Systems Security Certification Consortium
ISSMP	Information Systems Security Management Professional	(ISC)^2	International Information Systems Security Certification Consortium
LLE	Lymphedema Lower Extremity Certification	NAWCO	National Alliance of Wound Care and Ostomy
LLSA/MOC	Lifelong Learning and Self-Assessment/ Maintenance of Certification	ABPM	American Board of Preventive Medicine

(Continued)

Credential	Full Name	Organization Acronym	Organization Full Name
LNCC	Legal Nurse Consultant Certified	AALNC	American Association of Legal Nurse Consultants
M	Technologist in Microbiology	ASCP BOC	American Society for Clinical Pathology Board of Certification
MCDBA	Microsoft Certified Database Administrator		Microsoft
MCITP	Microsoft Certified IT Professional		Microsoft
MCP	Microsoft Certified Professional		Microsoft
MCPD	Microsoft Certified Professional Developer		Microsoft
MCSA	Microsoft Certified Solutions Associate		Microsoft
MCSD	Microsoft Certified Solutions Developer		Microsoft
MCSE	Microsoft Certified Systems Engineer		Microsoft
MCSM	Microsoft Certified Solutions Master		Microsoft
MCTS	Microsoft Certified Technology Specialist		Microsoft
MDxT	Molecular Diagnostics Technologist	ABOR	American Association of Bioanalysts (AAB) Board of Registry

(Continued)

Credential	Full Name	Organization Acronym	Organization Full Name
MLS	Medical Laboratory Scientist	ASCP BOC, NAACLS	American Society for Clinical Pathology Board of Certification, National Accrediting Agency for Clinical Laboratory Sciences
MLT	Medical Laboratory Technician	ABOR	American Association of Bioanalysts (AAB) Board of Registry
MLT	Medical Laboratory Technologist	ASCP BOC, AMT, NAACLS	American Society for Clinical Pathology Board of Certification, American Medical Technologists, National Accrediting Agency for Clinical Laboratory Sciences
MOS	Microsoft Office Specialist		Microsoft
MT (ASCP)	Certified Medical Technologist	ASCP, ABOR	American Society for Clinical Pathology, American Association of Bioanalysts (AAB) Board of Registry
MTA	Microsoft Technology Associate		Microsoft
NC-BC	NC-BC—Nurse Coach, Board Certified	AHNCC	American Holistic Nurses Credentialing Corporation
NCSN	Nationally Certified School Nurse	NBCSN	National Board for Certification of School Nurses

(*Continued*)

Credential	Full Name	Organization Acronym	Organization Full Name
NDTR	Nutrition and Dietetics Technician, Registered	CDR	Commission on Dietetics Registration
NEA	Nurse Executive, Advanced	ANCC	American Nurses Credentialing Center
NE-B	Nurse Executive	ANCC	American Nurses Credentialing Center
NNP-BC	Neonatal Nurse Practitioner	NCC	National Certification Corporation
NP-C	Nurse Practitioner–Certified	AANPCP	American Academy of Nurse Practitioners Certification Program
NSPM	Nonsurgical Pain Management	NBCRNA	National Board of Certification and Recertification for Nurse Anesthetists
OCN	Oncology Certified Nurse	ONCC	Oncology Nursing Certification Corporation
OCNS-C	Orthopaedic Clinical Nurse Specialist Certified	ONCB	Orthopaedic Nurses Certification Board
OMS	Ostomy Management Specialist	NAWCO	National Alliance of Wound Care and Ostomy
ONC	Orthopaedic Nurse Certified	ONCB	Orthopaedic Nurses Certification Board
ONP-C	Orthopaedic Nurse Practitioner Certified	ONCB	Orthopaedic Nurses Certification Board

(Continued)

Credential	Full Name	Organization Acronym	Organization Full Name
OTR	Occupational Therapist Registered	NBCOT	National Board for Certification in Occupational Therapy
PA-C	Physician Assistant–Certified	NCCPA	National Commission on the Certification of Physician Assistants
PATH A	Pathologists' Assistant	NAACLS	National Accrediting Agency for Clinical Laboratory Sciences
PBT	Phlebotomy Technician	ASCP BOC	American Society for Clinical Pathology Board of Certification
PCCN	(Adult) Progressive Care Nursing	AACN	American Association of Critical-Care Nurses Certification Corporation
PCNS	Pediatric Clinical Nurse Specialist	ANCC	American Nurses Credentialing Center
PfMP	Portfolio Management Professional	PMI	Project Management Institute
PgMP	Program Management Professional	PMI	Project Management Institute
PHCNS-BC	Public/Community Health Clinical Nurse Specialist	ANCC	American Nurses Credentialing Center
PI	Certified Principal Investigator	ACRP	Association of Clinical Research Professionals

(*Continued*)

Credential	Full Name	Organization Acronym	Organization Full Name
PMHCNS-BC	Adult Psychiatric-Mental Health Clinical Nurse Specialist	ANCC	American Nurses Credentialing Center
PMHCNS-BC	Child/Adolescent Psychiatric-Mental Health Clinical Nurse Specialist	ANCC	American Nurses Credentialing Center
PMHNP	Psychiatric–Mental Health Nurse Practitioner	ANCC	American Nurses Credentialing Center
PMHS	Pediatric Mental Health Specialist	PNCB	Pediatric Nurse Certification Board
PMI-ACP	PMI-Agile Certified Practitioner	PMI	Project Management Institute
PMP	Project Management Professional	PMI	Project Management Institute
PNP	Pediatric Nurse Practitioner	ANCC	American Nurses Credentialing Center
PPCNP-BC	Pediatric Primary Care Nurse Practitioner	ANCC	American Nurses Credentialing Center
RDCS	Registered Diagnostic Cardiac Sonographer	ARDMS	American Registry for Diagnostic Medical Sonography
RDMS	Registered Diagnostic Medical Sonographer	ARDMS	American Registry for Diagnostic Medical Sonography
RMSKS	Registered Musculoskeletal Sonographer	ARDMS	American Registry for Diagnostic Medical Sonography

(Continued)

Credential	Full Name	Organization Acronym	Organization Full Name
RN, BC/ RN-BC	Registered Nurse– Board Certified	ANCC	American Nurses Credentialing Center
RNC	Registered Nurse, Certified	NCC	National Certification Corporation
RNC-LRN	Certification in Low Risk Neonatal Nursing	NCC	National Certification Corporation
RNC-MNN	Certification in Maternal Newborn Nursing	NCC	National Certification Corporation
RNC-NIC	Certification for Neonatal Intensive Care Nursing	NCC	National Certification Corporation
RNC-OB	Credential in Inpatient Obstetric Nursing	NCC	National Certification Corporation
RPFT	Advanced Pulmonary Function Technologist	NBRC	National Board for Respiratory Care
RPT	Phlebotomy Technician	AMT	American Medical Technologists
RVT	Registered Vascular Technologist	ARDMS	American Registry for Diagnostic Medical Sonography
SANE-A	Sexual Assault Nurse Examiner–Adult/ Adolescent	IAFN	International Association of Forensic Nurses
SANE-P	Sexual Assault Nurse Examiner–Pediatric	IAFN	International Association of Forensic Nurses
SBB	Specialist in Blood Banking	ASCP BOC	American Society for Clinical Pathology Board of Certification

(*Continued*)

Credential	Full Name	Organization Acronym	Organization Full Name
SC	Specialist in Chemistry	ASCP BOC	American Society for Clinical Pathology Board of Certification
SCRN	Stroke Certified Registered Nurse	ABNN	American Board of Neuroscience Nursing
SCT	Specialist in Cytotechnology	ASCP BOC	American Society for Clinical Pathology Board of Certification
SH	Specialist in Hematology	ASCP BOC	American Society for Clinical Pathology Board of Certification
SM	Specialist In Microbiology	ASCP BOC	American Society for Clinical Pathology Board of Certification
SNP-BC	School Nurse Practitioner	ANCC	American Nurses Credentialing Center
SSCP	Systems Security Certified Practitioner	(ISC)^2	International Information Systems Security Certification Consortium
TCRN	Trauma Certified Registered Nurse	BCEN	Board of Certification for Emergency Nursing
VA-BC	Vascular Access–Board Certified	VACC	Vascular Access Certification Corporation
WCC	Wound Care Certified	NAWCO	National Alliance of Wound Care and Ostomy
WTA-C	Wound Treatment Associate	WOCNCB	Wound, Ostomy, Continence Nursing Certification Board

* This credential will sunset December 31, 2018.

II. Healthcare and Related Degrees

Designation	Full Name
AA	Associate of Arts
AAA	Associate of Applied Arts
AAB	Associate of Applied Business
AAS	Associate of Applied Science
AAS (R)	Associate of Applied Sciences in Radiography
AAS/ADN	Associate of Applied Science/Associate Degree Nursing
AAT	Associate in Applied Technology, Associate of Arts in Teaching
AB	Associate of Business
ABA	Associate of Business Administration
ABS	Associate in Business Science
ADN	Associate Degree in Nursing
AHS	Associate of Health Science
AIM	Applied Information Management
ALA	Associate of Liberal Arts
AOT	Associate in Occupational Technology
APRN	Advance Practice Registered Nurse
APT	Associate in Physical Therapy
ARM	Associate in Risk Management
AS	Associate of Science
ASc	Associate in Science
ASCIS	Associate of Science in Computer Information Systems
ASCNT	Associate of Science in Computer Network Technology
ASDH	Associate of Science in Dental Hygiene
ASMA	Associate of Science in Medical Assisting

(*Continued*)

Designation	Full Name
ASN	Associate of Science in Nursing
ASPT	Associate of Science in Physical Therapy
ASR	Associate of Science in Radiography
ASW	Associate Clinical Social Worker
AT	Associate of Technology
ATR	Art Therapist Registered
AuD	Doctor of Audiology
AyD	Doctor of Ayurvedic Medicine
B Comm	Bachelor of Commerce
BA	Bachelor of Arts
BABA	Bachelor of Arts of Business Administration
BAC	Baccalaureate Addictions Counselor
BAE, BAEd	Bachelor of Arts in Education
BAS	Bachelor of Applied Science
BBA	Bachelor in Healthcare or Business Administration
BBE	Bachelor of Biosystems Engineering
BD	Bachelor of Divinity
BDS	Bachelor of Dental Surgery
BDSc	Bachelor of Dental Science
BE	Bachelor of Education
BHS	Bachelor of Health Science
BHSA	Bachelor of Health Service Administration
BLD	Bioanalyst Laboratory Director
BMT	Bachelor of Medical Technology
BN	Bachelor of Nursing
BOT	Bachelor of Occupational Therapy

(*Continued*)

Designation	*Full Name*
BPH	Bachelor of Public Health
BPharm	Bachelor of Pharmacy
BPHS	Bachelor of Professional Health Science
BPod	Bachelor of Podiatry
BPT	Bachelor of Physical Therapy
BS, BSc	Bachelor of Science
BSBA	Bachelor of Science in Business Administration
BSBME	Bachelor of Science in Biomedical Engineering
BScN, BSN	Bachelor of Science in Nursing
BSCS	Bachelor of Science in Computer Science
BSEd	Bachelor of Science in Education
BSHCA	Bachelor of Science in Healthcare Administration
BSMicr	Bachelor of Science in Microbiology
BSPT	Bachelor of Science in Physical Therapy
BSRT	Bachelor of Science in Radiography
BSSW	Bachelor of Science in Social Work
BSW	Bachelor of Social Work
BSwE	Bachelor of Software Engineering
BTh	Bachelor of Theology
BVSC	Bachelor of Veterinary Science
CCC	Certificate of Clinical Competency
D	Diploma
DA	Doctor of Arts
DAOM	Doctor of Acupuncture and Oriental Medicine
DBA	Doctor of Business Administration
DC	Doctor of Chiropractic

(*Continued*)

Designation	Full Name
DCH	Doctor of Clinical Hypnotherapy
DCL	Doctor of Cannon Law, Doctor of Civil Law
DCLS	Doctor of Clinical Lab Science
DD	Doctor of Divinity
DDM	Doctor of Dental Medicine
DDS	Doctor of Dental Surgery
DEd	Doctor of Education
DHM	Doctor of Homeopathic Medicine
DIS	Doctor of Information Security
DM	Doctor of Management, Doctor of Music
DMA	Doctor of Musical Arts
DMD	Doctor of Dental Medicine, Doctor of Medical Dentistry
DMin	Doctor of Ministry
DMT	Doctor of Medical Technology
DNE	Doctor of Nursing Education
DNP	Doctor of Nursing Practice
DNS/DNSc/ DSN/DScN	Doctor of Nursing Science
DO	Doctor of Ostheopathy
DOS	Doctor of Ocular Science, Doctor of Optical Science
DP	Doctor of Podiatry
DPH/DrPH	Doctor of Public Health
DPhC	Doctor of Pharmaceutical Chemistry
DPM	Doctor of Podiatric Medicine
DPT	Doctor of Physical Therapy
Dr	Doctor
DrPH	Doctor of Public Health

(Continued)

Designation	*Full Name*
DS, DSc	Doctor of Science
DSC	Doctor of Surgical Chiropody
DScD	Doctor of Science in Dentistry
DScPT	Doctor of Science in Physical Therapy
DSCS	Doctorate of Science in Computer Science
DSN	Doctor of Science in Nursing
DSP	Doctor of Surgical Podiatry
DSSc	Doctor of Social Science
DSTh	Doctor of Sacred Theology
DSW	Doctor of Social Welfare, Doctor of Social Work
DTh	Doctor of Theology
DVM	Doctor of Veterinary Medicine
EdD	Doctor of Education
EdS	Education Specialist
JD	Doctor of Laws, Doctor of Jurisprudence, Juris Doctor
LAC, LicAc	Licenced Acupuncturist
LACMH	Licensed Associate Counselor of Mental Health
LCPC	Licensed Clinical Professional Counselor
LCSW	Licensed Clinical Social Worker
LD	Licensed Dietician
LDTC	Learning Disabilities Teacher Consultant
LL	Bachelor of Laws
LLD	Doctor of Laws
LLM	Master of Laws
LMFC	Licensed Marriage Family Counselor
LMFT	Licensed Marriage/Family Therapist

(Continued)

Designation	Full Name
LPC	Licensed Professional Counselor
LPN	Licensed Practical Nurse
LSW	Licensed Social Worker
LVN	Licensed Vocational Nurse
MA	Master of Arts
MAC	Master of Acupuncture, Master Addictions Counselor
MAEd	Master of Arts in Education
MAGD	Master of Academy of General Dentistry
MAcOM	Master of Acupuncture and Oriental Medicine
MAT	Master of Arts in Teaching
MBA	Master of Business Administration
MC	Master of Counseling
MCAT	Master of Creative Arts in Therapy
MCD	Master of Communication Disorders
MCS	Master of Computer Science
MD	Doctor of Medicine
MDiv	Master of Divinity
MDS	Master of Dental Surgery, Master of Dental Science
MEd	Master of Education
MFCC	Marriage, Family and Child Counseling License
MFT	Marriage and Family Therapist, Master of Family Therapy
MHA	Master of Health Administration
MHS	Master of Health Science, Masters in Human Services
MHSA	Master of Health Services Administration
MISM	Master of Information Systems Management
MMFT	Masters in Marriage and Family Therapy

(Continued)

Designation	Full Name
MN	Master of Nursing
MNA	Master of Nurse Anesthesia
MNS	Master of Nutrition Science
MP	Master of Psychotherapy
MPH	Master of Public Health
MPharm	Master of Pharmacy
MRad	Master of Radiology
MRC	Master of Rehabilitation Counseling
MS/MSc	Master of Science
MSBME	Master of Science in Biomedical Engineering
MSBMS	Master of Science in Basic Medical Sciences
MSC	Master of Science in Counseling
MSCIS	Master of Science in Computer Information Systems
MSCS	Master of Science in Computer Science
MSD	Master of Science in Dentistry
MSFS	Master of Science in Forensic Science
MSHA	Master of Science in Health Administration
MSHI	Master of Science in Health Informatics
MSIS	Master of Science in Information Systems
MSN	Master of Science in Nursing
MSOT	Master of Science in Occupational Therapy
MSPAS	Master of Science in Physician Assistant Studies
MSPH	Master of Science in Public Health
MSRD	Master of Science Registered Dietician
MSS	Master of Social Science, Master of Social Service
MSSE	Master of Science in Software Engineering

(*Continued*)

Designation	Full Name
MSSLP	Master of Science in Speech Language Pathology
MSW	Master of Social Work
MSwE	Master of Software Engineering
MTh	Master of Theology
MusD, DMus	Doctor of Music
ND	Doctor of Naturopathy
NP	Nurse Practitioner
OD	Doctor of Optometry
OT, OTR	Occupational Therapist, Occupational Therapist Registered
PA	Physician Assistant
PharmD	Doctor of Pharmacy
PhB	Bachelor of Philosophy
PhD	Doctor of Philosophy
PsyD	Doctor of Psychology
PsyM	Master of Psychology
PT	Physical Therapist, Physiotherapist
PTA	Physical Therapy Assistant
RD	Registered Dietician
RDA	Registered Dental Assistant
RDH	Registered Dental Hygienist
RDN	Registered Dietician Nutritionist
RHIA	Registered Health Information Administrator
RHIT	Registered Health Information Technician
RMA	Registered Medical Assistant
RN	Registered Nurse
RNA	Registered Nursing Assistant

(Continued)

Designation	Full Name
RNBSN	Registered Nurse Bachelor of Science Nursing
RNC	Registered Nurse Certified
RNMSN	Registered Nurse Master of Science Nursing
RPh	Registered Pharmacist
RRA	Registered Records Administrator
RRT	Registered Respiratory Therapist, Registered Radiologic Technologist
RT	Registered Technologist, Radiological Technologist, Respiratory Therapist
ScD, SD	Doctor of Science
SLP	Speech Language Pathologist
SScD	Doctor of Social Science
STB	Bachelor of Sacred Theology
STD	Doctor of Sacred Theology
ThB	Bachelor of Theology
ThD	Doctor of Theology

III. Professional Fellowships

Designation	Full Name
FAAFP	Fellow of the American Academy of Family Physicians
FACC	Fellow of the American College of Cardiology
FACEP	Fellow of the American College of Emergency Physicians
FACHE	Fellow of the American College of Healthcare Executives
FACMPE	Fellow of the American College of Medical Practice Executives
FACP	Fellow of the American College of Physicians
FASCP	Fellow, American Society of Clinical Pathologists

(Continued)

Designation	Full Name
FCAP	Fellow, College of American Pathologists
FCHIME	Fellow, College of Healthcare Information Management Executives
FHFMA	Fellow of the Healthcare Financial Management Association
FHIMSS	Fellow of the Healthcare Information and Management Systems Society
FIEEE	Fellow of the Institute of Electrical and Electronics Engineers
FNLM	Friends of the National Library of Medicine
LCHIME	Lifetime College of Healthcare Information Management Executives
LFHIMSS	Life Member and Fellow of the Healthcare Information and Management Systems Society
LHIMSS	Life Member of the Healthcare Information and Management Systems Society
SMIEEE	Senior Member of the Institute of Electrical and Electronics Engineers

IV. Honors Designations

ACMI	American College of Medical Informatics
FAAFP	Fellow of the American Academy of Family Physicians
FAAN	Fellow of the American Academy of Nursing
FACC	Fellow of the American College of Cardiology
FACEP	Fellow of the American College of Emergency Physicians
FACHE	Fellow of the American College of Healthcare Executives
FACMI	Fellow, American College of Medical Informatics
FACMPE	Fellow of the American College of Medical Practice Executives
FACP	Fellow of the American College of Physicians
FHAPI	Honorary Fellow, Association for Pathology Informatics

Acronyms

A

AA	Attribute authority
AAA	Authentication, authorization, and accounting
ABC	Activity-based costing
ABC codes	Alternative billing codes
ACA	Affordable Care Act
ACDF	Access control decision function
ACG	Ambulatory care group
ACI	Access control information
ACID	Atomicity, consistency, isolation, and durability
ACK	General acknowledgment message
ACL	Access control list
ACO	Accountable Care Organization
ACS	Access control service
AD	Active directory
AD	Addendum
ADE	Adverse drug event
ADG	Ambulatory diagnostic group
ADPAC	Automated data processing application coordinator
ADR	ADT response message
ADR	Adverse drug reaction
ADSL	Asymmetric digital subscriber line
ADT	Admission, discharge, and transfer
AE	Adverse event/adverse experience
AE Title	Application Entity Title
AEF	Access control enforcement function
AHT	Average handling time/average handle time
AIDC	Automatic identification and data capture
AIMS	Anesthesia information management system

AIS	Automated information system
ALOS	Average length of stay
ALU	Arithmetic logic unit
AMR	Ambulatory medical record
APACHE	Acute physiology and chronic health evaluation
APC	Ambulatory payment class
APG	Ambulatory patient group
API	Application program interface
APMs	Alternative payment model
ARI	Access to radiology information
ARP	Address resolution protocol
ARPANET	Advanced research projects agency network
ARRA	American Recovery and Reinvestment Act of 2009
ASA	Average speed of answer
ASCII	American standard code for information interchange
ASN	Abstract syntax notation
ASO	Administrative services only
ASP	Active server pages
ASP	Application service provider
ATA	Advanced technology attachment
ATCB	Authorized testing and certification body
ATM	Asynchronous transfer mode
ATNA	Audit trail and node authentication
AUI	Attachment unit interface
AUP	Acceptable use policy
AVR	Analysis, visualization, and reporting

B

B2B	Business-to-business
B2B2C	Business-to-business-to-consumer
B2C	Business-to-consumer
BAA	Business associate agreement
BAN	Body area network
BASIC	Beginner's all-purpose symbolic instruction code
BAT	Filename extension for a batch file
BCMA	Bar code medication administration
BCP	Business continuity plan
BDC	Backup domain controller
BEC	Business email compromise
BGI	Binary gateway interface
BGP	Border gateway protocol

BH	Behavioral health
BIA	Business impact analysis
BIOS	Basic input output system
BPS	Bits per second
BRFSS	Behavioral Risk Factor Surveillance System
BYOC	Bring your own cloud
BYOD	Bring your own device

C

CA	Certification authority
CAD	Computer-aided detection
CAH	Critical-access hospital
CAL	Computer-assisted learning
CAP	Common alerting protocol
CASE	Computer-assisted software engineering
CAT	Computerized axial tomography
CAT-1-7	Categories 1-7
CATH	Cardiac catheterization workflow
CBL	Computer-based learning
CCC	Clinical care classification
CCD	Continuity of care document
C-CDA	Consolidated clinical document architecture
CCO	Chief compliance officer
CCoM	Clinical context management
CCOW	Clinical context object workgroup
CCR	Continuity of care record
CD	Committee draft
CD	Compact disc
CDA	Clinical document architecture
CDMA	Code division multiple access
CDPD	Cellular digital packet data
CDR	Clinical data repository
CD-ROM	Compact Disc, read-only-memory
CDS	Clinical decision support
CDSS	Clinical decision support system
CDT	Current dental terminology
CDW	Clinical data warehouse
CE	Coded element
CEN	European Committee for Standardization
CERT	Computer emergency response team
CF	Conditional formatting/coded formatted element

CGI	Common gateway interface
CHAP	Challenge handshake authentication protocol
CHG	Charge posting
CHIN	Community health information network
C-HOBIC	Canadian Health Outcomes for Better Information and Care
CHV	Consumer health vocabulary initiative
CIA	Confidentiality/integrity/availability
CIO	Chief informatics officer
CIO	Chief information officer
CIS	Clinical information system
CISC	Complex instruction set computer processor
CM	Composite message/composite data type
CMD	Command
CMET	Common message element type
CMIO	Chief medical informatics officer
CMIO	Chief medical information officer
CMYK	Cyan, magenta, yellow, and black
CNCL	Cancelled
CNIO	Chief nursing informatics officer
CNIO	Chief nursing information officer
COA	Compliance-oriented architecture
COAS	Clinical observations access service
COB	Close of business
COB	Coordination of benefits
COMSEC	Communications security
CORBA	Common object request broker architecture
COW	Computer-on-wheels
CP	Certificate policy
CPI	Consistent presentation of images
CPM	Control program for microcomputers
CPOE	Computerized practitioner order entry
CPR	Computer-based patient record
CPRS	Computer-based patient record system
CPS	Certification practices statement
CPT	Current procedural terminology
CPU	Central processing unit
CQM	Clinical quality measures
CRA	Countermeasure response administration
CRM	Customer relationship management
CRUD	Create, read, update, and delete
CSMA/CD	Carrier sense multiple access with collision detection
CSO	Chief security officer
CSU/DSU	Channel sharing unit/data service unit

CT	Consistent time
CTI	Computer telephony integration
CTO	Chief technology officer
CTS	Common terminology services
CU	Control unit
CUI	Concept unique identifier
CVE	Common vulnerabilities and exposures
CVS	Concurrent versions system
CWE	Coded with exceptions
CWE	Common weakness enumeration
CxO	Corporate executives or C-level

D

DaaS	Data as a service
DBMS	Database management system
DDL	Data definition language
DEA	Data encryption algorithm
DEEDS	Data elements for emergency department systems
DES	Data encryption standard
DHCP	Data host configuration protocol
DI	Diagnostic imaging
DICOM	Digital imaging and communications in medicine
DLC	Dynamic link control
DLL	Dynamic link library
DMA	Direct memory access
DML	Data manipulation language
DNS	Domain name server
DNSSEC	Domain name system security extension
DOS	Disk operating system
DPI	Dots per square inch
DRAM	Dynamic random access memory
DRG	Diagnosis related group
DSA	Digital signature algorithm
DSG	Document digital signature
DSL	Digital subscriber line
DSLAM	Digital subscriber line access multiplexer
DSM	Diagnostic and Statistical Manual of Mental Disorders
DSML	Directory services markup language
DSMO	Designated Standard Maintenance Organization
DSS	Decision support system
DSSS	Direct sequence spread spectrum

DSTU	Draft standard for trial use
DSU	Data service unit
DSU/CSU	Data service unit/channel service unit
DT	Date data type (YYYYMMDD)
DTD	Document type definition
DTE	Data terminal equipment
DTR	Data terminal ready
DTR	Draft technical report
DVD	Digital video disk or digital versatile disk

E

e-[text] or e-text	Electronic text
E-1-3	European digital signal
EAI	Enterprise application integration
EAP	Extensible authentication protocol
EBB	Eligibility-based billing
EBCDIC	Extended binary coded decimal interchange code
EC	Electronic commerce
ECG	Electrocardiogram
ECN	Explicit congestion notifier
eCommerce	Electronic commerce
ED	Encapsulated data
ED	Evidence documents
EDC	Electronic data capture system
EDDS	Electronic document digital storage
EDI	Electronic data interchange
EDI gateway	Electronic data interchange gateway
EED	Early event detection
EDXL	Emergency data exchange language
EDXL–HAVE	Emergency data exchange language–hospital availability exchange
EEPROM	Electronically erasable programmable read-only memory
EGA	Enhanced graphics adapter
E-GOV	The "E-Government Act of 2002"
EHR	Electronic health record
EIDE	Enhanced or extended integrated drive electronics
EIN	Employer identification number
EIP	Enterprise information portal
EIS	Enterprise information system

EIS	Executive information system
eMAR	Electronic medication administration record
EMC	Electronic media claims
EMI	Electromagnetic interference
EMPI	Enterprise master patient index
EMR	Electronic medical record
EMRAM	Electronic medical record adoption model
EMSEC	Emanations security
EN	European standard
ENP	European nursing care pathways
EOB	Explanation of benefits
EOP	Explanation of payment
EP	Eligible professional
ePHI	Electronic protected health information
ePHR	Electronic personal health record
EPROM	Erasable programmable memory
ERA	Electronic remittance advice
ERD	Emergency repair disk
ERD	Entity relationship diagram
ERDA	Emergency respond data architecture
ERISA	Employee Retirement Income and Security Act of 1975
ERP	Enterprise resource planning
ESDI	Enhanced small device interface
ETL	Extraction, transformation, loading
EUA	Enterprise user authentication
EULA	End user license agreement

F

FAQ	Frequently asked questions
FAR	False acceptance rate
FCOE	Fiber channel over Ethernet
FDDI	Fiber distributed data interface
FFS	Fee for service
FHA	Federal Health Architecture
FHIR	Fast healthcare interoperability resources
FIFO	First in, first out
FIPS	Federal information processing standard
FQDN	Fully qualified domain name
FTP	File transfer protocol

G

GB	Gigabyte
GBps	Gigabytes per second
GELLO	Guideline Expression Language, Object Oriented
GIF	Graphics interchange format
GIG	Global information grid
GIGO	Garbage in, garbage out
GSM	Global system for mobile communications
GUDID	Global unique device identification database
GUI	Graphical user interface
GUID	Global unique identifier

H

HAN	Health alert network
HCPCS	Healthcare Common System Coding System
hData	A specification for exchanging electronic health data
HEDIS	Healthcare effectiveness data and information set
HIE	Health information exchange
HIEx	Health insurance exchange
HIO	Health information organization
HIPAA	Health Insurance Portability and Accountability Act of 1996
HIS	Health information system
HISP	Health information service provider
HIT	Health information technology
HITECH Act	Health Information Technology for Economic and Clinical Health Act
HITEP	Health Information Technology Expert Panel
HITPC	Health Information Technology Policy Committee
HITSC	Health Information Technology Standards Committee
HPID	(Unique) Health plan identifier
HTML	Hypertext markup language
HTTP	Hypertext transfer protocol
HUD	Heads-up display
Hz	Hertz

I

I/O	Input/output device
IAM	Identity access management

IAP	Internet access provider
ICC	Integrated circuit chip
ICD	International Classification of Diseases
ICIDH	International Classification of Impairments, Disability, and Health
ICMP	Internet control message protocol
ICR	Intelligent call routing
ICR	Intelligent character recognition
ICU	Intensive care unit
IDE	Integrated device electronics
IDM	Identity digital management
IDMS	Identity management system
IDN	Integrated delivery network
IDR	Intelligent document recognition
IDS	Integrated delivery system
IGP	Interior gateway protocol
IHE	Integrating the Healthcare Enterprise
IIF	Information in identifiable form
IIS	Immunization information systems
IIS	Internet information server
IKE	Internet key exchange
ILD	Injection laser diode
InterNIC	Internet Network Information Center
iOS	iPhone operating system
IoT	Internet of Things
IP	Internet protocol
IPA	Independent practice association
IRC	Internet relay chat
IRD	Information resource department
IrDA	Infrared Data Association
IRM	Information resource management
IRQ	Interrupt request
ISA	Industry standard architecture
ISA	Interoperability Standards Advisory
ISDN	Integrated service digital network
ISO/TC 215	International Organization for Standardization (ISO) Technical Committee for Health Informatics
ISP	Internet service provider
ITMRA	Information Technology Management Reform Act
ITSEC	Information technology security
IVR	Interactive voice response

J

JAD	Joint application development
JPEG	Joint photographic experts group
JSON	JavaScript Object Notation
JTC	Joint Technical Committee
JWG	Joint Working Group

K

KB	Kilobyte
Kbps	Kilobits per second
KHz	Kilohertz
KIN	Key image notes

L

LAN	Local area network
LAT	Local area transport
LEAP	Lightweight and efficient application protocol
LIFO	Last in, first out
LIS	Laboratory information system
LLC	Logical link control
LOINC	Logical observation identifiers names and codes
LQS	Lexicon query service
LSWF	Laboratory scheduled workflow
LTC	Long-term care
LTPAC	Long-term and post-acute care
LU	Logical unit

M

MAC	Mandatory access control
MAC	Media access control
MAC	Message authentication code
MACRA	Medicare Access and CHIP Reauthorization Act 2015
MAN	Metropolitan-area network
MAO	Maximum acceptable/allowable outage
MAU	Media access unit
Mb	Megabit

MBDS	Minimum basic data set
Mbps	Megabits per second
MDA	Model-driven architecture
MDI	Medical device interface
MDM	Master data management
MDM	Medical document management message
MDS	Minimum data set
MedDRA	Medical Dictionary for Regulatory Activities
MEDS	Minimum emergency data set
MeSH	Medical subject heading
mHealth	Mobile health
MHz	Megahertz
MIB	Medical information BUS
MID	Management information department
MIME	Multipurpose Internet mail extensions
MIPS	Merit based incentive payment system
MIPS	Millions of instructions per second
MIS	Management information system (services)
MITA	Medicaid information technology architecture
MLM	Medical logic model
MMIS	Medicaid management information system
MOLAP	Multidimensional online analytical processing
MOU	Memorandum of understanding
MPEG	Motion picture expert group
MPI	Master patient index
MPP	Massively parallel processing
MSA	Master services agreement
MSAU	Multiple station access unit
MSO	Management service organizations
MTBF	Mean time between failure
MTTD	Mean time to diagnose
MTTR	Mean time to repair
MU	Meaningful use
MUX	Multiplexer, multipleXer, or multipleXor

N

NAC	Network access control/network admission control
NAS	Network attached storage
NAT	Network address translation
NAV	Notification of document availability
NCPDP	National Council for Prescription Drug Programs

NDC	National Drug Code
NDIS	Network driver interface specification
NEDSS	National Electronic Disease Surveillance System
NEMSIS	National Emergency Medical System (EMS) Information System
NetBEUI	NetBIOS extended user interface
NetBIOS	Network basic input output system
NFS	Network file system
NHII	Nationwide Health Information Infrastructure
NHIN or NwHIN	Nationwide Health Information Network
NHRIC	National Health-Related Items Code
NIC	Network information center
NIC	Network interface card
NIC	Nursing intervention classification
NLP	Natural language processing
NM	Nuclear medicine image integration
NMB	National member body
NMDS	Nursing minimum data set
NMMDS	Nursing management minimum data set
NOC	Nursing outcome classification
NOC	Network operation center
NOI	Notice of Intent
NOS	Network operating system
NPF	National provider file
NPI	National provider identifier
NSF	National standard format
NSP	Network service provider
NSSN	National standards system network
NUMA	Nonuniform memory architecture
NWIP	New work item proposal

O

OASIS	Outcome and Assessment Information Set
OC	Optical carrier
OCR	Optical character recognition
OCSP	Online certificate status protocol
ODA	Open document architecture
ODS	Operational data store
OEID	Other entity identifier
OID	Object identifier
OLAP	Online analytical processing

OLE	Object linking and embedding
OLTP	Online transaction processing
OM	Outbreak management
OOA	Out of area
OON	Out of network
OOP	Object-oriented programming
OOP	Out of pocket
OpArc	Operational architecture
OS	Operating system
OS/2	Operating system/2
OSI	Open systems interconnection
OWL	Web ontology language

P

P2P	Peer-to-peer
PACS	Picture archiving and communication systems
PAN	Personal-area network
PAP	Password authentication protocol
PAS	Publicly available specification
PC	Personal computer
PCB	Printed circuit board
PCDS	Patient care data set
PCMCIA	Personal computer memory card international
PCMH	Patient-centered medical home
PCP	Primary care provider
PDC	Primary domain controller
PDF	Portable document format
PDI	Portable data for imaging
PDP	Policy decision point
PDQ	Patient demographic query
PEP	Policy enforcement point
PGP	Presentation of grouped procedures
PGP	Pretty good privacy
PHI	Protected/personal health information
PHIN	Public health information network
PHIN-MS	Public health information network-messaging system
PHMT	Personal health management tool
PHR	Personal health record
PIDS	Person identification service
PIM	Platform independent model
PIN	Personal identification number

PING	Packet Internet Groper
PIP	Policy information point
PIR	Patient information reconciliation
PIV	Personal identification verification
PIX	Patient identifier cross-referencing
PKC	Public key certificate
PKI	Public key infrastructure
PNDS	Perioperative nursing data set
PNG	Portable network graphics
POP	Post office protocol
POP server	Point-of-presence server
POSIX	Portable open systems interface
PPACA	Patient Protection and Affordable Care Act (Public Law 111-148)
PPO	Preferred provider organization
PPP	Point-to-point protocol
PPTP	Point-to-point tunneling protocol
PRAM	Parameter RAM
PRG	Procedure-related group
PROM	Programmable read-only memory
PSA	Patient synchronized applications
PVC	Permanent virtual circuit
PWF	Postprocessing workflow
PWP	Personnel White Pages

Q

QA	Quality assurance
QDM	Quality data model
QMF	Query management facility
QMR	Quick medical reference
QoS	Quality of service
QR codes	Quick response codes

R

RA	Registration authority
RAD	Rapid application development
RAID	Redundant array of independent disks
RAM	Random access memory
RARP	Reverse address resolution protocol

RAS	Remote access server
RBAC	Role-based access control
RDBMS	Relational database management system
RDF	Resource description framework
REC	Regional extension center
REST	Representational state transfer
RFI	Request for information
RFID	Radio frequency identification
RFP	Request for proposal
RGB	Red, green, blue color model
RHIN	Regional health information network
RHIO	Regional health information organization
RID	Retrieve information for display
RIM	Reference information model
RIP	Routing information protocol
RIS	Radiology information system
RISC	Reduced instruction set computer
RM	Records management
RMI	Remote method invocation
RM-ODP	Reference model for open distributed processing
RMON	Remote network monitor
ROI	Release of information
ROI	Return on investment
ROLAP	Relational online analytical processing
ROM	Read-only memory
RTF	Rich text format
RTLS	Real-time location service
RTM	Reference terminology model
RTO	Recovery time objective
RTS	Request to send
RVU	Relative value unit
RWF	Reporting workflow

S

S/MIME	Secure MIME
SaaS	Software as a Service
SAML	Security assertion markup language
SAN	Storage area network
SATA	Serial advanced technology application
SATAN	Security administrator tool for analyzing networks
SBAR	Situation–background–assessment–recommendation

SCOS	Smartcard operating system
SCSI	Small computer system interface
SCUI	Smartcard user interface
SDLC	System design lifecycle
SDO	Standards development organization
SDOH	Social determinants of health
SDXC	Secure digital extended capacity
SEC	Security
SET	Secure electronic transmission
sFTP	Secure file transport protocol
SGML	Standardized generalized markup language
SGMP	Simple gateway monitoring protocol
S-HTTP	Secure HTTP
SIG	Special interest group
SIMM	Single in-line memory module
SINR	Simple image and numeric report
SLIP	Serial line Internet protocol
SME	Subject-matter expert
SMP	Symmetrical multiprocessing
SMS	Short message service
SMTP	Simple mail transfer protocol
SNA	System network architecture
SNMP	Simple network monitoring protocol
SNMP	System network management protocol
SNOMED–CT	Systematized nomenclature of medicine–clinical terms
SOA	Service-oriented architecture
SOAP	Simple object access protocol
SONET	Synchronous optical network
SOP	Standard operating procedure
SOW	Statement of work
SP	Subportal
SPD	Summary plan description
SPIN	Standard prescriber identification number
SPOOL	Simultaneous peripheral operation online
SQL	Structured query language
SRAM	Static random access memory
SSH	Secure shell
SSL	Secure socket layer
SSO	Single sign-on
STP	Shielded twisted pair
SVC	Switched virtual circuit
SWF	Scheduled workflow

T

TC	Technical committee
TCO	Total cost of ownership
TCP/IP	Transmission control protocol/Internet protocol
TDR	Time-domain reflectometer
TELNET	TELecommunications NETwork
TFTP	Trivial file transfer protocol
TIFF	Tag image file format
TKIP	Temporal key integrity protocol
TPA	Third-party administrator
TPV	Third-party vendor
TTL	Time to live
TTP	Trusted third party

U

UART	Universal asynchronous receiver transmitter
UCC	Uniform Code Council
UDDI	Universal description, discover, and integration
UDI	Unique device identifier
UDK	User-defined keys
UDP	User datagram protocol
UI	User interface
UM	Utilization management
UMDNS	Universal medical device nomenclature system
UML	Unified Modeling Language
UMLS	Unified Medical Language System
UMS	Unified messaging system
UNC	Universal naming convention
UPC	Universal product code
UPI	Unique patient identifier
UPN	Universal product number
UPS	Uninterruptible power supply
URI	Uniform resource identifiers
URL	Uniform resource locator
USB	Universal serial bus
USHIK	United States Health Information Knowledgebase
UTP	Unshielded twisted pair

V

VAN	Value-added network
VAX	Virtual address extension
VistA	Veterans Health Information Systems Technology Architecture
VM	Virtual machine
VMM	Virtual machine monitor
VoIP	Voice over Internet protocol
VoxML	Voice markup language
VPN	Virtual private network
VRAM	Video RAM or video random access memory
VRML	Virtual reality modeling language
VRU	Voice response unit

W

WAI	Web accessibility initiative
WAIS	Wide-area information server
WAN	Wide area network
WAP	Wireless application protocol
WASP	Wireless application service provider
WAV or WAVE	Waveform audio format (.wav)
WEP	Wired equivalent privacy
WG	Work group
Wi-Fi	Wireless fidelity
WLAN	Wireless local area network
WORM	Write once, read many times
WOW	Workstation on wheels
WPA	Wi-Fi protected access
WSDL	Web services description language
WWW	World Wide Web
WYSIWYG	What you see is what you get
WYSIWYP	What you see is what you print

X

XDS	Cross-enterprise document sharing
XML	Extensible markup language
XSL	Extensible stylesheet language

References

1. Kessel, Richard. NIST. Glossary of Key Information Security Terms. Available at: http://nvlpubs.nist.gov/nistpubs/ir/2013/NIST.IR.7298r2.pdf. Last accessed May 2016.
2. WhatIs.com. Available at: whatis.techtarget.com. Last accessed August 2016.
3. HIMSS. (2013). *HIMSS Dictionary of Healthcare Information Technology Terms, Acronyms and Organizations*, 3rd ed. Chicago.
4. Business Dictionary. www.businessdictionary.com. Last accessed April 2016.
5. *2015 ANA Scope and Standards of Nursing Informatics Practice*, 2nd ed.
6. ABC Medical Coding. Outsource Strategies International. Available at: http://www.outsourcestrategies.com/blog/2008/02/abc-medical-coding.html. Last accessed May 2016.
7. IT Terminology. Available at: http://www.consp.com/it-information-technology-terminology-dictionary. Last accessed May 2016.
8. Wikipedia. www.wikipedia.org.
9. *The Free On-line Dictionary of Computing*. http://foldoc.org/. Denis Howe, Ed. Last accessed 2015.
10. Health Level Seven (HL7). 3300 Washtenaw Avenue, Suite 227, Ann Arbor, MI 48104. http://www.hl7.org/. Last accessed April 2016.
11. HIMSS Analytics. www.himssanalytics.com. Last accessed April 2016.
12. Oracle. www.orafaq.com. Last accessed October 2012.
13. Office of the National Coordinator for Health Information Technology. http://healthit.hhs.gov/portal. Last accessed August 2016.
14. www.dhs.gov. Last accessed April 2016.
15. Indiana University Knowledge Base. Available at: https://kb.iu.edu/d/aiuv. Last accessed January 2016.
16. NICCS. Explore Terms: A Glossary of Common Cybersecurity Terminology. Available at: https://niccs.us-cert.gov/glossary. Last accessed May 2016.
17. IT Law Wiki. //itlaw.wikia.com/. Last accessed October 2012.
18. Cisco. User Guide for the Cisco Secure Access Control System 5.1. Available at: http://www.cisco.com/c/en/us/td/docs/net_mgmt/cisco_secure_access_control_system/5-1/user/guide/acsuserguide/glossary.html.
19. National Committee on Vital and Health Statistics (NCVHS). www.ncvhs.hhs.gov. Last accessed October 2012.
20. Investopedia. www.investopedia.com. Last accessed July 2016.
21. ANSI. American National Standards Institute. www.ansi.org. Last accessed October 2012.

22. Health Insurance Portability and Accountability Act (HIPAA). https://www.hipaa.com/. Last accessed April 2016.
23. Department of Defense (DoD). Information Technology Security Certification and Accreditation Process (DITSCAP) definitions. www.csrc.nist.gov. Last accessed April 2016.
24. ACHC. achc.org. Last accessed July 2016.
25. HCSC. Health Care Glossary. Available at: http://www.hcsc.com/glossary.html. Last accessed July 2016.
26. ISO/TS 22600-3. HealthCare Information Privilege Management & Access Control P-3 (terms only). www.iso.org. Last accessed April 2016.
27. Access Control Information. Available at: https://publib.boulder.ibm.com/tividd/td/ITIM/SC32-1149-02/en_US/HTML/im451_poag45.htm. Last accessed July 2016.
28. Centers for Medicare & Medicaid Services (CMS). www.cms.gov. Last accessed August 2016.
29. Integrating the Healthcare Enterprise. www.ihe.net. Last accessed April 2016.
30. American Health Information Management Association (AHIMA). www.ahima.org. Last accessed March 2016.
31. www.merriam-webster.com. Last accessed March 2016.
32. www.technet.microsoft.com/en-us/library. Last accessed August 2016.
33. VA National Center for Patient Safety (NCPS). www.patientsafety.va.gov. Last accessed April 2016.
34. Health.gov. http://health.gov. Last accessed July 2016.
35. http://unix.stackexchange.com/questions/82934/what-is-a-background-process.
36. RACGP: Royal Australian College of General Practitioners (RACGP) RACGP College House, 1 Palmerston Crescent, South Melbourne, Victoria 3205.
37. U.S. Health and Human Services. www.hhs.gov. Last accessed August 2016.
38. International Organization for Standardization (ISO).1, ch. de la Voie-Creuse CP 56 CH-1211 Geneva 20, Switzerland. www.iso.org. Last accessed April 2016.
39. Vistapedia. http://vistapedia.net. Last accessed July 2016.
40. *Taber's Cyclopedic Medical Dictionary*. Donald Venes, MD, 2013.
41. Webopedia. www.webopedia.com. Last accessed August 2016.
42. http://www.optus.com.au/shop/broadband/home-broadband/network/internet-speed.
43. Food and Drug Administration. http://www.fda.gov. Last accessed August 2016.
44. TermWiki. Available at: www.termwiki.com/EN:application_entity_title_%28AE_title%29. Last accessed October 2012.
45. Report on Uniform Data Standards for Patient Medical Record Information (2000). National Committee on Vital and Health Statistics (NCVHS). Available at: www.ncvhs.hhs.gov/hipaa000706.pdf. Last accessed April 2016.
46. Dictionary.com. Last accessed August 2016.
47. Pfleeger, C. and Pfleeger, S. (2003). *Security in Computing*. New Jersey: Pearson Education, Inc. 2003.
48. CIGNA. www.cigna.com. Last accessed April 2016.
49. http://www.anesthesiologynews.com/download/AIMS_AN0909_WM.pdf. Last accessed July 2016.
50. Mastrian, K.G. and McGonigle, D. (2017). *Informatics for Health Professionals*. Burlington, MA: Jones & Bartlett Learning.
51. OECD Library. http://www.oecd-ilibrary.org. Last accessed July 2016.

52. University of Missouri. Available at: http://bppm.missouri.edu/chapter2/2_140.html. Last accessed August 2016.
53. http://www.centercode.com/blog/2011/01/alpha-vs-beta-testing/. Last accessed July 2016.
54. www.techopedia.com. Last accessed October 2012.
55. Healthcare Information and Management Systems Society (HIMSS). www.himss.org. Last accessed April 2016.
56. Ancillary Care Services. Available at: http://www.anci-care.com/about2.html. Last accessed August 2016.
57. http://medconditions.net/ancillary-information-system.html. Last accessed October 2012.
58. www.encyclopedia.com. Last accessed October 2012.
59. Infoway. www.infoway-inforoute.ca. Last accessed April 2016.
60. History of APACHE. www.salon.com. Last accessed October 2012.
61. University of Victoria (UVIC). www.uvic.ca. Last accessed October 2012.
62. The Free Dictionary. Available at: http://encyclopedia2.thefreedictionary.com/data+port. Last accessed October 2012.
63. World Wide Web Consortium (W3C) Portal to Glossaries. Available at: www.w3.org/Glossary. Last accessed April 2016.
64. www.openehr.org. Last accessed October 2012.
65. ISO/IS #13606-1. Electronic health record communication—Part 1: Reference model (terms only). www.iso.org. Last accessed October 2012.
66. Federal Identity Management. Available at: www.cio.gov/ficc/documents. Last accessed April 2016.
67. Coiera E. (2003). *Guide to Health Informatics*, 2nd ed. Arnold, London. www.coiera.com/glossatry.htm.
68. Informatics & Nursing: Opportunities & Challenges. Web supplement, 2003.
69. http://www.erg.abdn.ac.uk/users/gorry/course/inet-pages/arp.html. Last accessed July 2016.
70. Microsoft. www.microsoft.com. Last accessed April 2016.
71. www.creativyst.com/Prod/Glossary. Last accessed October 2012.
72. http://www.oss.com/asn1/resources/asn1-faq.html. Last accessed August 2016.
73. Kwantlen University College. Available at: www.kwantlen.bc.ca/home.html. Last accessed October 2012.
74. ISO/IS #17090-1. Public Key Infrastructure-1 Framework and Overview (terms only). www.iso.org. Last accessed October 2012.
75. www.techterms.com. Last accessed April 2016.
76. International Engineering Consortium. www.iec.org. Last accessed October 2012.
77. ISO/TS 17117 (revision). Criteria for the Categorization and Evaluation of Terminological Systems (terms only). www.iso.org. Last accessed October 2012.
78. ISO/IS #17115. Vocabulary for Terminological Systems (terms only). www.iso.org. Last accessed April 2016.
79. SNOMED. International Health Terminology Standards Development Organization (IHTSDO). Gammeltory 4, 1. 1457 Copenhagen K, Denmark. www.ihtsdo.org. Last accessed April 2016.
80. http://www.brighthub.com/computing/smb-security/articles/31234.aspx.
81. http://www.hipaasurvivalguide.com/hipaa-regulations/164-304.php.
82. CDC Centers for Disease Control. www.cdc.gov. Last accessed April 2016.

83. Institute of Electrical and Electronics Engineers (IEEE). Available at: www.ieee.org. Last accessed October 2012.
84. iHealthBeat. Available at: www.ihealthbeat.org. Last accessed January 2016.
85. Business Email Compromise. U.S. Department of Justice Federal Bureau of Investigation. Available at: https://www.fbi.gov/file-repository/email-compromise_508.pdf. Last accessed November 2016.
86. www.answers.com. Last accessed August 2016.
87. https://medanth.wikispaces.com/Behavioral+Health. Last accessed August 2016.
88. www.amia.org/applications-informatics/clinical-informatics. Last accessed April 2016.
89. ANSI/ASIS SPC.1-2009 Organizational Resilience: Security preparedness, and continuity management systems. www.ansi.org. Last accessed April 2016.
90. Bitcoin. https://bitcoin.org/en/. Last accessed November 2016.
91. IBM. www.ibm.com. Last accessed August 2016.
92. http://www.isaca.org/knowledge-center/documents/glossary/cybersecurity_funda mentals_glossary.pdf.
93. Castellino, Ronald A. "Computer aided detection (CAD): An overview." Available at: http://www.ncbi.nlm.nih.gov/pmc/articles/PMC1665219/.
94. American Hospital Association. www.aha.org. Last accessed April 2016.
95. Canon Group. Available at: www.pubmedcentral.nih.gov/articlerender.fcgi?artid =116200. Last accessed October 2012.
96. Federal Emergency Management Agency. www.fema.gov/. Last accessed April 2016.
97. Agency for Healthcare Research and Quality (AHRQ). Office of Communications and Knowledge Transfer. 540 Gaither Road, Suite 2000, Rockville, MD 20850. www.ahrq.gov. Last accessed April 2016.
98. www.treatment-now.com/resources/definitions. Last accessed January 2016.
99. Medicine Net. www.medicinenet.com. Last accessed January 2016.
100. https://www.vocabulary.com/. Last accessed August 2016.
101. Health Care Improvement Project (HCI); U.S. Agency for International Development (USAID). www.hciproject.org. Last accessed April 2016.
102. https://www.usaidassist.org/resources/cause-and-effect-analysis. Last accessed August 2016.
103. Techopedia. https://www.techopedia.com. Last accessed November 2016.
104. Virginia Saba, EdD, Honorary PhD, RN, FAAN, FACMI, LL, Distinguished Scholar, Georgetown University. www.sabacare.com. Last accessed January 2016.
105. www.openclinical.org. Last accessed August 2016.
106. ASTM. www.astm.org. Last accessed January 2016.
107. ISO/TR 22221. Good Principles and Practices for a Clinical Data Warehouse (terms only). www.iso.org. Last accessed October 2012.
108. CEN/ISSS e-Health Standardization Focus Group. Available at: www.who.int /classifications/terminology/prerequisites.pdf. Last accessed April 2016.
109. CERT. www.cert.org. Last accessed August 2016.
110. Success EHS. Available at: http://ehsmed.com/stimulus/body.cfm?id=158. Last accessed April 2016.
111. Pearson Software Consulting. Available at: http://www.cpearson.com/Excel/MainPage .aspx. Last accessed July 2016.
112. Los Angeles County, Department of Public Health, Los Angeles, California.

113. Canadian Health Outcomes for Better Information and Care. Available at: http://c -hobic.cna-aiic.ca/about/default_e.aspx. Last accessed April 2016.

114. Robert Wood Johnson Foundation. www.rwjf.org. Last accessed April 2016.

115. University of Utah. Available at: https://www.nlm.nih.gov/research/umls/sourcerelease docs/current/CHV/. Last accessed October 2012.

116. HIPAA Glossary. www.wedi.org. Last accessed April 2016. Available at: http:// dlthede.net/Informatics/Informatics.html. Last accessed March 2016.

117. Public Health Data Standards Consortium. www.phdsc.org. Last accessed October 2012.

118. Rosenbloom, S.T., Miller, R.A., Johnson, K.B. et al. (2008). A model for evaluating interface terminologies. *JAMIA*. 15:1; 65–76.

119. www.wisegeek.com. Last accessed October 2012.

120. National Institute for Standards Technology (NIST). Available at: www.nist.gov /healthcare/index.cfm. Last accessed April 2016.

121. Object Management Group. http://www.omg.org/. Last accessed August 2016.

122. Ohio Administrative Code: 5101:3 Division of Medical Assistance, Chapter 5101:3-1 General Provisions, 2007.

123. ISO/IS #21549-7. Patient Health Card Data Part 7 E-Prescription to Med Data (terms only). www.iso.org. Last accessed April 2016.

124. Behavioral Health Care Services (BHCS). Available at: http://www.acbhcs.org/HIPAA /Glossary.htm. Last accessed July 2016.

125. MITRE. Available at: https://www.mitre.org/publications/systems-engineering-guide /enterprise-engineering/enterprise-governance/communities-of-interest-andor -community-of-practice. Last accessed August 2016.

126. Medical Dictionary. http://medical-dictionary.thefreedictionary.com/. Last accessed August 2016.

127. ISO/TR 28380-1. IHE Global Standards Adoption—Part 1 The Process (terms only). www.iso.org. Last accessed April 2016.

128. Information Security Management Guidelines for Telecommunications, based on ISO/IEC 27002. ITU-T Study Gp 17 TD 2318.

129. Organization for Economic Co-operation and Development. www.oecd.org. Last accessed April 2016.

130. The City University of New York. www.cuny.edu. Last accessed April 2016.

131. Special Libraries Associations. www.sla.org. Last accessed October 2012.

132. Benefits of Computer on Wheels Solutions in Healthcare. Available at: http://www .remedi-tech.com/4-benefits-of-computer-on-wheels-solutions-in-healthcare/. Last accessed November 2016.

133. Government Technology. http://www.govtech.com/. Last accessed August 2016.

134. HL7 Definition. Caristix. Available at: http://hl7-definition.caristix.com:9010/Default .aspx?version=HL7%20v2.5.1&dataType=CWE. Last accessed November 2016.

135. ISO 18308:2011 Health informatics—Requirements for an electronic health record architecture. www.iso.org. Last accessed October 2012.

136. IBM. Available at: https://www.ibm.com/smarterplanet/global/files/the_value_of _analytics_in_healthcare.pdf. Last accessed August 2016.

137. https://www.reference.com/technology/data-capture-c3571dbc36b1021. Last accessed November 2016.

138. Microstrategy Glossary of Terms. Available at: http://www.microstrategy.com/News /Glossary/Letter_d.htm er_d.htm. Last accessed October 2012.

139. http://www.webopedia.com/TERM/D/data_logging.html. Last accessed November 2016.
140. McGonigle, D. and Mastrain, K. (2012). *Nursing Informatics and the Foundation of Knowledge*. Boston: Jones and Bartlett Publishing.
141. IT Law Wiki. Available at: http://itlaw.wikia.com/wiki/. Last accessed November 2016.
142. Data Provenance Glossary. S&I Framework. Available at: http://wiki.siframework.org/Data+Provenance+Glossary. Last accessed November 2016.
143. https://www.healthcatalyst.com/data-mining-in-healthcare. Last accessed August 2016.
144. Richesson, R.L. and Krischer, J. (2007). Data standards in clinical research: Gaps, overlaps, challenges and future directions. *JAMIA*. 14:6; 687–696.
145. http://www.signal.co/resources/tag-management-101/. Last accessed August 2016.
146. Gartner Group. Available at: www.gartner.com/it-glossary. Last accessed October 2012.
147. http://www.obitko.com/tutorials/ontologies-semantic-web/description-logics.html. Last accessed August 2016.
148. https://www.nlm.nih.gov/medlineplus/diagnosticimaging.html.
149. https://xlinux.nist.gov/dads//HTML/dictionary.html. Last accessed April 2016.
150. http://nvlpubs.nist.gov/nistpubs/FIPS/NIST.FIPS.186-4.pdf. Last accessed April 2016.
151. http://directproject.org/faq.php?key=faq. Last accessed April 2016.
152. www.isixsigma.com. Last accessed October 2012.
153. http://www.jefferson.edu/university/skmc/research/research-medical-education/Disease_Staging.html. Last accessed April 2016.
154. PC. Available at: http://www.pcmag.com/encyclopedia. Last accessed April 2016.
155. https://www.psychiatry.org/psychiatrists/practice/dsm/dsm-5. Last accessed April 2016.
156. National Information Standards Organization. http://www.niso.org/. Last accessed August 2016.
157. http://www.its.bldrdoc.gov/fs-1037. Last accessed April 2016.
158. https://www.standards.its.dot.gov/DeploymentResources/BriefStroll. Last accessed April 2016.
159. www.linux.about.com. Last accessed October 2012.
160. www.newworldencyclopedia.org. Last accessed October 2012.
161 www.oasis-open.org. Last accessed April 2016.
162. United States Congress. www.house.gov. Last accessed October 2012.
163. American Society for Quality. http://asq.org. Last accessed October 2012.
164. Wieteck, P. *International Nursing Review*, 55(3), September 2008. doi: 10-111/j.1466-7657.2008.00639x. Last accessed October 2012.
165. Clinger-Cohen Act of 1996. www.cio.gov. Last accessed August 2016.
166. http://definitions.uslegal.com/a/ancillary-services. Last accessed October 2012.
167. Hauenstein, L., Gao, t., Sze, T.W., Crawford, D., Alm, A. and White, D. (2006). A cross-functional service-oriented architecture to support real-time information exchange in emergency medical response. Conference Proceedings of the IEEE Engineering, Medicine, Biology and Society; Suppl: 6478–6481.
168. https://www.ncbi.nlm.nih.gov/pmc/articles/PMC3789163/. Last accessed November 2016.
169. Mulyar, N., Van der Aalst, W.M.P., and Peleg, M. (2007). A pattern-based analysis of clinical computer–interpretable guideline modeling languages. *JAMIA*.14:6; 781–797.

170. Van der Aalst, W.M.P., Hofstede, A.H.M., Russell, N. et al. Control Flow Patterns 2003, 2006. Available at: http://www.workflowpatterns.com/patterns/control. Last accessed October 2012.
171. How Stuff Works. http://computer.howstuffworks.com/. Last accessed April 2016.
172. American College of Physicians. www.acponline.org. Last accessed October 2012.
173. Federal Information Processing Standards Publications (FIPS PUBS). Available at: http://www.nist.gov/itl/fips.cfm. Last accessed March 2016.
174. www.linktionary.com. Last accessed October 2012.
175. ISO/TS #21298. Functional and Structural Roles (terms only). www.iso.org. Last accessed October 2012.
176. HL7 Standards Product Brief—GELLO (HL7 Version 3 Standard: Gello: A Common Expression Language, Release 2). (n.d.). Available at: http://www.hl7.org /implement/standards/product_brief.cfm?product_id=5. Last accessed March 2016.
177. National Human Genome Research Institute. Available at: https://www.genome .gov/19016904/faq-about-genetic-and-genomic-science/. Last accessed August 2016.
178. Business Intelligence. http://businessintelligence.com/. Last accessed November 2016.
179. Hubspot. http://blog.hubspot.com/. Last accessed November 2016.
180. Health Services Research Information Central. Available at: https://www.nlm.nih .gov/hsrinfo/informatics.html. Last accessed April 2016.
181. Health Information Confidentiality. (2012). American College of Healthcare Executives. Available at: https://www.ache.org/policy/hiconf.cfm. Last accessed August 2016.
182. "Apple's HealthKit Is Finally Here—After Bugs, Botches, and Boatloads of Apple Hype." Forbes. (n.d.). Available at: http://www.forbes.com/sites/dandiamond/2014/09/26 /apples-healthkit-finally-arrives-after-bugs-botches-and-boatloads-of-apple-hype /#4340d67e1bec. Last accessed April 2016.
183. iOS 9-Health-Apple. (n.d.). Available at: http://www.apple.com/ios/health/. Last accessed April 2016.
184. National Committee for Quality Assurance. Available at: http://www.ncqa.org/hedis -quality-measurement. Last accessed April 2016.
185. Best Practices for HISPs. The Direct Project. Available at: http://wiki.directproject .org/Best+Practices+for+HISPs. Last accessed November 2016.
186. What is Health IT? Health Resources and Services Administration. Available at: http:// www.hrsa.gov/healthit/toolbox/oralhealthittoolbox/introduction/whatishealthit.html. Last accessed November 2016.
187. National Quality Forum. www.qualityforum.org. Last accessed October 2012.
188. Hospital Review. Available at: www.beckershospitalreview.com/cms-hhs/hhs-attempts -to-establish-unique-health-plan-identifiers-under-hipaa.html. Last accessed October 2012.
189. World Health Organization (WHO). www.who.org. Last accessed August 2016.
190. International Council of Nurses (ICN). www.icn.ch. Last accessed August 2016.
191. Landis, Jared. (2014). Post-Acute Care Cheat Sheet: Integrated Delivery Networks. Advisory Board. Available at: https://www.advisory.com/research/post-acute-care -collaborative/members/resources/cheat-sheets/integrated-delivery-networks. Last accessed August 2016.
192. Intelligent Document Recognition (IDR) Software. Available at: http://www .informationmanagementcompare.com/Document-Management-Solutions/1277 -Intelligent-Document-Recognition-IDR-Software/. Last accessed August 2016.

193. KMWorld. www.kmworld.com. Last accessed October 2012.
194. www.dbmi.columbia.edu. Last accessed October 2012.
195. "25 Best Health Tech Infographics of 2014—HIT Consultant." (n.d.). Available at: http://hitconsultant.net/2015/01/12/25-best-health-tech-infographics-of -2014/. Last accessed April 2016.
196. National Security Council. www.whitehouse.gov/nsc. Last accessed October 2012.
197. ISO/IS #22307. Financial services—Privacy impact assessment (under development) (terms only). www.iso.org. Last accessed October 2012.
198. Substance Abuse and Mental Health Services Administration. Available at: http://www.integration.samhsa.gov/. Last accessed August 2016.
199. IEEE Standards Association. Available at: https://standards.ieee.org/findstds /standard/1012-2012.html. Last accessed February 2016.
200. Institute of Electrical and Electronics Engineers. *IEEE Standard Computer Dictionary: A Compilation of IEEE Standard Computer Glossaries.* New York: IEEE, 1990.
201. Mosby's Dental Dictionary, 2nd edition. Copyright 2008 Elsevier, Inc.
202. www.mathsisfun.com/definitions/discrete-data.html. Last accessed October 2012.
203. ISBT 128. https://iccbba.org/. Last accessed November 2016.
204. ITIM Groups. IBM. Available at: https://publib.boulder.ibm.com/tividd/td/ITIM /SC32-1149-02/en_US/HTML/im451_poag70.htm. Last accessed November 2016.
205. Glossary of Defense Acquisition Acronyms and Terms. Available at: https://dap.dau .mil/glossary/Pages/Default.aspx. Last accessed November 2016.
206. JSON. http://www.json.org/. Last accessed August 2016.
207. Arnold S. (Ed.). (2008). *Guide to the Wireless Medical Practice: Finding the Right Connections for Healthcare.* Chicago: HIMSS.
208. http://antivirus.about.com/od/combinations/a/What-Is-A-Logic-Bomb.htm. Last accessed August 2016.
209. Abdelhak, M., Grostick, S., and Hanken, M. (2013). *Health Information: Management of a Strategic Resource.* St. Louis, MO: Elsevier Inc., 2012.
210. Tomsho, Greg. (2015). *Guide to Networking Essentials.* Boston: Cengage Learning, 2016.
211. Logical Observation Identifiers Names and Codes (LOINC). http://www.loinc.org. Last accessed August 2016.
212. LTPAC HIT. http://www.ltpachealthit.org/. Last accessed August 2016.
213. HL7 Resources. (n.d.). Corepoint Health. Available at: http://corepointhealth.com /resource-center/hl7-resources. Last accessed August 2016.
214. American Academy of Pediatrics. www.medicalhomeinfo.org. Last accessed October 2012.
215. Deloitte LLP. www.deloitte.com. Last accessed October 2012.
216. Lundy, K.S. and Bergamini, A. (2003). *Essentials of Nursing Informatics.* Sudbury, MA: Jones & Bartlett Publishers.
217. Hayes, H., Parchman, M.L., and Howard, R. (2011). A logic model framework for evaluation and planning in a primary care practice-based research network (PBRN). *Journal of the American Board of Family Medicine.* 24(5); 576–582. doi: 10.3122 /jabfm.2011.05.110043
218. Definition of Master Services Agreement. Chron. Available at: http://smallbusiness .chron.com/definition-master-services-agreement-40141.html. Last accessed August 2016.

219. Understanding Management Services Organizations (MSOs). Available at: http://www.physicianspractice.com/practice-models/understanding-management-services-organizations-msos. Last accessed November 2016.
220. National Council on Prescription Drug Programs (NCPDP). www.ncpdp.org. Last accessed October 2012.
221. National Highway Traffic Safety Administration. www.nhtsa.gov; http://www.nemsis.org/documents/NEMSISSurveillancePresentation_draft01312012.pdf. Last accessed October 2012.
222. University of Iowa College for Nursing Centers. www.nursing.uiowa.edu; http://www.nursing.uiowa.edu/cncce/nursing-interventions-classification-overview. Last accessed October 2012.
223. The OMAHA System. Available at: www.omahasystem.org/systemo.htm. Last accessed October 2012.
224. Healthcare.gov. Available at: https://www.healthcare.gov/glossary/. Last accessed November 2016.
225. Military Health System Enterprise Architecture. Available at: www.tricare.osd.mil/Architecture.
226. SPARC. Available at: http://sparcopen.org/open-access/. Last accessed August 2016.
227. www.bitpipe.com. Last accessed October 2012.
228. http://hyperphysics.phy-astr.gsu.edu/hbase/electronic/or.html. Last accessed August 2016.
229. Computer Basics. Available at: http://www.gcflearnfree.org/computerbasics/. Last accessed November 2016.
230. Tufts Health Care Institute. www.thci.org. Last accessed October 2012.
231. State of Tennessee Office of eHealth. http://tn.gov/ehealth. Last accessed October 2012.
232. Federal Trade Commission. Available at: https://www.consumer.ftc.gov/. Last accessed August 2016.
233. Federal Health Architecture. Available at: https://www.healthit.gov/policy-researchers-implementers/federal-health-architecture-fha. Last accessed August 2016.
234. Plain Text. Available at: http://www.linfo.org/plain_text.html. Last accessed November 2016.
235. Joint Commission (formerly Joint Commission on Accreditation of Healthcare Organizations). www.jointcommission.org. Last accessed March 2016.
236. Kaiser Family Foundation. www.kff.org. Last accessed October 2012.
237. Precision Medicine Initiative. *National Institute of Health*. Available at: https://www.nih.gov/precision-medicine-initiative-cohort-program. Last accessed August 2016.
238. OECD. (2016). *OECD Health Policy Studies: Better Ways to Pay for Health Care*. Paris: OECD Publishing. http://dx.doi.org/10.178/9789264258211-en.
239. www.privacy.gov.au/materials. Last accessed October 2012.
240. Information Systems Audit and Control Association. (2015). *CISA Review Manual*, 26th ed.
241. Available at: www.ncbi.nlm.nih.gov/gquery/?term=glossary. Last accessed October 2012.
242. Available at: http://www.connectingforhealth.nhs.uk. Last accessed March 2016.
243. OASIS. Available at: https://www.oasis-open.org/. Last accessed August 2016.

244. Stockburger, David W. "Introductory Statistics: Concepts, Models, and Applications." 2013. Available at: http://www.psychstat.missouristate.edu/IntroBook3/sbk.htm. Last accessed February 2016.

245. https://cs.stanford.edu/people/eroberts/courses/soco/projects/risc/whatis/index.html.

246. Andison, M. and Moss, J. (2007) "What Nurses Do: Use of the ISO Reference Terminology Model for Nursing Action as a Framework for Analyzing MICU Nursing Practice Patterns." AMIA Annual Symposium Proceedings 2007; 2007: 21–25. Available at: http://www.ncbi.nlm.nih.gov/pmc/articles/PMC2942066/. Last accessed August 2016.

247. The Serial ATA International Organization. Available at: http://www.serialata.org/technology/why_sata.asp. Last accessed October 2012.

248. Mayo Clinic College of Medicine. www.mayo.edu. Last accessed October 2012.

249. http://dodcio.defense.gov/Portals/0/Documents/DIEA/Net-Centric-Data-Strategy-2003-05-092.pdf.

250. ISO/PAS 22399:2007—Societal security—Guideline for incident preparedness and operational continuity management. www.iso.org. Last accessed April 2016.

251. ISO/TS 22220. Identification of Subjects of Health Care (terms only). www.iso.org. Last accessed October 2012.

252. MITRE. www.mitre.org. Last accessed October 2012.

253. Center for Connected Health Policy. http://cchpca.org/. Last accessed August 2016.

254. www.hqda.army.mil/acsim_ca/FAQS.ASPX. Last accessed October 2012.

255. ECRI (formerly Emergency Research Care Institute). www.ecri.org. Last accessed October 2012.

256. Unified Medical Language System Fact Sheet. U.S. National Library of Medicine. Available at: https://www.nlm.nih.gov/pubs/factsheets/umls.html. Last accessed May 2016

257. Lewin's Change Theory. (n.d.). Available at: http://www.nursing-theory.org/theories-and-models/Lewin-Change-Theory.php. Last accessed May 2016.

258. Usability Testing. Available at: http://www.usability.gov/how-to-and-tools/methods/usability-testing.html. Last accessed May 2016.

259. United States Health Information Knowledgebase. www.ushik.org. Last accessed October 2012.

260. *Oxford Dictionary*. http://www.oxforddictionaries.com/us/. Last accessed March 2016.

261. Microsoft. Available at: https://www.microsoft.com/security/pc-security/virus-whatis.aspx. Last accessed February 2016.

262. US Department of Veterans Affairs. Available at: http://www.ehealth.va.gov/VistA_Monograph.asp. Last accessed March 2016.

263. http://searchservervirtualization.techtarget.com/definition/virtual-machine-monitor. Last accessed November 2016.

264. Dalhio, H.S. and Singh, J. (2010). VoIP signal processing in digital domain. *IUP Journal of Electrical & Electronics Engineering*. 3(4); 38–43.

265. Infolific. Available at: infolific.com/search/VoIP. Last accessed October 2012.

266. Goodbole, N.S. (2004). *Software Quality Assurance: Principles and Practice*. Pangbourne, UK: Alpha Science Intl Ltd. p. 288.

267. Patel, M., Asch, D., and Volpp, K. "Wearable Devices as Facilitators, not Drivers, of Health Behavior Change." *Journal of the American Medical Association*. 313(5). Available at: http://jama.jamanetwork.com/article.aspx?articleid=2089651.

268. https://www.sciencedaily.com/terms/web_crawler.htm. Last accessed May 2016.

269. https://www.laserfiche.com/ecmblog/whats-the-difference-between-wet-digital-and -electronic-signatures/. Last accessed May 2016.
270. https://www.itu.int/rec/T-REC-X.25-199610-I/en. Last accessed May 2016.
271. http://www.x12.org/about/asc-x12-about.cfm. Last accessed August 2016.
272. http://www.zigbee.org/what-is-zigbee/.

Index